Beginning
Database Design Solutions

Beginning
Database Design Solutions

Beginning
Database Design Solutions

Rod Stephens

WILEY

Wiley Publishing, Inc.

Beginning Database Design Solutions

Published by
Wiley Publishing, Inc.
10475 Crosspoint Boulevard
Indianapolis, IN 46256
www.wiley.com

Copyright © 2009 by Wiley Publishing, Inc., Indianapolis, Indiana

Published simultaneously in Canada

ISBN: 978-0-470-38549-4

Manufactured in the United States of America

10 9 8 7 6 5 4 3 2

Library of Congress Cataloging-in-Publication Data

Stephens, Rod, 1961-
   Beginning database design solutions / Rod Stephens.
      p. cm.
   Includes index.
   ISBN 978-0-470-38549-4 (978-0-470-38549-4)
   1.   Database design. 2.   Databases.   I. Title.
   QA76.9.D26S97 2008
   005.74 — dc22
                                              2008037282

About the Author

Rod Stephens started out as a mathematician but, while studying at MIT, discovered the joys of computer algorithms and programming and he's been programming professionally ever since. During his career, he has worked on a wide variety of applications in such diverse fields as telephone switching, billing, repair dispatching, tax processing, wastewater treatment, concert ticket sales, cartography, and training for professional football players.

Rod is a Microsoft Visual Basic Most Valuable Professional (MVP), consultant and author. He has written 18 books that have been translated into half a dozen different languages, and more than 250 magazine articles, mostly about Visual Basic. Currently he is a regular contributor of C# and Visual Basic articles at DevX.com (www.devx.com).

Rod's popular *VB Helper* Web site www.vb-helper.com receives several million hits per month and contains thousands of pages of tips, tricks, and example code for Visual Basic programmers, as well as example code for this book.

Credits

Executive Editor
Robert Elliott

Development Editor
Sydney Jones

Technical Editor
Steve Hoberman

Production Editor
Angela Smith

Copy Editor
Kim Cofer

Editorial Manager
Mary Beth Wakefield

Production Manager
Tim Tate

Vice President and Executive Group Publisher
Richard Swadley

Vice President and Executive Publisher
Joseph B. Wikert

Project Coordinator, Cover
Lynsey Stanford

Proofreader
Publication Services, Inc.

Indexer
Jack Lewis

Acknowledgments

Thanks to Bob Elliott, Sydney Jones, Steve Hoberman, and all of the others whose hard work went into producing this book.

Special thanks to Sydney Jones for putting up with my sometimes overly generous interpretation of the Wrox guidelines.

Contents

Contents

Contents

Contents

Contents

Contents

Contents

Introduction

It has been estimated that more than 80 percent of all computer programming is database-related. This is certainly easy to believe. After all, a database can be a powerful tool for doing exactly what computer programs do best: store, manipulate, and display data.

Even many programs that seem at first glance to have little to do with traditional business-oriented data use databases to make processing easier. In fact, looking back on more than 20 years of software development experience, I'm hard pressed to think of a single non-trivial application that I've worked on that didn't use some kind of database.

Not only do databases play a role in many applications, but they also often play a critical role. If the data is not properly stored, it may become corrupted and the program will be unable to use it meaningfully. If the data is not properly organized, the program may be unable to find what it needs in a reasonable amount of time.

Unless the database stores its data safely and effectively, the application will be useless no matter how well-designed the rest of the system may be. The database is like the foundation of a building: without a strong foundation, even the best crafted building will fail, sometimes spectacularly (the Leaning Tower of Pisa notwithstanding).

With such a large majority of applications relying so heavily on databases, you would expect everyone involved with application development to have a solid, formal foundation in database design and construction. Everyone including database designers, application architects, programmers, database administrators, and project managers should ideally understand what makes a good database design. Even an application's key customers and users could benefit from understanding how databases work.

Sadly that is usually not the case. Many IT professionals have learned what they know about databases through rumor, trial-and-error, and painful experience. Over the years, some develop an intuitive feel for what makes a good database design but they may still not understand the reasons why a design is good or bad, and they may leave behind a trail of rickety, poorly constructed programs built on shaky database foundations.

This book provides the tools you need to design a database. It explains how to determine what should go in a database and how a database should be organized to ensure data integrity and a reasonable level of performance. It explains techniques for designing a database that is strong enough to store data safely and consistently, flexible enough to allow the application to retrieve the data it needs quickly and reliably, and adaptable enough to accommodate a realistic amount of change.

With the ideas and techniques described in this book, you will be able to build a strong foundation for database applications.

Who This Book Is For

This book is intended for IT professionals and students who want to learn how to design, analyze, and understand databases. The material will benefit those who want a better high-level understanding of databases such as proposal managers, architects, project managers, and even customers. The material will also benefit those who will actually design, build, and work with databases such as database designers, database administrators, and programmers. In many projects, these roles overlap so the same person may be responsible for working on the proposal, managing part of the project, and designing and creating the database.

This book is aimed at IT professionals and students of all experience levels. It does not assume that you have any previous experience with databases or programs that use them. It doesn't even assume that you have experience with computers. All you really need is a willingness and desire to learn.

What This Book Covers

This book explains database design. It tells how to plan a database's structure so the database will be robust, resistant to errors, and flexible enough to accommodate a reasonable amount of future change. It explains how to discover database requirements, build data models to study data needs, and refine those models to improve the database's effectiveness.

The book solidifies these concepts by working through a detailed example that designs a realistic database. Later chapters explain how to actually build databases using two common database products: Access 2007 and MySQL.

The book finishes by describing some of the topics you need to understand to keep a database running effectively such as database maintenance and security.

What You Need to Use This Book

This book explains database design. It tells how to determine what should go in a database and how the database should be structured to give the best results.

This book does not focus on actually *creating* the database. The details of database construction are different for different database tools so, to remain as generally useful as possible, this book doesn't concentrate on any particular database system. You can apply the techniques described here equally to whatever database tool you use, whether it's Access, SQL Server, Oracle, MySQL, or some other database product.

Most database products include free editions that you can use for smaller projects. For example, SQL Server Express Edition, Oracle Express Edition, and MySQL Community Server are all free.

To remain database neutral, the book does not assume you are using a particular database so you don't need any particular software or hardware. To work through the Exercises, all you really need is a pencil and some paper. You are welcome to type solutions into your computer if you like but you may actually find working with pencil and paper easier than using a graphical design tool to draw pictures, at least until you are comfortable with database design and are ready to pick a computerized design tool.

Chapter 15, "Microsoft Access," explains how to build databases using the Microsoft Access 2007 database product. If you want to follow along with the examples in that chapter and work through the Exercises, you need to have Microsoft Access 2007 installed (although other versions of Access will also work with a few differences). You can use any operating system that will run Microsoft Access 2007.

Similarly Chapter 16, "MySQL," explains how to build databases using the MySQL Community Server database product. If you want to follow this chapter's examples and work through them, you will need to install MySQL Community Server. You can use any operating system that will run MySQL.

To experiment with the SQL database language described in Chapter 17, "Introduction to SQL," and Chapter 18, "Building Databases with SQL Scripts," you need any database product that supports SQL (that includes pretty much all relational databases) running on any operating system.

How This Book Is Structured

The chapters in this book are divided into five parts plus appendixes. The chapters in each part are described here. If you have previous experience with databases, you can use these descriptions to decide which chapters to skim and which to read in detail.

Part I: Introduction to Databases and Database Design

The chapters in this part of the book provide background that is necessary to understand the chapters that follow. You can skim some of this material if it is familiar to you but don't take it too lightly. If you understand the fundamental concepts underlying database design, it will be easier to understand the point behind important design concepts presented later.

Chapter 1, "Goals of Effective Database Design," explains the reasons why people and organizations use databases. It explains a database's purpose and conditions that it must satisfy to be useful. This chapter also describes the basic ACID (Atomicity, Consistency, Isolation, Durability) and CRUD (Create, Read, Update, Delete) features that any good database should have. It explains in high-level general terms what makes a good database and what makes a bad database.

Chapter 2, "Database Types," explains some of the different types of databases that you might decide to use. These include flat files, spreadsheets, hierarchical databases (XML), object databases, and relational databases. The relational database is one of the most powerful and most commonly used forms of database so it is the focus of this book, but it is important to realize that there are alternatives that may be more appropriate under certain circumstances. This chapter gives some tips on deciding which kind of database might be best for a particular project.

Chapter 3, "Relational Database Fundamentals," explains basic relational database concepts such as tables, rows, and columns. It explains the common usage of relational database terms in addition to the more technical terms that are sometimes used by database theorists. It describes different kinds of constraints that databases use to guarantee that the data is stored safely and consistently.

Part II: Database Design Process and Techniques

The chapters in this part of the book discuss the main pieces of database design. They explain how to understand what should be in the database, develop an initial design, separate important pieces of the database to improve flexibility, and refine and tune the design to provide the most stable and useful design possible.

Chapter 4, "Understanding User Needs," explains how to learn about the users' needs and gather user requirements. It tells how to study the users' current operations, existing databases (if any), and desired improvements. It describes common questions that you can ask to learn about users' operations, desires, and needs, and how to build the results into requirements documents and specifications. This chapter explains what use cases are and tells how to use them and the requirements to guide database design and to measure success.

Chapter 5, "Translating User Needs into Data Models," introduces data modeling. It explains how to translate the user's conceptual model and the requirements into other more precise models that define the database design rigorously. This chapter describes several database modeling techniques including user-interface models, semantic object models, entity-relationship diagrams, and relational models.

Chapter 6, "Extracting Business Rules," explains how a database can handle business rules. It explains what business rules are, how they differ from database structure requirements, and how you can identify business rules. This chapter explains the benefits of separating business rules from the database structure and tells how to achieve that separation.

Chapter 7, "Normalizing Data," explains one of the biggest tools in database design: normalization. Normalization techniques allow you to restructure a database to increase its flexibility and make it more robust. This chapter explains the various forms of normalization, emphasizing the stages that are most common and important: first, second, and third normal forms (1NF, 2NF, and 3NF). It explains how each of these kinds of normalization helps prevent errors and tells why it is sometimes better to leave a database slightly less normalized to improve performance.

Chapter 8, "Designing Databases to Support Software Applications," explains how databases fit into the larger context of application design and lifecycle. This chapter explains how later development depends on the underlying database design. It discusses multi-tier architectures that can help decouple the application and database design so there can be at least some changes to either without requiring changes to the other.

Chapter 9, "Common Design Patterns," explains some common patterns that are useful in many applications. Some of these techniques include implementing various kinds of relationships among objects, storing hierarchical and network data, recording temporal data, and logging and locking.

Chapter 10, "Common Design Pitfalls," explains some common design mistakes that occur in database development. It describes problems that can arise from insufficient planning, incorrect normalization, and obsession with ID fields and performance.

Part III: A Detailed Case Study

If you follow all of the examples and exercises in the earlier chapters, by this point you will have seen all of the major steps for producing a good database design. However, it's often useful to see all of the steps in a complicated process put together in a continuous sequence. The chapters in this part of the book walk through a detailed case study following all of the phases of database design for the fictitious Pampered Pet database.

Chapter 11, "User Needs and Requirements," walks through the steps required to analyze the users' problem, define requirements, and create use cases. It describes interviews with fictitious customers that are used to identify the application's needs and translate them into database requirements.

Chapter 12, "Building a Data Model," translates the requirements gathered in the previous chapter into a series of data models that precisely define the database's structure. This chapter builds user-interface models, entity-relationship diagrams, semantic object models, and relational models to refine the database's initial design. The final relational models match the structure of a relational database fairly closely so they are easy to implement.

Chapter 13, "Extracting Business Rules," identifies the business rules embedded in the relational model constructed in the previous chapter. It shows how to extract those rules in order to separate them logically from the database's structure. This makes the database more robust in the face of future changes to the business rules.

Chapter 14, "Normalization and Refinement," refines the relational model developed in the previous chapter by normalizing it. It walks through several versions of the database that are in different normal forms. It then selects the degree of normalization that provides a reasonable tradeoff between robust design and acceptable performance.

Part IV: Implementing Databases (with examples in Access and MySQL)

Though this book focuses on abstract database concepts that do not depend on a particular database product, it's also worth spending at least some time on more concrete implementation issues. The chapters in this part of the book describe some of those issues and explain how to build databases with two different database products: Access 2007 and MySQL.

Chapter 15, "Microsoft Access," explains how to build a database with Microsoft Access 2007. This chapter doesn't cover everything there is to know about Access, it just explains enough to get started and to use Access to build non-trivial databases. You can use other versions of Access to work through this chapter, although the locations of menus, buttons, and other Access features are different in different versions.

Chapter 16, "MySQL," explains how to build a database with MySQL. This chapter tells where to download a free version of MySQL. It explains how to use the MySQL Command Line Client as well as some useful graphical tools including MySQL Query Browser and MySQL Workbench.

Part V: Advanced Topics

Although this book does not assume you have previous database experience, that doesn't mean it cannot cover some more advanced subjects. The chapters in this part of the book explain some more sophisticated topics that are important but not central to database design.

Chapter 17, "Introduction to SQL," provides an introduction to SQL (Structured Query Language). It explains how to use SQL commands to add, insert, update, and delete data. By using SQL, you can help insulate a program from the idiosyncrasies of the particular database product that it uses to store data.

Chapter 18, "Building Databases with SQL Scripts," explains how to use SQL scripts to build a database. It explains the advantages of this technique, such as the ability to create scripts to initialize a database before performing tests. It also explains some of the restrictions on this method, such as the fact that the user must create and delete tables in specific orders to satisfy table relationships.

Chapter 19, "Database Maintenance," describes some of the database maintenance issues that are part of any database application. Though performing and restoring backups, compressing tables, rebuilding indexes, and populating data warehouses are strictly not database design tasks, they are essential to any working application.

Chapter 20, "Database Security," explains database security issues. It explains the kinds of security that some database products provide. It also explains some additional techniques that can enhance database security such as using database views to appropriately restrict the users' access to data.

Appendixes

The book's appendixes provide additional reference material to supplement the earlier chapters.

Appendix A, "Exercise Solutions," gives solutions to Exercises so you can check your progress as you work through the book.

Appendix B, "Sample Database Designs," includes the designs for a variety of common database situations. These designs store information about such topics as books, movies, documents, customer orders, employee timekeeping, rentals, students, teams, and vehicle fleets.

The Glossary provides definitions for useful database and software development terms. The Glossary includes terms defined and used in this book in addition to other useful terms that you may encounter while reading other database material. This appendix can be a useful reference when you encounter an unfamiliar term on the Web or in database articles.

How to Use This Book

Because this book is aimed at readers of all experience levels, you may find some of the material familiar if you have previous experience with databases. In that case, you may want to skim chapters covering material that you already thoroughly understand.

If you are familiar with relational databases, you may want to skim Chapter 1, "Goals of Effective Database Design," Chapter 2, "Database Types," and Chapter 3, "Relational Database Fundamentals."

If you have previously helped write project proposals, you may understand some of the questions you need to ask users to properly understand their needs. In that case, you may want to skim Chapter 4, "Understanding User Needs."

If you have built databases before, you may understand at least some of the data normalization concepts explained in Chapter 7, "Normalizing Data." This is a complex topic, however, so I would recommend that you not skip this chapter unless you have a really thorough understanding of data normalization.

If you have extensive experience with using the SQL database language, you may want to skim Chapter 17, "Introduction to SQL." (Many developers who have used but not designed databases fall into this category.)

In any case, I strongly recommend that you at least skim the material in every chapter to see if there are any new concepts you can pick up along the way. Look at the Exercises at the end of a chapter before you decide that you can safely skip that chapter. If you don't know how to outline the solutions to the Exercises, you should consider looking at the chapter more closely.

Different people learn best in different ways. Some learn best by listening to lecturers, others by reading, and others by doing. Everyone learns better by combining learning styles. You will get the most from this book if you read the material and then work through the Exercises. It's easy to think to yourself, "Yeah, that makes sense" and believe you understand the material but working through several of the Exercises will help solidify the material in your mind. It may also help you see new ways that you can apply the concepts covered in the chapter.

> *Normally, when I read a new technical book, I work through every example myself, modifying the problems to see what happens if I try different things not covered by the author. I work through as many questions and exercises as I can until I reach the point where more examples don't teach me anything new. Then I move on. It's one thing to read about a concept in the chapter; it's another to try to apply it to data that is meaningful to you.*

After you have mastered the ideas in the book, you can use it for a reference. When you are starting a new project, you may want to refer to Chapter 4, "Understanding User Needs," to refresh your memory about the kinds of questions you should ask users to really discover their true needs.

Visit the book's Web site to download supplementary material such as checklists of questions to ask users and quick summaries of key techniques. This material is included in the book but it is also available for easy download on the book's Web site.

Also visit the book's Web site to look for updates and addendums. If readers find typographical errors or places where a little additional explanation may help, I'll post updates on the Web site.

Finally, if you get stuck on a really tricky concept and need a little help, email me at `RodStephens@vb-helper.com` and I'll try to help you out.

Note to Instructors

Database programming is boring. Not for you and me who have discovered the ecstatic joy of database design, the thrill of normalization, and the slightly risqué elation brought by slightly de-normalizing a database to achieve optimum performance. But let's face it, to a beginner database design and development can be a bit dull.

There's little you can do about the basic concepts but you can do practically anything with the data. At some point it's useful to explain how to design a simple inventory system but that doesn't mean you can't use other examples designed to catch students' attention. Data that relates to the students' personal experiences or that is just plain outrageous keeps them awake and alert (and most of us know that it's easier to teach students who are awake).

The examples in this book are intended to demonstrate the topic at hand but not all of them are strictly business-oriented. I've tried to make them cover a wide variety of topics from serious to silly. To keep your students interested and alert, you should add new examples from your personal experiences and from your students' interests.

I've had great success in my classroom using examples that involve sports teams (particularly local rivalries), music (combining classics such as Bach, Beethoven, and Tone-Loc), the students in the class (but be sure not to put anyone on the spot), television shows and stars, comedians, and political candidates. (Be careful with politics, though, because some people can become really emotionally attached to a particular candidate, no matter how stupid that candidate is. I focus on things they do that are so stupid that even loyal followers have to admit, "Yeah, that was a mistake." Fortunately politicians make those kinds of mistakes daily so there's plenty to work with. Watch the evening comedians for material.)

For exercises, encourage students to design databases that they will find personally useful. I've had students build databases that track statistics for the players on their favorite football teams, inventory their DVD or CD collections, file and search recipe collections, store data on "Magic: The Gathering" trading cards, track role-playing game characters, record information about classic cars, and schedule athletic tournaments. (Although the tournament scheduler didn't work out too well — the scheduling algorithms were too tricky.) One student even built a small but complete inventory application for his mother's business that she actually found useful. I think he was as surprised as anyone to discover he'd learned something useful.

When students find an assignment interesting and relevant, they become emotionally invested and will apply the same level of concentration and intensity to building a database that they normally reserve for console gaming, *South Park*, and "World of Warcraft." They may spend hours crafting a database to track WoW alliances just to fulfill a five-minute assignment. They may not catch every nuance of domain/key normal form but they'll probably learn how to build a functional database.

Note to Students

If you're a student and you peeked at the previous section, "Note to Instructors," shame on you! If you didn't peek, do so now.

Building a useful database can be a lot of work but there's no reason it can't be interesting and useful to you when you're finished. Early in your reading, pick some sort of database that you would find useful (see the previous section for a few ideas) and think about it as you read through the text. When the book talks about creating an initial design, sketch out a design for your database. When the book explains how to normalize a database, normalize yours. As you work through the exercises, think about how they would apply to your dream database.

Don't be afraid to ask your instructor if you can use your database instead of one suggested by the book for a particular assignment. (Unless you have one of those instructors who hand out extra work to anyone who crosses their path. In that case, keep your head down.) Usually an instructor's thought process is quite simple: "I don't care what database you use as long as you learn the material." Your database may need to contain several related tables to create the complexity needed for a particular exercise but it's usually not too hard to make a database more complex.

When you're finished, you will hopefully know a lot more about database design than you do now and, if you're persistent, you might just have a database that's actually good for something. Hopefully you'll also know how to design other useful databases in the future. (And when you're finished, email me at RodStephens@vb-helper.com and let me know what you built!)

Conventions

To help you get the most from the text and keep track of what's happening, we've used a number of conventions throughout the book.

Try It Out

The *Try It Out* is an exercise you should work through, following the text in the book.

1. They usually consist of a set of steps.
2. Each step has a number.
3. Follow the steps through with your copy of the database.

How It Works

After most *Try It Out* sections, the process you've stepped through will be explained in detail.

Tips, hints, tricks, and asides to the current discussion are offset and placed in italics like this.

As for styles in the text:

- ❑ We *highlight* new terms and important words when we introduce them.
- ❑ We show keyboard strokes like this: Ctrl+A.
- ❑ We show file names, URLs, and code within the text like so: SELECT * FROM Students.
- ❑ We present blocks of code like this:

```
We use a monofont type with no highlighting for code examples.
```

Source Code

As you work through the examples in this book, you may choose either to type in all the code manually or to use the source code files that accompany the book. All of the source code used in this book is available for download at www.wrox.com. Once at the site, simply locate the book's title (either by using the Search box or by using one of the title lists) and click the Download Code link on the book's detail page to obtain all the source code for the book.

> *Because many books have similar titles, you may find it easiest to search by ISBN; this book's ISBN is 978-0-470-38549-4.*

Once you download the code, just decompress it with your favorite compression tool. Alternatively, you can go to the main Wrox code download page at . www.wrox.com/dynamic/books/download.aspx. to see the code available for this book and all other Wrox books.

The Book's Web Site

No book can possibly cover everything there is to know about any topic and this book is no exception. I have tried to make it as complete, correct, and understandable as possible but there isn't room for everything here.

To get the most out of this book, you should visit the book's Web page. There you will find additional useful information that didn't fit in the book such as checklists and user requirement surveys that you can download and print, corrections and clarifications, example SQL scripts, forums for questions and discussion, and other supplementary material.

To visit the book's Wrox Web site, go to . www.wrox.com and search for the book's title or ISBN, or for the author's name Rod Stephens. This Web site includes author information, excerpts, example programs that you can download, and so forth.

> *Please visit the book's Web site and look for additions and addendums. I also monitor the book's Wrox forum closely and answer questions as quickly as I can.*

The book's author web site, www.vb-helper.com/db_design.htm, contains similar material and links to the Wrox Web site. The main VB Helper Web site also contains thousands of tips, tricks, and examples written in various versions of Visual Basic.

To keep informed of changes to this book or my other books, you can sign up for one of my newsletters at . www.vb-helper.com/newsletter.html. The newsletters, which are sent every week or so, include Visual Basic tips, tricks, and examples, in addition to updates on my books and other thoughts about Visual Basic development.

If you have corrections or comments, please send them to me at RodStephens@vb-helper.com. I will try to help you out and do my best to keep the Web sites as up-to-date as possible.

Errata

We make every effort to ensure that there are no errors in the text or in the code. However, no one is perfect, and mistakes do occur. If you find an error in one of our books, like a spelling mistake or faulty piece of code, we would be very grateful for your feedback. By sending in errata you may save another reader hours of frustration and at the same time you will be helping us provide even higher quality information.

To find the errata page for this book, go to `www.wrox.com` and locate the title using the Search box or one of the title lists. Then, on the book details page, click the Book Errata link. On this page you can view all errata that has been submitted for this book and posted by Wrox editors. A complete book list including links to each book's errata is also available at `www.wrox.com/misc-pages/booklist.shtml`.

If you don't spot "your" error on the Book Errata page, go to `www.wrox.com/contact/techsupport.shtml` and complete the form there to send us the error you have found. We'll check the information and, if appropriate, post a message to the book's errata page and fix the problem in subsequent editions of the book.

p2p.wrox.com

For author and peer discussion, join the P2P forums at `p2p.wrox.com`. The forums are a Web-based system for you to post messages relating to Wrox books and related technologies and interact with other readers and technology users. The forums offer a subscription feature to email you topics of interest of your choosing when new posts are made to the forums. Wrox authors, editors, other industry experts, and your fellow readers are present on these forums.

At `p2p.wrox.com` you will find a number of different forums that will help you not only as you read this book, but also as you develop your own applications. To join the forums, just follow these steps:

1. Go to `p2p.wrox.com` and click the Register link.
2. Read the terms of use and click Agree.
3. Complete the required information to join as well as any optional information you wish to provide and click Submit.
4. You will receive an e-mail with information describing how to verify your account and complete the joining process.

You can read messages in the forums without joining P2P but in order to post your own messages, you must join.

Once you join, you can post new messages and respond to messages other users post. You can read messages at any time on the Web. If you would like to have new messages from a particular forum emailed to you, click the Subscribe to this Forum icon by the forum name in the forum listing.

For more information about how to use the Wrox P2P, be sure to read the P2P FAQs for answers to questions about how the forum software works as well as many common questions specific to P2P and Wrox books. To read the FAQs, click the FAQ link on any P2P page.

Contacting the Author

If you have questions, suggestions, comments, or just want to say "Hi," email me at RodStephens@vb-helper.com. I can't promise that I'll be able to help you with every problem, but I do promise to try.

Disclaimer

Many of the examples in this book were chosen for interest or humorous effect. They are not intended to disparage anyone. I mean no disrespect to police officers (or anyone else who regularly carries a gun), plumbers, politicians, jewelry store owners, street luge racers (or anyone else who wears helmets and Kevlar body armor to work), or college administrators. Or anyone else for that matter.

Well, maybe politicians.

Beginning
Database Design Solutions

Part I

Introduction to Databases and Database Design

Chapter 1: Goals of Effective Database Design

Chapter 2: Database Types

Chapter 3: Relational Database Fundamentals

The chapters in this part of the book provide background that is useful when studying database design.

Chapter 1 explains the reasons why database design is important. It discusses the goals that you should keep in mind while designing databases. If you keep those goals in mind, you can stay focused on the end result and not get bogged down in the minutiae of technical details. If you understand the goals, you can know when it might be useful to bend the rules a bit.

Chapter 2 describes several different kinds of databases. While this book (and most other database books) focuses on relational databases, there are other kinds of databases that are better suited to some tasks. If you know what alternatives are available, you can decide which will work best for you. (I once worked on a 40-developer project that failed largely because it used the wrong kind of database. Don't let that happen to you!)

Chapter 3 provides background on relational databases. It explains common relational database terms and concepts that you need to understand the chapters that follow. You won't get as much out of the rest of the book if you don't understand the terminology.

Even if you're somewhat familiar with relational databases, give these chapters at least a quick glance to make sure you don't miss anything important. Pay particular attention to the terms described in Chapter 3, because you'll need to know them later.

Goals of Effective Database Design

Using modern database tools, just about anyone can build a database. The question is, will the resulting database be useful?

A database won't do you much good if you can't get data out of it quickly, reliably, and consistently. It won't be useful if it's full of incorrect or contradictory data. It also won't be useful if it is stolen, lost, or corrupted by data that was only half written when the system crashed.

You can address all of these potential problems by using modern database tools, a good database design, and a pinch of common sense, but only if you understand what those problems are so you can avoid them.

Step one in the quest for a useful database is understanding database goals. What should a database do? What makes a database useful and what problems can it solve? Working with a powerful database tool without goals is like flying a plane through clouds without a compass: you have the tools you need but no sense of direction.

This chapter describes the goals of database design. By studying information containers such as files that can play the role of a database, it defines properties that good databases have and problems that they should avoid.

In this chapter, you learn:

- ❑ Why a good database design is important.
- ❑ Strengths and weaknesses of different kinds of information containers that can act as databases.
- ❑ How computerized databases can benefit from those strengths and avoid those weaknesses.
- ❑ How good database design helps achieve database goals.
- ❑ What CRUD and ACID are, and why they are relevant to database design.

Understanding the Importance of Design

Forget for a moment that this book is about designing databases and consider software design in general. Software design plays a critical role in software development. The design lays out the general structure and direction that future development will take. It determines which parts of the system will interact with other parts. It decides which subsystems will provide support for other pieces of the application.

If an application's underlying design is flawed, the system as a whole is at risk. Bad assumptions in the design creep into the code at the application's lowest levels, resulting in flawed subsystems. Higher-level systems built on those subsystems inherit the design flaws and soon their code is corrupted, too.

Sometimes a sort of decay pervades the entire system and nobody notices until relatively late in the project. The longer the project continues, the more entrenched the incorrect assumptions become and the more reluctant developers are to suggest scrapping the whole design and starting over. The longer problems remain in the system, the harder they are to remove. At some point, it may be easier to throw everything away and start over from scratch, a decision that few managers will want to present to upper management.

Project Management

A friend of mine who is an engineer was working on a really huge satellite project. After a while, the engineers all realized that the project just wasn't feasible given the current state of technology and the design. Eventually the project manager was forced to admit this to upper management and he was fired. The new project manager stuck it out for a while and then he, too, was forced to confess to upper management that the project was unfeasible. He, too, was fired.

This process continued for a while with a new manager taking over, realizing the hope-lessness of the design, and being fired until eventually even upper management had to admit the project wasn't going to work out and the whole thing collapsed.

They could have saved time, money, and several careers if they had spent more upfront time on the design and either fixed the problems or realized right away that the project wasn't going to work and scrapped it at the start.

Building an application is often compared to building a house or skyscraper. You probably wouldn't start building a multibillion dollar skyscraper without a comprehensive design that is based on well-established architectural principles. Unfortunately software developers often rush off to start coding as soon as they possibly can. Coding is more fun and interesting than design is. Coding also lets developers tell management and customers how many lines of code they have written so it seems like they are making progress even if the lines of code are corrupted by false assumptions. Only later do they realize that the underlying design is flawed, the code they wrote is worthless, and the project is in serious trouble.

Now back to database design. Few parts of an application's design are as critical as the database's design. The database is the repository of the information that the rest of the application manages and displays to the users. If the database doesn't store the right data, doesn't keep the data safe, or doesn't let the application find the data it needs, then the application has little chance for success. Here the GIGO (Garbage In, Garbage Out) principle is in full effect. If the underlying data is unsound, it doesn't matter what the application that uses it does; the results will be suspect at best.

For example, imagine that you've built an order tracking system that can quickly fetch information about a customer's past orders. Unfortunately every time you ask the program to fetch a certain customer's records it returns a slightly different result. Though the program can find data quickly, the results are not trustworthy enough to be usable.

Or imagine that you have built an amazing program that can track the thousands of tasks that make up a single complex job such as building a cruise liner or passenger jet. It can track each task's state of completion, determine when you need to order new parts for them to be ready for future phases of construction, and can even determine the present value of future purchases so you can decide whether it is better to buy parts now or wait until they are needed. Unfortunately the program takes hours to recalculate the complex task schedule and pricing details. Though the calculations are correct, they are so slow that users cannot reasonably make any changes. Changing the color of the fabric of a plane's seats or the tile used in a cruise liner's hallways could delay the whole project.

Or suppose you have built an efficient subscription application that lets customers subscribe to your company's quarterly newsletters and data services. It lets you quickly find and update any customer's subscriptions and it always shows the same values for a particular customer consistently. Unfortunately, when you change the price of one of your publications you find that not all of the customers' records show the updated price. Some customers' subscriptions are at the new rate, some are at the old rate, and some seem to be at a rate you've never seen before. (This example isn't as far-fetched as it may seem. Some systems allow you to offer sale prices or special incentives to groups of customers, or they allow sales reps to offer special prices to particular customers. That kind of system requires careful design if you want to be able to do things like change standard prices without messing up customized pricing.)

Poor database design can lead to these and other annoying and potentially expensive scenarios. A good design creates a solid foundation on which you can build the rest of the application.

Experienced developers know that the longer a bug remains in a system the harder it is to find and fix. From that it logically follows that it is extremely important to get the design right before you start building on top of it.

Database design is no exception. A flawed database design can doom a project to failure before it has begun as surely as ill-conceived software architecture, poor implementation, or incompetent programming can.

Information Containers

What is a database? This may seem like a trivial question, but if you take it seriously the result can be pretty enlightening. By studying the strengths and weaknesses of some physical objects that meet the definition of a database, you can learn about the features you might like a computerized database to have.

> **A database is a tool that stores data, and lets you create, read, update, and delete the data in some manner.**

This is a pretty broad definition and it includes a lot of physical objects that most people don't think of as modern databases. For example, an envelope full of business cards, a notebook, a filing cabinet full of customer records, and your brain all fit this definition. Each of these physical databases has advantages and disadvantages that can give insight into the features you might like in a computer database.

An envelope of business cards is useful as long as it doesn't contain too many cards. You can find a particular piece of data (for example, a person's phone number) by looking through all of the cards. The database is easy to expand by shoving more cards into the envelope, at least up to a point. If you have more than a dozen or so business cards, finding a particular card can be time consuming. You can even rearrange the cards a bit to improve performance for cards you use often. Each time you use a card, move it to the front of the pile. Over time, those that are used most will be in front.

A notebook is small, easy to use, easy to carry, doesn't require electricity, and doesn't need to boot before you can use it. A notebook database is also easily extensible because you can buy another notebook to add to your collection when the first one is full. However, a notebook's contents are arranged sequentially. If you want to find information about a particular topic, you'll have to look through the pages one at a time until you find what you want. The more data you have, the harder this kind of search becomes.

A filing cabinet can store a lot more information than a notebook and you can easily expand the database by adding more files or cabinets. Finding a particular piece of information in the filing cabinet can be easier than finding it in a notebook as long as you are searching for the type of data used to arrange the records. If the filing cabinet is full of customer information sorted by customer name, and you want to find a particular customer's data, you're in luck. If you want to find all of the customers that live in a certain city, you'll have to dig through the files one at a time.

Your brain is the most sophisticated database ever created. It can store an incredible amount of data and it allows you to retrieve a particular piece of data in several different ways. For example, right now you could probably easily answer the following questions about the restaurants that you visit frequently:

- ❑ Which is closest to your current location?
- ❑ Which has the best desserts?
- ❑ Which has the best service?
- ❑ Which is least expensive?
- ❑ Which is the best for a business lunch?
- ❑ Which is your overall favorite?

Your brain provides many different ways you can access the same information about restaurants. You can search the same base of information based on a variety of keys (location, quality of dessert, expense, and so forth). To answer these questions with an envelope of business cards (or restaurant matchbooks), a notebook, or a filing cabinet would require a long and grueling search.

Still your brain has some drawbacks, at least as a database. Most notably it forgets. You may be able to remember an incredible number of things but some of them become less reliable or disappear completely over time. Do you remember the names of all of your elementary school teachers? I don't. (I don't remember my own teachers' names, much less yours!)

Your brain also gets tired and when it is tired it is less accurate.

Although your brain is good at certain tasks such as recognizing faces or picking restaurants, it is not so good at other tasks such as providing an accurate list of every item a particular customer purchased in the last year. Those items have less emotional significance than, for example, your spouse's name, so they're harder to remember.

All of these information containers (business cards, notebooks, filing cabinets, and your brain) can become contaminated with misleading, incorrect, and contradictory information. If you write different versions of the same information in a notebook, the data won't be consistent. Later when you try to look up the data, you may find either version first and you may not even realize there is another version. (Your brain can become especially cluttered with inconsistent and contradictory information, particularly if you listen to politicians during an election year.)

The following section summarizes some of the strengths and weaknesses of these information containers.

Strengths and Weaknesses of Information Containers

By understanding the strengths and weaknesses of information containers such as those described in the previous section, you can learn about features that would be useful in a computerized database. So what are some of those strengths and weaknesses?

The following list summarizes the advantages of some information containers:

- ❑ None of these databases require electricity so they are safe from power failures. (Although your brain requires food. As the dormouse said, feed your head.)

- ❑ These databases keep their data fairly safe and permanent (barring fires). The data doesn't just disappear.

- ❑ These databases (excluding your brain) are inexpensive and easy to buy.

- ❑ These databases have simple user interfaces so almost anyone can use them.

- ❑ Using these databases, it's fairly easy to add, edit, and remove data.

- ❑ The filing cabinet lets you quickly locate data if you search for it in the same way it is arranged (for example, by customer name).

- ❑ Your brain lets you find data by using different keys (for example, by location, cost, or quality of service).

- ❑ All of these allow you to find every piece of information that they contain, although it may take a while to dig through it all.

- ❑ All of these (except possibly your brain) provide consistent results as long as the facts they store are consistent. For example, two people using the same notebook will find the same data. Similarly if you look at the same notebook at a later time, it will show the same data you saw before (if it hasn't been modified).

- ❑ All of these except the filing cabinet are portable.

- ❑ Your brain can perform complex calculations, at least of a limited type and number.

- ❑ All of these provide atomic transactions.

The final advantage is a bit more abstract than the others so it deserves some additional explanation. An *atomic transaction* is a possibly complex series of actions that is considered as a single operation by those who are not involved directly in performing the transaction.

The classic example is transferring money from one bank account to another. Suppose Alice writes Bob a check for $100 and you need to transfer the money between their accounts. You pick up the account book, subtract $100 from Alice's record, add $100 to Bob's record, and then put the notebook down. Someone else who uses the notebook might see it before the transaction (when Alice has the $100) or after the transaction (when Bob has the $100) but they won't see it during the transaction where the $100 has been subtracted from Alice but not yet given to Bob. The office bully isn't allowed to grab the notebook from your hands when you're halfway through. It's an all-or-nothing transaction.

In addition to their advantages, information containers such as notebooks and filing cabinets have some disadvantages. It's worth studying these disadvantages so you can try to avoid them when you build computerized databases.

The following list summarizes some of the disadvantages that these information containers have:

- ❏ All of these databases can hold incomplete, incorrect, or contradictory data.

- ❏ Some of them are easy to lose or steal. Someone could grab your notebook while you're eating lunch or read over your shoulder on the bus. You could even forget your notebook at the security counter as you dash to catch your flight.

- ❏ In all of these databases, correcting large errors in the data can be difficult. For example, it's easy to use a pen to change one person's address in an address notebook. It's much harder to update hundreds of addresses if a new city is created in your area. (This recently happened near where I live.) Such a circumstance requires a tedious search through a set of business cards, a notebook, or a filing cabinet. It may be years before your brain makes the switch completely.

- ❏ These databases are relatively slow at creating, retrieving, updating, and deleting data. Your brain is much faster than the others at some tasks but is not good at manipulating a lot of information all at once. For example, how quickly can you list your 20 closest friends in alphabetical order? Even picking your closest friends can be difficult at times.

- ❏ Your brain can give different results at different times depending on uncontrollable factors such as your mood, how tired you are, and even whether you're hungry.

- ❏ Each of these databases is located in a single place so it cannot be easily shared. Each also cannot be easily backed up so if the original is lost or destroyed, you lose your data.

The following section considers how you can translate these strengths and weaknesses into features to prefer or avoid in a computerized database.

Desirable Database Features

By looking at the advantages and disadvantages of physical databases, you can create a list of features that a computerized database should have. Some of these are fundamental characteristics that any database must have. ("You should be able to get data from it." How obvious is that?)

Most of these features, however, depend at least in part on good database design. If you don't craft a good design, you'll miss out on some or all of the benefit of these features. For example, any decent database provides backup features but a good design can make backup and recovery a lot quicker and easier.

The following sections describe some of the features that a good database system should provide and explain to what degree they depend on good database design.

CRUD

CRUD stands for the four fundamental database operations that any database should provide: Create, Read, Update, and Delete. If you read database articles and discussions on the Web, you will often see people tossing around the term CRUD. (They may be using the term just to sound edgy and cool. Now that you know the term, you can sound cool, too!)

You can imagine some specialized data gathering devices that don't support all of these methods. For example, the black box flight data recorders on airplanes record flight information and later play it back without allowing you to modify the data. In general, however, if it doesn't have CRUD it's not a database.

CRUD is more a feature of databases in general than it is a feature of good database design, but a good database design provides CRUD efficiently. For example, suppose you design a database to track times for your canuggling league (look it up online) and you require that the addresses for participants include a State value that is present in the States table. When you create a new record (the C in CRUD), the database must validate the new State entry. Similarly when you update a record (the U in CRUD), the database must validate the modified State entry. When you delete an entry in the States table (the D in CRUD), the database must verify that no Participant records use that state. Finally when you read data (the R in CRUD), the database design determines whether you find the data you want in seconds, hours, or not at all.

Many of the concepts described in the following sections relate to CRUD operations.

Retrieval

Retrieval is another word for "read," the R in CRUD. The database should allow you to find every piece of data. There's no point putting something in the database if there's no way to get it back later. (That would be a "data black hole," not a database.)

The database should allow you to structure the data so you can find particular pieces of data in one or more specific ways. For example, you should be able to find a customer's billing record by searching for customer name or customer ID.

Ideally the database will also allow you to structure the data so it is relatively quick and easy to fetch data in a particular manner.

For example, suppose you want to see where your customers live so you can decide whether you should start a delivery service in a new city. To get this information, it would be helpful to be able to find customers based on their addresses. Ideally you could optimize the database structure so you can quickly search for customers by address.

In contrast, you probably don't need to search for customers by middle name too frequently. (Imagine a customer calling you and saying, "Can you look up my record? I don't remember if I paid my bill last month. I also don't remember my account number or my last name but my middle name is 'Konfused'.") It would be nice if the common search by address was faster than the rare search by middle name.

Being able to find all of the data in the database quickly and reliably is an important part of database design. Finding the data you need in a poorly designed database can take hours or days instead of mere seconds.

Consistency

Another aspect of the R in CRUD is consistency. The database should provide consistent results. If you perform the same search twice in a row, you should get the same results. Another user who performs the same search should also get the same results. (Of course this assumes that the underlying data hasn't changed in the meantime. You can't expect your net worth query to return the same results every day when stock prices fluctuate wildly.)

A well-built database product can ensure that the exact same query returns the same result but design also plays an important role. If the database is poorly designed, you may be able to store conflicting data in different parts of the database. For example, you might be able to store one set of contact information in a customer's order and a different set of information in the main customer record. Later, if you need to contact the customer with a question about the order, which contact information should you use?

Validity

Validity is closely related to the idea of consistency. Consistency means different parts of the database don't hold contradictory views of the same information. Validity means data is validated where possible against other pieces of data in the database. In CRUD terms, data can be validated when a record is created, updated, or deleted.

Just like physical data containers, a computerized database can hold incomplete, incorrect, or contradictory data. You can never protect a database from users who can't spell or who just plain enter the wrong information, but a good database design can help prevent some kinds of errors that a physical database cannot prevent.

For example, the database can easily verify that data has the correct type. If the user sees a Date field and enters "No thanks, I'm married," the database can tell that this is not a valid date format and can refuse to accept the value. Similarly it can tell that "Old" is not a valid Age, "Lots" is not a valid Quantity, and "Confusion" is too long to be a two-letter state abbreviation (although that value may correctly reflect the user's state of mind).

The database can also verify that a value entered by the user is present in another part of the database. For example, a poor typist trying to enter CO in a State field might type CP instead. The database can check a list of valid states and refuse to accept the data when it doesn't find CP listed. (If the database needs to work with only certain states, you can restrict the list to include only those states and make the test even tighter.)

The database can also check some kinds of conditions on the data. Suppose the database contains a book ordering system. When the customer orders 500 copies of this book (who wouldn't want that many copies?), the database can check another part of the database to see if that many copies are available (most bookstores carry only a few copies of any given book) and refuse the order if there aren't enough copies.

A good database design also helps protect the database against incorrect changes. Suppose a cappuccino machine repair service is dropping coverage for a nearby city. When you try to remove that city from your list of valid locations, the database can tell you if you have existing customers in that city. Depending on the database's design, it could refuse to allow you to remove the city until you apologized to those customers and removed them from the database.

All of these techniques rely on a good, solid database design. They still can't protect you from a user who types first names in the last name field or who keeps accidentally bumping the CAPS LOCK KEY, but it can prevent many types of errors that a notebook can't.

Easy Error Correction

Even a perfectly designed database cannot ensure perfect validity. How can the database know that a customer's name is supposed to be spelled Pheidaux not Fido as typed by the user?

Correcting a single error in a notebook is fairly easy. Just cross out the wrong value and write in the new one.

Correcting systematic errors in a notebook is a lot harder. Suppose you hire a summer intern to go door-to-door selling household products and he writes up a lot of orders for "Duck Tape" not realizing that the actual product is "Duct Tape." Fixing all of the mistakes could be tedious and time-consuming. (Of course tedious and time-consuming jobs are what summer interns are for so you can make him fix it himself.) You could just ignore the problem and leave the orders misspelled, but then how would you tell when a customer really wants to tape a duck?

In a computerized database, this sort of correction is trivial. A simple database command can update every occurrence of the product name "Duck Tape" throughout the whole system. (In fact, this kind of fix is sometimes too easy to make. If you aren't careful, you may accidentally change the names of *every* product to Duct Tape, even those that were not incorrectly spelled Duck Tape. You can prevent this by building a safe user interface for the database or by being really careful.)

Easy correction of errors is a built-in feature of computerized databases, but to get the best advantage from this feature you need a good design. If order information is contained in a free-formatted text section, the database will have trouble fixing typos. If you put the product name in a separate field, the database can make this change easily.

Though easy corrections are almost free, you need to do a little design work to make them as efficiently and effectively as possible.

Speed

An important aspect of all of the CRUD components is speed. A well-designed database can create, read, update, and delete records quickly.

There's no denying that a computerized database is a lot faster than a notebook or a filing cabinet. Instead of processing dozens of records per hour, a computerized database can process dozens or hundreds per second. (I once worked with a billing center that processed around 3 million accounts every three days.)

Good design plays a critical role in database efficiency. A poorly organized database may still be faster than the paper equivalent but it will be a lot slower than a well-designed database.

Database Design

The billing center I mentioned in the previous paragraph had a simple problem: they couldn't find the customers who owed them the most money. Every three days the database would print out a list of customers who owed money. The list made a stack of paper almost three feet tall. Unfortunately the list was randomly ordered (probably ordered by customer ID or shoe size or something equally unhelpful) so they couldn't figure out who owed the most. The majority of the customers owed only a few dollars — too little to pursue — but a few customers owed tens of thousands of dollars.

We captured this printout electronically and sorted the accounts by balance. It turned out that the really problematic customers only filled a couple of pages and the first five or so customers owed more than all of the others combined.

I didn't include this story just to impress you with my programming prowess (to be completely honest, it was a pretty easy project) but to illustrate how database design can make a big difference in performance. Here a very simple change (which any database should be able to support) made the difference between finding the most troublesome customers in a few seconds or not at all.

Not all changes to a database's design can produce dramatic results, but design definitely plays an important role in performance.

Atomic Transactions

Recall that an atomic transaction is a possibly complex series of actions that is considered as a single operation by those not involved directly in performing the transaction. If you transfer $100 from Alice's account to Bob's account, no one else can see the database while it is in an intermediate state where the money has been removed from Alice's account and not yet added to Bob's.

The transaction either happens completely or none of its pieces happen — it cannot happen halfway.

Atomic transactions are important for maintaining consistency and validity, and are thus important for the R and U parts of CRUD.

Physical data containers such as notebooks support atomic transactions because typically only one person at a time can use them. Unless Derek the office bully grabs the notebook from your hands while you're writing in it, you can finish a series of operations before you let someone else have a turn.

Some of the most primitive kinds of databases, such as flat files and XML files (which are described later in this book) don't inherently support atomic transactions, but the more advanced relational database products do. Those databases allow you to start a transaction and perform a series of operations. You can then either *commit* the transaction to make the changes permanent or *rollback* the transaction to undo them all and restore the database to the state it had before you started the transaction.

These databases also automatically rollback any transaction that is open if the database halts unexpectedly. For example, suppose you start a transaction, take $100 from Alice's account, and then your company's mascot (a miniature horse) walks through the computer room, steps on a power strip, and kills the power to your main computer. When you restart the database (after sending the horse to the HR department), it automatically rolls the transaction back so Alice gets her money back. You'll need to try the transaction again but at least no money has been lost by the system.

Atomic transactions are more a matter of properly using database features than database design. If you pick a reasonably advanced database product and use transactions properly, you gain their benefits. If you decide to use flat files to store your data, you'll need to implement transactions yourself.

ACID

This section provides some more detail about the transactions described in the previous section rather than discussing a new feature of physical data containers and computerized databases.

ACID is an acronym describing four features that an effective transaction system should provide. ACID stands for Atomicity, Consistency, Isolation, and Durability.

Atomicity means transactions are atomic. The operations in a transaction either all happen or none of them happen.

Consistency means the transaction ensures that the database is in a consistent state before and after the transaction. In other words, if the operations within the transaction would violate the database's rules, the transaction is rolled back. For example, suppose the database's rules say that an account cannot make a payment that would result in a balance less than zero. Also suppose that Alice's account holds only $75. Now you start a transaction, add $100 to Bob's account, and then try to remove $100 from Alice's. That would put Alice $25 in the red, violating the database's rules, so the transaction is canceled and we all try to forget that this ugly incident ever occurred. (Actually we probably bill Alice an outrageous surcharge for writing a bad check.)

Isolation means the transaction isolates the details of the transaction from everyone except the person making the transaction. Suppose you start a transaction, remove $100 from Alice's account, and add $100 to Bob's account. Another person cannot peek at the database while you're in the middle of this process and see a state where neither Alice nor Bob has the $100. Anyone who looks in the database sees the $100 *somewhere*, either in Alice's account before the transaction or in Bob's account afterwards.

In particular, two transactions operate in isolation and cannot interfere with each other. Suppose one transaction transfers $100 from Alice to Bob and then a second transaction transfers $100 from Bob to Cindy. Logically one of these transactions occurs first and finishes before the other starts. For example, when the second transaction starts, it will not see the $100 missing from Alice's account unless it is already in Bob's account.

> Note that the order in which the transactions occur may make a big difference. Suppose Alice starts with $150, Bob starts with $50, and Cindy starts with $50.
>
> Now suppose the second Bob-to-Cindy transaction occurs first. If the transaction starts by removing $100 from Bob's account, Bob is overdrawn, this transaction is rolled back, we assess Bob a surcharge for being overdrawn, and we try to sell Bob overdraft protection for the low, low price of only $10 per month. After all of this, the Alice-to-Bob transaction occurs and we successfully move $100 into Bob's account.

> In contrast, suppose the Alice-to-Bob transaction occurs first. That transaction succeeds with no problem so, when the Bob-to-Cindy transaction starts, Bob has $150 and the second transaction can complete successfully.
>
> The database won't determine which transaction occurs first, just that each commits or rolls back before the other starts.

Durability means that once a transaction is committed, it will not disappear later. If the power fails, when the database restarts, the effects of this transaction will still be there.

The durability requirement relies on the consistency rule. Consistency ensures that the transaction will not complete if it would leave the database in a state that violates the database's rules. Durability means that the database will not later decide that the transaction caused such a state and retroactively remove the transaction.

Once the transaction is committed, it is final.

> A high-end database might provide durability through continuous shadowing. Every time a database operation occurs, it is shadowed to another system. If the main system crashes, the shadow database can spring instantly into service. Other databases provide durability through logs. Every time the database performs an operation, it writes a record of the operation into the log. Now suppose the system crashes. When the database restarts, it reloads its last saved data and then reapplies all of the operations described by the log. This takes longer than restarting from a shadow database but requires fewer resources so it's generally less expensive.
>
> To provide durability, the database cannot consider the transaction as committed until its changes are shadowed or recorded in the log so the database will not lose the changes if it crashes.

Persistence and Backups

The data must be persistent. It shouldn't change or disappear by itself. If you can't trust the database to keep the data safe, the database is pretty much worthless.

Database products do their best to keep the data safe, and in normal operation you don't need to do much to get the benefit of data persistence. When something unusual happens, however, you may need to take special action and that requires prior planning. For example, suppose the disk drives holding the database simply break. Or a fire reduces the computer to a smoldering puddle of slag. Or a user accidentally or intentionally deletes the database. (A user tried that once on a project I was working on. We were not amused!)

In these extreme cases, the database alone cannot help you. To protect against this sort of trouble, you need to perform regular backups.

Physical data containers such as notebooks are generally hard to back up, so they are hard to protect against damage. If a fire burns up your accounts receivable notebook, you'll have to rely on your customers' honesty in paying what they owe you. Though we like customers, I'm not sure most businesses trust them to that extent.

In theory you could make copies of a notebook and store them in separate locations to protect against these sorts of accidents, but in practice few businesses (except perhaps money laundering, smuggling, and other endeavors where it's handy to show law enforcement officials one set of books and the "shareholders" another) do.

Computerized databases, however, are relatively easy to back up. If the loss of a little data won't hurt you too badly, you can back up the database daily. If fire, a computer virus, or some other accident destroys the main database, you can reload the backup and be ready to resume operation in an hour or two.

If the database is very volatile or if losing even a little data could cause big problems (how much money do you think gets traded through the New York Stock Exchange in a busy hour?), then you need a different backup strategy. Many higher-end database products allow you to shadow every database operation as it occurs so you always have a complete copy of everything that happens. If the main database is destroyed, you can be back in business within minutes. Some database architectures can switch to a backup database so quickly the users don't even know it's happened.

Backup Plans

It's always best to store backups away from the computer that you're backing up. Then if a really big accident like a fire occurs and destroys the whole building holding the database, the backup is still safe.

I've known of several development groups that stored their backups right next to the computer they were backing up. That guards against some kinds of stupidity (in the teams I've worked on, about once every 10 person-years or so someone accidentally deleted a file that we needed to recover from backups) but doesn't protect against big accidents.

I've also known of companies that had an official backup plan, but once you submitted a backup for proper storage it was shipped off site and it took a long time to get it back if you needed it. A backup doesn't do much good if you can't use it!

In a very extreme example, I had a customer who was concerned that backups were stored only 30 miles from the database. Their thought was that the backups might not be safe in the event of a volcanic eruption or nuclear explosion.

Exactly how you implement database backups depends on several factors such as how likely you think a problem will be, how quickly you need to recover from it, and how disastrous it would be to lose some data and spend time to restore from a backup, but a computerized database gives you a lot more options than a notebook does.

Good database design can help make backups a bit easier. If you arrange the data so changes occur in a fairly localized area, you can back up that area fairly often and not waste time backing up data that changes only rarely.

Low Cost and Extensibility

Ideally the database should be easy to obtain and install, inexpensive, and easily extensible. If you discover that you need to process a lot more data per day than you had expected, you should be able to somehow increase the database's capacity.

Although some database products are quite expensive, most of them have reasonable upgrade paths so you can buy the least expensive license that will handle your needs, at least in the beginning. For example, SQL Server, Oracle, and MySQL provide free editions that you can use to get started building small single-user applications. They also provide more expensive editions that are suitable for very large applications that have hundreds of users.

Installing a database will never be as easy and inexpensive as buying a new notebook, but it also doesn't need to be a time-consuming financial nightmare.

Though expense and capacity are more features of the particular database product than database design, good design can help with a different kind of extensibility. Suppose you have been using a notebook database for a while and discover that you need to capture a new kind of information. Perhaps you decide that you need to track customers' dining habits so you know what restaurant gift certificate to give them on special occasions. In this case, it would be nice if you could extend the database design to hold this extra information.

Good database design can make this kind of extension possible.

Ease of Use

Notebooks and filing cabinets have simple user interfaces so almost anyone can use them effectively. (Although sometimes even they get messed up pretty badly. Should you file "United States Postal Service" under "United States?" "Postal Service?" "Snail Mail?")

A computer application's user interface determines how usable it is by average users. User interface design is not part of database design, so you may wonder why ease of use is mentioned here.

The first-level users of a database are often programmers and relatively sophisticated database users who understand how to navigate through a database. A good database design makes the database much more accessible to those users. Just by looking at the names of the tables, fields, and other database entities that organize the data, this type of user should be able to figure out how different pieces of data go together and how to use them to retrieve the data they need. If those sophisticated users can easily understand the database, they can build better user interfaces for the less advanced users.

Portability

A computerized database allows for a portability that is even more powerful than the portability of a notebook. It allows you to access the data from anywhere you have access to the Web *without actually moving the physical database*. You can access the database from just about anywhere while the data itself remains safely at home, far from the dangers of pickpockets, being dropped in a puddle, and getting forgotten on the bus.

In fact, the new kind of portability may be a little too easy. Though someone in the seat behind you on the airplane can't peek over your shoulder to read a computerized data the way he can a notebook (well, he can if you're using your laptop), a hacker located on the other side of the planet may try to sneak into your database and rifle through your customer data while you're asleep.

This leads to the next topic, security.

Security

A notebook is relatively easy to lose or steal but a highly portable database can be even easier to compromise. If you can access your database from all over the world, then so can cyber-banditos and other ne'er-do-wells.

Locking down your database is mostly a security issue that you should address by using your network's and database's security tools. However, there are some design techniques that you can use to make securing the database easier.

Information Theft

There have been a number of spectacular stories of lost or stolen laptops, hard drives, disks, and other media potentially exposing confidential information to bad guys.

- ❑ On January 22, 2005, a University of Northern Colorado hard drive containing personal information about 30,000 current and former University employees was apparently stolen.

- ❑ On December 22, 2005, a Ford Motor Company computer was stolen containing the names and Social Security Numbers of 70,000 current and former employees. Just three days later, on December 25, 2005, an Ameriprise Financial Inc. laptop containing sensitive information about 260,000 customers was stolen (the laptop was later recovered).

- ❑ On June 1, 2006, a laptop containing information about 243,000 Hotel.com customers was stolen.

- ❑ On January 13, 2007, a North Carolina Department of Revenue computer containing tax information from 30,000 taxpayers was stolen.

- ❑ On January 24, 2008, a Fallon Community Health Plan computer containing confidential information about 30,000 patients was stolen.

- ❑ Finally, in possibly the biggest data loss to date, on May 3, 2006, a U.S. Department of Veterans Affairs laptop containing information about 28.6 million veterans and active duty personnel was stolen.

I don't mean to single these victims out. This is a big issue and hundreds if not thousands of companies around the world have suffered similar data exposure. The Privacy Rights Clearinghouse Web page, "A Chronology of Data Breaches" at www.privacyrights.org/ar/ChronDataBreaches.htm, lists incidents totaling more than 230 million exposed records in the United States alone since the site began tracking incidents in 2005.

If you separate the data into categories that different types of users need to manipulate, you can grant different levels of permission to the different kinds of users. Giving users access to only the data they absolutely need not only reduces the chance of a legitimate user doing something stupid or improper, but it also decreases the chance that an attacker can pose as that user and do something malicious. Even if Clueless Carl won't mistreat your data intentionally, an online mugger might be able to guess Carl's password (which naturally is "Carl") and try to wreak havoc. If Carl doesn't have permission to trash the accounting data, neither does the mugger.

Yet another novel aspect to database security is the fact that users can access the database remotely without actually holding a copy of the database locally. You can use your palmtop computer to access a database without storing the data on your computer. That means if you do somehow lose your computer, the data may still be safe on the database's computer.

This is more an application architecture issue than a database design issue (don't store the data locally on laptops) but using a database design that restricts users' access to what they really need to know can help.

Sharing

It's not easy to share a notebook or envelope full of business cards among a lot of people. No two people can really use a notebook at the same time and there's some overhead in shipping the notebook back and forth among users. Taking time to walk across the room a dozen times a day would be annoying; express mailing a notebook across the country every day would be just plain silly.

Modern networks can let hundreds or even thousands of users access the same database at the same time from locations scattered across the globe. Though this is largely an exercise in networking and the tools provided by a particular database product, some design issues come into play.

If you compartmentalize the data into categories that different types of users need to use as described in the previous section, this not only helps with security but it also helps reduce the amount of data that needs to be shipped across the network.

Breaking the data into reasonable pieces can also help coordinate among multiple users. When your coworker in London starts editing a customer's record, that record must be locked so other users can't sneak in and mess things up before the edit is finished. Grouping the data appropriately lets you lock the smallest amount of data possible so more data is available for other users to edit.

Careful design can allow the database to perform some calculations and ship only the results to your boss who's working hard on the beaches of Hawaii instead of shipping the whole database out there and making the user's computer do all of the work.

Good application design is also important. Even after you prepare the database for efficient use, the application still needs to use it properly. But without a good database design, these techniques aren't possible.

Ability to Perform Complex Calculations

Compared to the human brain, computers are idiots. It takes seriously powerful hardware and frighteningly sophisticated algorithms to perform tasks that you take for granted such as recognizing faces, speaker-independent speech recognition, and handwriting recognition (although neither the human brain nor computers have yet deciphered doctors' prescriptions). The human brain is also self-programming, so it can learn new tasks flexibly and relatively quickly.

Though a computer lacks the adaptability of the human brain, it is great at performing a series of well-defined tasks quickly, repeatedly, and reliably. A computer doesn't get bored, let its attention wander, and make simple arithmetic mistakes (unless it suffers from the infamous Pentium FDIV bug, the f00f bug, the Cyrix coma bug, or a few others). The point is, if the underlying hardware and software works correctly, the computer can perform the same tasks again and again millions of times per second without making mistakes.

When it comes to balancing checkbooks, searching for accounts with balances less than zero, and performing a host of other number-crunching tasks, the computer is much faster and less error-prone than a human brain.

The computer is naturally faster at these sorts of calculations, but even its blazing speed won't help you if your database is poorly designed. A good design can make the difference between finding the data you need in seconds rather than hours, days, or not at all.

Consequences of Good and Bad Design

The following table summarizes how good and bad design can affect the features described in the previous sections.

Feature	Good Design	Bad Design
CRUD	You can find the data you need quickly and easily. The database prevents inconsistent changes.	You find the data you need either very slowly or not at all. You can enter inconsistent data or modify and delete data to make the result inconsistent. (Your products ship to the wrong address or the wrong person.)
Retrieval	You can find the correct data quickly and easily.	You cannot find the data you need quickly. (Your customer waits on hold for 45 minutes to get a simple account balance.)
Consistency	All parts of the database agree on common facts.	Different pieces of information hold contradictory data. (A customer's bills are sent to one address but late payment notices are sent to another.)
Validity	Fields contain valid data.	Fields contain gibberish. (Your company's address has the State value "Confusion." Although if the database does hold that value, it's probably correct on some level.)

Feature	Good Design	Bad Design
Error Correction	It's easy to update incorrect data.	Simple and large-scale changes never happen. (Thousands of your customers' bills are returned to you because their ZIP Code changed and the database didn't get updated.)
Speed	You can quickly find customers by name, account number, or phone number.	You can only find a customer's record if he knows his 37-digit account number. Searching by name takes half an hour.
Atomic Transactions	Related transactions either all happen or all don't happen.	Related transactions may occur partially. (Alice loses $100 but Bob doesn't receive it. Prepare for customer complaints.)
Persistence and Backups	You can recover from computer failure. The data is safe.	Recovering lost data is slow and painful or even impossible. (You lose all of the orders placed in the last week!)
Low Cost and Extensibility	You can move to a bigger database when your need grows.	You're stuck on a small-scale database. (When your Web site starts getting hundreds of orders per second, the database cannot keep up and you lose thousands per day. Don't we all wish we had this problem!)
Ease of Use	The database design is clear so developers understand it and build a great user interface.	The database design is confusing so the developers produce an "anthill" program — confusing and buggy. (I've worked on projects like that and it's no picnic!)
Portability	The design allows different users to download relevant data quickly and easily.	Users must download much more data than they need, slowing performance and giving them access to sensitive data (such as the Corporate Mission Statement, which proves management has no clue.)
Security	Users have access to the data they need and nothing else.	Hackers and disgruntled employees have access to everything.
Sharing	Users can manipulate the data they need.	Users lock data they don't really need and get in each others' way, slowing them down.
Complex Calculations	Users can easily perform complex analysis to support their jobs.	Poor design makes calculations take far longer than necessary. (I worked on a project where a simple change to a data model could force a 20-minute recalculation.)

Summary

This chapter explained the important position that database design plays in application development. If the database design doesn't provide a solid foundation for the rest of the project to build upon, the application as a whole will fail.

This chapter then described physical data containers that can behave as databases. It discussed the strengths and weaknesses of those objects and explained how a computerized database can provide the strengths while avoiding the weaknesses.

In this chapter you learned that a good database provides:

- ❏ CRUD
- ❏ Retrieval
- ❏ Consistency
- ❏ Validity
- ❏ Easy error correction
- ❏ Speed
- ❏ Atomic transactions
- ❏ ACID
- ❏ Persistence and backups
- ❏ Low cost and extensibility
- ❏ Ease of use
- ❏ Portability
- ❏ Security
- ❏ Sharing
- ❏ Ability to perform complex calculations

This chapter used physical objects such as notebooks and filing cabinets to study database goals and potential problems. These physical systems meet some but not all of the database goals fairly effectively.

The next chapter describes several different kinds of computerized databases. It explains which goals each type of database meets and which it does not.

Though this book focuses mostly on relational databases, some of these other kinds of databases are simpler and useful enough for some applications.

Before you move on, however, take a look at the following exercises and test your knowledge of database design goals described in this chapter. You can find the solutions to these exercises in Appendix A.

Exercises

1. Compare this book to a database (assuming you don't just use it as a notebook, scribbling in the margins). What features does it provide? What features are missing?

2. Describe two features that this book provides to help you look for particular pieces of data in different ways.

3. What does CRUD stand for? What do the terms mean?

4. How does a chalkboard implement the CRUD methods? How does a chalkboard's database features compare to those of this book?

5. Consider a recipe file that uses a single index card for each recipe with the cards stored alphabetically. How does that database's features compare to those of a book?

6. What does ACID stand for? What do the terms mean?

7. Suppose Alice, Bob, and Cindy all have account balances of $100 and the database does not allow an account's balance to ever drop below zero. Now consider three transactions: 1) Alice transfers $125 to Bob, 2) Bob transfers $150 to Cindy, and 3) Cindy transfers $25 to Alice and $50 to Bob. In what order(s) can the transactions be executed successfully?

8. Explain how a central database can protect your confidential data.

Database Types

Recall the question posed at the beginning of Chapter 1: What is a database? The answer given there was:

> **A database is a tool that stores data, and lets you create, read, update, and delete the data in some manner.**

This broad definition allows you to consider all sorts of odd things as databases including notebooks, filing cabinets, and your brain. If you're flexible about what you consider data, this definition includes even stranger objects such as a chess set (which stores board positions) or a parking lot (which stores car types and positions, although it might be hard for you to update any given car's position without the owner's consent).

This chapter moves into the realm of computerized databases. Relational databases are by far the most commonly used computerized databases today and most of this book (and other database books) focus on them, but it's still worth taking some time first to learn a bit about other kinds of computerized databases that are available. Relational databases are extremely useful in a huge number of situations but they're not the only game in town. Sometimes a different kind of database may make more sense for your particular problem.

Before you start frantically throwing tables together, building indexes, and normalizing everything in sight, it's worth taking some time to study some of the other kinds of databases that are available.

This chapter describes different types of databases including flat files, spreadsheets, hierarchical databases (XML), object databases, and relational databases. Relational databases are the most common of these, but this chapter describes the others and gives some tips on deciding whether one of the others would be more appropriate.

In this chapter, you learn:

- ❑ What kinds of databases are most common.
- ❑ The strengths and weaknesses of these database types.
- ❑ How to decide which kind of database to use.

Why Bother?

There's an expression, "If all you have is a hammer, everything looks like a nail." If the only kind of database you understand is the relational database, you'll probably try to hammer every kind of data into a relational database, and that can sometimes lead to trouble.

Comparing Database Types

I once worked on a fairly large database application with around 40 developers and more than 120,000 lines of code. The program loaded some fairly large relational databases and used their data to build huge tree-like structures. Those structures allowed sales representatives to design and modify extremely complicated projects for customers involving tens of thousands of line items.

The data was naturally hierarchical but was stored in relational databases, so the program was forced to spend a long time loading each data set. Many projects took 5 to 20 minutes to load. When the user made even a simple change to the data, the program's design required it to recalculate parts of the tree and then save the changes back into the database, a process that took another 5 to 30 minutes depending on the complexity of the model. The program was so slow that the users couldn't perform the kinds of experiments they really needed to optimize the projects they were building. You couldn't quickly see the effects of tweaking a couple of numbers here and there.

To make matters worse, loading and saving all of that hierarchical data in a relational database required tens of thousands of lines of moderately tricky code that was hard to debug and maintain.

At one point, I did a quick experiment to see what would happen if the data were stored in an XML database, a database that naturally stores hierarchical data. My test program was able to load and save data sets containing 20,000 items in three or four seconds.

At this point, the project was too big and the design too entrenched to make such a fundamental change. (After that, political pressure within the company pulled the project in too many directions and it eventually shredded like a tissue in a tug-of-war.)

The lesson is clear: before you spend a lot of time building the ultimate relational database and piling thousands of lines of code on top of it, make sure that's really the kind of database you need. Had this project started with an XML database, it probably would have had a simpler, more natural design with much less code and would probably have lasted for many years to come.

The following sections describe some of the most commonly used database types. They are listed more or less in order of increasing complexity, although it is possible to create very complicated flat files or relatively simple hierarchical databases.

Flat Files

Flat files are simply files containing text. Nothing fancy. No **bold**, *italic*, *different font faces*, or other special font tricks. Just text.

You can add structure to these files, for example by separating values with commas or using indentation to show structure, but the basic file is just a pile of characters. Some structured variations such as INI files and XML files are described later in this chapter.

Text files provide no special features. Flat files don't help you search for data and don't provide aggregate functions such as total, average, and minimum. Writing code to perform any one of those kinds of searches is fairly easy, but it's extra work and providing flexible ad hoc search capabilities is hard.

Programs cannot modify flat files in general ways. For example, you may be able to truncate a file, add data to the end, or change specific characters within the file, but you cannot insert or delete data in the middle of the file. Instead you must rewrite the entire file to make those sorts of changes.

Though flat files don't provide many services, don't scoff at their use. They are extremely simple and easy to understand, so they are a good choice for some kinds of data. You can open a flat file in any text editor and make changes without needing to write a complex user interface.

If a piece of data is relatively simple and seldom changes, a flat file may be an effective, simple way to store the data. For example, a flat file is a fine place to store a message of the day. Each day you can type in one of your favorite obscure quotes for a program to display when it starts. ("The next thing to saying a good thing yourself, is to quote one." –Ralph Waldo Emerson.)

Flat files are also good places to store configuration settings. A configuration file lists a series of named values that a program can read when it needs them. Often a program loads its configuration information when it starts and doesn't look at the configuration file again.

> *Lately some programming environments such as Microsoft's Visual Studio have started saving configuration information in XML files instead of flat files. This lets the application store values in a hierarchical arrangement. The section "XML" later in this chapter has more to say about XML.*

Flat files work well if:

- ❏ Values are fairly small and simple.
- ❏ Values don't change too often.
- ❏ You want to be able to change values with a simple text editor.
- ❏ You want to be able to distribute settings by copying files to new locations.
- ❏ You want to keep a simple historical list of previous values, such as a list of previous daily memos or welcome messages.
- ❏ You want to use tools to quickly compare two files.

Flat files don't work well if:

- ❏ You need to perform complex searches through the values.
- ❏ Values change often.
- ❏ You don't want others to be able to view and modify the values easily.
- ❏ The values are hierarchical.

Two particularly common places to store configuration information are INI files and the Windows system registry. The following sections describe these two approaches.

INI Files

One common type of flat file database is the INI file (INI stands for "initialization"). An INI file contains section names surrounded by square brackets. Each section can hold any number of setting names and values separated by an equal sign. For example, the following INI file contains configuration values for a fictitious application named RBP (Really Big Project):

```
[WebSites]
VbTips=http://www.vb-helper.com/whats_new.html
Quote=http://www.quotationspage.com/qotd.html
AstroPicture=http://antwrp.gsfc.nasa.gov/apod/
Comic=http://www.userfriendly.org/

[Directories]
Image=C:\RBP Project\Pictures
Text=C:\RBP Project\Documents
Data=C:\RBP Project\DB
```

The file's first section is called WebSites. It contains four values named VbTips, Quote, AstroPicture, and Comic that contain URLs leading to Web sites that the application might use. (These pages are my Web site's "what's new" page, a quote-of-the-day page, the astronomy picture-of-the-day site, and the User Friendly daily comic strip page.)

The file's second section is named Directories. It contains three directory paths that the program can use to locate different kinds of files.

When the RBP application starts, it opens this INI file, reads these values into variables, and uses those variables as it runs.

Later, if you need to change any of these settings, you can simply edit the INI file. For example, suppose your data files fill your 250GB C drive. Rather than replacing your C drive with a slightly bigger drive and filling it up in the next few weeks, you decide to add a new G drive that holds 10 petabytes (a petabyte is 1 million gigabytes so this should last you for a while) and move only your data files to that drive. To make the program use the new directory, you only need to change the value of the Directories section's Data setting to:

```
Data=G:\RBP Project\Data
```

Some applications store more volatile settings such as the MRU (Most Recently Used) file list in the File menu. That works if users have separate INI files but doesn't work if they all share the same INI file. To handle both common and individual settings, some programs use one INI file in a shared location to hold shared values and then other INI files in user-specific locations (for example, in each user's My Documents folder) for their personal settings.

Windows System Registry

The Windows system registry is actually not a flat file, although many applications use it as if it were one. The registry is a hierarchical database that holds configuration information for the operating system and many of the programs installed on the system. It contains information such as the locations of key executable programs and libraries.

The registry is extremely important to the operating system and if you mess it up you could seriously confuse the system. You can even make it unbootable, so it doesn't pay to fool around in there casually. However, some programming languages have tools that make using certain parts of the registry reasonably easy and safe. If you stick to those tools and don't get carried away, you should be able to store values with little risk of a serious meltdown.

The root of the registry contains several *hives* (that's what Microsoft calls the areas in the registry) that define branches for the local computer, users in general, and the current user. Those branches provide places for you to store both global and user-specific settings.

Many applications store shared settings in the `HKEY_LOCAL_MACHINE\SOFTWARE` branch of the registry. For example, the RBP application mentioned in the previous section might store its Text directory setting at the registry path `HKEY_LOCAL_MACHINE\SOFTWARE\RBP\Directories\Text`.

The registry automatically builds a separate `HKEY_CURRENT_USER` hive for each user so many applications store user-specific information there. The GBP application might store a user's color preferences so users who are color-deficient (color-blind) can adjust the colors so they are easy to see. The program can store the color settings in the `HKEY_CURRENT_USER\Software\GBP\Colors` area so different users see a different set of values.

Although if you provide this feature, some of the users will spend time fiddling with the colors to match their moods each day. Sooner or later, someone will set his foreground and background colors to black just to see what will happen. He won't be able to see anything and you'll have to fix it. (I knew someone who did this intentionally to her Windows system colors just to see what would happen. It took her most of a day to recover. Curiosity may not kill the programmer but it can sure make things interesting.)

The registry is hierarchical and you can build branches within other branches, but it really isn't intended for constructing elaborate data hierarchies. It also isn't intended for storing huge amounts of data or data that changes very frequently. It's a good place to store user-specific configuration information such as MRU lists that might change a few times per day, but it's not a good place to store customer orders and minute-to-minute stock prices.

Relational Databases

This book is mostly about relational databases. Chapter 3 provides an introduction to relational databases. This chapter needs to describe them in enough detail for you to decide whether they're the right choice for you.

Without getting into too much detail (I don't want to spoil the next chapter's surprise), a relational database contains tables that hold rows and columns. Each row holds related data about a particular entity (person, vehicle, sandwich, or whatever). Each column represents a piece of data about that entity (name, street address, number of pickles, and so forth).

Sometimes a piece of data naturally has more than one value. For example, a single customer might place lots of orders. To make it easy to add multiple values, those values are stored in a separate table linked to the first by some value that the corresponding records share.

For example, suppose you build a relational database to track your favorite street luge racers. The Racers table stores information about individual racers. Each row corresponds to a particular racer. The columns represent basic information for a racer such as name, age, height, weight, and so forth. A very important column stores each racer's ID number.

Over time, each racer will have lots of race results (although there will probably be lots of blank spots for bale chuckers — see `www.skateluge.com/lugetalk.htm`). You store race results in a separate RaceResults table. Each row records the final standings for a single racer in a single race. The columns record the racer's ID number, the race's name and date, the racer's finishing position, and the points that position is worth for overall ranking.

To find all of the finishing positions and points for a particular racer, you look up the racer's row in the Racers table, find the racer's ID number, and then find all of the rows in the RaceResults table that have this racer ID.

Figure 2-1 shows this simple database design. (No, this is not a finished design nor a very good one. It's just a start to give you the flavor of a relational database. Let's not get ahead of ourselves!)

Racers Table		
RacerName	Nationality	RacerId
Michael Serek	Austria	1
Chris McBride	United States	2
Sebastien Tournissac	France	3

RaceResults Table					
RaceName	Division	Dates	RacerId	FinishingPosition	Points
Go Fast Speed Days	Pro Classic Luge Mass	9/1/2007-9/2/2007	1	1	450.0024
Rock and Roll	Pro Classic Luge Mass	7/27/2007-7/28/2007	1	1	450.0024
Almabtrieb World Championships	Pro Classic Luge Mass	7/11/2007-7/14/2007	1	6	403.3633
Almabtrieb World Championships	Pro Classic Luge Mass	7/11/2007-7/14/2007	2	24	321.1366
Almabtrieb World Championships	Pro Classic Luge Mass	7/11/2007-7/14/2007	3	2	432.6154
Go Fast Speed Days	Pro Classic Luge Mass	9/1/2007-9/2/2007	2	2	432.6154
Go Fast Speed Days	Pro Classic Luge Mass	9/1/2007-9/2/2007	3	3	424.3687
Top Challenge	Pro Street Luge Mass	8/25/2007-8/26/2007	2	13	0

Figure 2-1

Relational databases have been around for a long time. (Edgar Codd started laying the foundations in 1970.) They are the most commonly used kind of database today and have been for years, so a lot of very powerful companies have spent a huge amount of time building them. All of that means that relational databases have been thoroughly studied and have evolved over time to the point where they are quite useful and effective.

Relational databases provide a number of features that make working with databases such as the street luge database easier. Some of the features they provide include:

- **Data types:** Each column has a particular data type (text, numeric, date, and so forth) and the database will not allow values of other types in a column.

- **Basic constraints:** The database can enforce constraints such as requiring that a luge racer's top speed be between 50 and 250mph (no one with a top speed less than 50 is worth recording) or it can require certain fields.

- **Referential integrity:** The database can prevent you from adding a RaceResults record for a racer who doesn't exist in the Racers table. Similarly, the database can prevent you from modifying a racer's ID if that would leave rows in the RaceResults table with invalid racer IDs, and it could prevent you from modifying a RaceResults row's racer ID to an invalid value.

- **Cascading deletes and updates:** If you delete a racer from the Racers table, the database can automatically delete all of that racer's RaceResults records. Similarly if you change a racer's ID number, the database can update the ID numbers in that racer's RaceResults records.

- **Joins:** The database can quickly gather related records from different tables. For example, it can easily list every racer with his or her corresponding finishing positions sorted alphabetically and by race date.

- **Complex queries:** Relational databases support all sorts of interesting query and aggregation functions such as SUM, AVG, MIN, COUNT, STDEV, and GROUP BY.

Relational databases work well if:

- You need to perform complicated queries and joins among different tables.
- You need to perform data validations such as verifying that related rows in other tables exist.
- You need to allow for any number of values for a particular piece of data (for example, race finishing positions).
- You want to be able to flexibly build new queries that you didn't plan when you started designing the project.

Relational databases don't work well if:

- You need to use a special data topology to perform the application's main function. For example, you can beat a hierarchy or network with a brick until it fits in a relational database but you may get better performance using a more specialized type of database.

Unless you have special needs, relational databases are usually an excellent choice. Hence the need for this book!

Some of the later sections in this chapter discuss variations on relational databases or other kinds of databases that provide relational features.

Spreadsheets

Spreadsheets display rows and columns of data. They allow the user to create formulas that depend on other data in the spreadsheet, make charts and graphs to visualize the data, print the data, and import and export the data in text and other formats. A spreadsheet may also support relatively sophisticated analysis tools such as statistical functions and iterated solution finding (basically making a bunch of guesses to see which ones work best).

Spreadsheets allow you to easily update some or all of the data and they automatically recalculate values that depend on the data you change.

Because many users understand spreadsheets and are comfortable with them, they can perform some of their own analysis, so you may be able to avoid some work generating a zillion different kinds of output.

> In most of the larger projects I've worked on, we tried to build in ad hoc query tools so the users could define their own reports. That not only lets you save all the time you would have spent building dozens of reports yourself (one application had more than 100 reports), but it also keeps the users busy so they have less time to dream up gratuitous feature change requests while you're trying to implement the basic functionality.

If these are the sorts of things you need to do with your data, using a spreadsheet may save you a lot of time and trouble building a more complicated database.

However, spreadsheets don't support complex queries. They also don't automatically check the data's integrity, so it's easy for you to enter incorrect or inconsistent values.

Some spreadsheets allow you to write scripting code that can add a lot of features such as integrity checks and complex analysis that isn't provided by the spreadsheet itself. If you're going to go to all that trouble, however, you may as well admit that you need more than the spreadsheet was intended to do and consider using a more powerful database such as a relational database.

> Many applications provide spreadsheet data as a form of output. They store their data in a relational or other kind of database and then dump results into a spreadsheet format for users to manipulate.

Spreadsheets work well if:

- ❑ The data fits naturally in a simple tabular format.
- ❑ You need to visualize the data in charts and graphs.
- ❑ The end users are comfortable with spreadsheets.
- ❑ The end users want to be able to experiment with the data on their own.

Spreadsheets don't work well if:

- ❑ You need complex relationships among the values on different worksheets.
- ❑ You need to perform complex calculations that a spreadsheet cannot easily handle.

❑   You need data validation.

❑   You need to perform complex queries.

❑   You need to update large amounts of data automatically.

Hierarchical Databases

Hierarchical data includes values that are naturally arranged in a tree-like structure. One piece of data somehow logically contains or includes other pieces of data.

Files on a disk drive are typically arranged in a hierarchy. The disk's root directory logically contains everything in the file system. Inside the root are files and directories or folders that break the disk into (hopefully) useful categories. Those folders may contain files and other folders that further refine the groupings.

The following listing shows a tiny part of the folders that make up a file system. It doesn't list the many files that would be in each of these folders.

```
C:\
    Documents and Settings
        Administrator
        All Users
        Ben Grim
        Groo
        Rod
    Temp
        Art
        Astro
    Windows
        Config
        Cursors
        Debug
        system
        system32
            1025
            1031
            1040 short form
            1099 int
```

The disk's root directory is called C:\. It contains the Documents and Settings, Temp, and Windows directories. Documents and Settings contains folders for the administrator and all users in general, in addition to folders for the system's other users.

The Temp directory contains temporary files. It contains Art and Astro folders that hold temporary files used for specific purposes.

The Windows directory contains various operating systems files that you should generally not mess with.

If your file system is designed logically, you should be able to tell from a file's position in the hierarchy what its purpose is. If you found the file iss_sts122.jpg in the folder C:\Temp\Astro, you could guess that this was a temporary astronomy image. (If you know your astronomy, you might also guess that it is a picture of the International Space Station taken on Space Shuttle mission TST-122. See antwrp.gsfc.nasa.gov/apod/image/0803/iss_sts122.jpg.)

Many other kinds of data can also be arranged hierarchically. Figure 2-2 shows a business organization chart that is arranged hierarchically. The lines indicate which people report to which others.

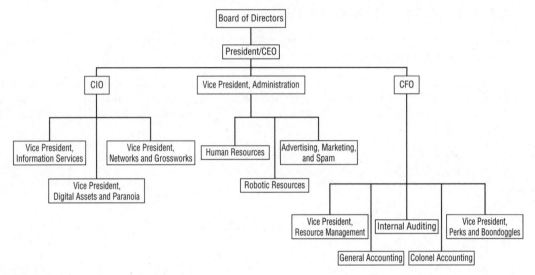

Figure 2-2

Figure 2-3 shows the same information in a slightly different format. This version is arranged more vertically in a way similar to that used by Windows Explorer to show a disk's file system.

In a pipe system, typically big pipes feed into smaller ones to form a hierarchy. Water flows from a treatment plant to large distribution pipes that break into smaller and smaller pipes that eventually feed into houses, bookstores, and coffee houses.

Similarly, electricity flows from a power plant across high-voltage long-distance transmission lines at a few hundred thousand volts (there's less power loss at higher voltages). Next a transformer lowers the voltage to 13,800 or so volts for more local transport. Some is used by factories and large businesses. The rest moves through more transformers that reduce the voltage to 110 or 220 volts (in the United States anyway) for use by your latte machine and desktop computer. (It doesn't even stop there. Your computer again reduces the voltage to 5 volts or so to power your USB plasma ball and missile launcher with Web camera.)

Some other examples of data that you can arrange hierarchically include a family tree tracing your ances-tors back in time (two parents, who each have two parents, who each have two parents, and so forth), the parts of any complicated object (a computer has a keyboard, mouse, screen, and system box; the system box includes a fan, power supply, peripherals, and a motherboard; the motherboard includes a chip, heat sink, memory, and so forth), and order tracking information (customers have orders; orders have basic information such as dates and addresses, in addition to order items and possibly sub-orders; order items have an inventory item and quantity; inventory item has description, part number, price, and in some applications sub-items).

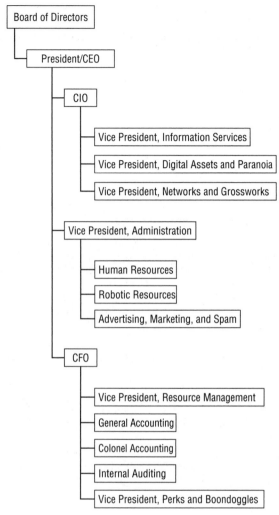

Figure 2-3

You can even think of the information in this book hierarchically. (It's made of chapters that contain paragraphs and sections; sections contain paragraphs and sub-sections; paragraphs contain sentences, which contain words, which contain characters.)

A hierarchical database stores these kinds of data in a way that makes it relatively easy to manipulate the data hierarchically. For example, it may be easy to add a new branch to the tree of data at a particular point. It may be easy to enumerate the "children" of a particular location in the tree. Or it may be easy to search the "ancestors" or "descendants" of a particular piece of data. (For example, in an organizational chart, you might want to list every employee in the Human Resources part of the hierarchy.)

At the same time, a hierarchical database may not support other operations as well as hierarchical operations. For example, it may be hard to search for every employee who filled in more than 60 hours on last week's timesheet (so you can buy these people cots to put in their offices so they can work even more). If this is a common search, a relational database could use an index to find these employees very quickly. A straightforward hierarchical database would need to examine every employee's data individually.

Hierarchical databases work well if:

❑ The data is naturally hierarchical.

❑ You need to perform operations that take advantage of the hierarchical structure.

Hierarchical databases don't work well if:

❑ The data is not naturally hierarchical.

❑ You need to perform complex calculations or searches that do not use the hierarchical structure.

❑ You need complex data validation.

❑ You need to update large amounts of data automatically.

In the past few years, the XML hierarchical data format has come into widespread use. XML is not actually a database; it's just a text-based method for storing hierarchical data. Although XML is not a database by itself, it's useful and common enough to deserve more in-depth coverage, so the following section provides a brief introduction to XML.

XML

XML (eXtensible Markup Language) is a language for storing hierarchical data. XML itself doesn't provide any tools for building, searching, updating, validating, or otherwise manipulating data and anyone who tells you otherwise is trying to sell you something.

However, XML is a fairly useful format for storing, transferring, and retrieving hierarchical data, and there are several common tools that can make working with XML files easy. This book doesn't explain everything there is to know about XML files. The following sections just provide an overview of XML to help you recognize when an XML database might be a better choice than other kinds of databases. Several other books cover XML in excruciating detail.

XML Basics

An XML file is a relatively simple text file that uses special tokens to define a structure for the data that it contains. People often compare XML to the Web language HTML (HyperText Markup Language) because both use tokens surrounded by pointy brackets, but the two languages have several large differences.

One major difference between XML and HTML is that XML is extensible (the X isn't part of the name just to sound edgy and cool). HTML commands are predefined by the language specification and if you try to invent new ones it's unlikely that a typical browser will know what to do with them. In contrast, XML defines some syntax and options but you get to make up the tokens that contain the data as you go along. All you need to do is start using a token surrounded by pointy brackets. You follow the token by whatever data it should contain and finish with a closing token that is the same as the opening token except it starts with a slash.

For example, the following text shows a single XML token called Name with value Rod Stephens:

```
<Name>Rod Stephens</Name>
```

Programs that read XML ignore whitespace (non-printing characters such as spaces, tabs, and carriage returns) so you can use them to make the data more readable. For example, you can use carriage returns and tabs to indent the data and show the hierarchical structure.

You can make new tokens at any time. For example, the following code shows a Person element that includes three fields called FirstName, LastName, and NetWorth. The text uses carriage returns and indentation to make the data easy to read:

```
<Person>
    <FirstName>Rod</FirstName>
    <LastName>Stephens</LastName>
    <NetWorth>$16.32</NetWorth>
</Person>
```

A second important way in which XML and HTML differ is that XML is much stricter about properly nesting and closing opened tokens. For example, the HTML <P> command tells a browser to start a new paragraph. Because this command cannot contain any text, there's no need to end it with a closing </P> token. The browser just assumes that the <P> token immediately ends with a corresponding </P> tag. Similarly, a browser assumes an immediate closing tag for a horizontal rule <HR> element, and assumes a closing tag for a list item element <LI> when it encounters another <LI> element or a list ending tag such as </OL> or </UL>.

In XML every opening token must have a corresponding closing token. (However, XML does allow you to use a shorthand syntax for tokens that immediately open and then close. Just put a slash before the closing pointy bracket as in <Closed />.)

XML requires that elements be properly nested. One element may completely contain another, but they may not overlap so one contains only part of another.

For example, the following text includes a FirstName element. While that element is open, the text defines a LastName element but the FirstName element closes before the LastName element does. (The indentation makes the overlap easier to see.) This violates XML's nesting rules, so this is not a properly formed piece of XML:

```
<Person>
    <FirstName>Rod
        <LastName>Stephens
    </FirstName>
        </LastName>
    <NetWorth>$16.32</NetWorth>
</Person>
```

An XML file can define *attributes* for an element. For example, in the following XML code, the Person element has an attribute named profession with value Dilettante:

```
<Person Profession="Dilettante">
    <FirstName>Rod</FirstName>
```

```
    <LastName>Stephens</LastName>
    <NetWorth>$16.32</NetWorth>
</Person>
```

You can enclose a comment in an XML file by starting it with the characters `<!--` and ending it with the characters `-->`. For example, the following XML code adds a comment to the previous code:

```
<!-- The book's author -->
<Person Profession="Dilettante">
    <FirstName>Rod</FirstName>
    <LastName>Stephens</LastName>
    <NetWorth>$16.32</NetWorth>
</Person>
```

The final XML rule covered here is that the file must have a single root element that contains all other elements. This makes the file an absolutely pure, true hierarchy of data. Actually, the file can also begin with an optional XML declaration that gives the XML version.

The following text shows a slightly more elaborate XML file:

```
<?xml version="1.0" encoding="UTF-8"?>
<ClassSchedule>
    <Class Name="Ascension for Beginners" Room="Atrium">
        <!-- Note: Requires Falling 101. -->
        <Instructor>Peter Parker</Instructor>
        <Students>
            <Student>
                <FirstName>Ben</FirstName>
                <LastName>Breaker</LastName>
            </Student>
            <Student>
                <FirstName>Carla</FirstName>
                <LastName>Crash</LastName>
            </Student>
            <Student>
                <FirstName>Dirk</FirstName>
                <LastName>Drop</LastName>
            </Student>
        </Students>
    </Class>

    <Class Name="Advanced Pyrotechnics" Room="Field 3">
        <!-- Note: Requires fire-retardant suit. -->
        <Instructor>Johnny Storm</Instructor>
        <Fees Materials="$45" />
        <Students>
            <Student>
                <FirstName>Erica</FirstName>
                <LastName>Enflame</LastName>
            </Student>
            <Student>
                <FirstName>Frank</FirstName>
                <LastName>Flammable</LastName>
                <NickName>Flamb&#xE9;</NickName>
```

```
            </Student>
          </Students>
        </Class>
    </ClassSchedule>
```

This file begins with an XML declaration indicating that it uses XML version 1.0 and the UTF-8 character encoding. It then starts a `ClassSchedule` element that holds all of the document's other content.

The `ClassSchedule` element contains two `Class` elements. Those elements have `Name` and `Room` attributes that give the class's name and location.

The `Class` elements contain `Instructor` and `Fees` elements that define basic information about the classes. Each also includes a `Students` element that contains information about all of the students enrolled in the class. The detailed student information is contained in `Student` elements that hold `FirstName` and `LastName` elements.

Note that the elements need not contain exactly the same kinds of content. For example, the second class contains a `Fees` element but the first does not. Similarly, the final `Student` element contains a `NickName` element but none of the other `Student` elements do. (The text `&#xE9;` in that value makes the `NickName` data include the character with Unicode hexadecimal value E9. That's the character "e" with an acute accent: é.)

Because you can make up XML elements as you go along, they allow more flexibility than some other kinds of databases. A relational database, for example, defines exactly what fields are contained in every record in a table. In an XML file, you can add new elements at any point in the file. The XML file's elements provide self-documenting names (if you give your elements reasonable names and not just "e1" and "N32"). This kind of flexible, self-describing database is called *semi-structured*.

XML schema files allow you to provide some validation. For example, they let you indicate that a particular element must contain certain other elements, that an element must contain a date or number, or that an element is required.

XML Structures

In practice I typically see XML files used most often in one of three ways.

First, XML files are hierarchical so it's natural to use them to hold hierarchical data. It's straightforward to map purely hierarchical data such as a simple family tree or organizational chart into an XML file.

Second, XML files are often used to hold table-like data. The basic structure closely follows the structure of a relational database. The root element holds several table elements. Each of those elements holds "records" that hold "fields."

For example, the following XML document holds data about a simple company's customers and their orders:

```
<AllData>
    <Customers>
        <Customer ID="1">
            <FirstName>Alfred</FirstName>
```

```
            <LastName>Gusenbauer</LastName>
        </Customer>
        <Customer ID="2">
            <FirstName>David</FirstName>
            <LastName>Thompson</LastName>
        </Customer>
        <Customer ID="3">
            <FirstName>Alberto</FirstName>
            <LastName>Selva</LastName>
        </Customer>
    </Customers>
    <Products>
        <Product ID="273645" Description="Toothbrush" Price="$1.95" />
        <Product ID="78463" Description="Pencil" Price="$0.15" />
        <Product ID="48937" Description="Notepad" Price="$0.75" />
    </Products>
    <CustomerOrders>
        <CustomerOrder Date="12/27/2008" CustomerId="2">
            <Item ID="1" ProductId="78463" Quantity="12" />
            <Item ID="2" ProductId="48937" Quantity="2" />
        </CustomerOrder>
    </CustomerOrders>
</AllData>
```

The file starts with an `AllData` root element. That element contains three more elements that define table-like structures holding customer, product, and customer order information.

Each of these "tables" defines "records." For example, the `Customers` element includes Customer "records" that hold `FirstName` and `LastName` values.

This XML document uses ID numbers to link records in different "tables" together. In this example, the single `CustomerOrder` element represents an order placed by customer 2 (David Thompson) who ordered 12 items with ID 78463 (pencils) and 2 items with ID 48937 (notepads).

The third XML file structure I've seen regularly is a simple list of values. The following XML document uses this structure to hold configuration settings for an application:

```
<Settings>
    <NormalColor>Black</NormalColor>
    <WarningColor>Green</WarningColor>
    <ErrorColor>Yellow</ErrorColor>
    <PanicSound>panic.wav</PanicSound>
    <BugEmail>bugs@panic.com</BugEmail>
</Settings>
```

This kind of XML file gives a little more structure than a flat text file used to hold settings and lets a program use XML tools to easily load and read setting values.

This flat structure is also useful when each XML document corresponds directly to some sort of object that a program will use. For example, the following XML file defines a letter. A program could load this data and use its fields to print and mail the letter.

```
<Letter>
    <ToName>Hulk Hogan</ToName>
    <ToStreet>2615 Grappler St, #12</ToStreet>
```

```
    <ToCity>Gripper</ToCity>
    <ToState>CA</ToState>
    <FromName>Yokozuna Hakuho</FromName>
    <Body>
Respected Sir,

Regarding your challenge: Bring it! Your dojo or mine?

Sincerely,
    </Body>
</Letter>
```

The following code shows the same data but in a more structured format:

```
<Letter>
    <To>
        <Name>Hulk Hogan</Name>
        <Address>
            <Street>2615 Grappler St, #12</Street>
            <City>Gripper</City>
            <State>CA</State>
        </Address>
    </To>
    <From>Yokozuna Hakuho</From>
    <Body>
Respected Sir,

Regarding your challenge: Bring it! Your dojo or mine?

Sincerely,
    </Body>
</Letter>
```

This version creates a To element that includes all of the information about the letter's recipient. The To element contains an Address element that holds the recipient's address information. You could add similar information for the sender.

XML Summary

XML files are hierarchical so they are a natural choice for storing hierarchical data. Though you can store hierarchical data in other types of databases, they are unlikely to be able to re-create the hierarchical object structure as quickly as XML tools can. (See the story in the "Why Bother?" section at the beginning of this chapter.)

XML files allow you to create elements within other elements just about anywhere you like, so they are semi-structured. This can be convenient if you're not sure of the data's exact format ahead of time. For example, you could easily add extra To, Cc, or Bcc elements to the previous letter example even if you didn't realize you would need them when you wrote the original letter. (Of course, the program that prints the letter may need some modifications to use the new fields but at least you can store valid data.)

Because XML files are plain old text files, they have some of the limitations of text files. In particular, you cannot add, delete, or modify data in the middle of an XML file. To update an XML file, a program typically reads the file into memory, makes its changes, and then writes the result back into the file.

This read-modify-write nature means XML documents are not great multi-user databases. An XML document works fine if many users need to read it but it's harder to allow them to update the file without interfering with each other.

Note that recent versions of some other kinds of databases provide XML support. For example, Excel workbooks can save their data in XML files. SQL Server and Oracle can execute queries to extract data and then return the result in an XML format for the program to manipulate or save into a file.

XML files work well if:

❑   The data is naturally hierarchical.

❑   Available XML tools provide the features you need.

❑   You want the kinds of validation that schema files can provide.

❑   You want to import and export the data in products that understand XML.

XML files don't work well if:

❑   You use non-hierarchical data such as networks (described in the following section).

❑   You need more complex data validation than schema files can provide.

❑   You need to perform relational rather than hierarchical queries.

❑   The database is very large so rewriting the entire file to update a small bit of data in the middle is cumbersome.

❑   You need to allow multiple users to frequently update the database without interfering with each other.

You can find lots of free tutorials covering XML and its related technologies such as XSL, XSLT, XPath, XQuery, and others on the W3 Schools Web site (www.w3schools.com).

Network

A network contains a collection of *nodes* that are connected by *links*. The nodes and links can represent all sorts of things such as telephone lines, streets, airline routes, and electrical circuits. Links can be unordered (you can travel either way across a link) or ordered (each link is one-way).

Figure 2-4 shows a simple ordered street network. The numbers on the links represent the average time in seconds to cross the link. The letters on the nodes are just there for identification.

A typical problem for this street network might be to find the shortest route from the police station at node A to the donut store at node D. The police will be using their lights and sirens so you don't need to worry about turn penalties (a common feature in shortest path algorithms makes it take longer to turn than to go straight). See if you can find the solution.

Often what appears to be a hierarchical database is really a network. For example, Figure 2-2 shows an idealized corporate organizational chart where lines indicate which people report to which others.

In practice, organizational charts are often more complex and convoluted. Many companies practice "matrix management" where employees may work in more than one department and have several managers for different purposes. Sometimes a person who normally reports to one superior also reports to someone else, either temporarily for the duration of a special project or permanently if more than one executive shares the same area of interest.

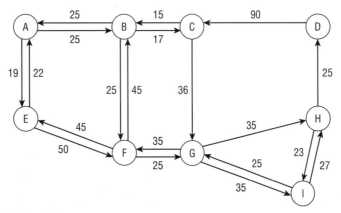

Figure 2-4

Figure 2-5 shows the organizational chart from Figure 2-2 with a few modifications. Here dashed lines indicate that the Robotics Resources director also reports to the CIO, and that the Vice President of Perks and Boondoggles also reports to the President, in addition to reporting through the normal chain of command.

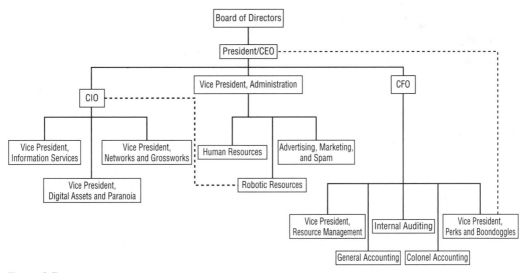

Figure 2-5

Some operating systems allow you to create links from one part of the file system to another. This lets you create a folder that seems to be inside one directory when really entering it warps you to a completely different part of the file system. In that case, the file system isn't really a hierarchy any more. Instead of a tree, it's more like a bush with grafts and intertwined branches that make strange backwards connections like some sort of alien hybrid, or the organizational chart shown in Figure 2-5. (Real organizational charts often look like the products of some bizarre alien intelligence or plates of spaghetti.)

Network databases are uncommon, although network data structures are very useful for operational algorithms such as shortest path finding, task scheduling, and network flow (think water flowing through pipelines).

Some XML tools allow you to easily save and restore networks in addition to hierarchical data. For example, Microsoft's Visual Studio programming languages C# (pronounced "C sharp") and Visual Basic include tools that can save and restore networks in XML files. The resulting files use automatically generated ID numbers to link nodes together and they can be hard to read, but if you only need to save and restore network structures they can be quite handy.

When you use a network file to store data, the program does all of the work. The file itself provides no special features.

Network files work well if:

❑ The data is naturally a network (or almost a hierarchy).

❑ You need to perform network operations on the data such as finding shortest paths or calculating network flows.

❑ You don't need to perform complex queries on the data.

Network files don't work well if:

❑ The data does not represent a network.

❑ You need to validate the data.

❑ You need to perform queries on the data.

❑ You need to allow multiple users to frequently update the data without interfering with each other.

Object

Modern programming languages are object-oriented. They use programming abstractions called objects to represent items such as customers, orders, penny stocks, and betting slips.

An *object database* manages objects. It provides some sort of query syntax for retrieving objects from the database. It also provides tools for saving changes to an object back into the database.

Object databases also provide some useful concurrency features. For example, if two users of a program need to work with an object representing the November 12th episode of the television show *Deal or No Deal*, the database gives them the same logical object. If the two users access the object simultaneously, the database referees so the users don't interfere with each other.

Object databases are also sometimes called object-oriented databases, object database management systems (ODBMS), and object stores. Some developers make a distinction among these different terms but at this level they're close enough to the same thing.

Object databases work well if:

❑ Your programming environment and architecture favors using objects.

❑ You don't need to perform complex queries on the data (which tend to slow these databases down considerably).

Object databases don't work well if:

❑ Your program needs to interact with external tools where storing the data in a more common format such as a relational database is an advantage.

❑ You need to perform complicated queries that will execute faster in a relational database.

❑ You aren't using an object-oriented language (for example, if a Microsoft Access database can do everything you need without any programming).

❑ You need to perform data validations that the object database cannot provide.

Object-Relational

An object-relational database (ORD) or object-relational database management system (ORDBMS) is a relational database that provides extra features for integrating object types into the data. Like a relational database, it can perform complex queries relatively quickly. Like an object database, it uses some special syntax to simplify the creation of objects.

Over time, many of the features originally designed for use by object-relational databases have been added to relational databases.

A closely related concept is the *object-relational mapping* system. An object-relational mapping system provides a layer between the object-oriented code and a relational database to convert between objects and relational data. If this layer does a good job of separating the objects and the database, programmers and database developers can ignore the details of each others' work. This lets them work more independently, makes them more productive, and makes it easier for either group to accommodate changes in the other group's work. (It may also help keep them from getting into brawls during project get-togethers.)

Object-relational databases and object-relational mappings work well if:

❑ Your programming environment and architecture favors using objects.

❑ You need to perform complicated relational-style queries.

❑ You need to perform relational-style data validations.

❑ Your program needs to interact with external tools where storing the data in a common relational format is an advantage.

❑ You have separate programmers and database developers so maintaining a strict separation can make the project more manageable.

Object-relational databases and object-relational mappings don't work well if:

❑ You aren't using an object-oriented language (for example, if a Microsoft Access database can do everything you need without any programming).

Exotic

These kinds of databases are more unusual than those described previously. They tend to be very specialized and work well only for a specific subset of database problems. Some are variations on other, less unusual kinds of databases.

Document-Oriented

A document-oriented database is designed to work with document-oriented applications. A typical document-oriented application allows the user to open a "document" that represents something. Usually this is an actual file such as a letter, video clip, or Web page, but it might be something more abstract such as student transcripts that are not actually stored in separate physical documents.

A good example of a document-oriented application might manage the files that make up a Web site. (My VB Helper Web site www.vb-helper.com holds more than 5,000 files in a dozen or so directories and keeping track of them all is quite a chore. I should build a document management system!)

Some document-oriented databases are simply constructs within a file system that use directories and subdirectories to hold the files that make up the documents. Unfortunately this kind of file system offers limited tools for sorting, searching, and performing other database-related tasks.

Other document-oriented databases are built as a layer on top of some other database system, for example, a relational database. The database might store the contents of the documents themselves or it might store the documents' locations on disk.

Deductive

A deductive database is one that can make deductions based on rules and facts contained within the database. They are a sort of cross between logic programming and relational databases. Some of these databases allow the programmer to guide the evaluation of a program.

Dimensional

A dimensional database (sometimes called a multi-dimensional database) represents different aspects of data as dimensions rather than as separate tables in a relational database.

You can think of dimensional data as forming a multi-dimensional rectangular box (also called a hyper-cube or multi-dimensional array) where each dimension represents some important facet of the data. For example, Figure 2-6 shows a three-dimensional picture with Year, Sales Rep, and Product Line as dimensions. Each little cube or *cell* in the larger box contains information relating to a particular selection of the dimensions. In other words, a particular cell would contain information about a selected sales rep's sales for a selected product line in a particular year (Crazy Bob's yo-yo sales for 2008).

Dimensional databases are particularly useful for scrounging through old data looking for patterns and they make useful data warehouses. However, if the data is sparse (a lot of the cells in Figure 2-6 are empty), they can waste a lot of space, so they are not usually appropriate for day-to-day use for new data entry. Truly native dimensional databases (as opposed to a dimensional database built on top of a relational database) may be optimized to handle sparse data and can save space while still providing fast results.

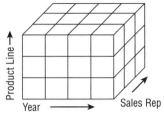

Figure 2-6

Temporal

A temporal database has built-in time information. One of the simplest pieces of temporal data that this kind of database stores is the data's *valid time*: the time during which it is valid.

For example, suppose you build an inventory and sales database for your jewelry store. To make mall visitors think they are getting a good deal, you constantly raise and lower prices. When you're ready for your bi-monthly vacation, you raise prices so the reduced sales load won't overwhelm your brother-in-law Joey (who's otnay ootay ightbray) while you're gone. When you get back, you have your bi-monthly "Once-In-A-Lifetime Blockbuster Overstock Sale!" to clear inventory. To be able to later track sales at various prices over time, you need to know the times during which different prices were in effect.

If you were on vacation from April 1 until April 14 and prices were "normal," then those prices have a valid time of those two weeks. If you return and cut prices by 40% from April 15 until your next vacation on May 22, the new prices have a valid time of April 15 through May 22.

For other examples, imagine tracking employee addresses as they move, mileage and fuel use in your fleet of rental scooters, or daily coffee prices. You could store only the latest information in each of these cases, but then you lose the ability to look back in time for important trends.

> *In fact, I've heard a reasonably plausible argument that a database should never delete or overwrite any information. Instead it should just mark the old data as deleted and optionally create a new record for the new data. With disk space as cheap as it is these days (as little as $0.22 or so per GB), it's easy to imagine saving every piece of data, at least for small- and medium-sized databases. (In this case, the database wouldn't need the D in CRUD (Create, Read, Update, Delete) so it goes from being CRUD to being CRU, a fine French wine.)*

It's not too hard to add time fields to other kinds of databases such as relational databases. You'll need a little extra programming to keep track of which values you should use at different times, but this technique can be very useful for data that changes frequently over time.

Summary

Before you launch into an exhausting year-long process of building a relational database, it's worth taking at least a few minutes to decide what kind of database would best fit your needs. Though you can probably use any kind of database for most purposes, some lend themselves more naturally to certain problems than others. Though you can store a data hierarchy or network in a relational database, it may be a lot faster to use a simpler XML file. Though you certainly can store simple configuration settings in an object-oriented database, a flat text file will do just as well with a lot less trouble.

In this chapter you learned how to pick the database type that will work best with your data. You learned that:

- ❑ Flat files are good for storing simple values or complete documents, although they lack features for concurrency and easy updating.

- ❑ INI files are good for storing simple values that are easy to look up, although they lack features for concurrency and easy updating.

- ❑ The Windows system registry is good for storing simple values that are easy to look up and can handle system-wide or user-specific settings.

- ❑ Relational databases are the workhorse of the database world. They allow complex data relations, sophisticated data validation, integrity constraints, cascading updates and deletes, ad hoc queries, and many more useful features.

- ❑ Spreadsheets are good for drawing charts and graphs, and are convenient for users who already know how to use them.

- ❑ Hierarchical databases are good for storing and manipulating hierarchical data such as organizational charts and family trees.

- ❑ XML files are good for storing hierarchical data, although they lack features for concurrency and easy updating.

- ❑ Network databases are good for storing network data such as street or telephone networks.

- ❑ Object databases are good for integrating programming objects into the database.

- ❑ Object-relational databases and object-relational mapping systems combine some of the best features of object-databases and relational databases. An object-relational mapping layered on top of a relational database can provide a useful separation between programmers and database developers.

- ❑ Document-oriented databases are useful in document management systems (such as the one I need to build some day to manage my Web site).

- ❑ Deductive databases can make logical deductions based on rules and data stored in the database.

- ❑ Dimensional databases consider data in hypercubes and make it easy to study data based on dimensional selections (such as sales by a particular representative or during a particular year).

- ❑ Temporal databases integrate time with the data so they can record and work with information that changes over time.

Relational databases are by far the most common type of database in use today and they are the topic of most of this book and the majority other database books. The next chapter describes relational databases in greater detail. It explains the basic relational concepts that you need to understand to design and build effective relational databases.

Before you move on to Chapter 3, however, use the following exercises to test your understanding of the material covered in this chapter. You can find the solutions to these exercises in Appendix A.

Exercises

For the following scenarios, list the type(s) of database that might make good choices for storing the data.

1. A dog breeding database that records the ancestors of a single dog for five generations.

2. A similar dog breeding database that records the ancestors and descendants of a single dog for five generations each way.

3. Application settings that record which windows a user had open and where they were positioned the last time the application was used.

4. Total sales figures by month, arranged to make it easy to see trends graphically.

5. The same as Exercise 4 but the users want to be able to draw similar data for several product lines on the same graph.

6. And they want to be able to print it and tweak the numbers to see what the graph would look like if they exceed expectations next quarter (wishful thinking).

7. A map showing the main vessels and arteries leaving the human heart.

8. A very large amount of sales data including information about customers, orders, inventory items, and sales representatives. You need to be able to perform ad hoc queries.

9. The same as Exercise 8 except your manager just returned from a technical seminar where he learned the phrase "object-oriented" and now he's determined to use object-oriented techniques in everything.

10. A simple recipe book. You should be able to find recipes by name, part of meal (entrée, aperitif, dessert, and so forth), or main ingredient.

11. A "Magic: The Gathering" game and trading card tracking system. You need to be able to sort cards by their monetary value, number of duplicates, and power in the game. You also want to be able to define "power decks" for competition.

12. A DVD, CD, or video collection. You want to be able to search by title, star rating (how good you thought it was), Motion Picture Association of America rating (G, PG, and so forth), actor, or director. And perhaps studio. And genre. And group titles by studio. And anything else you might think of later.

13. A database to hold statistics for your favorite sports teams: football, baseball, polo, hurling, or whatever. You need to be able to find all of the players on a particular team, find players with the best stats (most yards rushing, highest hitting percentage, most chuckers chucked, most ... uh ... hurls hurled?).

14. A database to hold the materials I use to write books. This includes author guidelines, chapters, figures, scheduling workbooks, and the like.

15. An inspirational message of the day database. Every day when the application starts, it should display a random message selected from the database.

Relational Database Fundamentals

The previous chapters discussed databases in general terms. Chapter 1 explained the general goals of database design. Chapter 2 described some of the many kinds of databases that you might decide to use.

With this chapter the book starts to focus on a particular kind of database: the relational database. Relational databases are very powerful, are the most commonly used kind of database in computer applications today, and are the focus of the rest of this book.

Before you can start learning how to properly design a relational database, you must understand the basic concepts and terms that underlie relational databases.

This chapter provides an introduction to relational databases. It explains the major ideas and terms that you need to know before you can start designing and building relational databases.

In this chapter, you learn about relational database terms such as:

- ❑   Table and relation
- ❑   Record, row, and tuple
- ❑   Column, field, and attribute
- ❑   Constraint, key, and index

Finally, you learn about the operations that you can use to get data out of a relational database.

Relational Points of View

Relational databases play a critical role in many important (that is, money-related) computer applications. As is the case whenever enormous amounts of money are at stake, people have spent a huge amount of time and effort building, studying, and refining relational databases. Database researchers usually approach relational databases from one of three points of view.

The first group approaches the problem from a database-theoretical point of view. These people tend to think in terms of provability, mathematical set theory, and propositional logic. You'll see them at the local rave throwing around phrases such as *relational algebra*, *Cartesian product*, and *tuple relational calculus*. This approach is intellectually stimulating (and looks good on a resume) but can be a bit intimidating. These researchers focus on logical design and idealized database principles.

The second group approaches the matter from a less formal "just build the database and get it done" point of view. Their terminology tends to be less precise and rigorous but more intuitive. They tend to use terms that you may have heard before such as table, row, and column. These people focus on physical database design and pay more attention to concrete bits-and-bytes issues dealing with actually building a database and getting the most out of it.

The third group tends to think in terms of flat files and the underlying disk structure used to hold data. Though these people are probably in the minority these days, their terms file, record, and field snuck into database nomenclature and stuck. Many of those who still use these terms are programmers and other developers who look at the database from a consumer's "how do I get my data out of it" point of view.

These differing points of view have led to several different and potentially confusing ways to view relational databases. This can cause some serious confusion, particularly because the different groups have latched on to some of the same terms but used for different meanings. In fact, they sometimes use the term "relation" in very different ways (that are described later in this chapter).

This chapter loosely groups these terms into "formal" and "informal" categories, where the formal category includes the database theoretical terms and the informal category includes everything else.

This chapter starts with informal terms. Each section initially focuses on informal terms and concepts, and then explains how they fit together with their more formal equivalents.

Table, Rows, and Columns

Informally you can think of a relational database as a collection of *tables*, each containing *rows* and *columns*. At this level, it looks a lot like a workbook containing several worksheets (or spreadsheets), although a worksheet is much less constrained than a database table is. You can put just about anything in any cell in a worksheet. In contrast, every entry in a particular column of a table is expected to contain the same kind of data. For example, all of the cells in a particular column might contain phone numbers or last names.

> *Actually a poorly designed database application may allow the user to sneak some strange kinds of data into other fields. For example, if the database and user interface aren't designed properly, you might be able to enter a string such as "none" in a telephone number field. That's not the field's intent, however. In contrast, a spreadsheet's cells don't really care what you put in them.*

The set of the values that are allowed for a column is called the column's *domain*. For example, a column's domain might be telephone numbers, bank account numbers, snowshoe sizes, or hang glider colors.

Domain is closely related to data type but it's not quite the same. A column's *data type* is the kind of data that the column can hold. The data types that you can use for a column depend on the particular database you are using but typical data types include integer, floating point number (a number with a decimal point), string, and date.

To see the difference between domain and data type, note that street address (323 Relational Rd) and jersey color (red) are both strings. However, the domain for the street address column is valid street addresses, whereas the domain for the jersey color column is colors (and possibly not even all colors if you only allow a few choices). (You can think of the data type as the highest level or most general possible domain. For example, an address or color domain is a more restrictive subset of the domain allowing all strings.)

The rows in a table correspond to column values that are related to each other according to the purpose of the table. For example, suppose you have a Competitors table that contains typical contact information for participants in your First (and probably Last) Annual Extreme Pyramid Sports Championship. This table includes columns to hold competitor name, address, event, blood type, and next of kin as shown in Figure 3-1. (Note that this is not a good database design. You'll see why in later chapters.)

Name	Address	Event	Blood Type	NextOfKin
Alice Adventure	6543 Flak Ter, Runner AZ 82018	Pyramid Boarding	A+	Art Adventure
Alice Adventure	6543 Flak Ter, Runner AZ 82018	Pyramid Luge	A+	Art Adventure
Bart Bold	6371 Jump St #27, Dove City, NV 73289	Camel Drafting	O−	Betty Bold
Bart Bold	6371 Jump St #27, Dove City, NV 73289	Pyramid Boarding	O−	Betty Bold
Bart Bold	6371 Jump St #27, Dove City, NV 73289	Sphinx Jumping	O−	Betty Bold
Cindy Copes	271 Sledding Hill, Ricky Ride CO 80281	Camel Drafting	AB−	John Finkle
Cindy Copes	271 Sledding Hill, Ricky Ride CO 80281	Sphinx Jumping	AB−	John Finkle
Dean Daring	73 Fighter Ave, New Plunge UT 78281	Pyramid Boarding	O+	Betty Dare
Dean Daring	73 Fighter Ave, New Plunge UT 78281	Pyramid Luge	O+	Betty Dare
Frank Fiercely	3872 Bother Blvd, Lost City HI 99182	Pyramid Luge	B+	Fred Farce
Frank Fiercely	3872 Bother Blvd, Lost City HI 99182	Sphinx Jumping	B+	Fred Farce
George Forman	73 Fighter Ave, New Plunge UT 78281	Sphinx Jumping	O+	George Forman
George Forman	73 Fighter Ave, New Plunge UT 78281	Pyramid Luge	O+	George Forman
Gina Gruff	1 Skatepark Ln, Forever KS 72071	Camel Drafting	A+	Gill Gruff
Gina Gruff	1 Skatepark Ln, Forever KS 72071	Pyramid Boarding	A+	Gill Gruff

Figure 3-1

A particular row in the table holds all of the values for a given competitor. For example, the values in the first row (Alice Adventure, 6543 Flak Ter, Runner AZ 82018, Pyramid Boarding, A+, Art Adventure) all apply to the competitor Alice Adventure.

Back in olden times when database developers worked with primitive tools by candlelight, everyone lived much closer to nature. In this case that means they needed to work more closely with the underlying file system. It was common to store data in "flat" files without any indexes, search tools, or other fancy modern luxuries. A file would hold the related information that you might represent at a higher level as a table. The file was divided into chunks called *records* that each had the same size and that each corresponded to a row in a table. The records were divided into fixed-length *fields* that corresponded to the columns in a table.

For example, if you think of the table shown in Figure 3-1 as a flat file, the first row corresponds to a record in the file. Each record contains Name, Address, Event, and other fields to hold the data.

Though relatively few people still work with flat files at this level, the terms file, record, and field are still with us and are often used in database documentation and discussions.

Relations, Attributes, and Tuples

The values in a row are *related* by the fact that they apply to a particular person. Because of this fact, the formal term for a table is a *relation*. This can cause some confusion because the word "relation" is also used informally to describe a relationship between two tables. This use is described in the section "Foreign Key Constraints" later in this chapter.

The formal term for a column is an *attribute* or *data element*. For example, in the Competitors relation shown in Figure 3-1, Name, Address, BloodType, and NextOfKin are the attributes of each of the people represented. You can think of this as in: "each person in the relation has a Name attribute."

The formal term for a row is a *tuple* (rhymes with "scruple"). This almost makes sense if you think of a two-attribute relation as holding data pairs, a three-attribute relation as holding value triples, and a four-attribute relation as holding data quadruples. Beyond four items, mathematicians would say 5-tuple, 6-tuple, and so forth, hence the name tuple.

Don't confuse the formal term *relation* (meaning table) with the more general and less precise use of the term that means "related to" as in "these fields form a relation between these two tables" (or "that psycho is no relation of mine"). Similarly, don't confuse the formal term *attribute* with the less precise use that means "feature of" as in "this field has the 'required' attribute" (or "don't attribute that comment to me!"). I doubt you'll confuse the term *tuple* with anything — it's probably confusing enough all by itself.

Theoretically a relation does not impose any ordering on the tuples that it contains nor does it give an ordering to its attributes. Generally the orderings don't matter to mathematical database theory. In practice, however, database applications usually sort the records selected from a table in some manner to make it easier for the user to understand the results. It's also a lot easier to write the program (and for the user to understand) if the order of the fields remains constant, so database products typically return fields in the order in which they were created in the table unless told otherwise.

Keys

Relational database terminology includes an abundance of different flavors of keys. In the loosest sense, a key is a combination of one or more columns that you use to find rows in a table. For example, a Customers table might use CustomerID to find customers. If you know a customer's ID, you can quickly find that customer's record in the table. (In fact, many ID numbers, such as employee IDs, student IDs, driver's licenses, and so forth, are invented just to make searching in database tables easier. My library card certainly doesn't include a 10-character ID number for my convenience.)

The more formal relational vocabulary includes several other more precise definitions of keys.

In general, a key is a set of one or more columns in the table that have certain properties. A *compound key* or *composite key* is a key that includes more than one column. For example, you might use the combination of FirstName and LastName to look up customers.

A *superkey* is a set of one or more columns in a table for which no two rows can have the exact same values. For example, in the Competitors table shown in Figure 3-1, the Name, Address, and Event columns together form a superkey because no two rows have exactly the same Name, Address, and Event values. Because superkeys define fields that must be unique within a table, they are sometimes called *unique keys*.

Because no two rows in the table have the same values for a superkey, a superkey can uniquely identify a particular row in the table. In other words, a program could use a superkey to find any particular record.

A *candidate key* is a minimal superkey. That means if you remove any of the columns from the superkey, it won't be a superkey anymore.

For example, you already know that Name/Address/Event is a superkey for the Competitors table. If you remove Event from the superkey, Name/Address is not a superkey because everyone in the table is participating in multiple events so they have more than one record with the same name and address.

If you remove Name, Address/Event is not a superkey because Dean Daring and his roommate George Foreman share the same address and are both signed up for Pyramid Luge. (They also have the same blood type. They became friends and decided to become roommates when Dean donated blood for George after a particularly flamboyant skateboarding accident.)

Finally if you remove Address, Name/Event is still a superkey. That means Name/Address/Event is not a candidate key because it is not minimal. However, Name/Event is a candidate key because no two rows have the same Name/Event values and you can easily see neither Name nor Event is a superkey, so the pair is minimal.

You could still have a problem if one of George's other brothers, who are all named George, moves in. If they compete in the same event, you won't be able to tell them apart. Perhaps we should add a CompetitorId column to the table after all.

Note that there may be more than one superkey or candidate key in a table. In Figure 3-1, Event/NextOfKin also forms a candidate key because no two rows have the same Event and NextOfKin values. (That would probably not be the most natural way to look up rows, however. "Yes sir, I can look up your record if you give me your event and next of kin.")

A *unique key* is a superkey that is used to uniquely identify the rows in a table. The difference between a unique key and any other candidate key is in how it is used. A candidate key *could* be used to identify rows if you wanted it to, but a unique key *is* used to constrain the data. In this example, if you make Name/Event be a unique key, the database will not allow you to add two rows with the same Name and Event values. A unique key is an implementation issue, not a more theoretical concept like a candidate key is.

A *primary key* is a superkey that is actually used to uniquely identify or find the rows in a table. A table can have only one primary key (hence the name "primary"). Again, this is more of an implementation issue than a theoretical concern. Database products generally take special action to make finding records based on their primary keys faster than finding records based on other keys.

Some databases allow alternate key fields to have missing values, whereas all of the fields in a primary key are required. For example, the Competitors table might have Name/Address/Event as a unique key and Name/Event as a primary key. Then it could contain a record with Name and Event but no Address value. (Although that would be a bit strange. We might want to require that all of the fields have a value.)

An *alternate key* is a candidate key that is not the primary key. Some also call this a *secondary key*, although others use the term secondary key to mean any set of fields used to locate records even if the fields don't define unique values.

That's a lot of keys to try to remember! The following list briefly summarizes the different flavors:

- **Compound key or composite key:** A key that includes more than one field.
- **Superkey:** A set of columns for which no two rows can have the exact same values.
- **Candidate key:** A minimal superkey.
- **Unique key:** A superkey used to require uniqueness by the database.
- **Primary key:** A unique key that is used to quickly locate records by the database.
- **Alternate key:** A candidate key that is not the primary key.
- **Secondary key:** A key used to look up records but that may not guarantee uniqueness.

One last kind of key is the *foreign key*. A foreign key is used as a constraint rather than to find records in a table, so it is described a bit later in the section "Constraints."

Indexes

An index is a database structure that makes it quicker and easier to find records based on the values in one or more fields. Indexes are not the same as keys, although the two are related closely enough that many developers confuse the two and use the terms interchangeably.

For example, suppose you have a Customers table that holds customer information: name, address, phone number, Swiss bank account number, and so forth. The table also contains a CustomerId field that it uses as its primary key.

Unfortunately customers usually don't remember their customer IDs, so you need to be able to look them up by name or phone number. If you make Name and PhoneNumber be two different keys, you can quickly locate a customer's record in three ways: by customer ID, by name, and by phone number.

> *Relational databases also make it easy to look up records based on non-indexed fields, although it may take a while. If the customer only remembers his address and not his customer ID or name, you can search for the address even if it that field isn't part of an index. It may just take a long time. Of course if the customer cannot remember his name, he's got bigger problems.*

Building and maintaining an index takes the database some extra time, so you shouldn't make indexes gratuitously. Place indexes on the fields that you are most likely to need to search and don't bother indexing fields such as apartment number that you are unlikely to need to search.

Constraints

As you might guess from the name, a *constraint* places restrictions on the data allowed in a table. In formal database theory, constraints are not considered part of the database. However, in practice constraints play such a critical role in managing the data properly that they are informally considered part of the database. (Besides, the database product enforces them!)

The following sections describe some of the kinds of constraints that you can place on the fields in a table.

Basic Constraints

Relational databases let you specify some simple basic constraints on a particular field. For example, you can make a field required. The special value *null* represents an empty value. For example, suppose you don't know a customer's income. You can place the value null in the Income field to indicate that you don't know the correct value. This is different from placing 0 in the field, which would indicate that the customer doesn't have any income.

Making a field required means it cannot hold a null value, so this is also called a *not null* constraint.

The database will also prevent a field from holding a value that does not match its data type. For example, you cannot put a 20-character string in a 10-character field. Similarly, you cannot store the value "twelve" in a field that holds integers.

These types of constraints restrict the values that you can enter into a field. They help define the field's domain so they are called *domain constraints*. Some database products allow you to define more complex domain constraints, often by using check constraints.

Check Constraints

A *check constraint* is a more complicated type of restriction that evaluates a Boolean expression to see if certain data should be allowed. If the expression evaluates to true, the data is allowed.

A *field-level* check constraint validates a single column. For example, in a SalesPeople table you could place the constraint `Salary > 0` on the Salary field to mean that the field's value must be positive.

A *table-level* check constraint can examine more than one of a record's fields to see if the data is valid. For example, the constraint `(Salary > 0) OR (Commission > 0)` requires that each SalesPeople record have a positive salary or a positive commission (or both).

Primary Key Constraints

By definition, no two records can have identical values for the fields that define the table's primary key. That greatly constrains the data.

In more formal terms, this type of constraint is called *entity integrity*. It simply means that no two records are exact duplicates (which is true if the fields in their primary keys are not duplicates) and that all of the fields that make up the primary key have non-null values.

Unique Constraints

A *unique constraint* requires that the values in one or more fields be unique. Note that it only makes sense to place a uniqueness constraint on a superkey. Recall that a superkey is a group of one or more fields that cannot contain duplicate values. It wouldn't make sense to place a uniqueness constraint on fields that can validly contain duplicated values. For example, it would be silly to place a uniqueness constraint on a Gender field.

Foreign Key Constraints

A *foreign key* is not quite the same kind of key defined previously. Instead of defining fields that you use to locate records, a foreign key refers to a key in another (foreign) table. The database uses it to locate records in the other table but you don't. Because it defines a reference from one table to another, this kind of constraint is also called a *referential integrity constraint*.

A foreign key constraint requires that a record's values in one or more fields in one table (the referencing table) must match the values in another table (the foreign or referenced table). The fields in the referenced table must form a candidate key in that table. Usually they are that table's primary key, and most database products try to use the foreign table's primary key by default when you make a foreign key constraint.

For a simple example, suppose you want to validate the entries in the Competitors table's Event field so the minimum wage interns manning the phones cannot assign anyone to an event that doesn't exist.

To do this with a foreign key, create a new table named Events that has a single column called Event. Make this the new table's primary key and make records that list the possible events: Pyramid Boarding, Pyramid Luge, Camel Drafting, and Sphinx Jumping.

Next, make a foreign key that relates the Competitors table's Event field with the Events table's Event field. Now whenever someone adds a new record to the Competitors table, the foreign key constraint will require that the new record's Event value be listed in the Events table.

The database will also ensure that no one modifies a Competitors record to change the Event value to something that is not in the Events table.

Finally, the database will take special action if you try to delete a record in the Events table if its value is being used by a Competitors record. Depending on the type of database and how you have the relationship configured, the database will either refuse to remove the Events record or it will automatically delete all of the Competitors records that use it.

This example uses the Events table as a lookup table for the Competitors table. Another common use for foreign key constraints is to make sure related records always go together. For example, you could build a NextOfKin table that contains information about the competitors' next of kin (name, phone number, email address, beneficiary status, and so forth). Then you could make a foreign key constraint to ensure that every Competitor record's NextOfKin value is contained in the Name fields in some NextOfKin table record. That way you know that you can always contact the next of kin for anyone in the Competitors table.

Figure 3-2 shows the Competitors, Events, and NextOfKin tables with lines showing the relationships among their related fields.

Name	Address	Event	Blood Type	NextOfKin
Alice Adventure	6543 Flak Ter, Runner AZ 82018	Pyramid Boarding	A+	Art Adventure
Alice Adventure	6543 Flak Ter, Runner AZ 82018	Pyramid Luge	A+	Art Adventure
Bart Bold	6371 Jump St #27, Dove City, NV 73289	Camel Drafting	O−	Betty Bold
Bart Bold	6371 Jump St #27, Dove City, NV 73289	Pyramid Boarding	O−	Betty Bold
Bart Bold	6371 Jump St #27, Dove City, NV 73289	Sphinx Jumping	O−	Betty Bold

Event
Camel Drafting
Pyramid Boarding
Pyramid Luge
Sphinx Jumping

Name	Phone	Email	Beneficiary
Art Adventure	507-387-2738	art@adventure.com	Yes
Betty Bold	302-288-9278	bettybopper@mns.com	Yes
Gill Gruff	614-376-2378	gillyweed@hp.net	No

Figure 3-2

Foreign keys define associations between tables that are sometimes called *relations*, *relationships*, or *links* between the tables. The fact that the formal database vocabulary uses the word *relation* to mean table sometimes leads to confusion. Fortunately, the formal and informal database people usually get invited to different parties so the terms usually don't collide in the same conversation.

Database Operations

The final topic in this chapter covers database operations. (I'll save the rest so I have something for the rest of the book.)

Eight operations were originally defined for relational databases and they form the core of modern database operations. The following list describes those original operations:

❑ **Selection:** This selects some or all of the records in a table. For example, you might want to select only the Competitors records where Event is Pyramid Luge so you can know who to expect for that event (and how many ambulances to have standing by).

❑ **Projection:** This drops columns from a table (or selection). For example, when you make your list of Pyramid Luge competitors you may only want to list their names and not their addresses, blood types, events (which you know is Pyramid Luge anyway), or next of kin.

❑ **Union:** This combines tables with similar columns and removes duplicates. For example, suppose you have another table named FormerCompetitors that contains data for people who participated in previous years' competitions. Some of these people are competing this year and some are not. You could use the union operator to build a list of everyone in either table. (Note that the operation would remove duplicates, but for these tables you would still get the same person several times with different events.)

❑ **Intersection:** This finds the records that are the same in two tables. The intersection of the FormerCompetitors and Competitors tables would list those few who competed in previous years and who survived to compete again this year (the slow learners).

❑ **Difference:** This selects the records in one table that are not in a second table. For example, the difference between FormerCompetitors and Competitors would give you a list of those who competed in previous years but who are not competing this year (so you can email them and ask them what the problem is).

❑ **Cartesian Product:** This creates a new table containing every record in a first table combined with every record in a second table. For example, if one table contains values 1, 2, 3 and a second table contains values A, B, C, then their Cartesian product contains the values 1/A, 1/B, 1/C, 2/A, 2/B, 2/C, 3/A, 3/B, and 3/C.

❑ **Join:** This is similar to a Cartesian product except records in one table are paired only with those in the second table if they meet some condition. For example, you might join the Competitors records with the NextOfKin records where a Competitors record's NextOfKin value matches the NextOfKin record's Name value. In this example, that gives you a list of the competitors together with their corresponding next of kin data.

❑ **Divide:** This operation is the opposite of the Cartesian product. It uses one table to partition the records in another table. It finds all of the field values in one table that are associated with every value in another table. For example, if the first table contains the values 1/A, 1/B, 1/C, 2/A, 2/B, 2/C, 3/A, 3/B, and 3/C and a second table contains the values 1, 2, 3, then the first divided by the second gives A, B, C. (Don't worry, I think it's pretty weird and confusing, too, so it won't be on the final exam. Probably.)

The workhorse operation of the relational database is the join, often combined with selection and projection. For example, you could *join* Competitors records with NextOfKin records that have the correct name. Next you could *project* to select only the competitors' names, the next of kin names, and the next of kin phone numbers. You could then *select* only Bart Bold's records. Finally, you could *select* for unique records so the result would contain only a single record containing the values Bart Bold, Betty Bold, 302-288-9278.

The following SQL query produces this result:

```
SELECT DISTINCT Competitors.Name, NextOfKin.Name, Phone
FROM Competitors, NextOfKin
WHERE Competitors.NextOfKin = NextOfKin.Name
  AND Competitors.Name = 'Bart Bold'
```

The SELECT clause performs selection, the FROM clause tells which tables to join, the first part of the WHERE clause (Competitors.NextOfKin = NextOfKin.Name) gives the join condition, the second part of the WHERE clause (Competitors.Name = 'Bart Bold') selects only Bart's records, and the DISTINCT keyword selects unique results.

The results of these operations are table-like objects that aren't permanently stored in the database. They have rows and columns so they look like tables, but their values are generated on the fly when the database operations are executed. These result objects are called *views*. Because they are often generated by SQL queries, they are also called *query results*. Because they look like tables that are generated as needed, they are sometimes called *virtual tables*.

Chapter 20 has more to say about relational database operations as they are implemented in practice.

Summary

Before you can start designing and building relational databases, you need to understand some of the basics. This chapter provided an introduction to relational databases and their terminology.

In this chapter you learned about:

❑   Formal relational database terms such as relation, attribute, and tuple.

❑   Informal terms such as table, row, record, column, and field.

❑   Several kinds of keys including superkeys, candidate keys, and primary keys.

❑   Different kinds of constraints that you can place on columns or tables.

❑   Operations defined for relational databases.

The following chapters change the book's focus from general database concepts and terminology to design techniques. They describe the tasks you must perform to design a database from scratch. Chapter 4 starts the process by explaining how to gather user requirements so the database you design has a good chance of actually satisfying the users' needs.

Before you move on to Chapter 4, however, use the following exercises to test your understanding of the material covered in this chapter. You can find the solutions to these exercises in Appendix A.

Exercises

1.   What does the following check constraint on the SalesPeople table mean?

```
((Salary > 0) AND (Commission = 0)) OR ((Salary = 0) AND (Commission > 0))
```

2.   In Figure 3-3, draw lines connecting the corresponding terms.

Attribute	Row	File
Relation	Column	Relationship
Foreign Key	Table	Virtual Table
Tuple	Foreign Key	Record
View	Query Result	Field

Figure 3-3

For questions 3 through 6, suppose you're a numismatist and you want to track your progress in collecting the 50 state quarters created by the United States Mint. You start with the following table and plan to add more data later (after you take out the trash and finish painting your lead miniatures).

State	Abbr	Title	Engraver	Year	Got
Arizona	AZ	Grand Canyon State	Joseph Menna	2008	No
Idaho	ID	Esto Perpetua	Norm Nemeth	2007	No
Iowa	IA	Foundation in Education	John Mercanti	2004	Yes
Michigan	MI	Great Lakes State	Donna Weaver	2004	Yes
Montana	MT	Big Sky Country	Don Everhart	2007	No
Nebraska	NE	Chimney Rock	Charles Vickers	2006	Yes
Oklahoma	OK	Scissortail Flycatcher	Phebe Hemphill	2008	No
Oregon	OR	Crater Lake	Charles Vickers	2005	Yes

3. Is State/Abbr/Title a superkey? Why or why not?
4. Is Engraver/Year/Got a superkey? Why or why not?
5. What are all of the candidate keys for this table?
6. What are the domains of each of the table's columns?

For questions 7 through 10, suppose you are building a dorm room database. Consider the following table. For obscure historical reasons, all of the rooms in the building have even numbers. The Phone field refers to the number of the phone in the room. Rooms that have no phone cost less but students in those rooms are required to have a cell phone (so you can call them and nag if they miss too many classes).

Room	FirstName	LastName	Phone	CellPhone
100	John	Smith	Null	202-837-2897
100	Mark	Garcia	Null	504-298-0281
102	Anne	Johansson	202-237-2102	Null
102	Sally	Helper	202-237-2102	Null
104	John	Smith	202-237-1278	720-387-3928
106	Anne	Uumellmahaye	Null	504-298-0281
106	Wendy	Garcia	Null	202-839-3920
202	Mike	Hfuhruhurr	202-237-7364	Null
202	Jose	Johansson	202-237-7364	202-839-3920

7. If you don't allow two people with the same name to share a room (due to administrative whimsy), what are all of the possible candidate keys for this table?

8. If you do allow two people with the same name to share a room, what are all of the possible candidate keys for this table?

9. What field-level check constraints could you put on this table's fields? Don't worry about the syntax for performing the checks, just define them.

10. What table-level check constraints could you put on this table's fields? Don't worry about the syntax for performing the checks, just define them.

Part II
Database Design Process and Techniques

The chapters in this part of the book contain the bulk of the information about the database design process. They discuss the major steps in database design starting from the beginning of a project and working through various design and refinement stages to provide a fully functional database.

Chapter 4 explains how you can learn about the customers' needs. If you don't understand the customers' needs, how can you possibly build a database that satisfies them? This chapter also explains how to ensure that the customers agree with you on what the database should do so everyone is happy with the final result.

Chapter 5 shows how to translate the customer needs defined in Chapter 4 into several different kinds of data models. The data models allow you to represent the database's needs formally. They let you study the data and rearrange the pieces to build toward a flexible design.

Chapter 6 explains how to identify business rules. It tells how to modify the data models you developed in Chapter 5 to make it easier to manage business rules, which may change relatively frequently.

Chapter 7 describes one of the best known steps in designing a database: normalization. A properly normalized database is more robust and resistant to certain kinds of potential data errors.

Chapter 8 discusses some database design issues that affect the database's use and maintenance in a larger application. The techniques described in this chapter make it easier for application developers to build an effective, flexible user interface for the database.

Chapter 9 describes some patterns that occur in many applications. It explains solutions that you can use to make handling those patterns simple.

Chapter 10 describes some common pitfalls that often hinder database designers. Avoiding these problems can make database design easier, faster, and more effective.

After you finish working through these chapters, you will have a good understanding of database design. You will know how to decide what data belongs in a database, how to build data models, and how to convert those models into powerful, flexible database designs.

Understanding User Needs

The previous chapters discussed databases in general terms. Chapters 1 and 2 explained the goals of database design and described some of the types of databases that are available. Chapter 3 described the most common type of database, relational databases, in slightly greater detail. With this basic understanding of databases, you're ready to take the first step in designing an actual database to solve a particular problem: understanding the user's needs.

Designing any custom product, whether it's a database, beach house, or case mod (see www.neatorama.com/case-mod/index.php for some amazing examples), is largely a translation process. You need to translate the customers' needs, wants, and desires from the sometimes fuzzy ideas floating around in their heads into a product that meets the customers' needs.

The first step in the translation process is understanding the user's requirements. Unless you know what the user needs, you cannot build it. Designing the best order processing database imaginable won't do you a bit of good if the customer really wants a circuit design database or an ostrich race handicapping system.

Just as the database design forms the foundation upon which the rest of the application's development stands, your understanding of the user's needs form the foundation of the database design. If you don't know what the user needs, how can you possibly design it?

If you don't understand the customer's needs thoroughly and completely, you may as well pack it in now. There's little satisfaction in wasting months of your life and a pile of your company's money to build something unusable. Make sure you're on the right road before you stomp on the accelerator and burn rubber down a dead-end alley.

This chapter explains techniques that you can use to learn about the customer's needs. It describes methods that you can use to record those needs in a concrete and verifiable way.

The sections that follow describe some of the steps you can take to better understand the customers' needs. In some projects, you may not need to follow all of these steps. For example, if your customer is a single person with very concrete ideas about what needs to be done, you may not need to spend much time learning who's who or brainstorming. If your customer works with government classified data, you may not be allowed to "walk a mile in the user's shoes" and you may have access to only some of the business's documentation.

I once knew a developer who was working on a classified project. He had clearance to see the source code but not the data, so every week his customer brought him a giant printout of the latest run with all of the data carefully clipped out with scissors. He would try to guess what was going on and make some suggestions so the customer's developers could try to fix the code. Then the cycle repeated the next week. What an odd way to work!

In other projects, the steps may work best in a different order. You may find it better to brainstorm before visiting the customers' site and watching them work.

These are just steps that I've found most useful in trying to understand the customers' situation. You'll have to adjust them as necessary to fit each of your projects.

In this chapter, you learn how to:

- ❑ Understand the customers' needs and motivations.
- ❑ Gather and document user requirements.
- ❑ Cull requirements from existing practices and information.
- ❑ Build use cases to understand the user's needs and to measure success or failure.
- ❑ Anticipate changes and future needs to build the most flexible database possible.

After you master these techniques, you'll be ready to move on to the next step and actually start designing the database.

Make a Plan

Though the steps described in this chapter sometimes occur in different orders, the following list summarizes the order that's most typical. Feel free to add, remove, and rearrange them as necessary.

- ❑ Bring a List of Questions
- ❑ Meet the Customers
- ❑ Learn Who's Who
- ❑ Pick the Customers' Brains
- ❑ Walk a Mile in the User's Shoes
- ❑ Study Current Operations
- ❑ Brainstorm
- ❑ Look to the Future
- ❑ Understand the Customers' Reasoning
- ❑ Learn What the Customers Really Need
- ❑ Prioritize
- ❑ Verify Your Understanding
- ❑ Write the Requirements Document

❑ Make Use Cases

❑ Decide Feasibility

This list isn't perfect but it makes a good meta-plan — a plan for making the project's plan. (Hopefully it won't be as useless as the traditional pre-meeting agenda planning meeting.)

Bring a List of Questions

From the very first day, you should start thinking of questions to ask the customers to get a better idea of the project's goals and scope.

The following sections list some questions that you can ask your customers to help understand their needs. You'll see many of them described in greater detail later in this chapter.

This list is by no means complete — the questions that you need to ask will depend to a large extent on the type of project. Use them only as a starting point. It's helpful to have something to work from when you start, however. Then you can then wander off in promising directions as the discussions continue.

Functionality

These questions deal with what the system is supposed to accomplish and, to a lesser extent, how. It is usually best to avoid deciding how the system should do anything until you thoroughly understand what it should do so you don't become locked into one idea too early, but it's still useful to record any impressions the customers have of how the system should work.

❑ What should the system do?

❑ Why are you building this system? What do you hope it will accomplish?

❑ What should it look like? Sketch out the user interface.

❑ What response times do you need for different parts of the system? (Typically, interactive response times should be under five seconds, whereas reports and other offline activities may take longer.)

❑ What reports are needed?

❑ Do the end users need to be able to define new reports?

❑ Who are the players? (ties to previous section)

❑ Do power users and administrators need to be able to define new reports?

Data Needs

These questions help clarify the project's data needs. Knowing what data is needed will help you start defining the database's tables.

❑ What data is needed for the user interface?

❑ Where should that data come from?

❑   How are those pieces of data related?

❑   How are these tasks handled today? Where does the data come from?

Data Integrity

These questions deal with data integrity. They help you define some of the integrity constraints that you will build into the database.

❑   What values are allowed in which fields?

❑   Which fields are required? (For example, does a customer record need a phone number? A fax number? An email address? One of those but not all of them?)

❑   What are the valid domains (allowed values) for various fields? What phone number formats are allowed? How long can customer names be? Addresses? Do addresses need extra lines for suite or apartment number? Do addresses need to handle U.S. ZIP Codes such as 12345? ZIP+4 Codes such as 12345-6789? Canadian postal codes such as T1A 6G9? Or other countries' postal codes?

❑   Which fields should refer to foreign keys? (For example, an address's State field might need to be in the States table and a CustomerID field might need to be in the Customers table. I've seen customers with a big list of standard comments and a Comments field can only take those values.)

❑   Should the system validate cities against postal codes? (For example, should it verify that the 10005 ZIP Code is in New York City, New York? That's cool but a bit tricky and can involve a lot of data.)

❑   Do you need a customer record before you can place orders?

❑   If a customer cancels an account, do you want to delete the corresponding records or just flag them as inactive?

❑   What level of system reliability is needed?

     ❑   Does the system need 24/7 access?

     ❑   How volatile is the data? How often does it need to be backed up?

     ❑   How disastrous will it be if the system crashes?

     ❑   How quickly do you need to be back up and running?

     ❑   How painful will it be if you lose some data during a crash?

Security

These questions focus on the application's security. The answers to these questions will help you decide which database product will work best (different products provide different forms of security) and what architecture to use.

❑   Does each user need a separate password? (Generally a good idea.)

❑   Do different users need access to different pieces of data? (For example, sales clerks might need to access customer credit card numbers but order fulfillment technicians probably don't.)

❑   Does the data need to be encrypted within the database?

❑   Do you need to provide audit trails recording every action taken and by whom? (For example, you can see which clerk increased the priority of a customer who was ordering the latest iPod and then ask that clerk why that happened.)

❑   What different classes of users will there be?

I often use three classes of users. First, clerks do most of the regular work. They enter orders, print invoices, discuss the latest Oprah around the water cooler, and so forth. Second, supervisors can do anything that clerks can and they also perform managerial tasks. They can view reports, logs, and audit trails; assign clerks to tasks; grant bonuses; and so forth. Third, super users or key users can do everything. They can reset user passwords, go directly into database tables to fix problems, change system parameters such as the states that users can pick from dropdowns, and so forth. There should only be a couple of super users and they should usually log in as supervisors, not as super users, to prevent accidental catastrophes.

❑   How many of each class of user will there be? Will only one person need access to the data at a time? Will there be hundreds or even thousands (as is the case with some Web applications)?

❑   Is there existing documentation describing the users' tasks and responsibilities?

Environment

These questions deal with the project's surrounding environment. They gather information about other systems and processes that the project will replace or with which it will interact.

❑   Does this system enhance or replace an existing system?

  ❑   Is there documentation describing the existing system?

  ❑   Does the existing system have paper forms that you can study?

  ❑   What features in the existing system are required? Which are not?

  ❑   What kinds of data does the existing system use? How is it stored? How are different pieces of data related?

  ❑   Is there documentation for the existing system's data?

❑   Are there other systems with which this one must interact?

  ❑   Exactly how will it interact with them?

  ❑   Will the new project send data to existing systems? How?

  ❑   Will the new project receive data from existing systems? How?

  ❑   Is there documentation for those systems?

❑   How does your business work? (Try to understand how this project fits into the bigger picture.)

Meet the Customers

Before you can start any project, you need to know what it is about. Are you building an inventory system, a supply chain model, or a stock price tracker and predictor (also called a random number generator)?

The best way to understand the system you need to design and build is to interrogate the customers. I use the rather unfriendly word "interrogate" because, to do the job right, you need much more than a simple chat over tea and crumpets. Learning about the customers' requirements can be a long and grueling process. It can take days or even weeks of cross-examination, studying existing practices, poring over dusty scrolls and other corporate documentation, and spying on the customers while they do their daily jobs.

When it's over, the customers shouldn't hate you outright but they might wish you would go away and leave them alone for a while. A good question and answer session should leave everyone exhausted but with the warm glow of satisfaction that comes with moving a lot of information from their brains to yours.

Customers who are truly dedicated to the company are usually willing to field even the most obtuse questions as long as you're willing to dish them out. Benjamin Disraeli once said, "Talk to a man about himself, and he will listen for hours." Most customers are more than happy to share the ins and outs of their corner of the business universe with you for as long as you can stand it.

> *It may sound boring listening to customers drone on about their supply chains but I've found that once you dig deeply enough, almost any business can be pretty interesting. I've worked on projects spanning such topics as fuel tax collection, wastewater treatment, ticket sales, and school enrollment. Every time, after I'd learned enough, I discovered hidden complexity that I would never have imagined.*

The goal isn't to torture the customers (although it may sometimes seem like it to them) but to give you an absolute and complete understanding of the problem you're attempting to solve. You want as few surprises as possible after you're done researching the problem. Unexpected difficulties and feature requests are the biggest reasons why software projects finish late, come in over budget, or fail completely.

The sooner you can identify potential problems and the more completely you can identify the system's features, the easier it will be for you to plan for them and the less they will mess up your meticulously crafted plan. Your initial encounters with the customer give you your first chance to address these issues so they don't bite you later.

So when you first start a project, meet the customers. Get to know them and what they do. Even if the problem you are trying to solve is only a small part of their business, get a feel for the overall picture. Sometimes you'll find unexpected connections that may make your job easier or that may lead to surprising benefits in a completely unrelated area.

When you first meet the customers, it usually doesn't hurt to warn them that you're going to be a major pest for a while. This can also help you figure out who's who. Those who are committed to the project and are eager to succeed will take your warning well. Those who are less than dedicated may tip their hands at this point. This idea leads naturally to the next section.

Learn Who's Who

Ideally a project team works well together, everyone does the best possible job without conflict, and the project moves along smoothly to create a finished product that meets the customers' needs. In practice, however, it doesn't always work out that way. Like the bickering superheroes in an X-Men movie, everyone has his or her own personal abilities, agenda, and motivation that don't always coincide with those of the other team members.

As you get to know the customers (and your team members), it's important to realize that not everyone shares the same vision of the product. You need to figure out which customer is the leader, which are team players, which have little or no say in specifying the project, and which will be super villains.

> *No one wants a super villain on their project, but you should be aware that they are out there. I've worked on projects where customers ostracized members of the project team, tried to delete all of our project files, spread dark rumors among senior management, and even slashed tires. Hopefully you won't encounter any of these types but it's best that you know about these people as early as possible.*

The following list describes some of the roles that customers (and developers) often play in a project. Naturally these cannot categorize everyone, but they define some characteristics that you should look for.

- ❏ **Executive Champion:** This is the highest ranking customer driving the project. Often this person doesn't participate in the project's day-to-day trials and tribulations. The Executive Champion will fight for truth, justice, and getting you that extra laptop you need. In the end, the Executive Champion must be able to take on any bored super villains or you might be in trouble.

- ❏ **Customer Champion:** This person has a thorough understanding of the customers' needs. Lesser champions may help define pieces of the project but this is the person you run to when the others are unclear. For the purposes of this chapter ("Understanding User Needs"), this is the most important person on the project. This person must have enough time and resources (also known as "people") to help you define the project and answer your questions. Ideally this person also has enough clout to make decisions when the heroes start bickering over who has to fight Magneto and who gets to fly the invisible plane.

- ❏ **Customer Representative:** A Customer Representative is someone assigned to answer your questions and help define the project. Often these are people who do the day-to-day work of your customers' business. Sometimes they are experts in only parts of the business so you need more than one to cover all of the issues.

- ❏ **Stakeholder:** This is anyone who has an interest in the project. Some of these fall into other categories such as Customer Champion or Customer Representative. Others are affected by the outcome but have no direct say in the design of the system. For example, front-line clerks rarely get to toss in their two cents when you design a point-of-sales system. They are like the civilians whose fate is determined by the battling superheroes and who are easily crushed by falling debris and pieces of robot monsters. Though many of them have no direct power over the outcome, you should keep them in mind and try to minimize collateral damage. (In a really well-run company, these people have their own representatives to watch out for them.)

- ❏ **Sidekick/Gopher:** This is someone who can help you get the more mundane resources you need such as conference rooms, airline tickets, donuts, and kryptonite. Though this isn't a glamorous job, an effective Sidekick can make everything run more smoothly. (Sometimes they also provide comic relief. On one project, the Sidekick invited everyone out to a huge celebratory lunch on him, only to find that the restaurant didn't take credit cards, so we all had to pitch in. In all fairness, though, it could have happened to any of us.)

- ❏ **Short-Timer:** This is someone who is only going to be around for a short while. This may be someone who is about to be promoted to a new division, who will retire soon, or who is just plain fed up and about to walk. A dedicated short-timer can be a huge asset, particularly those who are about to retire and take a lifetime's worth of experience with them. Others don't care all that much whether the project succeeds or fails after they're gone. (These are like the red-shirts on *Star Trek* who don't contribute much. When Kirk says, "Spock, Bones, and Smith, meet me in the transporter room," guess who isn't coming back?)

❑ **Devil's Advocate:** This is an important role for avoiding groupthink. Left unchecked, some groups become irrationally optimistic and can make extremely poor decisions. A Devil's Advocate can help bring the hopeless dreamers back to earth and keep the project realistic... as long as the Devil's Advocate doesn't get out of hand. The purpose of the Devil's Advocate is to maintain a reality check, not to defeat the entire project. If this person shoots down every idea anyone comes up with, you might gently mention that eventually you need to decide on an approach and get something done.

❑ **Convert:** This is someone who originally is against the project but who you convert to your cause. Strangely, both finding and converting this person are usually surprisingly easy, at least for bigger projects. If you talk to the disenfranchised stakeholders (the front-line users who have no say in the matter), you can usually find some who are dead-set against the project, if for no other reason than it represents a change from the way they have always worked. Take one of these people who has a fair amount of experience and make him a Stakeholder Representative. Get him involved early in the process and take his suggestions very seriously. If you act on some of those suggestions, you'll show that you have the Stakeholders' interests in mind and you'll win his loyalty. He'll tell the rest of the Stakeholders and, if all goes well, you'll have more support than you can imagine. And who knows, you may build a better product with this person's input.

❑ **Generic Bad Guy:** These range from simple defeatists and layabouts to Arch Super Villains actively trying to sabotage the project. Try to identify these people early so you know what you're up against. (On one project, we had a super villain at the Vice Presidential level. We also had an Executive Champion at the same level, so we were able to hold our own, but it was pretty tough going. It's easy to get squashed when such heavy-hitters collide.)

Don't feel constrained by this list. These are just some of the characters that I've encountered and you may meet others.

I don't mean to imply that every project is subject to continual harassment, interference, and sabotage. I've worked on lots of projects where everyone really was pulling for the common good and we achieved impressive results. Just keep your eyes open. Identify the main players as quickly as possible so you know who to ask questions and where to run when the fighting erupts.

Try It Out   Know the Players

If you're familiar with the Dilbert comic strip, think about the main characters Dilbert, Alice, Wally, Asok the Intern, and the Pointy-Haired Boss. Assume they are your customers and you need to design them a database.

Who will play which customer roles? In particular, who will be:

❑   Executive Champion

❑   Customer Representative

❑   Sidekick

❑   Bad Guy

What are your chances for success?

How It Works

Unfortunately the only candidate for Executive Champion is the Pointy-Haired Boss. He's incompetent and unable to defend against any attacks from bad guys so you're in trouble from the start.

Alice and Dilbert generally know what's going on and try to do the right thing. They will be your best bets for Customer Representatives.

Asok means well and is competent but he's new to the company and doesn't know how everything works, so he won't be the best Customer Representative. He might make a good Sidekick, however.

Wally is a serious layabout. He actively seeks to avoid work even if doing the work would be easier. He's a bad guy, although on a minor scale. He won't destroy the project single-handedly but he may waste other people's time.

Your overall chances depend entirely on whether the project will face outside attack. If any serious bad guy appears, the Pointy-Haired Boss will crumble and the project will fail.

If no one else is interested in taking over or ruining the project, you might have a chance to finish before the Pointy-Haired Boss plays too active a role and messes everything up. (But then again, how long do things run without interference in a Dilbert cartoon?)

Pick the Customers' Brains

Once you figure out more or less who the movers and shakers are, you can start picking their brains. Sit down with the Customer Champion and find out what the customers think they need. Find out what they think the solution should look like. Find out what data they think it should contain, how that data will be presented, and how different parts of the data are related.

Get input from as many Stakeholders as you can. Always keep in mind, however, that the Customer Champion is the one who understands the customers' needs thoroughly and has the authority to make the final decisions. Though you should consider everyone's opinions, the Customer Champion has the final word.

Depending on the scope of the project, this can take a while. I've been on projects where the initial brain-picking sessions took only a few hours and I've been on others where we spent more than a week talking to the customers. One project was so complex that part of the project was still defining requirements after other parts of the project had been underway for months.

Take your time and make sure the customers have finished telling you what they think they need.

Walk a Mile in the User's Shoes

Often following the customers' day-to-day operations can give you some extremely helpful perspective. Ideally you could do the customers' jobs for them for a while to thoroughly learn what's involved. Unless your customers aren't in your industry (and if they are, why are they hiring you?), however, you probably aren't qualified to do their jobs.

I was once saddened to read an article about ice cream testers. I eat a lot of ice cream and thought I had a good sense of what tastes good and what tastes bad, but professional ice cream testers can isolate and identify individual flavors in recipes that include dozens of ingredients. I'm not even competent to eat ice cream professionally!

Though you may not be able to actually do the customers' jobs, you may be able to sit next to them while they do it. Warn them that you will probably reduce productivity slightly by asking stupid and annoying questions. Then ask away. Take notes and learn as much as you can. Sometimes your outsider's point of view can lead to ideas that the customers would never have discovered.

Another Point of View

On one project, we visited a billing center responsible for a couple million accounts. Every three days they processed 1/10th of their accounts and one of the things they did was print out a pile of paper almost three feet tall listing all of the accounts that owed money.

Unfortunately the accounts were arranged by ID, not balance, so they couldn't figure out which ones owed the most. In fact, by state law they were not allowed to do anything about accounts that owed less than $50, and those included the vast majority.

Because of our outsider computer nerd viewpoint, we knew there was a better approach. We installed a printer emulator (a program that looks like a printer to the system but actually captures the data instead of killing trees with it) and dumped the data into a file. We sorted the file by account balance and displayed the result to the user. The first two or three pages listed all of the accounts that needed action. (In fact, the first four or five accounts usually owed more than all of the other accounts combined.)

We were actually there looking at a different problem but when we saw this one we jumped all over it and in about a week we were heroes.

Take notes while you're watching the customers do their jobs. Draw pictures and diagrams if that helps you visualize what they're doing. Pictures can also be very helpful in asking the customers if you have the right idea. If the customers will let you, print screen shots and even take photographs. (However, keep in mind that many businesses are required to safeguard the privacy of their clients' data, so don't expect them to let you walk out with screen shots or photographs showing credit information, medical histories, or records of political contributions. Be sure you ask before you try to take any material away and ask before you even bring a camera in the building.)

Study Current Operations

After you've walked a mile or two in the customers' shoes, see if there are other ways that you can study the current operation. Often companies have procedure manuals and documentation that describes the customers' roles and responsibilities. (In fact, that kind of documentation is required for certain kinds of ISO certifications. Some bigger companies like to display huge banners that say things like "ISO-9000

Certified.'' These may just be there to cover holes in the wall, but if they have such a banner they probably have more documentation than you can stomach.)

Look around for any existing databases that the customers use. Don't forget the lesson of Chapter 2 that there are many different kinds of databases. Don't just look for relational databases. Look also for note files, filing cabinets, boxes of index cards, tickler files (cubbies where they can place items that should be examined on a certain date), and so forth. Generally, snoop around and find out what information is kept where.

Figure out how that information is used and how it relates to other pieces of information. Often different physical databases contain redundant information and that forms a relationship. For example, a filing cabinet holding information about customers includes all of the customers' data. A pile of invoices also includes the customers' names, addresses, ID numbers, and other information that is duplicated in the customer files. Paper orders probably contain the same information. These are the sorts of pieces of data that tie the whole process together.

Brainstorm

At this point, you should have a decent understanding of the customers' business and needs. To make sure the customer hasn't left anything out, you can hold brainstorming sessions. Bring in as many Stakeholders as you can and let them run wild. Don't rule out anything yet. If a stakeholder says the database should record the color of customers' shoes when they make a purchase, write it down. If someone else says they need to track the number of kumquats eaten by assembly line workers, write it down.

Continue brainstorming until everyone has had their say and it's clear that no new ideas are appearing.

Occasionally extra creative people (sometimes known to management as "troublemakers") look like they're going to go on forever. Let them go for a while but if it's clear they really can't stem the flood of ideas, split up. Have everyone go off separately and write down anything else relevant that they can think of. Then come back and dump all of the ideas in a big pile.

Try not to let the Customer Champion suppress the others' creativity too early. Though the Customer Champion has the final say, the goal right now is to gather ideas, not to decide which ones are the best.

The goal at this point isn't to accept or eliminate anything as much as it is to write everything down. You want to be sure that everything relevant is considered before you start designing. Later, when you've started laying out tables and indexes and changes are more difficult to make, you don't want someone to step in and say, "Owl voltages! Why didn't someone think of owl voltages?" Hopefully you have owl voltages written down somewhere and crossed out so you can say they were considered and everyone agreed they were not a priority.

> *Different development shops take different approaches if this earth-shatteringly important requirement somehow got missed during brainstorming. I prefer to grudgingly add it to the requirements, while making sure that the customers understand that this sort of last minute change might affect the schedule. If you grumble a little, they usually take the hint and only insist on changes that really are important. Other shops simply say, "Sorry, that wasn't in the original requirements and we're not doing it so there!" Though this is technically correct, it increases the chances that the final product won't meet the customers' needs.*

Look to the Future

During the brainstorming process, think about future needs. Explicitly ask the customers what they might like to have in future releases. You may be able to include some of those ideas in the current project, but even if you can't it's nice to know where things are headed. That will help you design your database flexibly so you can more easily incorporate changes in the future.

For example, suppose your customer Paula Marble runs a plumbing supply shop but thinks some day it might be nice to add a little café and call the whole thing "Paula's Plumbing and Pastries." After you hide your snickers behind a cough, think about how this might affect the database and the rest of the project.

Plumbing supplies are generally non-perishable, but pastries must be baked fresh daily and the ingredients that go into pastries are perishable. You may want to think about using separate inventory tables to hold information about non-perishable plumbing items that clients can purchase (gaskets, thread tape, pipe wrenches) and perishable cooking items that the clients won't buy directly (flour, eggs, raisins).

You might not even track quantity in stock for finished pastries (the clients either see them in the case or not) but you probably want to be able to record prices for them nonetheless. In that case, you will have entries in an inventory table that will contain prices but that will never hold quantities.

You don't necessarily need to start planning the future database just yet (after all, Paula may decide to go with "Paula's Plumbing and Tattoo Palace" instead), but you can keep these future changes in mind as you study the rest of the problem.

Understand the Customers' Reasoning

Occasionally you'll come across a customer who thinks he knows something about database design. He may say that you should use a particular table structure, an object-relational hierarchical data model, or an acute polar space modulator.

Sometimes these suggestions make perfect sense. Other times you'll think the customer clicked the Google "I'm Feeling Lucky" link and stumbled into the endless morass of techno-babble.

Even if the suggestions seem to make no sense whatsoever, don't dismiss them out of hand. Remember that the customer has a different perspective than you do. The customer knows a lot more than you about his particular business. He may or may not know anything about database design, but it's entirely possible that he has a reason for his obscure requests.

For example, suppose you're trying to design a sales and inventory system for Thor's Thimbles. The president and CEO Thor says he thinks you need to use a temporal database, although the way he pronounces it makes you think he probably doesn't understand what that means (or perhaps it's just his Scandinavian accent). You think, "How hard can it be to sell thimbles?" and ignore him.

After you spend a month building a really slick relational database you discover that old Thor isn't so naive after all. It turns out that the company sells hundreds of different models of thimbles made from such materials as stainless steel, anodized aluminum, gold, and platinum. The value of the more exotic models changes daily with precious metal prices. Almost as volatile are the collectors' models such as the

Great Scientists of History series and the Sports Immortals (the Pete Rose Hall of Fame model can bring up to $200 at auction).

Suddenly what you thought was a simple problem really does have hundreds of variables changing rapidly over time and you realize that you probably should have built a temporal database. You have egg on your face and Thor decides that his brother-in-law, who originally suggested the temporal database to Thor, might be able to do a better job than you.

Even if a customer's suggestion seems odd, take it seriously. Dig deeper to find out why the customer thinks that will be useful. Take the approach my doctor takes when I tell him that I think I have scurvy or the plague or some other nonsense. He keeps an absolutely straight face and asks, "Why do you think that?" I won't be right but the symptoms I used in my incorrect diagnosis may help him decide that I really have a cold. (I envision him with the other doctors sitting in the break room later laughing and saying, "You'll never guess what my patient thought he had today! Ha, ha, ha!")

Try It Out   **Who's Right?**

Suppose you have a customer who says you should use an XML-enabled object-relation database. You look into the problem and don't think that makes any sense. You ask the customer and he gives you a bunch of half-justifications that don't really add up. In the end he says, "Just do it."

How should you respond?

How It Works

This is a tricky situation. Everyone dreads the customer who tells you point-blank to do something that you know doesn't make sense. Do you waste the customer's time and money to pursue the wrong course? Or do you tell the customer that you won't do it and risk getting fired?

Everyone has to make this call for him- or herself. You're the one who has to be able to sleep at night after making the decision.

My personal philosophy is that I put the customer's needs first. If I think the customer is telling me to do something incorrect, I'll say so. But if the customer insists and I think I can do what he wants, I'll go ahead and do my best. In the end, it's the customer's money after all. If I make a big deal out of it and get fired, he'll probably just go out and find someone less experienced who blunders in without seeing the consequences of following the misguided advice and will make matters worse than I would.

However, I've rarely come to this point with a customer. Usually if you can explain your concerns in terms that customers can understand, they'll either convince you that there's a reason to their madness or they'll realize that the issues you've raised make sense.

Learn What the Customers Really Need

Sometimes the customers don't really understand what they need. They think they do and they almost certainly understand the symptoms of their problems, but they don't always make the right cause-and-effect connections.

Sometimes customers think a database or a new computer program will magically increase their sales, reduce their costs, walk their dogs, and wash their cars. In fact, a well-designed database will increase consistency, reduce data entry errors, provide reports, and otherwise help the customers manage their data, but that won't necessarily translate into higher profits.

As you look over the customers' operation, keep in mind that their real goals may not be exactly what they think they are. Their real goals probably include things such as making bigger profits, making fewer mistakes so they don't get yelled at as much by managers and clients, and finishing their daily work in time to go watch junior's soccer practice.

Look for the real causes of the customers' problems and think about ways you can address them. If you can see a way to improve operations, suggest it (always keeping in mind that they probably know a whole lot more about their business than you do so there's a good chance that your idea won't fly).

> *By the way, never ever tell a customer, "What you really need is a slap in the head and a better product." That sort of non-constructive criticism may be gratifying but usually generates an unfavorable response.*

Prioritize

At this point, you should have a fair understanding of the customers' business, at least the pieces that are relevant to your project. You should understand at least roughly which customers will be playing which roles during the upcoming drama. At a minimum, you should know who the Customer Champion and Customer Representatives are so you know who to ask questions.

You should also have a big list of desired features. This list will probably include a lot of unicorns and pixie dust — things that would be nice to have but that are obviously unrealistic. It may also include things that are reasonable but that would take too much time for your current project.

To narrow the wish list to manageable scope, sit down with the customers and help them prioritize. You'll need the Customer Representatives who understand what is needed so they can make the decisions. Sometimes you may need the Customer Champion either in the meeting or available for consultation to make the tough calls.

Group the features into three categories. Priority 1 (or release 1) features are things that absolutely must be in the version of the project that you're about to start building. This should be the bare-bones essentials without which the project will be a failure.

Priority 2 (or release 2) features are those that the customers can live without until the first version is in use and you have time to start working on the next version. If development goes well, you may be able to pull some of these features into the first release but the customers should not count on it.

Priority 3 (or release 3) features are those that the customers think would be nice but that are less important than the priority 1 and 2 features. This is where you put the unicorns and pixie dust so you can ignore them for now.

> *You don't need to tell the customers but the priority 3 features are unlikely to ever make it into production. By the time release 1 is finished, the customers will have thought of a plethora of other priority 1 and 2 features that they want in release 2 so the release 3 features will remain unimplemented in the next version, and so on forever by induction.*

This is another place where different development shops take different approaches. In the more flexible approach that I prefer, these categories are somewhat flexible. If, during development, you discover that some priority 2 feature would be really easy to implement, you can pull it into the current release. In contrast, if some priority 1 feature turns out to be unexpectedly hard, you might ask the customers how important it really is and suggest that it be bumped to the priority 2 list to avoid endangering the schedule.

To make this sort of shuffling easier, it can be helpful to further prioritize the items within each category. If an item is high up on the list of priority 1 items, it is not a likely candidate for deferral to the next release. Similarly, if an item is high up in the priority 2 list, you might be willing to spend a little extra effort to bring it into the first release.

In a hard-line development approach, the categories are fixed after the requirements phase ends and items never move from one category to another. This prevents the customers from promoting items from priority 2 to priority 1, so it can save you some trouble. However, this approach also makes it hard for you to downgrade a feature that turns out to be a real project albatross.

Verify Your Understanding

With your notebook (and brain) bursting at the seams with all of this information, it's almost time to move on to the next chapter and start building a data model. Before you do, you should verify one last time that you really understand the customers' needs. This may be your last chance to avoid a painful catastrophe, so be sure you've gotten it right.

Walk through your understanding of the system and explain it to the customers as if they were building the system for you and not the other way around. They should make comforting grunts and noises such as "yup" and "uh huh."

Watch out for words such as "but," "except," and "sort of." When they use those words, make sure they're only emphasizing something that you already know and not adding a new twist to things. Often at this stage the customers think of new situations and exceptions that they didn't think of before.

Pay particular attention to exceptions — cases where things mostly work one way but occasionally work in another. Exceptions are the bane of database designers and, as you'll see in the following chapter, you need to handle them in a special way.

For example, suppose you need to allow for returns. (A client might decide that the Kathryn Janeway sculpture he ordered is too short or clashes with his Predator statue.) While reviewing your understanding of the project, you say, "So the receiving clerk enters the RMA (Return Merchandize Authorization number) and clicks Done, right?" Your customer representatives look sheepishly at each other and say, "Well... usually but sometimes they don't have an RMA. Then they just write in 'None.'" This is an important exception that the customers didn't tell you about before and you need to write it down.

For another example, suppose your customers currently use paper order forms that have shipping and billing address sections. You say, "So the form needs to hold one shipping address and one billing address?" Your customer replies, "Well, sometimes we need two shipping addresses because different parts of the order go to different addresses." Someone pulls out an order form where a second address and additional instructions have been scribbled in the margin.

This is a huge exception. It's easy enough to add little notations to a paper form but it's impossible to add more than one address value to a single set of fields in a database. You can work around the issue if you plan for it, but it can be a major headache if you don't learn about it ahead of time.

For a final example, suppose a customer record needs a billing address. While you're reviewing your understanding the customer says, "Oh yeah, and a shipping address because sometimes they buy one as a gift." Now you have to wonder if sometime later someone will decide that you also need a contact address in case you have questions about the order. Or a corporate address where you can send legal correspondence. Or perhaps a whole slew of branch office addresses. Or an executive address where you can send golf clubs to bribe the client's executives.

When your customer expands a single field (or a group of fields such as an address), you should ask seriously whether it's going to happen again. If the record needs to hold many copies of the same field, you can easily pull them into a separate table if you plan ahead of time, but it can be hard to add new copies of fields to a table after you build it and its user interface. A single customer record can hold one or two addresses but not an ill-defined, ever-expanding number. It's better to know ahead of time and plan for an arbitrary number of related addresses.

Sometimes in database design it's better to only allow one or many related items. There's no such thing as two.

Write the Requirements Document

The *requirements document* describes the system that you are going to build. This document is sometimes called the *product requirements document* (PRD), the *requirements specification*, *specification*, or *spec*. As all of these names imply, this document specifies the project's requirements.

At a minimum, the requirements document needs to spell out what you're planning to build and what it will do. It needs to explain the problems that it will solve and it should describe how the customers will use it to solve their problems. It can also include any design or architecture that you've already done, and it can include (possibly as attachments or appendixes) summaries of the discussions you've had while deciding on the project's features.

The requirements document keeps everyone on track during later design and development. It can also prevent finger-pointing when someone starts yelling about how you forgot to include the telepathic user interface. You can simply point to the requirements document and say, "Sorry but the telepathic interface isn't in here." In fact, if you considered this issue during brainstorming and dumped the telepathic interface into the priority 3 "unicorns and pixie dust" category, having it listed there will probably allow you to skip the whole argument. The potential wave-maker can see that the issue has been shelved for now and will probably not bother stirring up trouble on a dead issue.

(I've worked on some projects that had enormous requirements documents, sometimes running to 500 or more pages. In that case, it's hard for anyone to remember everything that's in there and you may end up revisiting some issues occasionally.)

The requirements document should define *deliverables* (also called *milestones*, not to be confused with millstones) that the customers can use to gauge the project's progress. These should be tasks that you complete along the way that you can show the customer and *that can be verified in some meaningful way*. It's important that they be verifiable. Saying you're 25 percent done thinking about the design doesn't do the user any good. Saying that you will have a database built and you will have filled it with test data drawn from a legacy system is much more useful and verifies that the database can hold that kind of data.

If you make the database design a deliverable (usually a good idea), then you need to be able to somehow verify that the design meets the customers' needs. Usually that means an extensive review where a lot of people put their heads together and try to poke holes in your carefully crafted design.

Prototypes also make excellent deliverables. Customers can experiment with a prototype to better understand what the system will do and they can give you feedback if you're not heading in the right direction. If you're building a full-blown user interface for the database, you could mock-up some prototype screens (probably with no error checking and possibly with just a little concocted data) to give the customers a feel for the completed application.

Some of the deliverables defined by the requirements document should be *final deliverables*. These are deliverables that determine whether the project is finished. Like all of the other deliverables, they must be measurable to be useful.

A particularly useful technique for deciding when a project has met its goals is to create use cases. Use cases are described in the following section.

Make Use Cases

A *use case* is a script that the users can follow to practice solving a particular problem that they will face while using your finished product. These can range in complexity from the very simple such as logging in or closing the application, to the extremely complex such as scheduling a fleet of trucks to perform in-home dog grooming.

Depending on how complete the user interface design is when you are writing the use cases, these may be sketchy or extremely detailed. They may spell out every keystroke and mouse movement that the user must make or they may provide vague instructions such as, "The user will use the Order Entry form to place a new order."

When the project is finished, the customers should review all of the use cases and verify that the finished project can handle them all. (In self-defense, you should run through the use cases before you tell the customers that you're finished. That way you don't look silly when the product cannot handle simple chores during an executive dog and pony show.)

Some of the things that you might specify when writing up use cases include:

- ❑ **Goals:** A summary of what the use case should achieve.
- ❑ **Summary:** An executive overview that your Executive Champion can understand.
- ❑ **Actors:** Who will do what? This includes people, your finished system, other systems, and so forth. Anyone or anything that will do something.
- ❑ **Pre- and post-conditions:** The conditions that should be true before and after the use case is finished. For example, a pre-condition to placing a new order might be that the client placing the order already exists.

❏   **Normal Flow:** The normal steps that occur during the use case.

❏   **Alternative Flow:** Other ways the use case might proceed. For example, when a user tries to look up a customer, what happens if the customer isn't there?

❏   **Notes:** Just in case there are special considerations that the person following the use case needs to know.

Many developers like to draw use case diagrams to show what actors perform what tasks. These seem to usually work at one of two levels.

A higher level use case shows which actors perform which tasks. For example, the Student actor enrolls in a class and takes the class, the Instructor actor teaches the class and assigns grades, and so forth. This type of use case diagram provides little detail about how the actors accomplish their tasks. It's useful early on when you know what you want to do but don't yet know how the system will do it.

Figure 4-1 shows a high-level use case diagram. Actors are shown as stick figures, tasks are shown in ellipses, and lines connect actors to tasks. More elaborate use case diagrams use other kinds of arrows, lines, and annotations to provide more detail.

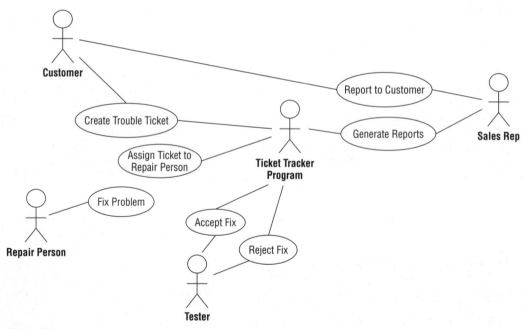

Figure 4-1

The second kind of use case lists more specific steps that actors take to perform a task, although the steps are still listed at a fairly high level.

Neither of these kinds of use case diagram provides enough detail to use as a script for testing, although they do list the cases that you must test. Because they are shown at such a high level, they are great for executive presentations. For more information on use case diagrams, look for books about UML (Universal Modeling Language), which includes use case diagrams, or search the Web for "use case diagram." Two links that provide introductions are:

❏ atlas.kennesaw.edu/~dbraun/csis4650/A&D/UML_tutorial/use_case.htm

❏ www.developer.com/design/article.php/10925_2109801_1

Typical use cases might include:

❏ The user logging in.

❏ The user logging out.

❏ Switching users (if the program allows that).

❏ Creating a new customer record.

❏ Editing a customer record.

❏ Marking a customer record as inactive.

❏ Creating a new order for an existing customer.

❏ Creating a new order for a new customer.

❏ Creating an invoice for an order.

❏ Sending out late payment notices.

❏ Creating a replacement invoice in case the customer lost one.

❏ Receiving a payment.

❏ Defining a new inventory item (when the CEO decides that you should start selling Rogaine for Dogs).

❏ Adding new items to inventory (for example, when you restock your fuzzy dice supply).

❏ Etc.

The list can go on practically forever. A large project can include hundreds of use cases and it may take quite a while to write them all down and then later verify that the finished project handles them all.

In addition to being measurable (you want to be able to tell whether the program can pull its weight), use cases should be as realistic as possible. There's no point in verifying that the program can handle a situation that will never occur in real life.

In one project, the program we were writing needed to be able to handle 20 simultaneous users. One customer performed a test where 20 people all sitting in the same room walked step-by-step through the same use case at the same time. They all typed in the same text and clicked the Find button at the same time. The program gave terrible performance because every user's computer tried to access the same database records at the same time. In a more realistic test, every user tried to access a different record and everything was fine.

Try It Out   Use Cases

Suppose you are building a program to let students log on over the Internet and enroll in classes. All enrollments are tentative until a specific date on which they are all processed. (That gives the school a chance to juggle schedules; for example, if a graduating student really needs a class, another student might get bumped for now.) To accommodate this flexibility, students should enter alternate choices.

For this exercise, make a list of database use cases that you could use to look for data that you have not built into the design and to later test to ensure that all of the data is present. You don't need to explain how a user will perform a certain task, just briefly describe the task and list the kinds of data that must be stored or accessed during that task. Add any questions that need further study or feedback from the customers.

How It Works

You should perform use cases covering every task that the final users of the system would perform. Here's the list that I've come up with.

Task	Data Needs
Log on successfully or unsuccessfully	Verify UserName and Password in Students table. (How do we generate these? How do we guarantee security?)
Enter desired schedule	Let students pick from dropdown lists so we don't need to verify that they typed meaningful choices. Refer to course schedule tables to give students choices. Save student selections in student selections tables. (Allow students to prioritize their selections?)
Generate final schedules	Refer to course schedule tables to get Capacity. Refer to global tables to learn minimum enrollment to not cancel a class. (Or does this vary by class? By department?) Process student selections tables, adding students to desired classes in the course tables. If a class fills, bump lower priority students, consult their selections, and assign a replacement course. If a class has too few students, notify the administrator to cancel the class. Consult the selections of any students in the class and assign replacement courses. When finished, review the course tables and copy student course assignments into student data tables. Check global tables (vary by department?) to learn minimum and maximum normal course load. If a student falls outside of those bounds, look up the student's counselor in the student tables and notify that counselor via email.
Send schedules to students	Get student schedule and email address from student tables. Email the schedule.

Task	Data Needs
Email course rosters	Get course roster data from course tables. Get the name and email address of each course's instructor from the course tables. Get the instructor's email address from the instructor tables. Email the class's roster to the instructor.
Manually adjust schedules	Allow administrators to manually adjust schedules to handle special circumstances. This will require free access to course tables, student data tables, and student course assignment tables.

Decide Feasibility

At some point, you should step back, take a deep breath, and decide whether the project is feasible. Is it even possible to design a database to do everything that the customer wants it to do?

Can you really build a database to hold records for 17 million customers, provide simultaneous access for 80 service representatives, log every transaction with timestamps and user IDs, give interactive responses to queries in less than 2 seconds 90 percent of the time, and still fit it all on a 16MB flash drive?

Okay, the last condition is pretty unrealistic but seriously, someone needs to think about the project's viability at some point. No one will be happy to hear that you can't solve all of the customers' problems, but everyone will be a lot happier if the project is canceled early instead of after you've waste a year of everyone's time and a king's ransom in funding.

If it really looks like you can't complete the project, make the tough call and ask everyone to rethink. Perhaps the customers can give up some features to make the project possible. Or perhaps everyone should just walk away and move on to a more realistic project.

Summary

Building any custom product is largely a translation process whether you're building a small database, a gigantic Internet sales system similar to the one used by Amazon, or a really tricked-out snowboard. You need to translate the half-formed ideas floating around in the minds of your customers into reality.

The first step in the translation process is understanding the customers' needs. This chapter explained ways you can gather information about the customers' problems, wishes, and desires so you can take the next step in the process.

In this chapter you learned how to:

❑ Try to decide which customers will play which roles.

❑ Pick the customers' brains for information.

- ❑ Look for documentation about user roles and responsibilities, existing procedures, and existing data.

- ❑ Watch customers at work and study their current operations directly.

- ❑ Brainstorm and categorize the results into priority 1, 2, and 3 items.

- ❑ Verify your understanding of the customers' needs.

- ❑ Write a requirements document with verifiable deliverables including use cases.

After you've achieved a good understanding of the customers' needs and expectations, you can start turning them into data models. The following chapter explains how to convert those needs into informal data models that help you better understand the database, and then how to convert the informal models into more formal ones that you can actually use to build a database.

Before you move on to Chapter 5, however, use the following exercises to test your understanding of the material covered in this chapter. You can find the solutions to selected exercises in Appendix A.

Exercises

1. In Figure 4-2, draw lines connecting the customer roles with their corresponding descriptions.

Customer Role	Description
Convert	Someone who won't be around for long. May be helpful or may not care all that much.
Customer Champion	Answers your questions about the project.
Customer Representative	Anyone who has an interest in the project.
Devil's Advocate	Makes things generally run smoothly. Not glamorous but very useful.
Executive Champion	Provides a reality check and prevents groupthink.
Generic Bad Guy	Ranges from annoying naysayer to malicious saboteur/super villain.
Short-Timer	A user who originally was against your project that you include in the development process to bring them onto your side.
Sidekick/Gopher	The highest ranking customer driving the project. Willing to fight super villains.
Stakeholder	Thoroughly understands the customers' needs. Has the authority to make decisions that stick.

Figure 4-2

2. Which of the following does *not* describe a use case?

   a. A script for performing some task.

   b. Should describe a realistic operation.

   c. Should cover the customer's entire operation from start to finish.

   d. Should be verifiable.

3. Brainstorming sessions should ideally include:

   a. Customer Representatives.

   b. A Devil's Advocate.

   c. All interested Stakeholders.

   d. All of the above.

4. If a customer says you should use a hierarchical XML database, you should:

   a. Politely say, "Thank you," and ignore this nugget of wisdom.

   b. Ask the customer why he thinks that.

   c. Do as the customer says. (It's his money.)

   d. Study the problem to see if that kind of database makes sense.

5. During a visit to view the customers' operation, you see someone repeatedly stamping the front of an order with the current date, turning the order over, turning it over again, and stamping the front with the date again. You should:

   a. Ask someone what that's all about.

   b. Suggest that the manager fire this crazy and possibly dangerous employee.

   c. Ignore the whole issue and stay focused on your own tasks.

   d. Avoid eye contact with this employee at all costs.

6. Look at the ZIP Code lookup form at zip4.usps.com/zip4/welcome.jsp. What are this form's data needs? Which fields are required? (How does the user know those fields are required?) What are the domains for the fields? Which *could* involve a foreign key validation?

7. Which of the following is *not* a security issue that you should consider when studying the project?

   a. The number of classes of users the database must support.

   b. Whether you need to provide audit trails to record changes to the data.

   c. The frequency with which you need to perform backups.

   d. Whether the users should have individual passwords.

8. You are called upon to design a database for a florist shop named "Frank's Floral Fantasies." Frank thinks that he might want to track the medicinal and homeopathic properties of his plants because he thinks that might improve his sales of echinacea, St. John's Wort, and other plants. What priority should this requirement get?

a.   Priority 1, definitely in this release.

b.   Priority 2, probably in the next release.

c.   Priority 3, with the unicorns and pixie dust.

d.   It depends (you need more information).

9.   Write a use case for logging in to your computer's operating system.

10.   You're halfway finished designing your database when a Vice Presidential Super Villain says your project is doomed to failure because you didn't include a sufficient allowance for farbulistic granilation. You need to cancel the whole thing and start over with him in control. How should you handle this attack?

Translating User Needs into Data Models

Chapter 4 discussed ways you can work with customers to gain a full understanding of the problem at hand. The result should be a big pile of facts, goals, needs, and requirements that should be part of the new database and its surrounding ecosystem. You may already have made some connections among various parts of this information, but mostly it should be a big heap of requirements that doesn't say too much about the database's design and construction.

This kind of pile of information is sometimes called a *contextual list*. It's basically just a list of important stuff (although it may be fairly elaborate and include requirements documents, diagrams, charts, and all sorts of other supporting documentation).

The next step in turning the conceptual list into a database is converting it into a more formal model. You can compare the formal model to the contextual list and make sure that the model can handle all of your requirements.

You can also use the model to verify that you're on track. You can explain the model to the customers and see if they think it will handle all of their needs or if they forgot to mention something important while you were following the procedures described in Chapter 4.

> *Constantly verifying that you're on track is an important part of any project. It's much easier to hit a target if you're constantly checking the map and making any necessary adjustments. You wouldn't aim your car at a parking space, close your eyes, and step on the pedal, would you? It's much easier to park if you keep an eye on your progress, the other cars, the skateboarders slamming nosegrinds off the curb, kids riding on shopping carts, and everything else in the parking lot.*

After you build a data model (or possibly more than one), you can use it to build a relational model. The relational model is a specific kind of formal model that has a structure very similar to the one used by relational databases. That makes it relatively easy to convert the relational model into an actual database in Access, SQL Server, MySQL, or some other database product.

In this chapter you learn how to:

- ❑ Create user interface models
- ❑ Create semantic object models
- ❑ Create entity-relationship models
- ❑ Convert those types of models into relational models

After you master these techniques, you'll be ready to start pulling the models apart and rearranging the pieces to improve the design by making it lean and flexible.

What Are Data Models?

Despite what some managers occasionally seem to believe, a model isn't a silver bullet or enchanted wand that will magically make a project succeed. A model by itself doesn't do anything. It doesn't build a database, it isn't a piece of software (although there are software tools that can help you build a model), and the final user of your database never sees a model.

A model is a plan. It's a blueprint for building something, in this case a database. The purpose of the model isn't to do anything by itself. Instead it gives you a concrete way to think about the database that you are going to build. By studying the pieces of the model, you can decide whether it represents all of the data that you need to meet your customers' needs.

A model is also useful for ensuring that everyone on the project has the same understanding of what needs to be done. If everyone understands the model, then everyone should have the same ideas about what data should be stored, which tables should contain it, and how the tables are related. They should also agree on the business rules that determine how the data is used and constrained.

Note that it's important that everyone actually understands the model. I've seen developers build remarkably complicated models and then dump them on hapless end users, expecting those users to understand the models' every subtle nuance. The developers ended up walking the users through the models until the users' heads were spinning and the developers could have convinced them of just about anything. The models are for those who know how to understand them, not necessarily for everyone.

After you build a model, you can look at it and ask questions such as:

- ❑ Where do we store customer information?
- ❑ How many contact names can we store for a customer?
- ❑ Where do we store the contacts' favorite colors?
- ❑ What if we need to store multiple price points for the same product?
- ❑ How do we store the seventeen kinds of addresses we need for customers?
- ❑ Where do we store supplier information?
- ❑ If someone asks about an order they placed but haven't received, how can we figure out where it is?

❏ Where can we enter special instructions for an order?

❏ How do we know when we need to restock left-handed cable stretchers?

You should also work through any use cases or current scenarios and see if the model can handle them. You can't actually fill out insurance claim forms and look in the warehouse for missing orders yet, but you should be able to say, "this table contains the data we need to do that."

The end users can help a lot with this part. Though they may not understand the models, they do understand their business and can ask these sorts of questions while you and the other developers try to figure out if the model can handle them.

If the model cannot handle all of your (and the users') questions, you need to adjust the model. You might need to add fields or tables, change a field's data type, make new connections between tables, or make other changes to satisfy the requirements. In extreme cases, it may be easiest to start a new model from scratch.

This chapter discusses four kinds of models that grow successively closer to the final database implementation.

First, a user interface model views the database at a very high level as seen from the final user's point of view. Depending on how you are going to use the database, this might be as the user will view the database through forms on a computer screen. This model is very far from the final database implementation and it doesn't tell much about the database design. This model is useful for understanding what data is needed by the project and how you might use it to navigate through the user interface.

The second and third types of models described in this chapter are semantic object models and entity-relationship models. These are roughly at the same distance from the final database. They are at a slightly lower level than the user interface model and show relationships among data entities more explicitly. They are still at a moderately high logical level, however, and do not provide quite enough detail to build the final database.

The fourth type of model described in this chapter is the relational model. This model mimics the structure of a relational database closely enough that you can actually sit down and start building the database.

In a typical database design project, you might start with a user interface model. I like to start there because I figure if the user is going to see something, we better have a place for it in the database. Conversely, if the user isn't going to see it in some manner, do we really need it in the database? (But that's just me. I like designing user interfaces. Some people prefer to skip that and let someone else worry about the user interface.)

Next you use what you learned from the user interface model to build either a semantic object model or an entity-relationship model. These models serve the same purpose so you generally don't need to build them both. Work through this chapter and the exercises at its end and decide which one you prefer.

Finally, you convert the semantic object model or entity-relationship model into a relational model. Now you have something that could be turned into a database. There are still some steps to go as you refine the relational model to improve the final database's reliability and performance, but those are subjects for later chapters.

Remember, these models are intended to better your understanding of the data and the ways in which different bits are related, so with that in mind, anything that increases understanding is beneficial. Don't be afraid to add notes that clarify confusing issues. Feel free to modify the basic modeling techniques described here. There's some benefit to sticking close to standard notations because it lets others who have studied the same notation understand what you are doing, but if adding a number in a box by each link or a colored triangle helps you and your team get a better handle on the design, do it. Just be sure to make a note of your additions and changes so everyone is on the same page.

User Interface Models

In most database applications, a user will eventually see the data in some form. For example, an order entry and tracking application might use a series of screens where the user can perform such chores as entering orders, tracking orders, marking an order as paid, looking up available inventory, and so forth. Those screens form the database's user interface.

Some databases don't have their own user interfaces, at least not that a human will see. Some databases are designed to store data for other applications to manipulate. In that case, it is the interfaces that those other applications provide that the human user sees. If possible, you should consider what those applications will need to display and plan accordingly. Sometimes it is useful to build throwaway interfaces to view the data on forms, in spreadsheets such as Microsoft Excel, or in text files.

You should also consider how those other applications will get the data from your database. The way in which those applications interact with your database forms a non-human interface and you should plan for that one, too. For example, suppose you know that a dispatch system will need to fetch information about employees from your database and information about pending repair jobs from another system. You should think about the kinds of employee data that the dispatch system will need (things such as a repairperson's skills, equipment, assigned vehicle, and so forth). Then you can design your database to make fetching this data easy and efficient.

To build the user interface model, start by making rough sketches of the screens that the user will see. Often these first sketches can come directly from paper forms if any exist.

Include the fields with sample data to make it easier to understand what belongs on each screen. These sketches can be anything from crayon scribbles on bar napkins, to forms drawn with your favorite computerized drawing tool, to full user interface prototypes. Figure 5-1 shows a mocked-up Find Orders screen built with Visual Basic. This form holds only controls and doesn't include any code to do anything more than just sit there and look pretty.

In addition to the image in Figure 5-1, you should include text explaining what the various parts of the form do. In this case, that text might say:

❑   The user enters selection criteria in the upper part of the form and clicks the Search button.

❑   The program displays a list of matching order records in the bottom of the form.

❑   The user can select an order from the list and click Open to open that order's detail form.

At this level, the user probably thinks of each order as containing all of the information on this form. If you were to fill out an order on a piece of paper, that paper would include blanks for you to fill in customer name, customer ID, contact name, order date, and so forth. The order would also have a status, although you might represent that by putting the order in boxes on your desk labeled Pending, Open, Closed, and so forth rather than by having a status box on the paper form.

Figure 5-1

The form and its description also raise some important questions:

❑ What fields should be allowed as selection criteria?

❑ Should we index the selection criteria fields to make searching faster? Some or all fields?

❑ When the user selects an order and clicks Open, how does the program open the Orders record? (Searching for the exact combination of fields shown in the list would be slow and there might even be two entries with the same values if someone placed two orders on the same day. It might be wise to add an order ID field to make finding the record again easier.)

When you select an order from the form shown in Figure 5-1 and click Open, the program displays the form shown in Figure 5-2.

This form shows the fields that should be associated with an order. These include:

❑ Various dates such as the date the order was placed, the date the products were shipped, the date the customer paid, and so forth

❑ The order's current status

❑ The shipping method (Priority, Overnight, Armored Courier, and so forth)

❑ The billing method (credit card, invoice net 30)

❑ Various addresses such as the shipping and billing addresses

❑ Contact information for when we get confused (or want to send spam to the unsuspecting contact)

❑ The order's line items

❑ Subtotal, taxes, shipping, and grand total

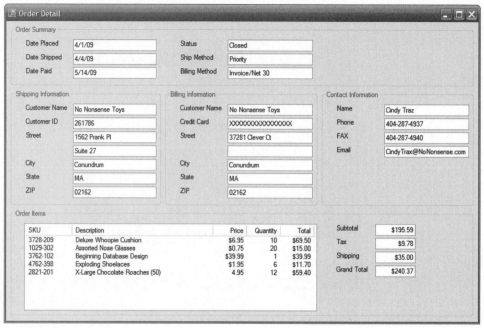

Figure 5-2

Both of these forms involve orders and both provide some information about the order data. The Order Detail form includes a lot of the fields that must be stored to represent an order. The Find Orders screen tells which order fields should be allowed as search criteria (and thus may make good keys) and which order fields should be displayed in the result list.

Each of these forms tells a little bit more about the order data. Other mocked-up forms would give even more information about the order data. For example, the application would need an order entry form and a form to update order information (such as changing the addresses or setting order status to Closed). Depending on how the work was divided among employees, there might be special forms for performing a single specific task. For example, an order fulfillment clerk (who puts things in a box and ships them) would need to be able to change an order's status to Shipped but probably doesn't need to be able to change credit card numbers. In fact, going through the screens and deciding which employees should be able to do which tasks gives you an initial indication of the application's security requirements.

Still other forms would give hints about other parts of the database. A full-fledged database for this application would need to include forms for managing inventory. (For example, how do we know there are any more whoopee cushions to sell and how do we know when to order more?) It might also include supplier information (who sells us our nose glasses?), employee information (who is assigned to pester delinquent customers this week?), advertising data (which spam campaigns gave us the most new contacts?), and so forth.

A large application might include dozens or even hundreds of forms, each of which gives only a partial glimpse of the information contained in the database. Together these mocked-up screens form a user interface model that shines spotlights into the data needed to support the application.

With the user interface model in hand, you are now ready to build a more formal model that shows the entities used by the application in greater detail. The first of those models discussed in this chapter is the semantic object model.

User Interface Models

Sketch out a form where the user could enter shift information for employees. What data must be displayed on the form?

How It Works

Figure 5-3 shows a mocked-up employee shift form.

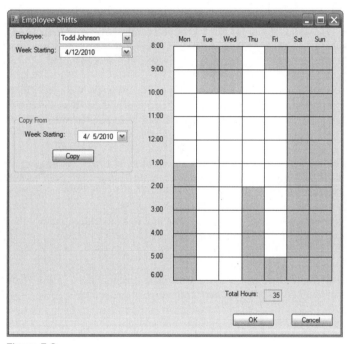

Figure 5-3

This form includes the following data:

❑   Employee name (selected from a combo box).

❑   The starting day of the week the user is viewing and editing for this employee (selected from a combo box). (Which weeks will we allow the user to pick? How far in the future?)

❑   The user should also be able to select past weeks (from a combo box) from which to copy.

❑   The hours that the employee is scheduled to work. These records (in the EmployeeShifts table?) will include employee, date, start time, and stop time.

❑   Total hours scheduled. This can be calculated from the shift data.

The form will also need to look up minimum and maximum normal hours so we can warn the user if something is unusual. For example, if the user is scheduled to work 70 hours in a week, the form can ask the user to verify before accepting the changes.

Semantic Object Models

A semantic object model (SOM) is intended to represent a system at a fairly high level. Though the ideas are somewhat technical, they still relate fairly closely to the way people think about things, so semantic object models are relatively understandable to users.

Classes and Objects

Intuitively a *semantic class* is a type of thing that you might want to represent in your system. This can include physical objects such as people, furniture, inventory items, and invoices. It can also include logical abstractions such as report generators, tax years, and work queues.

Technically a semantic class is a named collection of attributes that are sufficient to identify a particular entity. For example, a PERSON class might have FirstName and LastName attributes. If you can identify members of the PERSON class by using their FirstName and LastName attribute values, then that's good enough.

By convention, the names of semantic classes are written in ALL CAPS as in EMPLOYEE, WORK_ORDER, or PHISHING_ATTACK. Some prefer to use hyphens instead of underscores so the last two would be WORK-ORDER and PHISHING-ATTACK.

A *semantic object* (SO) is an instance of a semantic class. It is an entity instance that has all of the attributes defined by the class filled in. For example, an instance of the PERSON class might have FirstName "David" and LastName "Letterman."

Traditionally the attributes that define a semantic class and that distinguish semantic objects are written in mixed case as in LastName, InvoiceDate, and DaysOfConfusion.

Attributes come in three flavors: simple, group, and object.

A *simple attribute* holds a simple value such as a string, number, or date. For example, LastName holds a string and EmployeeId holds a number.

A *group attribute* holds a composite value — a value that is composed of other values. For example, an Address attribute might contain a Street, Suite, City, State, and ZipCode. You could think of these as separate attributes but that would ignore the structure built into an address. These values really go together so, to represent them together, you use a group attribute.

An *object attribute* represents a relationship with some other semantic object. For example, a relationship may represent logical containment. A COURSE class would have a STUDENT object attribute to represent the students taking the course. Similarly the STUDENT class would have a COURSE object attribute representing the courses that a student was taking. Each of these classes is related to the other so they are called *paired classes*. Similarly their related attributes are called *paired attributes*.

Cardinality

An attribute's *cardinality* tells how many values of that attribute an object might have. For example, at the start of some volleyball tournaments each team's roster must contain between 6 and 12 players.

You write the lower and upper bounds beside the attribute to which they apply separated by a period. The volleyball team roster's `Players` attribute would have cardinality 6.12. (I have no idea why it's a single period and not a dash or ellipsis.)

Usually the minimum cardinality is 0 if the value is optional or 1 if it is required.

The maximum cardinality is usually 1 if at most one value is allowed or N if any number of values is allowed.

Probably the most common cardinalities are:

- ❑ **1.1:** Exactly one value required. For example, suppose you are building a database to track restaurant orders. In the `ORDER` class, the `ServerName` attribute would have cardinality 1.1 because every order must have exactly one server.

- ❑ **1.N:** Any number of values but at least one required. For example, the `ORDER` class's `Item` attribute would hold the items ordered by the diners and would have cardinality 1.N. It wouldn't make sense to send an order to the kitchen if it didn't contain any items, but it could contain any number of items. (Although in practice I might double-check with the server if the kitchen received an order for 13,000 hamburgers.)

- ❑ **0.1:** An optional single value. For example, the server might want to record a comment to go with the order. ("Extra cheese on the milkshake.")

- ❑ **0.N:** Any number of optional values. For example, a series of comments. ("Dressing on the side for salad 1. No mayo on burger 2. Recognize poor tipper, use day-old breadsticks.")

Identifiers

An *object identifier* is a group of one or more attributes that the users will typically use to identify an object in the class.

An object identifier can include a single attribute such as `CustomerId` or a group of attributes such as `FirstName`, `MiddleName`, and `LastName`.

You indicate an identifier by writing the text "ID" to the left of its attributes. Often identifiers contain unique values so every item in the class will have different values for the identifier. For example, `CustomerId`, `SocialSecurityNumber`, and `Isbn` are unique identifiers for customers, employees, and books, respectively. You can indicate a unique identifier by underlining the "ID" to its left.

Sometimes non-unique identifiers are used to find groups of objects. For example, suppose the users of your system will want to find customers in a particular city. Then the `CUSTOMER` class's `City` attribute would be a non-unique identifier.

Putting It Together

Figure 5-4 shows a simple representation of a `CUSTOMER` class that demonstrates these notational features.

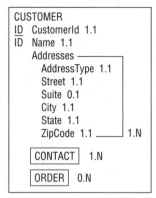

Figure 5-4

A big box surrounds the whole class definition. The class name, CUSTOMER, goes at the top.

CustomerId is a simple attribute that is used to identify customers so it gets the ID notation. CustomerId values are unique so the ID is underlined. This value is required and a customer can have only one ID so its cardinality is 1.1.

Users sometimes want to search for customers by name so the Name attribute is also an identifier. It is possible that two customers could have the same name, however, so here ID isn't underlined. (Duplicate customer names could also lead to a trademark battle if your customers are companies. Fortunately that's their problem, not yours.)

The CUSTOMER class includes address information stored in the Addresses attribute. Each address has the attributes AddressType (this will be something like Shipping or Billing), Street, Suite, City, State, and ZipCode. All of these except Suite are required and can hold only one value. The Suite attribute is optional. Lines show the attributes contained inside the Addresses value. The 1.N to the lower right of the group indicates that a CUSTOMER object must have one or more Addresses values (each containing a Street, Suite, City, State, and ZipCode).

Finally, the class has two object attributes named CONTACT and ORDER. The CONTACT attribute represents one or more contact people for the customer. The box around the attribute tells you that this is an object attribute. Its cardinality 1.N indicates that the CUSTOMER must have at least one contact.

The ORDER attribute represents the orders placed by this customer. You might think that this should have cardinality 1.N. After all, why would you need a customer who doesn't place any orders? However, when you first create a customer record it will have no associated orders. You might also want to be able to make a customer record in anticipation of future orders. For both of those reasons, this design sets the cardinality of ORDER to 0.N.

> *This is a design decision and in your application you could take the other route. You can look at the user interface model to see which would be more natural. Do you want to provide a screen where a user can create a customer record without an order or do you want to make the order entry screen allow for creating a new customer?*

Try It Out   **Semantic Object Model**

Make a semantic object model for an EMPLOYEE_WEEK class that holds information about employees scheduled for a week. This class should have object identifier fields EmployeeId and StartDate. It should also have a group attribute named Shift that includes StartTime and StopTime, and it should hold one Shift for each of the seven days of the week.

How It Works

Figure 5-5 shows the semantic object model for the EMPLOYEE_WEEK class.

Figure 5-5

Semantic Views

Sometimes it is useful to define different views into the same data. For example, consider the kinds of information a company typically tracks for its employees. That information might include:

❏   Normal contact information such as name, address, phone number, and next of kin.

❏   Work-related contact information such as title, office number, extension, pager number, and locker number at the country club (if you're an executive).

❏   Confidential salary information including your complete salary and annual bonus history.

❏   Other confidential information such as your stock plan and 401K program participation, insurance selections, annual performance reviews, and golf handicap.

Some of this information, such as your name and title, is freely available to anyone who wants it.

Other semi-public information is available to anyone within the company but not outside the company. (Many companies worry that executive recruiters with the company phonebook could steal employees away with all of their valuable skills and the proprietary information locked inside their heads.) This information includes your office number, extension, project history, and birth date (excluding the year). It does not include your home address, annual performance reviews, salary history, or other financial data.

Other more sensitive information should be available to your manager and other superiors but not to the general population of coworkers. This information includes such things as your annual performance reviews and work history. However, your manager does not need to know how much you are having deducted for retirement contributions, whether you participate in the company stock plan, and whether you are deducting the extra $750 a month for the dental plan. Those sorts of information should be hidden from your manager. (Depending on the way your company is structured, your manager might not even need to know your exact salary.)

The people in the Human Resources department are the ones who arrange to siphon money out of your paycheck for such perks as the stock plan and dental insurance so they obviously need to know that information. However, they probably don't need access to your annual performance reviews.

Figure 5-6 shows an EMPLOYEE class and four views that give access to different parts of the employee data. For simplicity I've shown each attribute as if it were a simple attribute when actually most of these are group or object attributes. For example, the OfficeData attribute is really a compound attribute including Title, Office, Extension, BirthDate, and so forth.

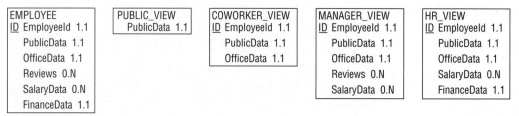

Figure 5-6

Defining these different views allows you to make data available only to those who need it. (This notion of *view* maps directly to the relational database concept of *view* so defining views now will help you later.)

After you finish building a complete semantic object model, you should check each of the views to ensure that they contain all of the information needed for each class of user and nothing else. For example, you should run through all of the use cases for managers and see if the EMPLOYEE class's MANAGER_VIEW provides enough information to handle those use cases. You should also check that every piece of data included in the MANAGER_VIEW is actually used. If something isn't used in some use case, then managers might not need it and it might not belong in the MANAGER_VIEW.

Class Types

The following sections describe some of the types of classes that you may need to use while building semantic object models. Some of these are little more than names for simple cases. Others such as association classes and derived classes introduce new concepts that are useful for building models.

Simple Objects

A *simple* or *atomic object* is one that contains only single-valued simple attributes. For example, an inventory item class might include the attributes Sku, Description, UnitPrice, and QuantityInStock. Each inventory item's data must include exactly one value for each of these attributes.

Figure 5-7 shows a simple INVENTORY_ITEM class.

```
INVENTORY_ITEM
ID Sku  1.1
    Description  1.1
    UnitPrice  1.1
    QuantityInStock  1.1
```

Figure 5-7

Composite Objects

A *composite object* contains at least one multi-valued, non-object attribute. For example, suppose you allow online customers to provide product reviews for inventory items. Then you could add a multi-valued `Reviews` attribute to the class shown in Figure 5-7 to get the composite object shown in Figure 5-8.

> *There's some difference among developers over these terms. Some call an object with a multi-valued, non-object attribute a "complex object" or "complex type" and use "composite" to mean an object that contains more than one data element. I think the terms defined here are more common but if there's any doubt in your discussion with other developers, you should agree on common definitions.*

```
INVENTORY_ITEM
ID  Sku  1.1
    Description  1.1
    UnitPrice  1.1
    QuantityInStock  1.1
    Reviews  1.N
```

Figure 5-8

Note that the multi-valued attribute need not be a simple attribute. For example, suppose you decide not to use a simple attribute to hold customer comments. Instead for each comment you store the customer's user name, a numeric rating, and comments. Figure 5-9 shows the revised INVENTORY_ITEM class.

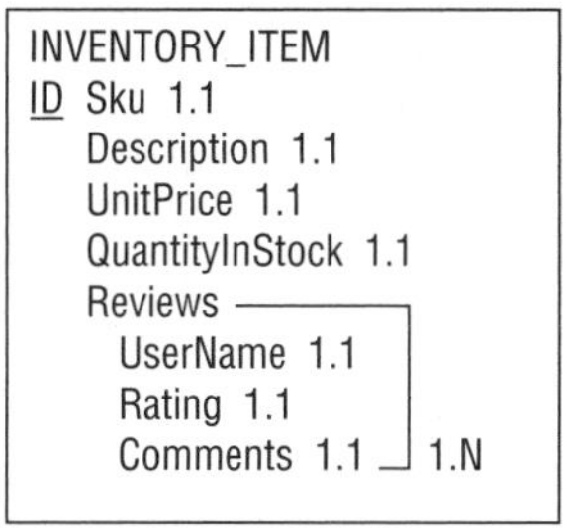

```
INVENTORY_ITEM
ID  Sku  1.1
    Description  1.1
    UnitPrice  1.1
    QuantityInStock  1.1
    Reviews ─────────
       UserName  1.1 │
       Rating  1.1   │
       Comments  1.1 ┘ 1.N
```

Figure 5-9

Compound Objects

A *compound object* contains at least one object attribute. For example, consider the CUSTOMER class shown in Figure 5-10. This class contains basic information such as a customer name and shipping and billing addresses. Its CONTACT object attribute stores information about the person we should contact if we have a question about this customer. (This is also the person who gets our junk mail.) The SALES_REPRESENTATIVE object attribute refers to another object representing the sales representative who is charged with keeping this customer happy. (Okay, not too much junk mail.)

```
CUSTOMER
ID  CustomerId  1.1
    Name  1.1
    Addresses
        AddressType  1.1
        Street  1.1
        Suite  0.1
        City  1.1
        State  1.1
        ZipCode  1.1 _____ 1.N

    CONTACT  1.1
    SALES_REPRESENTATIVE  1.1
```

Figure 5-10

Hybrid Objects

A *hybrid object* contains a combination of the other kinds of attributes. For example, it might contain a multi-valued group that contains an object attribute. The ORDER class shown in Figure 5-11 contains a LineItems group attribute to represent the items in the order. Each LineItems entry contains an INVENTORY_ITEM object attribute that refers to an object of the type shown in Figure 5-9.

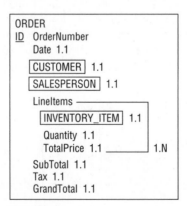

```
ORDER
ID  OrderNumber
    Date  1.1
    CUSTOMER  1.1
    SALESPERSON  1.1
    LineItems
        INVENTORY_ITEM  1.1
        Quantity  1.1
        TotalPrice  1.1 _____ 1.N
    SubTotal  1.1
    Tax  1.1
    GrandTotal  1.1
```

Figure 5-11

Association Objects

An *association object* represents a relationship between two other objects and stores extra information about the relationship.

Association objects are particularly useful for many-to-many relationships where an object of one class can be associated with many objects of a second and an object of the second class can be associated with many objects of the first.

For example, consider the PROJECT and DEVELOPER classes. A PROJECT may include many DEVELOPERs and a DEVELOPER may work on many PROJECTs, so the two classes have a many-to-many relationship. Figure 5-12 shows this relationship modeled with straightforward object attributes.

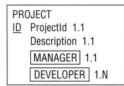

Figure 5-12

If this is all there is to the relationship, then this model is fine. However, if there is extra information that should be stored with the relationship, this model has no place to store that information.

For example, suppose developers play different roles in a project. A developer might be a technical lead, toolsmith, tester, writer, generic project member, or even the project's manager. In that case, there's no place to store this information in Figure 5-12. You cannot place it in the PROJECT class because data in that class applies to the project as a whole and not to a specific developer on the project. You cannot place the information in the DEVELOPER class because a developer might play different roles on different projects.

The solution is to create an association class to connect these classes and store the extra information. Figure 5-13 shows the new design. A PROJECT_ROLE object connects the PROJECT and DEVELOPER classes to represent the relationship that a particular developer has with a particular project. The RoleName attribute stores the information about the type of role that a particular developer plays in the project (technical lead, tester, and so forth).

Figure 5-13

For a concrete example, consider Dr. Frankenstein's famous Build-a-Friend project. The following table shows this PROJECT object's attribute values.

ProjectId	Description	PROJECT_ROLE
Build-a-Friend	Make a friend out of spare parts.	Role1
		Role2

The following table shows the attribute values for the two DEVELOPER objects.

DeveloperId	FirstName	LastName	PROJECT_ROLE
Dr. Frankenstein	Ted	Frankenstein	Role1
Igor	Igor	Johnson	Role2

Finally, the following table shows the values for PROJECT_ROLE objects.

RoleId	RoleName	DEVELOPER	PROJECT
Role1	Mad Scientist	Dr. Frankenstein	Make-a-Friend
Role2	Flunky	Igor	Make-a-Friend

From this data, you can figure out which developers play which roles on what projects.

Try It Out   Association Objects

Suppose you're putting together a database to record World of Warcraft adventures. You want to remember which player participated in which adventure. You also want to know what character they played during the adventure.

Make a semantic object model to record this information.

1. Create PLAYER and ADVENTURE classes.
2. Make a PLAYER_CHARACTER association class to fit between PLAYER and ADVENTURE. This class should store the character in addition to data linking the other two classes.

How It Works

1. Create PLAYER and ADVENTURE classes.

    The PLAYER class stores player information (PlayerId, FirstName, LastName, and so forth), plus an object attribute pointing to one or more PLAYER_CHARACTER objects. Those objects represent this player's characters in various adventures.

    The ADVENTURE class stores adventure information (AdventureId, Description), plus another object attribute pointing to one or more PLAYER_CHARACTER objects. Those objects represent all of the characters in the adventure.

2. Make a PLAYER_CHARACTER association class to fit between PLAYER and ADVENTURE. This class should store the character in addition to data linking the other two classes.

    The PLAYER_CHARACTER class stores the name of the character that the player used in this adventure. An object attribute points to the single PLAYER who played this character. Another object attribute points to the single ADVENTURE in which the player used this character.

Figure 5-14 shows the classes.

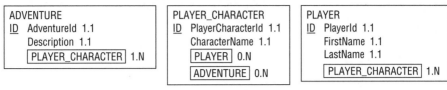

Figure 5-14

Inherited Objects

Sometimes one class might share most of the characteristics of another class but with a few differences.

For example, you've built a CAR class that has typical automobile attributes: Make, Model, Year, NumberOfCupholders, and so forth.

Now suppose you decide you need a RACECAR class. A racecar is a type of car so it has all of the same attributes that a car has. In addition, it has some racecar-specific attributes such as ZeroTo60Time, ZeroTo100Time, TopSpeed, and QuarterMileTime. You could build a whole new class that duplicates all of the CAR attributes but that would not only be extra work (something any self-respecting database designer should avoid), it also doesn't acknowledge the relationship between the two classes.

Instead you can make RACECAR a subclass or subtype of the CAR class. To denote a subclass in a semantic object model, create a RACECAR class that contains only the new attributes not included in CAR. Include an object attribute in CAR linking to the RACECAR class and using the notation 0.ST in place of the cardinality to indicate that RACECAR forms an optional subtype for CAR. Then place an object attribute in the RACECAR class linking it back to the CAR class and using the notation p in place of the cardinality to indicate that the link refers to the parent class.

Figure 5-15 shows a CAR class and a RACECAR subclass. In this case, the RACECAR class is said to inherit from the CAR class. CAR is called the *parent class*, *superclass*, or *supertype*.

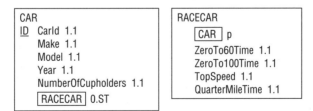

Figure 5-15

In more complicated models, a class can have multiple subclasses, nested subclasses, or multiple parent classes.

For example, suppose you decide you also want to store information about motorcycles. Motorcycles and cars share some information but one isn't really a special type of the other, so you create a new VEHICLE class to hold the common features. You then pull the common attributes from the CAR class into VEHICLE and make both CAR and MOTORCYCLE subclasses of VEHICLE. In this example, you have multiple classes (CAR and MOTORCYCLE) inheriting from a common parent class (VEHICLE). You also have a nested class RACECAR inheriting from the CAR subclass.

Comments and Notes

Semantic object models are fairly good at capturing the basic classes involved in a project, and through object attributes they do a decent job of showing which classes are related to other classes. However, they don't capture every possible scrap of information about a project.

For example, semantic object models don't indicate an attribute's domain. There's nothing in Figure 5-15 that shows that the CAR class's Make attribute must take values from an enumerated list (Ford, GM, Yugo, De Lorean, and so forth), that Model must come from a list that depends on Make, and that NumberOfCupholders should be an integer between 0 and 99 (some of the bigger minivans may need three-digit numbers).

For an even stranger example, suppose you build a VOLLEYBALL_TEAM class to represent volleyball teams. Depending on the tournament, a volleyball team might have 2, 4, or 6 players but other values are not allowed. (Although I've seen some really weird formats including as the "executive retreat" event where as many 12 people wearing slacks and dress shirts but no shoes squeeze onto the court.) A semantic object model lets you specify a minimum and maximum for the PLAYER object attribute but it cannot handle the special case of 2, 4, or 6.

A semantic object model also doesn't necessarily capture all of the meaning of the relationships between classes. For example, suppose you build BAND and ARTIST classes to store information about your favorite heavy metal bands. You would like to make separate fields in the BAND class to represent lead vocal, lead guitar, lead trombone, and other key band members but, because these are all object attributes, you need to represent them in the model as ARTIST. You'd really like to make LeadVocal, LeadGuitar, and LeadTrombone attributes that have as their domain ARTIST objects.

Though you cannot make those kinds of attributes, you can jot down notes saying what each of the ARTIST objects in the BAND class represent. You can add them as a footnote to the class, in a separate document, or in any other way that will make it easy for you to remember the meanings of these associations.

> *Note that you can also work around this problem by making an association class* BAND_MEMBER *that has a* Role *attribute in addition to* BAND *and* ARTIST *object attributes. Then, for example, you could use a* BAND_MEMBER *object to associate the* BAND *Spiñal Tap with the* ARTIST *David St. Hubbins with* Role *set to* Lead Vocal.

Remember that the point of a semantic model (or any model for that matter) is to help you understand the problem. If the model alone doesn't capture the full scope of the problem, add comments, notes, attachments, video clips, dioramas, and other extras. The model can only do so much and if it's missing something, write it down. You may not need this information now to build the initial model, but you'll need it later to build the database so write it down.

Entity-Relationship Models

An *entity-relationship diagram* (ER diagram or ERD) is another form of object model that in many ways is similar to a semantic object model. It also allows you to represent objects and their relationships, although it uses different symbols. ER diagrams also have a different focus, providing a bit more emphasis on relations and a bit less on class structure.

The following sections explain how to build basic ER diagrams to study the entities and relationships that define a project.

Entities, Attributes, and Identifiers

An *entity* is similar to a semantic object. It represents a specific instance of some thing that you want to track in the object model. Like semantic objects, an entity can be a physical thing (employee, work order, espresso maker) or a logical abstraction (appointment, discussion, excuse).

Similar entities are grouped into *entity classes* or *entity sets*. For example, the employee entities Bowb, Phrieda, and Gnick belong to the Employee entity set.

Like semantic objects, entities include attributes that describe the object that they represent.

There are a couple of different methods for drawing entity sets. In the first method, a set is contained within a rectangle. Its attributes are drawn within ellipses and attached to the set with lines. If one of the attributes is an identifier (also called a *key* or *primary key*), its name is underlined. Figure 5-16 shows a simple Employee entity set with three attributes. (Some developers write entity set names in ALL CAPS, whereas others use Mixed Case.)

Figure 5-16

One problem with this notation is that it takes up a lot of room. If you add all of the attributes to the Employee class (EmployeeId, FirstName, LastName, SocialSecurityNumber, Street, Suite, City, State, ZipCode, HomePhone, CellPhone, Fax, Email, and so forth), you'll get a pretty cluttered picture. If you then try to add Department, Project, Manager, and other classes to the picture with all of their attributes, you can quickly build an incomprehensible mess.

A second approach is to draw entity sets in a manner similar to the one used by semantic object models and then place only the set's name in the ER diagram. Lines and other symbols, which are described shortly, connect the entity sets to show their relationships. This approach allows you greater room for listing attributes while removing them from the main ER diagram so it can focus on relationships.

Relationships

An ER diagram indicates a relationship with a diamond containing the relationship's name. The name is usually something very descriptive such as Contains, Works For, or Deceives, so often the relationship is perfectly understandable on its own. If the name isn't enough, you can add attributes to a relationship just as you can add them to entities: by placing the attribute in an ellipse and attaching it to the relationship with a line.

Normally entity names are nouns such as Voter, Person, Forklift, and Politician. Relationships are verbs such as Elects, Drives, and Deceives. When you see entities and relationships connected in an

ER diagram, they appear as easy-to-read caveman phrases such as `Voter Elects Politician`, `Person Drives Forklift`, and `Politician Deceives Voter`.

Figure 5-17 shows the `Person Drives Forklift` relationship.

Figure 5-17

Note that every relation implicitly defines a reverse relation. The phrase `Person Drives Forklift` implicitly defines the relation `Forklift IsDrivenBy Person`. Usually you can figure out the relation's direction from the context. You can help by drawing the relationships from left-to-right and top-to-bottom whenever possible.

I've also seen ER diagrams that include arrows above or beside a relationship to show its direction. For example, Figure 5-18 shows an ER diagram that includes three objects and two relationships. The arrows make it easier to see that `Customer Places Order` and `Shipper Ships Order`.

Figure 5-18

Cardinality

To add cardinality information, ER diagrams add one or more of three symbols to the lines leading in and out of entity sets. The three symbols are:

- ❏ **ring:** A ring (or circle or ellipse) means zero.
- ❏ **line:** A short line (or dash or bar) means one.
- ❏ **crow's foot:** A crow's foot (or teepee or whatever you call it) means many.

These aren't too hard to remember because the number 0 looks like a circle, the number 1 looks a line, and the crow's foot looks like several 1s.

If two of these symbols are present, they give the minimum and maximum number of entities that can be associated with the relation. For example, if the line entering an entity includes a circle and line, then zero or one of those items is associated with the relation.

For a concrete example, consider Figure 5-19. The relationship `Swallows` connects the classes `SwordSwallower` and `Sword`. The two lines beside `SwordSwallower` mean that the relationship involves between 1 and 1 `SwordSwallower`. In other words, the relationship requires exactly one `SwordSwallower`.

The circle and crow's foot beside `Sword` mean that the relationship involves between 0 and many swords. That means this is a one-to-many relationship.

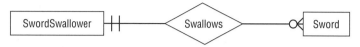

Figure 5-19

ER diagrams only have three symbols for representing three cardinalities: 0, 1, and many. (It reminds me of those primitive tribes that only have words for the numbers 1, 2, and many. I wonder if they played a role in developing ER diagrams?) This means you cannot specify cardinality as precisely as you can with semantic object models, which let you explicitly give upper and lower bounds.

For example, suppose you want to represent 2 to 4 jugglers juggling 5 or more flaming torches. (It's hardly juggling if two people just stand there holding four torches. Even I could do that, if they're not too heavy.) In a semantic object model, you would give the jugglers the cardinality 2.4 and the torches 5.N. Because ER diagrams don't have symbols for 2, 4, or 5, you're out of luck if you're building an ER diagram.

But wait! The point of these models is to gain an understanding of the system, not to rigidly follow the rules to their ridiculous conclusions, so I see no reason why you shouldn't merge the best of both systems and use ER diagrams that specify cardinality in the semantic object model style.

Figure 5-20 shows how I would model the jugglers. You won't find many people who use this combined notation on the Internet so you should understand the normal ER symbols, too, but this version seems easy enough to understand.

Figure 5-20

Inheritance

Like a semantic object model, an ER diagram can represent inheritance. An ER diagram represents inheritance as a special relationship named `IsA` (read as "is a") that's drawn inside a triangle. One point of the triangle points toward the parent class. Other lines leading into the triangle attach on the triangle's sides.

For example, a space shuttle crew contains several different kinds of astronauts including Commander, Pilot, Mission Specialist, and Payload Specialist. All of these have the common crew member attributes plus additional attributes that relate to their more specialized roles. For example, a Commander, Pilot, and Mission Specialist have special NASA space training (I'll call them "space trained").

A Payload Specialist is a doctor, physicist, database design book author, or other professional who comes along for the ride to perform some specific mission such as watching spiders spin webs in microgravity.

Figure 5-21 shows one way you might model this inheritance hierarchy in an ER diagram. The PayloadSpecialist inherits directly from Astronaut. SpaceTrained also inherits from Astronaut, although the relationship diagram probably will include only subclasses of SpaceTrained and not any SpaceTrained entities. Commander, Pilot, and MissionSpecialist inherit from SpaceTrained.

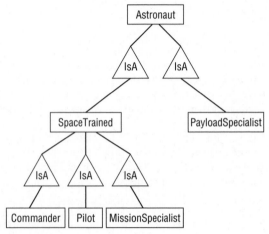

Figure 5-21

Sometimes you may see the IsA symbol shared by more than one inherited entity. The result implies a sibling relationship that probably doesn't mean much (for example, SpaceTrained and PayloadSpecialist are related only by the fact that they inherit from a common parent entity) but it does make the diagram less cluttered.

Figure 5-22 shows the same inheritance diagram shown in Figure 5-21 but with this new notation.

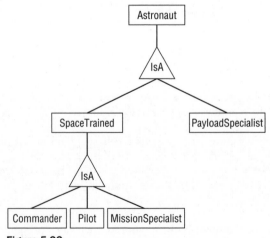

Figure 5-22

Try It Out   ER Diagrams

Make an ER diagram to represent the `Passenger`, `Driver`, and `Car` entities.

1. Make a `Person` class with `PersonId`, `FirstName`, and `LastName` fields.
2. Show `Passenger` and `Driver` inheriting from `Person`.
3. Display the relationships between the `Driver` and `Passenger` classes and the `Car` class.

How It Works

1. Make a `Person` class with `PersonId`, `FirstName`, and `LastName` fields.

    Draw `Person` in a rectangle. Attach ellipses holding `PersonId` (underlined because it's the key), `FirstName`, and `LastName`.

2. Show `Passenger` and `Driver` inheriting from `Person`.

    Place a triangular `IsA` symbol below `Person`. Draw lines out of the bottom of that symbol to connect to the `Driver` and `Passenger` classes.

3. Display the relationships between the `Driver` and `Passenger` classes and the `Car` class.

    Connect `Driver` with `Car` via a `Drives` relationship. This relationship must involve exactly one `Driver` and one `Car`. (This model doesn't allow backseat drivers.)

    Connect `Passenger` with `Car` via a `Rides In` relationship. This relationship must involve exactly one `Car` but may involve any number of `Passengers` (even none).

    Figure 5-23 shows the finished diagram.

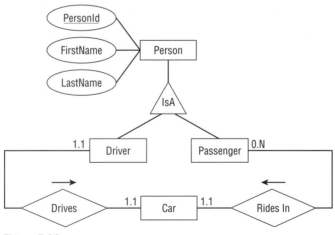

Figure 5-23

Additional Conventions

ER diagrams use a few other conventions to add fine shades of meaning to a model.

If every entity in an entity set *must* participate in the relationship, the diagram includes a thick or double line. This is called a *participation constraint* because each entity must participate.

For example, consider the Pilot Flies Airplane relationship. During flight, every airplane must have a pilot (otherwise it's called a "smoking pile of metal" instead of an "airplane"). This is a participation constraint on the Airplane entity set because all entities in that set must participate in the relationship (that is, have a pilot).

If an entity can participate in *at most one* instance of the relationship set, the diagram uses an arrow to connect the entity to the relationship. This is called a *key constraint*. For example, during flight a pilot can fly at most one airplane so the Pilot entity set has a key constraint on the Flies relationship. (Although I suppose a pilot could throw a paper airplane while in the cockpit and thus fly two planes at the same time.)

If an entity must be involved in exactly one instance of a relationship set, it gets a thick or double arrow to indicate both participation and key constraints. For example, during flight an airplane must have one and only one pilot so it would get the thick or double arrow.

Figure 5-24 shows the Pilot Flies Airplane relationship. Each Pilot can fly at most one airplane so Pilot is connected to the relationship with an arrow (key constraint). A Pilot might sometimes be a passenger who's not flying the airplane so there's no participation constraint on Pilot for this relationship. On the other side of the relationship, the Airplane must have one and only one Pilot so it gets the double arrow to indicate both key and participation constraints. The cardinalities are between 1 and 1 for both entities because there's a one-to-one relationship between Pilot and Airplane (ignoring copilots) in this relationship.

Figure 5-24

A *weak entity* is one that cannot be identified by its attributes alone. For example, consider a database to store submarine race results. A Race entity holds information about particular race. A Result entity holds information about how a submarine performed in a race. The Result entity has attributes to store a reference to the Race entity, a reference to a Sub entity, and result information such as Time, FinishPosition, and TorpedoesFired.

Alone, there's no reasonable way to find a specific Result entity. There is no combination of Result attributes that really makes sense as a search key. You could search for a combination of Time and FinishPosition but that doesn't identify a particular Result.

Instead you would either search for a particular Race and use it to find its associated Results, or search for a particular Sub and use it to find its associated Results.

In an ER diagram, you draw a weak entity with a thick rectangle and connect it to its identifying relationship with a thick arrow. Figure 5-25 shows the Race, Sub, and Result entity sets and their relationships.

Figure 5-25

Comments and Notes

As is the case with semantic object models, you shouldn't be afraid to add notes, comments, scribbles, and anything else to make an ER diagram easier to understand. Annotate entity set definitions to show the domain and cardinality of an entity's attributes. Add notes to further explain confusing entities and relationships.

The purpose of an ER diagram is to help you understand a project, not to become a technically correct but uninformative doodle.

Relational Models

Chapter 3 explained basic concepts of relational databases such as tables, tuples, rows, and columns. (If you don't remember Chapter 3, go back and skim through it quickly to refresh your memory.)

Converting semantic object models and ER diagrams into a relational version isn't too difficult once you know how the concepts described in Chapter 3 map to those described so far in this chapter. The following table shows the how key terms from Chapter 3 map to the terms used in semantic object models and ER diagrams.

Theory	Database	File	SOM	ER
Relation	Table	File	Class	Entity Set
Tuple	Row	Record	Object	Entity
Attribute	Column	Field	Attribute	Attribute

To convert semantic object models and ER diagrams into relational models, you simply map the classes or entity sets to tables. You then figure out which columns in the tables form the foreign key relationships among the tables.

The following sections work through examples of converting SOM and ER models into relational ones.

Converting Semantic Object Models

Consider the simple semantic object model shown in Figure 5-26. A CUSTOMER object has one or more Addresses, one or more CONTACTs, and one or more ORDERs. The CONTACT class contains only simple attributes. The ORDER class contains a simple Date and a group attribute to hold information about Items ordered.

This model leads immediately to three relational tables: Customers, Contacts, and Orders.

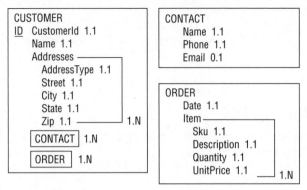

Figure 5-26

If the semantic object model includes inheritance relationships, build a table for each of the object sets. Use the parent class's primary key as a foreign key in the child class to connect the two in a one-to-one relationship. For example, if CUSTOMER inherits from PERSON, add a PersonId field in the Customers table to associate the corresponding records in the two tables.

The CUSTOMER class's CONTACT and ORDER attributes indicate that there should be a link from the Customers table to the Contacts and Orders tables. To do this, you can place foreign key fields in the Contacts and Orders tables to hold the CustomerId values of their corresponding Customer records. To make understanding the relational model easier, call those fields CustomerId so they match the name in the Customers table.

At this point, the relational model is practically finished. Only one little problem remains: a relational record cannot hold a potentially unlimited number of columns. In this case, a row in the Customers table cannot have an unlimited number of columns to hold multiple address values for every row. Similarly, the Orders table cannot have an unlimited number of columns to hold item data.

The solution is similar to the one used to allow a Customers record to correspond to multiple Contacts and Orders records. Create new tables to hold the repeated items. Then use foreign key fields to link those records back to their owning Customers and Orders records.

Figure 5-27 shows the resulting relational model.

Each table's primary key is underlined (only the Customers and Orders tables have primary keys).

Lines connect the fields that form foreign key relationships. The numbers at the ends of these lines give the numbers of items participating in the relationship (the infinity symbol ∞ means "many"). In this example, all of the relationships are one-to-many relationships.

This diagram shows relationships among tables but doesn't show much other detail. In particular, it doesn't show the fields' data types or whether they are required. If you expand each table's representation, you can add some of this information. Figure 5-28 shows the same model with columns to show the fields' data types and whether each is required.

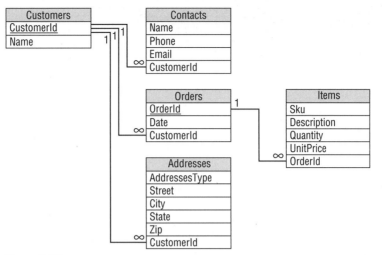

Figure 5-27

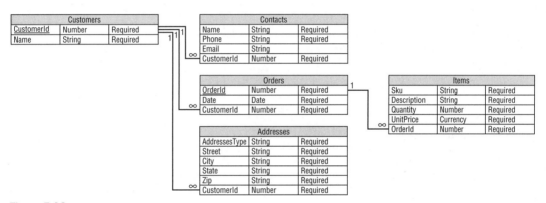

Figure 5-28

There's only so much information you can add to one of these diagrams, however. Even this relatively simple diagram is pretty big if you add data type and required data. Usually it's better to stick to the simpler version and put additional information in separate documents.

As is the case with all models, you should write down notes to record any information that is not fully captured by the diagram alone. For example, Figure 5-28 does not show which fields are required, their meanings (what does Sku mean, anyway?), more precise cardinalities (what if "one-to-many" should really be "one-to-four"), and so forth.

Though the figure gives data types for each of the tables' fields, that does not necessarily completely specify the fields' domains. For example, the Zip field should contain a 5-digit ZIP Code or a Zip+4 Code similar to 12345-5678, UnitPrice should be a positive monetary value, and the Email field should hold a properly formatted email address such as `comments@whitehouse.gov`.

You should write down all of these and any other constraints that are not obvious from the diagram. (In case you're curious, Sku stands for "stock keeping unit" and is pronounced "skew." It's like a serial number you can use to identify products.)

Converting ER Diagrams

Figure 5-29 shows an ER diagram that covers a situation similar to the one modeled by semantic object model shown in Figure 5-26.

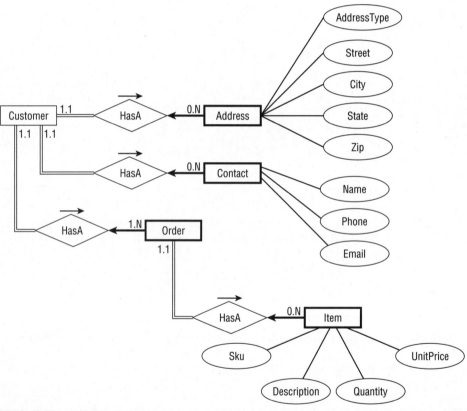

Figure 5-29

Each `Customer` entity has at least one `Address`, `Contact`, and `Order`. Those are all participation constraints so they are drawn with double lines.

The `Address`, `Contact`, and `Order` entities are accessed through their corresponding `Customer` entities. That makes them weak entities so they are drawn with thick rectangles and they have thick arrows pointing to their identifying relationships. (If you want to allow the users to search for orders directly, perhaps by an OrderId, then Order would not be a weak entity.)

The Order entity must be associated with at least one Item so it has a participation constraint drawn with a double line. The Item entity is also weak so it is drawn with a thick rectangle and it uses a thick arrow to connect to its identifying relationship.

The entities in the ER diagram lead directly to the relational tables Customers, Addresses, Contacts, Orders, and Items.

To connect a weak entity with its owner, make sure the owner's table has a primary key. Then add a foreign key field to the weak entity's table that refers back to the owner's primary key.

The resulting relational model is the same as the one generated by the semantic object model and is shown in Figure 5-27.

You can handle inheritance the same way you did for semantic object models. Build a table for each of the entities. Use the parent class's primary key as a foreign key in the child class to connect the two in a one-to-one relationship. For example, if Politician inherits from Weasel, then add a WeaselId field in the Politicians table to link the corresponding records in the two tables.

As is the case when translating a semantic object model into a relational model, you will need to write down any extra conditions, constraints, or other information that is not completely captured by the model. See the end of the previous section for some examples of things you might want to write down.

Summary

Different kinds of models help define a problem. They identify the entities that are significant to the problem and they clarify the relationships among those entities. You can then use the models to test your understanding of the problem and to verify that the models provide the data you need to satisfy the problem's use cases and other requirements.

This chapter explained how to build different kinds of models.

In this chapter you learned how to:

- ❏ Build user interface models to learn what kind of data the database will need to store.
- ❏ Build semantic object models to study the objects that will interact while solving the problem.
- ❏ Build entity-relationship diagrams to study the entities that are involved in the problem and to examine their interactions.
- ❏ Convert semantic object models and entity-relationship diagrams into relational models.

After you've built a relational model, you can use it to start building a database. Before you begin, however, there are several techniques that you can use to make the model more efficient. The first of these techniques, extracting business rules, is described in the following chapter.

Before you move on to Chapter 6, however, use the following exercises to test your understanding of the material covered in this chapter. You can find the solutions to these exercises in Appendix A.

Exercises

1. Draw a semantic object model for a small college with the classes STUDENT, INSTRUCTOR, COURSE, and PROJECT. The rules are:

    a. All students must be enrolled in at least one course or one project (or they're dropped).

    b. Similarly an instructor must teach at least one course or supervise at least one project.

    c. A student cannot be working on more than one project (they're too time-consuming).

    d. An instructor can teach any number of courses and supervise any number of projects.

    e. A project or course must have an instructor.

    f. A course must have at least 5 students (or it's canceled).

    g. A project must have between 1 and 5 students.

    h. STUDENT and INSTRUCTOR should be subclasses of a PERSON class that contains common elements such as name, address, and phone number.

    i. Student data must include past courses and projects, and grades for them.

    Write down any special conditions and features that the semantic object model cannot handle with its normal notation.

2. Draw two ER diagrams for the situation described in Exercise 1, one to show the inheritance relationships and one to show the main entity relationships. Write down descriptions of any constraints and any special conditions that are not represented by the diagram alone.

3. Convert either the semantic object model that you built for Exercise 1 or the ER diagram you built for Exercise 2 into a relational model.

4. Mike's Trikes sells tricycles. Not the little kiddie models, the giant motorized half-ton behemoths you occasionally see on the road that are somewhere between a motorcycle with an extra wheel and a car with one missing.

    Draw a semantic object model for Mike with the classes CUSTOMER, SALESPERSON, MANAGER, CONTRACT, PAYMENT, and SHIFT. Use the following assumptions:

    a. CUSTOMER and SALESPERSON are subclasses of the PERSON class that holds contact information (name, address, phone). MANAGER is a subclass of SALESPERSON.

    b. A salesperson sells a payment contract to a customer. The salesperson gets a commission so you need to keep track of who sold the contract.

    c. A customer doesn't have a record until that customer buys a contract.

    d. SHIFT objects track dates and times that a salesperson works.

    e. Customers make payments that should be subtracted from the customer's balance. A PAYMENT object should record the payment's date and amount, and the customer who made it.

f. You should be able to find all of the contracts that a particular salesperson sold.

g. You should be able to find all of the contracts that a particular customer purchased. You should also be able to check the customer's current balance.

Write down any special conditions and features that the semantic object model cannot handle with its normal notation.

5. Draw two ER diagrams for the situation described in Exercise 3, one to show the inheritance relationships and one to show the main entity relationships. Write down descriptions of any constraints and any special conditions that are not represented by the diagram alone.

6. Convert either the semantic object model that you built for Exercise 4 or the ER diagram you built for Exercise 5 into a relational model.

7. Suppose you want to make a database to represent your most expensive purchases. These include your house and vehicles so you make HOUSE and VEHICLE classes. You decide to expand the model to include CAR and TRUCK classes. Then you buy a camper. Because it shares attributes with both HOUSE and TRUCK, you decide that it should inherit from both of those classes.

Draw a semantic object model showing these inheritance relations. Add a few additional non-object attributes of your choosing to each class.

8. Draw an ER diagram representing the inheritance hierarchy described in Exercise 7.

Extracting Business Rules

Chapter 5 explained how to build models to represent the entities involved in a database project and to study the interactions among those entities. The final kind of model described in that chapter, the relational model, has a structure that closely mimics the organization of a relational database. You can easily convert a relational model into a working relational database.

Before you do, however, you should optimize the relational model to make the final database as flexible and efficient as possible. Optimizing the model now is easier than reorganizing the database later, so it's worth taking some time to make sure you get the database design right the first time.

The first step in optimizing the database is extracting business rules. Keeping business rules separate from other database constraints and relations, at least logically, makes later changes to the database easier.

In this chapter you learn:

- ❏   Why business rules are important.
- ❏   How to identify business rules.
- ❏   How to modify a relational model to isolate business rules.

After you understand business rules, you'll be able to use them to make the database more flexible and easier to maintain.

What Are Business Rules?

Business rules describe the objects, relationships, and actions that a business finds important and worth writing down. They include rules and policies that define how a business operates and handles its day-to-operations. They generally help a business satisfy its goals and meet its obligations.

For example, some general business rules might be:

❑ The nearest clerk greets customers by saying "Welcome to Cloud Nine" when they enter the store.

❑ Clerks ask to see a customer's ID when writing a check for more than $20 or charging more than $50. No signature is required when charging less than $25.

❑ Whoever unlocks the door in the morning makes the first pot of coffee (or risks mutiny).

❑ Save the good scotch for the landlord.

Because this is a database design book, this chapter is only concerned with the database-related business rules. Some examples of those are:

❑ Don't make a Customer record until the customer buys something and has an associated order.

❑ Customer records must have first and last names. (If Bono, Everlast, or Madonna buys something, get an autograph and make up a last name.)

❑ If a student doesn't enroll in at least one class, change the Status field to Inactive.

❑ If a salesperson sells more than 10 hot tubs in one month, award a $200 bonus.

❑ All Contact records must have at least one phone number or email address.

❑ If an order totals more than $100 before taxes and shipping, give a 10 percent discount.

❑ If an order totals more than $50 before taxes and shipping, give free shipping.

❑ Employees get a 1 percent discount.

❑ If the in-stock quantity of an inventory item drops below the number of items sold during the last month, order more.

From a database point of view, business rules are constraints. Some are simple constraints such as:

❑ All orders must have a ContactPhoneNumber.

Simple rules such as this one map easily to the features provided by a relational database. It's easy to indicate that a field has a certain data type or that it is required (as in this case).

Other business rules may represent quite complex constraints such as:

❑ A student's number of course hours plus number of project hours must be between 1 and 14.

You can implement some of these more complex rules with check constraints or foreign key constraints. Recall from Chapter 3 that check constraints include field-level constraints that apply to a single field in a table, and table-level constraints can examine more than one field in the same record.

Still other business rules are even more complex:

❑ An instructor must have a combination of classes, labs, and office hours totaling at least 30 contact hours with up to 1/2 office hour per hour of class, 1 office hour per hour of lab, and thesis supervision counts as 2 hours.

This constraint may require you to gather data from several different tables. This kind of very complex check is probably best performed by code either in the database itself or in external software.

All of these rules are implemented as constraints in one form or another, whether as easy database features (requiring a field), as harder database features (check constraints and foreign keys), or in code (inside or outside of the database).

Identifying Key Business Rules

Writing down all of the business rules is worthwhile in its own right so you can make sure they all get implemented somehow in the database. It's also worth categorizing the business rules so you can build them properly.

How you implement a business rule depends not only on how tricky it is to build, but also on how likely it will be to change later. If a rule is likely to change later, you may be better off building it by using a more complicated but more flexible method.

For example, suppose you only ship orders to states where you have a warehouse and those include Wyoming, Nebraska, Colorado, and Kansas. A business rule requires that the State field in an order's shipping address must be WY, NE, CO, or KS. You can implement this as a simple field-level check constraint in the Orders table. Three minutes' work and you're a hero! No big deal.

But now suppose you open a new warehouse in Utah. To allow for this change, you'll need to edit this check constraint. This isn't the end of the world, but this change requires that you modify the structure of the database.

Now suppose the company policy changes so some warehouses are allowed to ship to certain other states. You'll need to change the database's check constraints again to allow for the change. This still isn't the end of the world, but once more you're required to change the structure of the database to accommodate a change to a business rule.

Now consider an alternative approach. Suppose instead of making this business rule a field-level check constraint on the State field, you make it a foreign key constraint. You create a ShippingStates table and fill it with the values WY, NE, CO, and KS. Then you make the Orders table's State field a foreign key referring to the new States table. Now the Orders table will accept only records that have a State value that is listed in the States table.

If you need to change the states that are allowed, you only need to add or remove records from the States table. Admittedly the difference in difficulty between this approach and the previous one is small. The previous approach required changing the database's structure, whereas the new approach only requires changing the data.

Not only does changing the data take a bit less effort, but it also requires less skill. This rule implemented as a check constraint might look like this:

```
State = 'WY' Or State = 'NE' Or State = 'CO' Or State = 'KS'
```

This isn't terribly difficult code, but it is code and only someone familiar with database programming will be able to make changes to it.

Data in the States table, however, is relatively easy to understand. Even your customers can add entries to this table (possibly with a few hints from you).

Placing the validation data in a separate table also allows the users to understand it more easily. Most users would be intimidated by the previous check constraint (even if they can find it), but they can easily understand a list of allowed values in a table.

To identify these key business rules, ask yourself two questions. First, how easy is it to change a rule? If a rule is very complex, it will be difficult to change without messing it up. If implementing the rule is as simple as making a field required or not in a table, you won't lose a huge amount of time if the customer later decides that the Lumberjacks table's PreferredAxe field isn't required after all.

Second, how likely is the rule to change? If a rule is likely to change frequently, it's probably worth some extra planning to make changing the rule easier.

Types of rules that make good candidates for extra attention include:

- ❏ **Enumerated values:** For example, allowed shipping states, order statuses (Pending, Approved, Shipped), and service names (Installation, Repair, Dog Washing).

- ❏ **Calculation parameters:** For example, suppose you give free shipping on orders over $50. Will you later change that to $75? $100?

- ❏ **Validity parameters:** For example, suppose full-time students must take between 8 and 16 credits. Will we ever make this 12 to 16 hours? 8 to 20 hours? Or suppose you require that all projects include between 2 and 5 students. Will you ever want to allow a single student to have a project? Or will you allow a bigger team if a group of friends wants to work together badly enough to bribe you with donuts and latte?

- ❏ **Cross-record and cross-table checks:** These kinds of checks are more complicated. For example, you might require that the date and time of a poker game be after the date the tournament started. (Although the Olympics schedules competitions before the opening ceremony. They probably use some sort of time-warp effect at international levels.)

- ❏ **Generalizable constraints:** If you think you may need to apply a similar constraint later, you should think about generalizing the constraint and moving it out of the database proper. For example, suppose your buyer slipped a decimal point and ordered 100 sets of crampons (those spiky things that ice climbers wear on their boots) instead of 10. To move the excess inventory, you offer a $50 bonus to any salesperson who can sell 10 pairs in a week. That's fine, but next month you might end up with an excess inventory of ice axes. After you fire your buyer, you might want to change the incentive to give a $30 bonus to any salesperson who sells 5 ice axes. You can make these changes easier if you pull the product name or ID, number of sales, bonus amount, and duration (weekly) out into another table and then use those parameters to calculate bonuses.

❏ **Very complicated checks:** Some checks are so complex that it's just easier to move them into code, either stored within the database or in external code modules. For example, suppose you can only register for the course Predicate Calculus (in the Mathematics department) if you have already taken (and passed) Propositional Calculus (in the Mathematics department) or Logic I and Logic II (in the Philosophy department). Or you have the instructor's permission. Or your advisor's. You can probably implement this as a table-level check constraint, but it may be worth thinking about moving this rule somewhere else, particularly because you may be able to generalize it to handle prerequisites for other courses.

Types of rules that are usually not worth special attention and can be just implemented directly in the database include:

❏ **Enumerated types with fixed values:** Though it might make sense to move allowed values for a State field into a new table, it probably doesn't make sense to do the same for a Handedness field. Unless you're planning to start marketing to octopi and squids, Left Handed and Right Handed are probably the only values you'll ever need for this field.

❏ **Data type requirements:** Requiring specific data types for a field is one of the bigger advantages to using a database. It hardly ever makes sense to use a very generic data type such as string because you're not sure whether the field will need to be a currency amount or a date. If you are that unsure, you probably need to study this field some more or split it into multiple fields.

❏ **Required values:** If a GolfRound record really needs a Caddie entry (so the golfer knows who to blame for using the 3-wood on that 124-yard par 3 hole), just make it required and worry about something more complicated.

❏ **Sanity checks:** For example, all inventory items should have a price of at least 0. You might want to allow 0 cost for loss leaders (or perhaps not) but if I ever find a store that sells a product for less than nothing (that is, pays me), I'm going down there with a dump truck and cleaning them out. (Now that I think about it, I've bought a few products that would have been overpriced at negative amounts. I might have to think a bit harder depending on what the product is.) If the sanity checks are so broad that they'll never need to be changed, just wire them in and don't worry about it.

Somewhere in the middle ground are business rules that have never changed in the past but that you cannot swear won't change in the future. They may be easy to implement as checks within the database but there still might be some advantage to extracting them to accommodate changes.

For example, suppose you require that Resident Advisors (RAs) have passed all of their general education requirements. It's been that way for five years, but before that the rule was different. Chances are the rule won't change again, at least not for a long time, but you never know. There has been talk about exempting RAs from the writing requirement ('cause riting ain't emportunt enuff).

In cases such as this one, you need to rely on the judgment of those who make the rules. Then when the unexpected happens, you can blame them.

So write down all of the business rules you can discover. Include the domains of every field and any simple bounds checks such as Price > 0 in addition to more complicated rules.

Group the rules by how likely they are to change and how hard they would be to change. Then take a closer look at the ones that are likely to change and that will be hard to change and see if you shouldn't pull them out of the database's structure.

Try It Out   **Find the Business Rules**

Consider this partial list of business rules for a custom woodworking shop:

- ❑   Accept no new orders if the customer has an unpaid balance on completed work.
- ❑   All customer records must include daytime and evening phone numbers.
- ❑   Always wear proper eye protection.
- ❑   Clean the shop thoroughly at the end of the day.
- ❑   Create a customer record when the customer places his or her first order.
- ❑   Don't use non-portable power tools alone.
- ❑   Give a 10% discount if the customer pays in full in advance.
- ❑   If there is less than 1 pound of standard size screws, add them to the reorder list.
- ❑   If we have fewer than 3 bottles of glue, add it to the reorder list.
- ❑   Leave no power tool plugged in when not in use, even for a minute.
- ❑   No customer can ever have an outstanding balance greater than $10,000.
- ❑   No customers allowed in the painting area.
- ❑   Order 25% extra material for stock items.
- ❑   Replace a tool if you won't need it in the next hour. Replace all tools at the end of the day.
- ❑   Require half of an order's payment up front (so we can buy materials) if the order is more than $1,000.
- ❑   Walt is not allowed to use the nail gun. Ever!
- ❑   When we have fewer than 2 pounds of standard size nails, add them to the reorder list.

1.   Identify the database-related rules and indicate when they would apply.
2.   Identify the rules that are simple or that seem unlikely to change so they can be built into the database.
3.   Identify the rules that may change or that are complicated enough to deserve special attention.

How It Works

1.   The following are the database-related rules:

     ❑   Accept no new orders if the customer has an unpaid balance on completed work.

       Applies when the customer tries to place a new order.

     ❑   All customer records must include daytime and evening phone numbers.

       Applies when the customer places a new order.

     ❑   Create a customer record when the customer places his or her first order.

       When the customer places a new order, try to look up the customer's record. If there is no record, create one.

❑ Give a 10% discount if the customer pays in full in advance.

When the customer places a new order, give this discount if he or she pays in advance. (You should also mention the discount at this time.)

❑ If there is less than 1 pound of standard size screws, add them to the reorder list.

When we use screws, check this. (In practice, we'll probably check weekly or whenever we notice we're running low.)

❑ If we have fewer than 3 bottles of glue, add it to the reorder list.

When we use up a bottle of glue, check this.

❑ No customer can ever have an outstanding balance greater than $10,000.

When the user tries to place a new order, check the outstanding balance and place the order on hold until the balance is under $10,000. Also when we receive a payment, check for orders on hold (so we can release them if the customer's balance is low enough).

❑ Order 25% extra material for stock items.

When ordering supplies, see if an item is in stock and if so add 25% to the order.

❑ Require half of an order's payment up front (so we can buy materials) if the order is more than $1,000.

When the user places a new order, check the cost and require this payment if necessary.

❑ When we have fewer than 2 pounds of standard size nails, add them to the reorder list.

When we use nails, check this. (In practice, we'll probably check weekly or whenever we notice we're running low.)

2. The following rules are simple or seem unlikely to change, so they can be built into the database:

❑ Accept no new orders if the customer has an unpaid balance on completed work.

This seems unambiguous and unlikely to change, although if we need an exception mechanism (for brother-in-law Frank), this rule cannot be built into the database's structure.

❑ All customer records must include daytime and evening phone numbers.

This seems unambiguous and unlikely to change. (Will we ever need more than two phone numbers?)

❑ Create a customer record when the customer places his or her first order.

This seems unambiguous and unlikely to change.

3. The following rules seem likely to change or are complicated enough to deserve special attention:

❑ Give a 10% discount if the customer pays in full in advance.

The parameter "10%" might change.

❑ If there is less than 1 pound of standard size screws, add them to the reorder list.

The parameter "1 pound" might change.

❑ If we have fewer than 3 bottles of glue, add it to the reorder list.

The parameter "3 bottles" might change.

❏ No customer can ever have an outstanding balance greater than $10,000.

The parameter "$10,000" might change. (Do we need an exception mechanism?)

❏ Order 25% extra material for stock items.

The parameter "25%" might change.

❏ Require half of an order's payment up front (so we can buy materials) if the order is more than $1,000.

The parameters "half" and "$1,000" might change.

❏ When we have fewer than 2 pounds of standard size nails, add them to the reorder list.

The parameter "2 pounds" might change.

A few of these rules follow the pattern, "If we have less than X, reorder." It might be worthwhile to generalize this rule and apply it to all inventory items. The item's record would have fields ReorderWhen (to indicate the quantity on hand that triggers a supply order) and ReorderQuantity (to indicate how much to order).

Extracting Key Business Rules

Now that you've identified the business rules that will be tricky to implement within the database or that may change frequently, pull them out of the database. There are a couple of standard approaches for doing that.

First, if the rule is a validation list, convert it into a foreign key constraint. Only shipping to a set of specific states is the perfect example. Simply make a States table, enter the allowed states, and then make the Orders table's State field be a foreign key referring to the States table.

Second, if the rule is a fairly straightforward calculation with parameters that may change, pull the parameters out and put them in a table. For example, if you want to give salespeople who sell at least $250,000 worth of cars in a month a $5 bonus, pull the parameters $250,000 and $5 out and put them in a table. In some businesses, you might even want to pull out the duration one month.

I've written several applications that had a special Parameters table containing all sorts of oddball parameters that were used to perform calculations, check constraints, and otherwise determine the system's behavior. The records had two fields: Name and Value. To see if a salesperson should get the bonus, you would look up the BonusSales parameter and see if his or her sales totaled at least that much. If so, you would look up the BonusAward parameter and give the salesperson that big a bonus. (This approach works particularly well when program code performs the checks. When the program starts, it can load all of the parameters into a collection. Later it can look up values in the collection without hitting the database.)

Third, if a calculation is complicated, extract it into code. That doesn't necessarily mean you need to write the code in C++, C#, Ada, or the latest programming language flavor-of-the-month. Many database products can store and execute stored procedures. A stored procedure can select and iterate through records, perform calculations, make comparisons, and do just about anything that a full-fledged programming language can.

So what's the point of moving checks into a stored procedure? Partly it's a matter of perception. Pulling the check out of the database's table structure and making it a stored procedure separates it logically from the tables. That makes it easier to divide up maintenance work on the database into structural work and programming work.

Of course you can also build the check into code written in a traditional programming language. You may be able to invoke that code from the database or you might use it in the project's user interface.

Finally, if you have a rule that you might want to generalize, well, you're going to have to use your judgment and imagination. For example, suppose an author of a database design book earns a 5% royalty on the first 5,000 copies sold, 7% on the next 5,000, and 10% on any copies after that. You could code those numbers into a stored procedure to calculate royalties but then later, when Steven Spielberg turns the book into a movie, you better believe the author will want better terms for the sequel.

Rather than writing these values into the code, put them in a table. In this case, those values are associated with a particular record in the Books table. You may want more or less than three percentage values for different royalty points so you'll need to pull the values into their own table (in ER diagram terms, the new table will be a weak entity with identifying relationship to the Books table).

Figure 6-1 shows a tiny part of the relational model for this database. To find the royalty rates for a particular book, you would look up the RoyaltyRates records for that book's BookId.

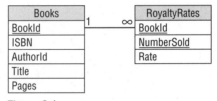

Figure 6-1

Now it will be a little more work calculating royalty payments than before (although you can still hide the details in a stored procedure), but it is easy to create new royalty schedules for future books.

Multi-Tier Applications

A multi-tier application uses several different layers to handle different data-related tasks. The most common form of multi-tier application uses three tiers. (The tiers are also often called layers, so you'll hear talk of three-layer systems.)

The first tier (often called the *user interface tier* or *user interface layer*) is the user interface. It displays data and lets the user manipulate it. It might perform some basic data validation such as ensuring that required fields are filled in and that numeric values are actually numbers, but it doesn't implement complicated business rules.

The third tier (often called the *data* or *database tier* or *layer*) is the database. It stores the data with as few restrictions as possible. Normally it provides basic validation (NumberOfRockets is required, MaximumTwistyness must be between 0.0 and 1.0) but it doesn't implement complicated business rules, either.

The middle tier (often called the *middle* or *business tier* or *layer*) is a service layer that moves data between the first and third tiers. This is the tier that implements all of the business rules. When the user interface tier tries to send data back to the database, the middle tier verifies that the data satisfies the business rules and either sends the data to the data tier or complains to the user interface tier. When it fetches data from the database, the middle tier may also perform calculations on the data to create derived values to forward to the user interface tier.

Figure 6-2 shows the three-tier architecture graphically.

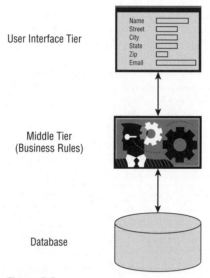

User Interface Tier

Middle Tier
(Business Rules)

Database

Figure 6-2

The main goal of a multi-tier architecture is to increase flexibility. The user interface and database tiers can work relatively independently while the middle tier provides any necessary translation. For example, if the user interface changes so a particular value must be displayed differently (perhaps in a dropdown instead of in a text box), it can make that change without requiring any changes to the database. If the database must change how a value is stored (perhaps as a string Small/Medium/Large instead of as a numeric size code), the user interface doesn't need to know about it. The middle tier might need to be adjusted to handle any differences but the first and third tiers are isolated from each other.

The middle tier also concentrates most of the business logic. The user interface and database perform basic validations but the middle tier does all of the heavy lifting.

Another advantage of multi-tier systems is that the tiers can run on different computers. The database might run one a computer at corporate headquarters, the middle tier libraries might run on a second computer (or even split across two other computers), and the user interface can run on many users' computers. Or all three tiers might run on the same computer. Separating the tiers lets you shuffle them around to fit your computing environment.

In practice, there's some benefit to placing at least some checks in the database tier so, if there's a problem in the rest of the application, the database has the final say. For example, if the user interface contains an obscure bug so customers who order more than 999 pencils on leap year day are charged $–32,767, the database can save the day by refusing that obviously harebrained price.

There's also some value to placing basic checks in the user interface so the application doesn't need to perform unnecessary round trips to the database. For example, it doesn't make a lot of sense to ship an entire order's data across the network to the corporate database only to have it rejected because the order is for –10 buggy whips. The user interface should be smart enough to know that customers cannot order less than zero of something.

Adding validations in both the user interface and the database requires some redundancy, but it's worth it. (Also notice that the user interface developers and database programmers can do their work separately so they can work in parallel.)

Although multi-tier architecture is far outside the scope of this book, it's worth knowing a little about it so you understand that there's another benefit to extracting complex business rules from the database's table structure. Even if you implement those rules in stored procedures within the database, you still get some of the benefits of a logical separation and flexibility almost as if you had a hidden extra tier.

Try It Out   Multi-Tier Applications

Consider the following database-related business rules:

- ❏   All Customers records must have at least one associated Orders record.
- ❏   All Orders records must have at least one associated OrderItems record.
- ❏   In a Customers record, Name, Street, City, State, and Zip are required.
- ❏   In an Orders record, Customer, Date, and DueDate are required.
- ❏   In an OrderItems record, Item and Quantity are required.
- ❏   In an OrderItems record, Quantity must be at least 1.
- ❏   In an OrderItems record, Quantity must normally (99% of the time) be no greater than 100. In very rare circumstances, it might be greater.
- ❏   Only one order can be assigned a particular DueDate. (We have special products that take an entire day to install and only enough staff to handle one installation per day.)

Decide where each of these rules should be implemented in a three-tier application.

1.   Identify the rules that should be implemented in the database's structure.
2.   Identify the rules that should be implemented in the middle tier.
3.   Identify the rules that should be implemented in the user interface.

Note that there will be some overlap. For example, the user interface may validate a required field to avoid a round-trip to the database if the field is missing.

How It Works

1. Identify the rules that should be implemented in the database's structure.

   Whether a rule should be implemented in the database's structure depends on whether it will change. For example, if the users decide that it might be useful to create a Customers record with no associated Orders records after all, then that rule should not be implemented in the database layer. The following list shows the rules that seem extremely unlikely to change, so they can be implemented in the database's structure:

   ❏ In Customers record, Name, Street, City, State, and Zip are required.

   ❏ In an Orders record, Customer, Date, and DueDate are required.

   ❏ In an OrderItems record, Item and Quantity are required.

   ❏ In an OrderItems record, Quantity must be at least 1.

   ❏ Only one order can be assigned a particular DueDate.

   The last one might be a bit iffy if the customer decides to add new staff so they can perform more than one installation per day. I'd check with the customer on this, but this rule seems to belong here.

2. Identify the rules that should be implemented in the middle tier.

   The rules in the middle tier are the most complicated and the most subject to change. The following list shows the rules that should probably be implemented in the middle tier:

   ❏ All Customers records must have at least one associated Orders record.

   ❏ All Orders records must have at least one associated OrderItems record.

   ❏ In an OrderItems record, Quantity must normally (99% of the time) be no greater than 100. In very rare circumstances it might be greater.

3. Identify the rules that should be implemented in the user interface.

   Whether a rule should be implemented in the user interface depends mostly on the rule's simplicity and the likelihood that it will change. These rules can prevent unnecessary trips to the middle and database tiers so they can save time. However, the user interface shouldn't be unduly constrained so we have to make changes to it when business rules change. (Hint: if it's implemented in the middle tier, there's probably a reason, so you might not want to implement it here, too.) The following list shows the rules that probably should be enforced in the user interface:

   ❏ In Customers record, Name, Street, City, State, and Zip are required.

   ❏ In an Orders record, Customer, Date, and DueDate are required.

   ❏ In an OrderItems record, Item and Quantity are required.

   ❏ In an OrderItems record, Quantity must be at least 1.

   The following table summaries the places where these rules are implemented.

Rule	Database	Middle Tier	UI
All Customers records must have at least one associated Orders record.		X	
All Orders records must have at least one associated OrderItems record.		X	
In Customers record, Name, Street, City, State, and Zip are required.	X		X
In an Orders record, Customer, Date, and DueDate are required.	X		X
In an OrderItems record, Item and Quantity are required.	X		X
In an OrderItems record, Quantity must be at least 1.	X		X
In an OrderItems record, Quantity must normally (99% of the time) be no greater than 100. In very rare circumstances it might be greater.		X	
Only one order can be assigned a particular DueDate.	X		

The final rule demonstrates an unusual combination: a rule that is easy to implement in the database but hard to implement in the middle tier or user interface. Only the database has ready access to every order at all times so it can see if a new order's DueDate will conflict with a different order's DueDate.

Summary

Business rules are, quite simply, the rules that govern how a business runs. They cover everything from a list of acceptable attire for Casual Fridays to the schedule of performance bonuses.

As far as databases are concerned, business rules help define the data model. They define every field's domain (what values and ranges of values they can contain), whether fields are required, the fields' data types, and any special conditions on the fields.

Some rules are simple and unlikely to change so they can be easily implemented by using the database's features. Other rules are complex or subject to occasional change. You can make changing those rules easier by separating them from the database's structure either physically or logically.

In this chapter you learned how to:

❑   Understand business rules.

❑   Identify key business rules that may deserve special attention.

❑   Isolate key business rules physically or logically by extracting their data into tables, moving them into stored procedures, and moving them into a middle tier.

Separating business rules from the database's table structure is one way to make a database more efficient and flexible. Chapter 7 describes another important way to improve the database's behavior: normalization.

Before you move on to Chapter 7, however, use the following exercises to test your understanding of the material covered in this chapter. You can find the solutions to these exercises in Appendix A.

Exercises

For Exercises 1 through 3, consider Happy Sherpa Trekking, a company that sells and rents trekking equipment (boots, backpacks, llamas, yaks). They also organize guided adventure treks. Figure 6-3 shows a relational model for that part of the business.

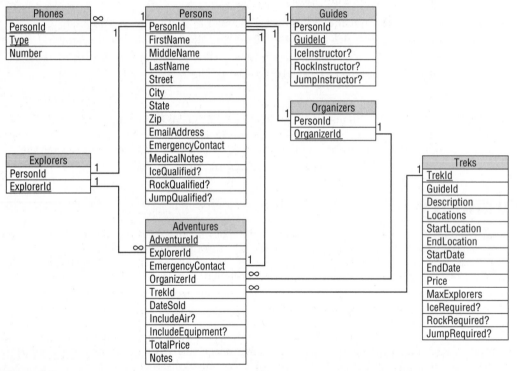

Figure 6-3

The company uses the following terminology to try to get everyone in an Indiana Jones mood:

❑ **Explorer:** A customer. Must be qualified to go on a trek.

❑ **Adventure:** A particular explorer's trek. This is basically the contract with the customer.

❑ **Guide:** The person who will lead the trek. Must be qualified and an instructor for any needed skills for a particular trek.

- ❑ **Organizer:** A salesperson who sells adventures to explorers.

- ❑ **Ice/Rock/Jump:** These refer to ice climbing, rock climbing, and parachute jumping skills.

- ❑ **Qualified?:** These indicate whether an explorer or guide has training in a particular skill. For example, if IceQualified? is Yes, then this person has ice climbing training.

- ❑ **Instructor?:** These indicate whether a guide is qualified to teach a particular skill. For example, if RockInstructor? is Yes, then this guide can teach rock climbing.

- ❑ **Required?:** These indicate whether a trek requires a particular skill. For example, if JumpRequired? is Yes, then this trek requires parachute jumping skills (for example, the popular "Parachute into the Andes and Hike Out" trek).

The company requires an emergency contact for all explorers and that contact cannot be going on the same trek (in case an avalanche takes out the whole group).

The company gives a 10% discount if the explorer purchases airline flights with the adventure. Similarly the company gives a 5% discount if the explorer rents equipment with the adventure. (During requirements gathering, one of the company's owners asks which gives the customer the biggest discount: applying a 10% discount followed by a 5% discount, applying a 5% discount followed by a 10% discount, or adding the two and applying a 15% discount. What do you think?)

If the explorer purchases airfare with the adventure, the organizer uses the Notes field to record flight information such as the explorer's starting airport and meal preferences.

1. For each of the database's tables, make a chart to describe the table's fields. Fill in the following columns for each field:

   - ❑ **Field:** The field's name.

   - ❑ **Required:** Enter Yes if the field is always required, No if it is not, or ? if it is sometimes required and sometimes not.

   - ❑ **Data Type:** The field's data type as in String or Yes/No.

   - ❑ **Domain:** List or describe the allowed values. If the allowed values are a list that might need to change, write "List:" before the list. You will extract these values into a new table. If the value must be in another table, list the foreign field as in Persons.PersonId.

   - ❑ **Sanity Checks:** List any basic sanity checks such as MaxExplorers > 0. Remember that these just verify extremely basic information such as a price is greater than $0.00. Don't enter more complex checks such as looking up a value in a list. Also don't enter data type validations such as the fact that an ID really is an ID or that a date is a date. (Note that this kind of sanity check has nothing to do with the explorers' sanity. If it did, we'd never get any customers to purchase the "Tubing over Niagara Falls" or "August in Tampa" packages.)

2. For each of the database's tables, list the related business rules that are unlikely to change (and that are not too horribly complicated) so they should be implemented in the table's field or table checks. (For example, before the database creates a new Adventures record, it should verify that the corresponding trek has space available.)

   Include any fields that can be validated against a list of values that will never change (such as Gender) and more complex format validations (such as phone numbers).

Do not include fields that are foreign key constraints because that validates them completely. For example, a Phones record's PersonId value must be in the Persons table so it needs no further validation.

3.   List any business rules that are likely to change, that fit better in a lookup table, that are really complicated, or that are just too weird to build irrevocably into the database. Next to each, describe how you might extract that business rule from the database's structure.

4.   List the new tables (and their fields) that you would create to implement these changes.

Normalizing Data

Chapter 6 explained how you can make a database more flexible and robust by extracting certain business rules from the database's structure. By removing some of the more complex and changeable rules from the database's check constraints, you make it easier to change those rules later.

Another way to make a database more flexible and robust is to "normalize" it. Normalization makes the database more able to accommodate changes in the structure of the data. It also protects the database against certain kinds of errors.

This chapter explains what normalization is and tells how you can use it to improve your database design.

In this chapter you learn:

- ❑ What normalization is.
- ❑ What problems different types or levels of normalization address.
- ❑ How to normalize a database.
- ❑ How to know what level of normalization is best for your database.

After you normalize your relational model, you'll be ready to build the database.

What Is Normalization?

Depending on how you design a relational database, it may be susceptible so all sorts of problems. For example:

- ❑ It may contain lots of duplicated data. This not only wastes space but it also makes updating all of those duplicated values a time-consuming chore.
- ❑ It may incorrectly associate two unrelated pieces of data so you cannot delete one without deleting the other.

❑ It may require a piece of data that shouldn't exist in order to represent another piece of data that should exist.

❑ It may limit the number of values that you can enter for what should be a multi-valued piece of data.

In database terminology, these issues are called *anomalies*. (Anomaly is a euphemism for "problem." I'm not sure why this needs a euphemism — I doubt the database's feelings would be hurt by the word "problem.")

Normalization is a process of rearranging the database to put it into a standard (normal) form that prevents these kinds of anomalies.

There are seven different levels of normalization. Each level includes those before it. For example, a database is in Third Normal Form if is in Second Normal Form plus it satisfies some extra properties. That means if a database is at one level of normalization, then by definition it gets the advantages of the "lower" levels.

The different levels of normalization in order from weakest to strongest are:

❑ First Normal Form (1NF)

❑ Second Normal Form (2NF)

❑ Third Normal Form (3NF)

❑ Boyce-Codd Normal Form (BCNF)

❑ Fourth Normal Form (4NF)

❑ Fifth Normal Form (5NF)

❑ Domain/Key Normal Form (DKNF)

A database in DKNF has amazing powers of protection against anomalies, can leap tall buildings, and has all sorts of other super-database powers.

The following sections explain the properties that a database must satisfy to officially earn one of these coveted uber-database titles. They also explain the data anomalies that each level of normalization prevents.

First Normal Form (1NF)

First Normal Form basically says that the data is in a database. It's sort of the price to play the game if you want be a relational database.

Most of the properties needed to be in 1NF are enforced automatically by any reasonable relational database. There are a couple of extra properties added on to make the database more useful, but mostly these rules are pretty basic. The official qualifications for 1NF are:

1. Each column must have a unique name.

2. The order of the rows and columns doesn't matter.

3. Each column must have a single data type.

4. No two rows can contain identical values.

5. Each column must contain a single value.

6. Columns cannot contain repeating groups.

The first two rules basically come for free when you use a relational database product such as Access, SQL Server, or MySQL. All of these require that you give columns different names. They also don't really care about the order of rows and columns, although when you select data you will probably want to specify the order in which it is returned for consistency's sake.

Rule 3 means two rows cannot store different types of data in the same column. For example, the Value field in a table cannot hold a string in one row, a date in another, and a currency value in a third. This is almost a freebie because database products won't let you say, "This field should hold numbers or dates."

One way to run afoul of Rule 3 is to store values with different types converted into a common form. For example, you could store a date written as a string (such as "3/14/2012") and a number written as a string (such as "17") in a column designed to hold strings. Though this is an impressive display of your cleverness, it violates the spirit of the rule. It makes it much harder to perform queries using the field in any meaningful way. If you really need to store different kinds of data, split them apart into different columns that each holds a single kind of data. (In practice, many databases end up with just this sort of field. In particular, users often enter key data in comment or notes fields and a program must later search for values in those fields. Not the best practice but it does happen.)

Rule 4 makes sense because, if two rows *did* contain identical values, how would you tell them apart? The only reason you might be tempted to violate this rule is if you don't need to tell the rows apart. For example, suppose you fill out an order form for a pencil, some paper, and a tarantula. Oh, yeah, you also need another pencil so you add it at the end.

> *This reminds me of the joke where some guy wants to buy two new residents for his aquarium by mail-order (this was before Internet shopping) but he doesn't know whether the plural of octopus is octopi or octopuses. So he writes, "Dear Sirs, please send me an octopus. Oh and please send me another one."*

Now the form's list of items contains two identical rows listing a pencil. You don't care that the rows are identical because the pencils are identical. In fact, all you really know is that you want two pencils. That observation leads to the solution. Instead of using two identical rows, use one row with a new Quantity field and set Quantity to 2.

Note that Rule 4 is equivalent to saying that the table can have a primary key. Recall from Chapter 3 that a primary key is a set of columns that you can use to uniquely identify rows. If no two rows can have exactly the same values, then you must be able to pick a set of columns to uniquely identify the rows, even if it includes every column.

In fact, let's make that a new rule:

> 4. (continued). Every table has a primary key.

Rule 5 is the one you might be most tempted to violate. Sometimes a data entity includes a concept that needs multiple values. The semantic object models described in Chapter 5 even let you explicitly set an attribute's cardinality so you can make one attribute that holds multiple values.

For example, suppose you are building a recipe table and you give it the fields Name, Ingredients, Instructions, and Notes (which contains things such as "Sherri loves this recipe" and "For extra flavor, increase ants to 3 tbl."). This gives you enough information to print out a recipe and you can easily follow it (assuming you have some talent for cooking and a garden full of ants).

However, the Ingredients, Instructions, and Notes fields contain multiple values. Two hints that this might be the case are the fact that the column names are plural and that the column values are probably broken up into sub-values by commas, periods, carriage returns, or some other delimiter.

Storing multiple values in a single field limits the usefulness of that field. For example, suppose you decide that you want to find all of your recipes that use ants as an ingredient. Because the Ingredients field contains a bunch of different values all glommed together, you cannot easily search for a particular ingredient. You might be able to search for the word "ants" within the string, but you're likely to get extraneous matches such as "currants." You also won't be able to use indexes to make these searches in the middle of a string faster.

The solution is to break the multiple values apart, move them into a new table, and link those records back to this one with this record's primary key. For the recipe example, you would create a RecipeIngredients table with fields RecipeId, Ingredient, and Amount. Now you can search for RecipeIngredients records where Ingredient is "ants."

Similarly, you could make a RecipeInstructions table with fields RecipeId, StepNumber, and Instruction. The StepNumber field is necessary because you want to perform the steps in the correct order. (I've tried rearranging the steps and it just doesn't work! Baking bread before you mix the ingredients gives you a strange little brick-like puddle.) Now you can search for Recipes records and matching RecipeInstructions records that contain the word "preheat" to see how hot the oven must be.

Note that you only need to separate a field's values if they are logically distinct for whatever purposes you will use them. For example, you might want to search for individual ingredients. It's a bit less clear that you'll need to search for particular instructions. It's even less sure that you'll want to search for specific values within a Notes field. Notes is more or less a free-format field, and it's not clear that any internal structure is important.

For an even more obvious example, consider an Authors table's Biography field. This field contains a brief biography of the author. You could break it into sentences (or words, or even letters), but the individual sentences don't have any real context, so there's little point. You will display the Biography as a whole anyway so there's little benefit in chopping it up arbitrarily.

Rule 6 means you cannot have multiple columns that contain values that are not distinguishable. For example, suppose you decide that each Exterminators record should be able to hold the animals for which an exterminator is qualified to remove (muskrat, ostrich, platypus, and so forth). (Don't worry, this is a humane pest control service, so the exterminators catch the critters and release them far away so they can bug someone else.)

You already know from Rule 5 that you can't just cram all of the animals into a single Critters field. Rule 6 says you also cannot create columns named Critter1, Critter2, and Critter3 to hold different animals. Instead you need to split the values out into a new table and use the Exterminators table's primary key to link back to the main records.

Figure 7-1 shows a relational model for the recipe data. The ingredients and instructions have been moved into new tables but the Notes field remains as it was originally.

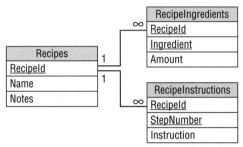

Figure 7-1

Try It Out   **Arranging Data in the First Normal Form**

The following table contains information about airline flights. It contains data about a party of two flying from Denver to Phoenix and a party of three flying from San Diego to Los Angeles. The first two columns give the start and destination cities. The final column gives the connection cities (if any) or the number of connections. The rows are ordered so the frequent flyer passengers are at the top, in this case in the first three rows.

City	City	Connections
DEN	PHX	1
SAN	LAX	JFK, SEA, TPA
SAN	LAX	JFK, SEA, TPA
DEN	PHX	1
SAN	LAX	JFK, SEA, TPA

Your mission, should you decide to accept it, is to put this atrocity into First Normal Form:

1. Make sure every column has a unique name. This table has two columns named City. To fix these problems (sorry, I mean "anomalies"), rename those columns to StartCity and DestinationCity.

2. Make sure the order of the rows and columns doesn't matter. If the order of the rows matters, add a column to record the information implied by their positions. In this example, make a new Priority column and explicitly list the passengers' priorities.

3. Make sure each column holds a single data type. If a column holds more than one type of data, split it into multiple columns, one for each data type. In this case, list the connecting cities, and don't even record the number of cities. Just count them when necessary.

4. Make sure no two rows can contain identical values. If two rows contain identical values, add a field to differentiate them. In this case, add a CustomerId column so you can tell the customers apart.

5. Make sure each column contains a single value. If a column holds multiple data values, split them out into a new table. Make a new Connections table and move the connection data there. To tie those records back to their original rows in this table, add columns that correspond to the primary key columns in the original table (CustomerId and Date).

6. Make sure multiple columns don't contain repeating groups. In this example, you need to think about the two city fields and decide whether they contain distinguishable values.

How It Works

1. Make sure every column has a unique name.

   Rule 1 says each column must have a unique name, but this table has two columns named City. This also sort of violates the rule that the order of the columns cannot matter because we're using the ordering to know which is the start city and which is the destination city.

   After you rename the columns, the table looks like this:

StartCity	DestinationCity	Connections
DEN	PHX	1
SAN	LAX	JFK, SEA, TPA
SAN	LAX	JFK, SEA, TPA
DEN	PHX	1
SAN	LAX	JFK, SEA, TPA

2. Make sure the order of the rows and columns doesn't matter. If the order of the rows matters, add a column to record the information implied by their positions.

   Rule 2 says the order of the rows and columns doesn't matter. After making the first change, the order of the columns doesn't matter any more because you can use the column names rather than their order to tell which city is which. However, you're using the order of the rows to determine which passengers have the highest priority (frequent flyers get the caviar and pheasant while the others get Twinkies and Spam).

   To fix this, take whatever concept the row ordering represents and move it into a new column. After you make a new Priority column and explicitly list the passengers' priorities, the ordering of the rows doesn't matter because you can retrieve the original idea of who has higher priority from the new column. Now the table looks like this:

StartCity	DestinationCity	Connections	Priority
DEN	PHX	1	1
SAN	LAX	JFK, SEA, TPA	1
SAN	LAX	JFK, SEA, TPA	1
DEN	PHX	1	2
SAN	LAX	JFK, SEA, TPA	2

3. Make sure each column holds a single data type. If a column holds more than one type of data, split it into multiple columns, one for each data type.

Rule 3 says each column must have a single data type. Here the Connections column holds either a list of connecting cities or the number of connections, two different kinds of data. There are at least two reasonable solutions for this problem (at least for right now).

First, you could make two columns, ConnectingCities and NumberOfConnections, and split these values into their proper columns. This would be the better solution if you really needed both of these types of values.

In this case, however, the number of connections is just a count of the number of connecting cities so, if you knew the cities, you could just count them to get the number of cities. The better solution in this case is to list the connecting cities and calculate the number of those cities when necessary. Here's the new table:

StartCity	DestinationCity	Connections	Priority
DEN	PHX	LON	1
SAN	LAX	JFK, SEA, TPA	1
SAN	LAX	JFK, SEA, TPA	1
DEN	PHX	LON	2
SAN	LAX	JFK, SEA, TPA	2

4. Make sure no two rows can contain identical values. If two rows contain identical values, add a field to differentiate them.

Rule 4 says no two rows can contain identical values. Unfortunately this table's second and third rows are identical. The question now becomes, "Do you care that you cannot tell these records apart?"

143

If you are a cold, heartless, big corporation airline and you don't care who is flying, just that *someone* is flying, then you don't care. In that case, add a Count field to the table and use it to track the number of identical rows. This would be the new design:

StartCity	DestinationCity	Connections	Priority	Count
DEN	PHX	LON	1	1
SAN	LAX	JFK, SEA, TPA	1	2
DEN	PHX	LON	2	1
SAN	LAX	JFK, SEA, TPA	2	1

However, if you're a warm, friendly, mom-and-pop airline, then you do care who has which flight. In that case, what is the difference between the two identical rows? The answer is that they represent different customers so the solution is to add a column to differentiate between the customers. If you add a CustomerId column, then you don't need the Count column and the table becomes:

StartCity	DestinationCity	Connections	Priority	CustomerId
DEN	PHX	LON	1	4637
SAN	LAX	JFK, SEA, TPA	1	12878
SAN	LAX	JFK, SEA, TPA	1	2871
DEN	PHX	LON	2	28718
SAN	LAX	JFK, SEA, TPA	2	9287

This works for now, but what if one of these customers wants to make the same trip more than once on different dates? In that case the table will hold two identical records again. Again you can ask yourself, what is the difference between the two identical rows? The answer this time is that the trips take place on different dates so you can fix it by adding a Date column.

StartCity	DestinationCity	Connections	Priority	CustomerId	Date
DEN	PHX	LON	1	4637	4/1/10
SAN	LAX	JFK, SEA, TPA	1	12878	6/21/10
SAN	LAX	JFK, SEA, TPA	1	2871	6/21/10
DEN	PHX	LON	2	28718	4/1/10
SAN	LAX	JFK, SEA, TPA	2	9287	6/21/10

Rule 4a says the table should have a primary key. The combination of CustomerId and Date can uniquely identify the rows. This seems like a safe combination because one customer cannot take two flights at the same time (although customers have been known to book multiple flights at the same time and then cancel all but one).

5. Make sure each column contains a single value. If a column holds multiple data values, split them out into a new table.

Rule 5 says each column must contain a single value. This table's Connections column clearly violates the rule. To solve this problem, make a new Connections table and move the connection data there. To tie those records back to their original rows in this table, add columns that correspond to the primary key columns in the original table (CustomerId and Date).

That single change leads to a big problem, however. The values in the combined Connections column implicitly defined the connections' order. Using the new table, you cannot tell which connections come before which. (Unless you use the ordering of the rows to decide which comes first, and you know that's not allowed!)

The solution is to add a ConnectionNumber field to the new table so you can figure out how to order the connections.

Figure 7-2 shows the tables together with lines connecting the corresponding records.

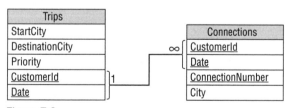

Figure 7-2

Figure 7-3 shows a relational model for these tables. (In the context of airline connections, that infinity symbol is kind of depressing.)

Trips
StartCity
DestinationCity
Priority
CustomerId
Date

Connections
CustomerId
Date
ConnectionNumber
City

Figure 7-3

6. Make sure multiple columns don't contain repeating groups. In this example, you need to think about the two city fields and decide whether they contain distinguishable values.

Rule 6 says that multiple columns don't contain repeating groups. In this example, the two city fields contain very similar types of values: cities. Unlike the exterminator example described earlier, however, these values are distinguishable. Starting and ending destination are not the same thing, and they are not the same as connecting cities. (Although I had a travel agent once who may not have fully understood the difference, judging by where my rental car was reserved.)

Database purists would say that having two fields containing the same kind of data is a bad thing and you should move the values into a new table.

My take on the issue is that it depends on how you are going to use the values. Will you ever want to ask, "Which customers ever visit San Jose?" If so, then having these cities in two separate fields is cumbersome because you'll have to ask the same question about each field. In fact, you'll also have to ask about the connecting cities. In this case, it might be better to move the start and destination cities out of this table.

In contrast, suppose you never ask what cities customers visit and instead ask, "Which customers start from Berlin?" or "Which customers finish in Madrid?" In that case, keeping these values in separate fields does no harm.

For now I'll leave them alone and take up this issue again in the next section.

As a quick check, you should also verify that the new table is in 1NF. If you run through the rules, you'll find that most of them are satisfied trivially but a few are worth a moment of reflection.

Rules 4 says no two rows can contain identical values and the table must have a primary key. Assuming no customer takes more than one trip per day, then the Trips table's CustomerId/Date fields and the Connections table's CustomerId/Date/ConnectionNumber fields make reasonable primary keys. If you need to allow customers to take more than one trip per day (which happens in the real world), you probably need to add another TripNumber field to both tables.

Rule 5 says every column must contain a single value. If we split apart the values in the original table's Connections column, the new table should be okay.

But we'll need a separate table to track where the luggage goes.

Second Normal Form (2NF)

A table is in 2NF if:

1. It is in 1NF.

2. All of the non-key fields depend on all of the key fields.

To see what this means, consider the alligator wrestling schedule shown in the following table. It lists the name, class (amateur or professional), and ranking for each wrestler, together with the time when this wrestler will perform. The Time/Wrestler combination forms the table's primary key.

Time	Wrestler	Class	Rank
1:30	Annette Cart	Pro	3
1:30	Ben Jones	Pro	2
2:00	Sydney Dart	Amateur	1

Time	Wrestler	Class	Rank
2:15	Ben Jones	Pro	2
2:30	Annette Cart	Pro	3
3:30	Sydney Dart	Amateur	1
3:30	Mike Acosta	Amateur	6
3:45	Annette Cart	Pro	3

Though this table is in 1NF (don't take my word for it, verify it yourself), it is trying to do too much work all by itself and that leads to several problems.

Note that the Wrestler field contains both first and last names. This would violate 1NF if you consider those as two separate pieces of information. For this example, assume you only need to display first and last name together and will never need to perform searches on last name only, for example. This is confusing enough without adding extra columns.

First, this table is vulnerable to update anomalies. An *update anomaly* occurs when a change to a row leads to inconsistent data. In this case, update anomalies are caused by the fact that this table holds a lot of repeated data. For example, suppose Sydney Dart decides to turn pro, so you update the Class entry in the third row. Now that row is inconsistent with the Class entry in row 6 that still shows Sydney as an amateur. You'll need to update every row in the table that mentions Sydney to fix this problem.

Second, this table is susceptible to deletion anomalies. A *deletion anomaly* occurs when deleting a record can destroy information that you might need later. In this example, suppose you cancel the 3:30 match featuring Mike Acosta. In that case you lose the entire 7th record in the table, so you lose the fact that Mike is an amateur, that he's ranked 6th, and even that he exists (presumably he disappears in a puff of smoke).

Third, this table is subject to insertion anomalies. An *insertion anomaly* occurs when you cannot store certain kinds of information because it would violate the table's primary key constraints. Suppose you want to add a new wrestler Nate Waffle to the roster but you have not yet scheduled any matches for him. (Nate's actually the contest organizer's nephew so he doesn't really wrestle alligators; he just wants to be listed in the program to impress his friends.) To add Nate to this table, you would have to assign him a wrestling match, and Nate would probably have a heart attack. Similarly, you cannot create a new time for a match without assigning a wrestler to it.

Okay, I confess I pulled a fast one here. You *could* create a record for Nate that had Time set to null. That would be really bad form, however, because all of the fields that make up a primary key should have non-null values. Many databases require that all primary key fields not allow nulls. Because Time/Wrestler is the table's primary key, you cannot give Nate a record without assigning a Time and you're stuck.

The underlying problem is that some of the table's columns do not depend on all of the primary key fields. The Class and Rank fields depend on Wrestler but not on Time. Annette Cart is a professional whether she wrestles at 1:30, 2:30, or 3:45.

The solution is to pull the columns that do not depend on the *entire* primary key out of the table and put them in a new table. In this case, you could create a new Wrestlers table and move the Class and Rank fields into it. You would add a WrestlerName field to link back to the original table.

Figure 7-4 shows a relational model for the new tables.

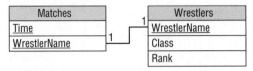

Figure 7-4

Figure 7-5 shows the new tables holding the original data. Here I've sorted the matches by wrestler name to make it easier to see the relationship between the two tables. (It's a mess if you sort the matches by time.)

Matches	
Time	WrestlerName
1:30	Annette Cart
2:30	Annette Cart
3:45	Annette Cart
1:30	Ben Jones
2:15	Ben Jones
3:30	Mike Acosta
2:00	Sydney Dart
3:30	Sydney Dart

Wrestlers		
WrestlerName	Class	Rank
Annette Cart	Pro	3
Ben Jones	Pro	2
Mike Acosta	Amateur	6
Sydney Dart	Amateur	1

Figure 7-5

The new arrangement is immune to the three anomalies described earlier. To make Sydney Dart a professional, you only need to change her Wrestlers record. You can cancel the 3:30 match between Mike Acosta and Hungry Bob without losing Mike's information in the Wrestler's table. Finally, you can make a row for Nate in the Wrestlers table without making one in the Matches table.

You should also verify that all of the new tables satisfy the 2NF rule, "All of the non-key fields depend on all of the key fields." The Matches table contains no fields that are not part of the primary key so it satisfies this requirement trivially.

The primary key for the Wrestlers table is the WrestlerName field, and the Class and Rank fields depend directly on the value of WrestlerName. If you move to a different WrestlerName, you get different values for Class and Rank. Note that the second wrestler might have the same Class and Rank but that would be mere coincidence. The new values belong to the new wrestler.

Intuitively, the original table had problems because it was trying to hold two kinds of information: information about matches and information about wrestlers. To fix the problem, we broke the table into two tables to hold those two kinds of information separately.

If you ensure that every table represents one single, unified concept such as wrestler or match, the table will be in 2NF. It's when a table tries to play multiple roles, such as storing wrestler and match information at the same time, that it is open to data anomalies.

Try It Out   **Arranging Data in the Second Normal Form**

Suppose you just graduated from the East Los Angeles Space Academy and you rush to the posting board to find your ship assignments:

Cadet	Position	Ship
Ash, Joshua	Fuse Tender	Frieda's Glory
Barker, Sally	Pilot	Scrat
Barker, Sally	Arms Master	Scrat
Cumin, Bil	Cook's Mate	Scrat
Farnsworth, Al	Arc Tauran Liaison	Frieda's Glory
Farnsworth, Al	Interpreter	Frieda's Glory
Major, Major	Cook's Mate	Scrat
Pickover, Bud	Captain	Athena Ascendant

This table uses the Cadet/Position combination as a primary key. Note that some cadets have more than one job.

To earn your posting as Data Minder First Class:

1.   Describe the table's update, deletion, and insertion anomalies.

2.   Put it in 2NF. Find any fields that don't depend on the entire primary key and move them into a new table. In this case, split the table into two new tables: CadetPositions and CadetShips. The CadetPositions table is similar to the original table with the Ship field removed. The CadetShips table links the cadets with their ships.

How It Works

1.   Describe the table's update, deletion, and insertion anomalies.

This table allows update anomalies because it contains repeated values. For example, if you change Sally Barker's Ship in row 2 to Athena Ascendant, it would conflict with the Ship value in row 3 that says Sally is on the Scrat.

This table also allows deletion anomalies. If you delete the last row, you no longer know that the Athena Ascendant is a Courier class ship or that she even exists. (Her crew will be mad when headquarters stops sending paychecks.)

Finally, the table allows insertion anomalies because you cannot store information about a cadet without a ship or a ship without a cadet.

2.   Put it in 2NF. Find any fields that don't depend on the entire primary key and move them into a new table.

This table has problems because some of the fields don't depend on the entire primary key. In particular, the Ship field depends on the Cadet (it's the ship where this cadet is assigned) but it does not depend on the Position. You could solve the problem if you could remove Position from the primary key but we need both Cadet and Position to uniquely identify a record.

The solution is to split the table into two new tables: CadetPositions and CadetShips, and move the ship information (which doesn't depend on the entire primary key) into the new table. Figure 7-6 shows the relational model for this new design.

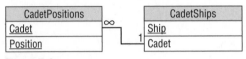

Figure 7-6

Figure 7-7 shows the new tables and their data.

CadetPositions			CadetShips	
Cadet	Position		Cadet	Ship
Ash, Joshua	Fuse Tender		Ash, Joshua	Frieda's Glory
Barker, Sally	Pilot		Barker, Sally	Scrat
Barker, Sally	Arms Master		Cumin, Bil	Scrat
Cumin, Bil	Cook's Mate		Farnsworth, Al	Frieda's Glory
Farnsworth, Al	Arc Tauran Liaison		Major, Major	Scrat
Farnsworth, Al	Interpreter		Pickover, Bud	Athena Ascendant
Major, Major	Cook's Mate			
Pickover, Bud	Captain			

Figure 7-7

You can easily verify that these tables are in 1NF.

The CadetPositions table is in 2NF trivially because every field is part of the primary key.

The CadetShips table is in 2NF because the only field that is not part of the primary key (Ship) depends on the single primary key field (Cadet).

Third Normal Form (3NF)

A table is in 3NF if:

1. It is in 2NF.
2. It contains no transitive dependencies.

A *transitive dependency* is when one non-key field's value depends on another non-key field's value.

For example, suppose you and your friends decide to start a book club. To see what kinds of books people like, you put together the following table listing everyone's favorite books. It uses Person as the primary key. (Again the Author field might violate 1NF if you consider it as containing multiple values: first and last name. For simplicity, and because you won't ever want to search for books written by authors with the first name "Orson," I'll treat this as a single value.)

Person	Title	Author	Pages	Year
Amy	Support Your Local Wizard	Duane, Diane	473	1990
Becky	Three to Dorsai!	Dickson, Gordon	532	1975
Jon	Chronicles of the Black Company	Cook, Glen	704	2007
Ken	Three to Dorsai!	Dickson, Gordon	532	1975
Wendy	Support Your Local Wizard	Duane, Diane	473	1990

You can easily show that this table is 1NF. It uses a single field as primary key so every field in the table depends on the entire primary key, so it's also 2NF. (Each row represents that Person's favorite book so every field must depend on that Person.)

However, this table contains a lot of duplication, so it is subject to modification anomalies. (At this point you probably knew that!) If you discover that the Year for *Support Your Local Wizard* is wrong and fix it in row 1, it will conflict with the last row.

It's also subject to deletion anomalies (if Jon insults everyone and gets kicked out of the group so you remove the third row, you lose all of the information about *Chronicles of the Black Company*) and insertion anomalies (you cannot save Title, Author, Pages, and Year information about a book unless it's someone's favorite, and you cannot allow someone to join the group until he or she decides on a favorite).

The problem here is that some of the fields are related to others. In this example, Author, Pages, and Year are related to Title. If you know a book's Title, you could look up its Author, Pages, and Year.

In this example, the primary key Person doesn't exactly drive the Author, Pages, and Year fields. Instead it selects the Person's favorite Title and then Title determines the other values. This is a *transitive dependency*. Title depends on Person and the other fields depend on Title.

The main clue that there is a transitive dependency is that there are lots of duplicate values in the table.

You can fix this problem in a way similar to the way you put a table into 2NF: find the fields that are causing the problem and pull them into a separate table. Add an extra field to contain the original field on which those were dependent so you can link back to the original table.

In this case, you could make a Books table to hold the Author, Pages, and Year fields. You would then add a Title field to link the new records back to the original table.

Figure 7-8 shows a relational model for the new design.

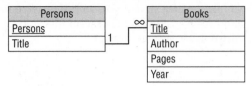

Figure 7-8

Figure 7-9 shows the new tables containing the original data.

Persons	
Person	Title
Jon	Chronicles of the Black Company
Amy	Support Your Local Wizard
Wendy	Support Your Local Wizard
Becky	Three to Dorsai!
Ken	Three to Dorsai!

Books			
Title	Author	Pages	Year
Chronicles of the Black Company	Cook, Glen	704	2007
Support Your Local Wizard	Duane, Diane	473	1990
Three to Dorsai!	Dickson, Gordon	532	1975

Figure 7-9

Try It Out   Arranging Data in the Third Normal Form

Suppose you're helping to organize the 19,524th Jedi Olympics. Mostly the contestants stand around bragging about how they don't need to use violence because the Force is strong in them. You also often hear the phrases, "I was just following the Force," and "The Force made me do it."

But to keep television ratings up, there are some athletic events. The following table shows the day's schedule. It uses Contestant as the primary key.

Contestant	Time	Event	Venue
Boyce Codd	2:00	Monster Mayhem	Monster Pit
General Mills	1:30	Pebble Levitating	Windy Plains Arena
Master Plethora	4:00	X-wing Lifting	Windy Plains Arena
Master Tor	1:00	Monster Mayhem	Monster Pit
Glenn	5:00	Poker	Dark Force Casino
Xzktp! Krffzk	5:00	Poker	Dark Force Casino

As part of your data processing padawan training:

1. Describe the data anomalies that this table allows.

2. Put the table in 3NF. If some fields are dependent on other non-key fields, pull the dependent fields out into a new table.

How It Works

1. Describe the data anomalies that this table allows.

   This table allows update anomalies because it contains lots of repeated values. For example, if you changed the Venue for Monster Mayhem in row 1, it would conflict with the Venue for Monster Mayhem in row 4. It also allows deletion anomalies (if Master Plethora is caught metaclorian doping and he drops out, you lose the fact that X-wing Lifting occurs in the Windy Plains Arena) and insertion anomalies (you cannot add a new contestant without an event or an event without a contestant).

2. Put the table in 3NF. If some fields are dependent on other non-key fields, pull the dependent fields out into a new table. Pull the dependent Venue field out into a new table. Add the field it depends upon (Event) as a key to link back to the original table.

   The problem is that the Event and Venue fields are dependent on each other in some manner.

   The solution is to pull the dependent fields out and put them in a new table. Then add a field linking back to the field on which they depend. The next question is, "Which of these two related fields should be the one that you leave in the original table to use as the link?" Does Venue depend on Event? Or does Event depend on Venue? Or does it matter which one you consider dependent on the other?

   In this example, it does matter.

   Notice that Event determines Venue. In other words, each particular Event occurs in only one Venue, so if you know the Event, you know the Venue. For example, all Pebble Levitating events occur in Windy Plains Arena. This means Venue is dependent on Event.

   However, the reverse is not true. Venue does not determine Event. If you know the Venue, you do not necessarily know the Event. For example, the Windy Plains Arena is the venue for both Pebble Levitating and X-wing Lifting. This means Event is not dependent on Venue.

   (If there were a one-to-one mapping of Event to Venue, each field would determine the other so you could use either as the key field. Although to me it makes more intuitive sense to use Event as the key.)

   Figure 7-10 shows the new model.

ContestantAssignments		EventVenues
Contestant	1	EventName
Time		Venue
EventName	∞	

Figure 7-10

Figure 7-11 shows the tables containing the original data.

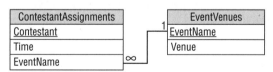

Contestants				EventVenues	
ContestantName	Time	Event		Event	Venue
Boyce Codd	2:00	Monster Mayhem		Monster Mayhem	Monster Pit
Master Tor	1:00	Monster Mayhem		Pebble Levitating	Windy Plains Arena
General Mills	1:30	Pebble Levitating		Poker	Dark Force Casino
Glenn	5:00	Poker		X-wing Lifting	Windy Plains Arena
Xzktp! Krffzk	5:00	Poker			
Master Plethora	4:00	X-wing Lifting			

Figure 7-11

Stopping at Third Normal Form

Many database designers stop normalizing the database at 3NF because it provides the most bang for the buck. It's fairly easy to convert a database to 3NF and that level of normalization prevents the most common data anomalies. It stores separate data separately so you can add and remove pieces of information without destroying unrelated data. It also removes redundant data so the database isn't full of a zillion copies of the same information that waste space and make updating values difficult.

However, the database may still be vulnerable to some less common anomalies that are prevented by the more complete normalizations described in the following sections. These greater levels of normalization are rather technical and confusing. They can also lead to unnecessarily complicated data models that are hard to implement, hard to maintain, and hard to use. In some cases, they can give worse performance than less completely normalized designs.

Though you may not always need to use these super-normalized databases, it's still good to understand them and the problems that they prevent. Then you can decide whether those problems are a big enough issue to justify including them in your design. (Besides, they make great ice breakers at parties. "Hey everyone! Let's see who can put the guest list in 4NF the fastest!")

Boyce-Codd Normal Form (BCNF)

This one is kind of technical, so to understand it you need to know some terms.

Recall from Chapter 3 that a *superkey* is a set of fields that contain unique values. You can use a superkey to uniquely identify the records in a table.

Also recall that a *candidate key* is a minimal superkey. In other words, if you remove any of the fields from the candidate key, it won't be a superkey anymore.

Now for a new term. A *determinant* is a field that at least partly determines the value in another field. Note that the definition of 3NF worries about fields that are dependent on another field that is not part of the primary key. Now we're talking about fields that might be dependent on fields that *are* part of the primary key (or any candidate key).

A table is in BCNF if:

1. It is in 3NF.
2. Every determinant is a candidate key.

For example, suppose you are attending the Wizards, Knights, and Farriers Convention hosted by three nearby castles: Castle Blue, Castle Green, and Le Château du Chevalier Rouge. Each attendee must select a track: Wizard, Knight, or Farrier. Each castle hosts three seminars, one for each track.

During the conference, you may attend seminars at any of the three castles, but you can only attend the one for your track. That means if you pick a castle, I can deduce which session you will attend there.

Here's part of the attendee schedule. The letters in parentheses show the attendee and seminar tracks to make the table easier to read and they are not really part of this data.

Attendee	Castle	Seminar
Agress Profundus (w)	Green	Poisons for Fun and Profit (w)
Anabel (k)	Blue	Terrific Tilting (k)
Anabel (k)	Rouge	Clubs 'N Things (k)
Frock Smith (f)	Blue	Dealing with Difficult Destriers (f)
Lady Mismyth (w)	Green	Poisons for Fun and Profit (w)
Sten Bors (f)	Blue	Dealing with Difficult Destriers (f)
The Mighty Brak (k)	Green	Siege Engine Maintenance (k)
The Mighty Brak (k)	Rouge	Clubs 'N Things (k)

This table is susceptible to update anomalies because it contains duplicated data. If you moved the Poisons for Fun and Profit seminar to Castle Blue in the first record, it would contradict the Castle value in row 5.

It's also vulnerable to deletion anomalies because the relationship between Castle and Seminar is stored implicitly in this table. If you deleted the second record, you would lose the fact that the Terrific Tilting seminar is taking place in Castle Blue.

Finally, this table suffers from insertion anomalies. For example, you cannot create a record for a new seminar without assigning an attendee to it.

In short, this table has a problem because it has multiple overlapping candidate keys.

This table has two candidate keys: Attendee/Castle and Attendee/Seminar. Either of those combinations will uniquely identify a record.

The remaining combination, Castle/Seminar, cannot identify the Attendee so it's not a candidate key.

The Castle and Seminar fields have a dependency: Seminar determines Castle (but not vice versa). In other words, Seminar is a determinant of Castle.

This table is not in BCNF because Seminar is a determinant but is not a candidate key.

You can put this table in BCNF by pulling out the dependent data and linking it to the determinant. In this case, that means moving the Castle data into a new table and linking it back to its determinant, Seminar.

Figure 7-12 shows the new design.

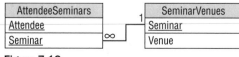

Figure 7-12

Figure 7-13 shows the new tables containing the original data.

AttendeeSeminars	
Attendee	Seminar
Anabel (k)	Clubs 'N Things (k)
The Mighty Brak (k)	Clubs 'N Things (k)
Frock Smith (f)	Dealing with Difficult Destriers (f)
Sten Bors (f)	Dealing with Difficult Destriers (f)
Agress Profundus (w)	Poisons for Fun and Profit (w)
Lady Mismyth (w)	Poisons for Fun and Profit (w)
The Mighty Brak (k)	Siege Engine Maintenance (k)
Anabel (k)	Terrific Tilting (k)

SeminarVenues	
Castle	Seminar
Rogue	Clubs 'N Things (k)
Blue	Dealing with Difficult Destriers (f)
Green	Poisons for Fun and Profit (w)
Green	Siege Engine Maintenance (k)
Blue	Terrific Tilting (k)

Figure 7-13

Now you can move the Poisons for Fun and Profit seminar to Castle Blue by changing a single record in the SeminarVenues table. You can delete Anabel's record for Terrific Tilting without losing the fact that Terrific Tilting takes place in Castle Blue because that information is in the SeminarVenues table. Finally, you can add a new record to the SeminarVenues table without assigning any attendees to it.

For another example, suppose you have an Employees table with columns EmployeeId, FirstName, LastName, SocialSecurityNumber, and Phone. Assume you don't need to worry about weird special cases such as roommates sharing a phone number or multiple employees with the same name.

This table has several determinants. For example, EmployeeId determines every other field's value. If you know an employee's ID, then all of the other values are fixed. This doesn't violate BCNF because EmployeeId is also a candidate key.

Similarly SocialSecurityNumber and Phone are each determinants of all of the other fields. Fortunately they, too, are candidate keys.

So far so good. Now for a stranger case. The combination FirstName/LastName is a determinant for all of the other fields. If you know an employee's first and last names, the corresponding EmployeeId, SocialSecurityNumber, and Phone values are set. Fortunately FirstName/LastName is also a candidate key so even that doesn't break the table's BCNF-ness.

This table is in BCNF because every determinant is also a candidate key. Intuitively the table is in BCNF because it represents a single entity: an employee.

The previous example was not in BCNF because it represented two concepts at the same time: attendees and the seminars they're attending, and the locations of the seminars. We solved that problem by splitting the table into two tables that each represented only one of those concepts.

Generally if every table represents a single concept or entity, it will be in pretty good shape. It's when you ask a table to do too much that you run into problems.

Try It Out   Arranging Data in the BCNF

Consider an EmployeeAssignments table with the fields EmployeeId, FirstName, LastName, and Project. Each employee can be assigned to multiple projects and each project can have multiple employees. Ignore weirdnesses such as two employees having the same name.

To become a Data Wizard:

1. Explain why this table is not in BCNF. (Find a determinant that this not also a candidate key.)

2. Describe data anomalies that might befall this table.

3. Put this table in BCNF by pulling the FirstName and LastName fields out of the table and moving them into a new EmployeeData table. Add an EmployeeId field to link the new table's records back to the original records.

How It Works

1. Explain why this table is not in BCNF. (Find a determinant that this not also a candidate key.)

Intuitively the problem with this table is that it includes two different concepts. It contains multiple pieces of employee data (EmployeeId, FirstName, LastName) together with employee project assignment data.

More technically, this table's candidate keys are EmployeeId/Project and FirstName/LastName/Project. (Take a few minutes to verify that these combinations specify the records uniquely, that you cannot remove any fields from them, and that the remaining combination EmployeeId/FirstName/LastName doesn't work.)

The problem occurs because these two candidate keys are partially overlapping. If you subtract out the overlapping field (Project), you get EmployeeId and FirstName/LastName. These are in the two candidate keys because they specify the same thing: the employee. That means they are determinants of each other. Unfortunately neither of these is a candidate key by itself so the table is not in BCNF.

2. Describe data anomalies that might befall this table.

Suppose an employee is involved with multiple projects. If you change the employee's FirstName in one of that employee's rows, it will contradict the FirstName in the employee's other rows. This is a modification anomaly.

Suppose you delete the only record containing employee Milton Waddams. You no longer have a record of his EmployeeId. In fact, you no longer have a record of him at all. (Perhaps that's the way he got deleted from the database in the movie *Office Space*.) This is a deletion anomaly.

You also can't add an employee record without assigning the employee to a project, and you can't create a project without assigning an employee to it. These are insertion anomalies.

3. Explain how to put this table in BCNF.

The solution is to move one of the dependent fields into a new table. In this case, you could pull the FirstName and LastName fields out of the table and move them into a new EmployeeData table. Add an EmployeeId field to link the new table's records back to the original records.

Figure 7-14 shows the new model.

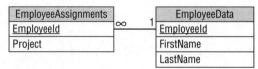

Figure 7-14

Fourth Normal Form (4NF)

Suppose you run a home fixit service. Each employee has a set of skills and each drives a particular truck that contains useful special equipment. They are all qualified to use any of the equipment. The following table shows a really bad attempt to store this information.

Employee	Skills	Tools
Gina Harris	Electric, Plumbing	Chop saw, Impact hammer
Pease Marks	Electric, Tile	Chain saw
Rick Shaw	Plumbing	Milling machine, Lathe

You should instantly notice that this table isn't even in 1NF because the Skills and Tools columns contain multiple values.

The following table shows an improved version. Here each row holds only one skill and tool.

Employee	Skill	Tool
Gina Harris	Electric	Chop saw
Gina Harris	Electric	Impact hammer
Gina Harris	Plumbing	Chop saw
Gina Harris	Plumbing	Impact hammer
Pease Marks	Electric	Chain saw
Pease Marks	Tile	Chain saw
Rick Shaw	Plumbing	Milling machine
Rick Shaw	Plumbing	Lathe

Unfortunately, to capture all of the data about each employee, this table must include a lot of duplication. To record the fact that Gina Harris has the electric and plumbing skills, and that her truck contains a chop saw and an impact hammer, you need four rows showing the four possible combinations of values.

In general, if an employee has S skills and T tools, the table would need S × T rows to hold all of the combinations.

This leads to the usual assortment of problems. If you modify the first row's Skill to Tile, it contradicts the second row, causing a modification anomaly. If Gina loses her impact hammer, you must delete two rows to prevent inconsistencies. If Gina takes classes in Painting, you need to add two new rows to cover all of the new combinations. If she then decides to add a spray gun, too, you need to add three more rows.

Something strange is definitely going on here. And yet this table is in BCNF!

You can easily verify that it's in 1NF.

Next note that every field must be part of the table's primary key because there can be duplicates of every other combination.

The table is in 2NF because all of the non-key fields (there are none) depend on all of the key fields (all of them). It's in 3NF because there are no transitive dependencies (every field is in the primary key so there no field is dependent on a non-key field). It's in BCNF because every determinant is a candidate key (the only determinant is Employee/Skill/Tool, which is also the only candidate key).

In this table, the problem arises because Employee implies Skill and Employee implies Tool but Skill and Tool are independent. This situation is called an *unrelated multi-valued dependency*.

A table is in 4NF if:

1. It is in BCNF.
2. It does not contain an unrelated multi-valued dependency.

A particular Employee leads to multiple Skills and for any given Skill there can be many Employees, so there is a many-to-many relationship between Employee and Skill. Similarly there is a many-to-many relationship between Employee and Tool. (Note that there is no relationship between Skill and Tool.)

Figure 7-15 shows an ER diagram for the entities involved: Employee, Skill, and Tool.

The solution to the problem is to find the field that drives the unrelated multi-valued dependency. In this case, Employee is the central field. It's in the middle of the ER diagram shown in Figure 7-15 and it forms one part of each of the many-to-many relationships.

Figure 7-15

To fix the table, pull one of the other fields out into a new table. Add the central field (Employee) to link the new records back to the original ones.

Figure 7-16 shows the new model.

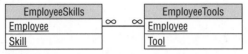

Figure 7-16

Figure 7-17 shows the original data in the new tables.

EmployeeSkills		EmployeeTools	
Employee	Skill	Employee	Tool
Gina Harris	Electric	Gina Harris	Chop saw
Gina Harris	Plumbing	Gina Harris	Impact hammer
Pease Marks	Electric	Pease Marks	Chain saw
Pease Marks	Tile	Rick Shaw	Milling machine
Rick Shaw	Plumbing	Rick Shaw	Lathe

Figure 7-17

Try It Out   Arranging Data in Fourth Normal Form

Consider the following artist's directory that lists artist names, genres, and shows they will attend this year.

Artist	Genre	Show
Ben Winsh	Metalwork	Makers of the Lost Art
Ben Winsh	Metalwork	Tribal Confusion
Harriette Laff	Textile	Fuzzy Mountain Alpaca Festival
Harriette Laff	Textile	Tribal Confusion
Harriette Laff	Sculpture	Fuzzy Mountain Alpaca Festival
Harriette Laff	Sculpture	Tribal Confusion
Mark Winslow	Sculpture	Green Mountain Arts Festival

A true database artist should be able to:

1. Identify the table's unrelated multi-valued dependency.
2. Draw an ER diagram showing the table's many-to-many relationships.

3. Put the table into 4NF by pulling the Show field out into a new table and adding an Artist column to link back to the original records. Then draw a relational model for the result.

4. Display the new tables with their data.

How It Works

In this example, there is a many-to-many relationship between Genre and Artist, and a second many-to-many relationship between Show and Artist.

1. Identify the table's unrelated multi-valued dependency.

   The Artist determines Genre and Show but Genre and Show are unrelated.

2. Draw an ER diagram showing the table's many-to-many relationships.

   Figure 7-18 shows an ER diagram for this situation.

```
          ←                              →
┌───────┐ 0.N ╱───────╲ 0.N ┌────────┐ 0.N ╱─────────────╲ 0.N ┌──────┐
│ Genre │─────│ Works In │─────│ Artist │─────│  Will Attend  │─────│ Show │
└───────┘     ╲───────╱      └────────┘      ╲─────────────╱      └──────┘
```

Figure 7-18

3. Put the table into 4NF and draw a relational model for the result.

   The central entity is Artist. One solution to this puzzle is to pull the Show field out into a new table and add an Artist column to link back to the original records. Figure 7-19 shows the result.

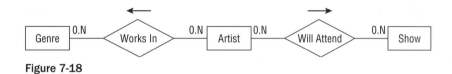

Figure 7-19

4. Display the new tables with their data.

   Figure 7-20 shows the new tables holding the original data.

ArtistGenres	
Artist	Genre
Ben Winsh	Metalwork
Harriette Laff	Textile
Harriette Laff	Sculpture
Mark Winslow	Sculpture

ArtistShows	
Artist	Show
Ben Winsh	Makers of the Lost Art
Ben Winsh	Tribal Confusion
Harriette Laff	Fuzzy Mountain Alpaca Festival
Harriette Laff	Tribal Confusion
Mark Winslow	Green Mountain Arts Festival

Figure 7-20

Fifth Normal Form (5NF)

A table is in 5NF (also called "Project-Join Normal Form") if:

1. It is in 4NF.

2. It contains no related multi-valued dependencies.

For example, suppose you run an auto repair shop. The grease monkeys who work there may be certified to work on particular makes of vehicles (Honda, Hummer, Yugo) and on particular types of engines (gas, diesel, hybrid, matter-antimatter).

If a grease monkey is certified for a particular make and for a particular engine, that person *must* provide service for that make and engine (if that combination exists). For example, suppose Joe Quark is certified to repair Hondas and Diesel. Then he must be able to repair Diesel engines made by Honda.

Now consider the following table showing which grease monkey can repair which combinations of make and engine.

GreaseMonkey	Make	Engine
Cindy Oyle	Honda	Gas
Cindy Oyle	Hummer	Gas
Eric Wander	Honda	Gas
Eric Wander	Honda	Hybrid
Eric Wander	Hummer	Gas
Joe Quark	Honda	Diesel
Joe Quark	Honda	Gas
Joe Quark	Honda	Hybrid
Joe Quark	Toyota	Diesel
Joe Quark	Toyota	Gas
Joe Quark	Toyota	Hybrid

In this case, GreaseMonkey determines Make. For a given GreaseMonkey, there are certain Makes that this person can repair.

Similarly, GreaseMonkey determines Engine. For a given GreaseMonkey, there are certain Engines that this person can repair.

Up to this point, the table is very similar to the Employee/Skill/Tool table described in the previous section about 4NF. Here comes the difference.

In the Employee/Skill/Tool table, Skill and Tool were unrelated. In this table, however, Make and Engine are related. For example, Eric Wander is certified in the Makes Honda and Hummer. He is also certified in the Engines Gas and Hybrid. The rules state that he must repair Gas and Hybrid engines for Honda and Hummer vehicles, if they provide those Makes. But Hummer doesn't make a hybrid, so Eric doesn't need to service that combination.

There's the dependency between Make and Engine. While the GreaseMonkey determines the Make and Engine, Make also influences Engine.

So how can you remove this dependency? Break the single table into three new tables that record the three different relationships: GreaseMonkey/Make, GreaseMonkey/Engine, and Make/Engine.

Figure 7-21 shows the new relational model.

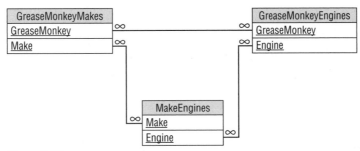

Figure 7-21

Figure 7-22 shows the new tables holding the original data. I haven't drawn lines connecting related records because it would make a big mess.

GreaseMonkey	Make
Cindy Oyle	Honda
Cindy Oyle	Hummer
Eric Wander	Honda
Eric Wander	Hummer
Joe Quark	Honda
Joe Quark	Toyota

GreaseMonkey	Engine
Cindy Oyle	Gas
Eric Wander	Gas
Eric Wander	Hybrid
Joe Quark	Diesel
Joe Quark	Gas
Joe Quark	Hybrid

Make	Engine
Honda	Diesel
Honda	Gas
Honda	Hybrid
Hummer	Gas
Hummer	Diesel
Toyota	Diesel
Toyota	Gas
Toyota	Hybrid

Figure 7-22

Try It Out   Working with the Fifth Normal Form

Remember the artist's directory from the previous sections about 4NF? The rules have changed slightly. The directory still lists artist names, genres, and shows they will attend, but now each show allows only certain genres. Now the Fuzzy Mountain Alpaca Festival includes only textile arts and Tribal Confusion includes only metalwork and sculpture. (Also, Ben Winsh started making sculptures.)

Here's the new schedule:

Artist	Genre	Show
Ben Winsh	Metalwork	Makers of the Lost Art
Ben Winsh	Metalwork	Tribal Confusion
Ben Winsh	Sculpture	Makers of the Lost Art
Harriette Laff	Textile	Fuzzy Mountain Alpaca Festival
Harriette Laff	Sculpture	Tribal Confusion
Mark Winslow	Sculpture	Green Mountain Arts Festival

To prove you're a true database artist:

1. Identify the table's related multi-valued dependency.
2. Draw an ER diagram showing the table's many-to-many relationships.
3. Put the table into 5NF and draw a relational model for the result.
4. Display the new tables with their data.

How It Works

1. Identify the table's related multi-valued dependency.

   Artist determines Genre, Artist determines Show, and Show determines Genre.

2. Draw an ER diagram showing the table's many-to-many relationships.

   Figure 7-23 shows an ER diagram for this situation.

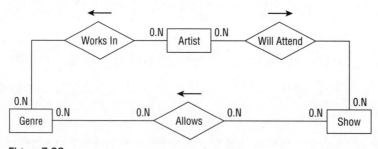

Figure 7-23

3. Put the table into 5NF and draw a relational model for the result.

   The new model should make separate tables to store the relationships between Artist and Genre, Artist and Show, and Show and Genre. Figure 7-24 shows this 5NF model.

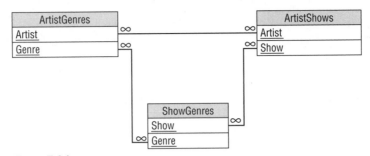

Figure 7-24

4. Display the new tables with their data.

Figure 7-25 shows the new tables holding the original data.

ArtistGenres	
Artist	Genre
Ben Winsh	Metalwork
Ben Winsh	Sculpture
Harriette Laff	Sculpture
Harriette Laff	Textile
Mark Winslow	Sculpture

ArtistShows	
Artist	Show
Ben Winsh	Markers of the Lost Art
Ben Winsh	Trible Confusion
Harriette Laff	Fuzzy Mountain Alpaca Festival
Harriette Laff	Tribal Confusion
Mark Winslow	Green Mountain Arts Festival

ShowGenres	
Show	Genre
Fuzzy Mountain Alpaca Festival	Textile
Green Mountain Arts Festival	Sculpture
Markers of the Lost Art	Metalwork
Markers of the Lost Art	Sculpture
Tribal Confusion	Metalwork
Tribal Confusion	Sculpture

Figure 7-25

Domain/Key Normal Form (DKNF)

A table is in DKNF if:

1. The table contains no constraints except domain constraints and key constraints.

In other words, a table is on DKNF if every constraint is a consequence of domain and key constraints.

Recall from Chapter 3 that a field's domain consists of its allowed values. A domain constraint simply means that a field has a value that is in its domain. It's easy to check that a domain constraint is satisfied by simply examining all of the field's values.

A key constraint means the values in the fields that make up a key are unique.

So if a table is in DKNF, to validate all constraints on the data it is sufficient to validate the domain constraints and key constraints.

For example, consider a typical Employees table with fields FirstName, LastName, Street, City, State, and Zip. There is a hidden constraint between Street/City/State and Zip because a particular Street/City/State defines a ZIP Code and a ZIP Code defines City/State. You could validate new addresses in a table-level check constraint that looked up Street/City/State/Zip to make sure it was a valid combination.

This table contains a constraint that is neither a domain constraint nor a key constraint so it is not in DKNF.

You can make the table DKNF by simply removing the Zip field. Now instead of validating a new Street/City/State/Zip, you look up the address's ZIP Code whenever you need it. (You would use whatever method you had been using before to validate the ZIP Code. For example, if the table-level check constraint was looking it up in a table, you would use that table to look it up now.)

It can be proven (although not by me) that a database in DKNF is immune to all data anomalies. So why would you bother with lesser forms of normalization? Mostly because it can be confusing and difficult to build a database in DKNF. (For example, there are about 45,000 U.S. ZIP Codes and they are constantly changing. That would make a whopper of a table and a maintenance nightmare!)

Lesser forms of normalization also usually give good enough results for most practical database applications so there's no need for DKNF under most circumstances.

However, it's nice to know what DKNF means so you won't feel left out at cocktail parties when everyone else is talking about DKNF.

Try It Out   Arranging Data in the Domain/Key Normal Form

Consider the following student/class assignment table:

Student	Class	Department
Annette Silver	First Order Logic	Philosophy
Annette Silver	Real Analysis II	Mathematics
Janet Wilkes	Fluid Dynamics I	Physics
Janet Wilkes	Real Analysis II	Mathematics
Mark Hardaway	First Order Logic	Philosophy
Mark Hardaway	Topology I	Mathematics

This table has a dependency between Class and Department because each class is within a single department.

To ace this class:

1. Explain why this table is not in DKNF.
2. Explain how you could put the table in DKNF.
3. Draw a relational model for the result.
4. Show the table(s) you create containing the original data.

How It Works

1. Explain why table is not in DKNF.

    The dependency between Class and Department is not a domain constraint or a key constraint.

2. Explain how you could put the table in DKNF.

    Pull the Department data out of the table and make a new table to relate Department and Class. Now instead of storing the Department data in the original table, you store only the Student and Class. When you need to know the Department, you look it up in the new table.

3. Draw a relational model for the result.

    Figure 7-26 shows a relational model in DKNF.

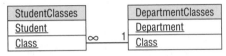

Figure 7-26

4. Show the table(s) you create containing the original data.

    Figure 7-27 shows the new tables holding the original data.

StudentClasses			DepartmentClasses	
Student	Class		Class	Department
Annette Silver	First Order Logic		First Order Logic	Philosophy
Mark Hardaway	First Order Logic		Fluid Dynamics I	Physics
Janet Wilkes	Fluid Dynamics I		Real Analysis II	Mathematics
Annette Silver	Real Analysis II		Topology I	Mathematics
Janet Wilkes	Real Analysis II			
Mark Hardaway	Topology I			

Figure 7-27

Essential Redundancy

One of the major data anomaly themes is redundancy. If a table contains a lot of redundant data, it's probably vulnerable to data anomalies, particularly modification anomalies.

However, this is not true if the redundant data is in keys. For example, look again at Figure 7-27. The StudentClasses table contains several repeated student names and class names. Similarly the DepartmentClasses table contains repeated Department names. You might think these create a modification anomaly hazard.

In fact, if you look at Figure 7-26, you'll see that all of these fields are all part of the tables' keys. Their repetition is necessary to represent the data that the tables hold. For example, the repeated Department values in the DepartmentClasses table are part of the data showing which departments hold which classes. Similarly the repeated Student and Class data in the StudentClasses table is needed to represent the students' class assignments.

Though these repeated values are necessary, they do create a different potential problem. Suppose you want to change the name of the class "Real Analysis II" to "Getting Real, the Sequel" because you think it will make more students sign up for it.

Unfortunately you're not supposed to change the value of a primary key. If you could change the value, you might need to update a large number of records and that could lead to problems like any other modification anomaly would.

The real problem here is that you decided that the class's name should be changed. Because you can't change key values, the solution is to use something else instead of the class's name for the key. Typically a database will use an arbitrary ID number to represent the entity and then move the real data (in this case the class's name) into another table. Because the ID is arbitrary, you should never need to change it.

Figure 7-28 shows one way to replace these fields used as keys with arbitrary IDs that you will never need to change.

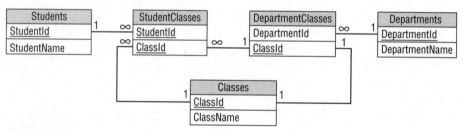

Figure 7-28

For bonus points, you can notice that you can combine the DepartmentClasses and Classes tables to give the simpler model shown in Figure 7-29.

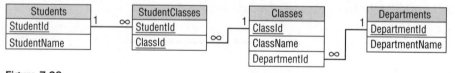

Figure 7-29

This is a reasonable model. Each table represents a single, well-defined entity (student, class, department, and the relationship between students and classes).

The Best Level of Normalization

Domain/Key Normal Form makes a database provably immune to data anomalies, but it can be tricky to implement and it's not usually necessary. The higher levels of normalization may also require you to split tables into many pieces, making it harder and more time-consuming to reassemble the pieces when you need them.

For example, the previous section explained that an Employees table containing Street, City, State, and Zip fields was not in DKNF because the Street/City/State combination duplicates some of the information in the Zip field. The solution was to remove the Zip field and to look up an employee's ZIP Code whenever it was needed. To see whether this change is reasonable, look at the costs and benefits.

The extra cost is that you must perform an extra lookup every time you need to display an employee's address with the ZIP Code. Just about any time you display an employee's address you will need the ZIP Code, so you will probably perform this lookup a lot.

The benefit is that it makes the data less susceptible to data modification anomalies if you need to change a ZIP Code value. But how often do ZIP Codes change? On a national level, ZIP Codes change all the time but unless you have millions of employees, your employees' ZIP Codes probably won't change all that frequently. This seems like a rare problem. It is probably better to use a table-level check constraint to validate the Street/City/State/Zip combination when the employee's data is created or modified and then leave well enough alone. On the rare occasion when a ZIP Code really does change, you can do the extra work to update all of the employees' ZIP Codes.

Often 3NF reduces the chances of anomalies to a reasonable level without requiring confusing and complex modifications to the database's structure.

When you design your database, put it in 3NF. Then look for redundancy that could lead to anomalies. If the kinds of changes that would cause problems in your application seem like they may happen often, then you can think about using the more advanced normalizations. If those sorts of modifications seem rare, you may prefer to leave the database less normalized.

Summary

Normalization is the process of rearranging a database's table designs to prevent certain kinds of data anomalies. Different levels of normalization protect against different kinds of errors.

If every table represents a single, clearly defined entity, you've already gone a long way toward making your database safe from data anomalies. You can use normalization to further safeguard the database.

In this chapter you learned about:

❑   Different kinds of anomalies that can afflict a database.

❑   Different levels of normalization and the anomalies they prevent.

❑   Methods for normalizing database tables.

The next chapter discusses another way you can reduce the chances of errors entering a database. It explains design techniques other than normalization that can make it safer for a software application to manipulate the database.

Before you move on to Chapter 8, however, use the following exercises to test your understanding of the material covered in this chapter. You can find the solutions to these exercises in Appendix A.

Exercises

1. Suppose a student contact list contains the fields Name, Email, Email, Phone1, PhoneType1, Phone2, PhoneType2, and MajorOrSchool. The student's preferred email address is listed in the first Email field. Similarly the preferred phone number is in the Phone1 field. The MajorOrSchool field stores the student's major if he or she has picked one and the student's school (School of Engineering, School of Liberal Arts, School of Metaphysics, and so forth) otherwise.

    a. Explain why this list isn't in 1NF.

    b. Convert it into 1NF. Draw a relational diagram for it.

2. Consider the following table that lists errands that you need to run. The list shows the most important items at the top.

Location	Items
Grocery store	milk, eggs, bananas
Office supply store	paper, pencils, divining rod
Post Office	stamps
Computer store	flash drive, 8″ floppy disks

    a. Explain why this list isn't in 1NF.

    b. Convert this list into a single 1NF table. Be sure to define a primary key.

3. For the table you built for Exercise 2:

    a. Explain why the table isn't in 2NF.

    b. Convert the table into 2NF.

4. Consider the following employee assignments table, which uses Employee as its primary key.

Employee	Project	Department
Alice Most	Work Assignment	Network Lab
Bill Michaels	Network Routing	Network Lab
Deanna Fole	Survey Design	Human Factors
Josh Farfar	Work Assignment	Network Lab

Employee	Project	Department
Julie Wish	Survey Design	Human Factors
Mandy Ponem	Network Routing	Network Lab
Mike Mix	New Services Analysis	Human Factors

    a. Explain why the table isn't in 3NF.

    b. Convert the table into 3NF.

5. One of your friends has decided to start a breakfast club. What each member can cook depends on his or her skills and equipment. Your friend built the following table to record all of the combinations.

Person	Food	Tool
Alice	Muffins	Muffin tin
Alice	Muffins	Omelet pan
Alice	Muffins	Pancake griddle
Alice	Omelets	Muffin tin
Alice	Omelets	Omelet pan
Alice	Omelets	Pancake griddle
Alice	Pancakes	Muffin tin
Alice	Pancakes	Omelet pan
Alice	Pancakes	Pancake griddle
Bob	Muffins	Omelet pan
Bob	Omelets	Omelet pan
Bob	Pancakes	Omelet pan
Cyndi	Omelets	Muffin tin
Cyndi	Omelets	Pancake griddle

Fortunately you know all about normalization, so help your friend by:

    a. Explaining why the table isn't in 5NF.

    b. Converting the table into 5NF.

6. In Figure 7-30, match the normal forms on the left with their corresponding rules on the right.

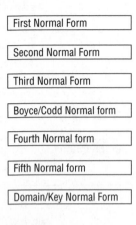

First Normal Form

Second Normal Form

Third Normal Form

Boyce/Codd Normal form

Fourth Normal form

Fifth Normal form

Domain/Key Normal Form

• It contains no transitive dependencies.
• It does not contain an unrelated multi-valued dependency.
• Each column must have a unique name.   • The order of the rows and columns doesn't matter.   • Each column must have a single data type.   • No two rows can contain identical values.   • Each column must contain a single value.   • Columns cannot contain repeating groups.
• All of the non-key fields depend on all of the key fields.
• Every determinant is a candidate key.
• It contains no related multi-valued dependencies.
• The table contains no constraints except domain constraints and key constraints.

Figure 7-30

Designing Databases to Support Software Applications

The previous chapters showed how to gather user requirements, build a database model, and normalize the database to improve its performance and robustness. Those chapters showed how to look at the database from the customers' perspective, from the end user's perspective, and from a database normalization perspective, but there's one other point of view that you should consider before you open your database product and start slapping tables together: the programmer's.

You may not be responsible for writing a program to work with a database. The database may not ever directly interact with a program (although that's rare). In any case, the techniques that you would use to make a database easier for a program to use often apply to other situations. Learning how to help a database support software applications can make the database easier to use in general.

In this chapter you learn:

❑   Steps you can take to make the database more efficient in practical use.

❑   Methods for making validation easier in the user interface.

❑   Ways to easily manage non-searchable data.

This chapter describes several things that you can do to make the database more program-friendly.

A few of these ideas (such as multi-tier architecture) have been covered in earlier chapters. They are repeated in brief here to tie them together with other programming-related topics, but you should refer to the original chapters for more detailed information.

Plan Ahead

Any complicated task benefits from prior planning, and software development is no exception. It has been shown that the longer an error remains in a project the longer it takes to fix it. Database design occurs very early in the development process, so mistakes made here can be very costly. A badly designed database provides the perfect proving ground for the expression, "Act in haste, repent at leisure." Do your work up front or be prepared to spend a lot of extra time fixing mistakes.

Practically all later development depends directly or indirectly on the database design. The database design acts like a building's foundation. If you build a weak foundation, the building on top of it will be wobbly and unsound. The Leaning Tower of Pisa is a beautiful result built on a weak foundation, but it's the result of luck more than planning and people have spent hundreds of years trying to keep it from falling down. If you try to build on a wobbly foundation, you're more likely to end up with a pile of broken rubble than an interesting building.

After you get some experience with database design, it's very tempting to just start cranking out table and field definitions without any prior planning, but that's almost always a mistake. Don't immediately start building a database or even creating a relational object model. At least sketch out an ER diagram to better understand the entities that the database must represent before you start building.

Document Everything

Write everything down. This helps prevent disagreements about who promised what to whom. ("But you promised that the database could look up a customer's credit rating and Amazon password.")

Good documentation also keeps everyone on the same wavelength. If you have done a good job of writing requirements, use cases, database models, design specifications, and all of the other paperwork that describes the system, the developers can scurry off into their own little burrows and start working on their parts of the system without fear of building components that won't work together.

You can make programmers' lives a lot easier if you specify table and field definitions in great detail. Write down the fields that belong in each table. Also write down each field's properties: name, data type, length, whether it can be null, string format (such as "mm/dd/yyyy" or "###-####"), allowed ranges (1–100), default values, and other more complex constraints.

Programmers will need this information to figure out how to build the user interface and the code that sits behind it (and the middle tiers if you use a multi-tier architecture). Make sure the information is correct and complete at the start so the programmers don't need to make a bunch of changes later.

For example, suppose Price must be greater than $1.00. The programmers get started and build a whole slew of screens that assume Price is greater than $1.00. Now it turns out that you meant Price must be *at least* $1.00 not *greater than* $1.00. This is a trivial change to the design and to the database but the programmers will need to go fix the whole bunch of screens that contain the incorrect assumption. (Actually, good programming practices will minimize the problem, but you can't assume everyone is a top-notch developer.)

After you have all of this information, don't just put it in the database and assume that everyone can get the information from there. Believe it or not, some developers don't know how to use every conceivable type of database product (MySQL, SQL Server, Access, Informix, Oracle, DB2, Paradox, Sybase, PostgreSQL, FoxPro — there are hundreds) so making them dig this information out of the database can be a time-consuming hassle. Besides, writing it all up gives you something to show management to prove that you're making progress.

Consider Multi-Tier Architecture

A multi-tier architecture can help isolate the database and user interface development so programmers and database developers can work independently. This approach can also make a database more flexible and amenable to change. Unless you're a project architect, you probably can't decide to use this kind of architecture by yourself but you can make sure it is considered. See Chapter 6 for more details about multi-tier architectures.

Convert Domains into Tables

It's easy enough to validate a field against its domain by using check constraints. For example, suppose you know that the Addresses table's State field must always hold one of the values CA, OR, or WA. You can verify that a field contains one of those values with a field-level check constraint. In Access, you could set the State field's Validation Rule property to:

```
='CA' Or ='OR' Or ='WA'
```

Other databases use different syntax.

Although this is simple and it's easy for you to change, it's not easily visible to programmers building the application. That means they need to write those values into the code. Later if you change the list, the programmers need to change the code.

Even worse, someone needs to remember that the code needs to be changed! It's fairly common to change one part of an application and forget to make a corresponding change elsewhere. Those kinds of mistakes can lead to some bugs that are very hard bugs.

A better approach is to move the domain information into a new table. Create a States table and put the values CA, OR, and WA in it. Then make a foreign key constraint that requires the Addresses table's States field to allow only values that are in the States table. Programmers can query the database at run time to learn what values are allowed and can then do things such as making a combo box that allows only those choices. Now if you need to change the allowed values, you only need to update the States table's data and the program automatically picks up the change.

Wherever possible, convert database structure into data so everyone can read it easily.

Try It Out   **Lookup Tables**

Okay, this is really easy but it's important so bear with me. Suppose your Phoenician restaurant offers delivery service for customers with ZIP Codes between 02154 and 02159. In Access, you could validate the customer's Zip field with the following field-level check constraint:

```
>='02154' And <='02159'
```

Unfortunately that constraint is hidden from the programmers building the user interface. These checks may also not be in a form that's easy for the program to understand. Most programmers don't know how to open Access, read a field's check constraints, and parse an expression such as this one to figure out what it does.

How could you make this condition easier for programmers to discover and use at run time?

How It Works

Though reading and parsing check constraints is hard, it's fairly easy for a program to read the values from a table. The answer is to make a DeliveryZips table that lists the ZIP Codes in the delivery area:

Zip
02154
02155
02156
02157
02158
02159

This seems less elegant than the field-level check constraint but it's a lot easier for the program to understand.

Keep Tables Focused

If you keep each table well-focused, there will be fewer chances for misunderstandings. Different developers will have an easier time keeping each table's purpose straight so different parts of the application will use the data in the same (intended) way.

Modern object-oriented programming languages also use objects and classes that are very similar to the objects and classes used in semantic object modeling and that are similar to the entities and entity sets used by entity-relationship diagrams. If you do a good job of modeling, and keep object and table definitions well-focused, those models practically write the code by themselves. There are still plenty of other things for the programmers to do but at least they'll be able to make programming object models that closely resemble the database structure.

Use Three Kinds of Tables

One tip that can help you keep tables focused is to note that there are three basic kinds of tables. The first kind stores information about objects of a particular type. These hold the bulk of the application's data.

The second kind of table represents a link between two or more objects. For example, the association tables described in Chapter 5 represent a link between two types of objects.

Figure 8-1 shows an ER diagram to model employees and projects. Each employee can be assigned to multiple projects and each project can involve multiple employees. The EmployeeRoles table provides a link between the other two object tables. It also stores additional information about the link. In this case, it stores the role that an employee played on each project.

Figure 8-1

The third basic kind of table is a lookup table. These are tables created simply to use in foreign key constraints. For example, the States table described in the earlier section "Convert Domains into Tables" is a lookup table.

When you build a table, ask yourself whether it represents an object, a link, or a lookup. If you cannot decide or if the table represents more than one of those, the table's purpose may not be clearly defined.

Try It Out   **Well-Focused Tables**

Take a look at the following table of extra-terrestrial animals:

Animal	Size	Planet	PlanetaryMass
Hermaflamingo	Medium	Virgon 4	1.21
Shunkopotamus	Large	Dilbertopia	0.88
Mothalope	Medium	Xanth	0.01
Shunkopotamus	Large	Virgon 4	1.21
Platypus	Small	Australia	1.00

The table's primary key is the combination of Animal/Planet. (The PlanetaryMass field is measured in Earth masses.)

This isn't a very well-focused table.

1. What ideas is this table is trying to capture?
2. What types of ideas are these (object, link, or lookup)?
3. Suggest a better design that keeps the table's separate purposes separate.

How It Works

1. What ideas is this table is trying to capture?

    This table is trying to capture three different ideas: information about the animals (Animal and Size), information about planets (Planet and PlanetaryMass), and the associations between the animals and planets. The fact that this table holds information about three different concepts is a sign that it is not well-focused.

(Also note this table is not in Second Normal Form because it has non-key fields that do not depend on the entire key. Recall that the primary key is Animal/Planet. The Size field depends on Animal but not Planet, and the PlanetaryMass field depends on Planet but not Animal.)

2. What types of ideas are these (object, link, or lookup)?

Information about the animals and information about the planets represent objects. Information about the associations between animals and planets is a link.

3. Suggest a better design that keeps the table's separate purposes separate.

The key is to move the three kinds of information into three different tables. Figure 8-2 shows one relational design that separates the three sets of information into three tables.

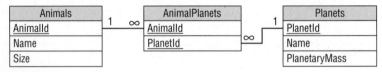

Figure 8-2

Figure 8-3 shows the tables holding their original data.

Animals				AnimalPlanets			Planets		
Size	Animal	AnimalId		AnimalId	PlanetId		PlanetId	HomePlanet	PlanetaryMass
Medium	Hermaflamingo	1		1	101		101	Virgon 4	1.21
Large	Shunkopotamus	2		2	102		102	Dilbertopia	0.88
Medium	Mothalope	3		3	103		103	Xanth	0.01
Small	Platypus	4		2	101		104	Australia	1.00
				4	104				

Figure 8-3

Use Naming Conventions

Use consistent naming conventions when you name database objects. It doesn't matter too much what conventions you use as long as you use something consistent.

Some database developers prefix table names with tbl and field names with fld as in, "The tblEmployees table contains the fldFirstName and fldLastName fields." For simple databases, I prefer to omit the prefixes because it's usually easy enough to tell which names represent objects (tables) and which represent attributes (fields).

Some developers also use a lnk prefix for tables that represent a link between objects as in, "The lnkAnimalsPlanets table links tblAnimals and tblPlanets." These developers are also likely to use lu or lup as a prefix for lookup tables.

Some developers prefer to use UPPERCASE_LETTERS for table names and lowercase_letters for field names. Others use MixedCase for both.

Some prefer to make table names singular (the Employee table) and others prefer to make them plural (the Employees table).

As I said, it doesn't matter too much which of these conventions you use as long as you pick some conventions and stick to them.

However, there are three "mandatory" naming rules that you should follow or the other developers will snicker behind your back and openly mock you at parties.

First, don't use special characters in table names, field names, or anywhere else in database objects. For example, some databases (such as Access) allow you to include spaces in table and field names. For example, you can make a field named "First Name." Those databases also provide some mechanism for making these weird names readable to the database. For example, in Access you need to use square brackets to surround a field with a name containing spaces as in "[First Name]." This produces hard-to-read expressions in check constraints and anywhere else you use the field. It also makes programmers using the field take similar annoying steps and that makes their code less readable, too.

Second, if two fields in different tables contain the same data, give them the same name. For example, suppose you use an ID field to link the Employees table to the EmployeePhones table. Don't call this linking field Id in the Employees table and EmpId in the EmployeePhones table. That's just asking for trouble. Call the field EmployeeId in both tables. (A corollary to this rule is that you cannot name an ID field something vague such as Id. It may make sense in the main table such as Employees but that name won't make sense in a related table such as EmployeePhones.)

The third mandatory naming rule is to use meaningful names. Don't abbreviate to the point of obscurity. It shouldn't take a team of National Security Agency cryptographers to decipher a table's field names. StudPrfCrs is much harder to read than StudentPreferredCourses. Don't be afraid to spell things out so everyone can understand them. (The exception here seems to be the military where everyone would understand "SecInt visited NavSpecWarGru" but saying "the Secretary of the Interior visited the Naval Special War Group" would brand you as an outsider.)

The section "Poor Naming Standards" in Chapter 10 has more to say about naming conventions and includes a few links that you can follow to learn about some specific standards that you can adopt if you like.

Allow Some Redundant Data

Chapter 7 explained that it is not always best to normalize a database as completely as possible. The higher forms of normalization usually spread data out into tables that are linked by their fields. When a program needs to display that data, it must reassemble all of that scattered data and that can take some extra time.

For example, if you allow customers to have any number of phone numbers, email addresses, postal addresses, and contacts, then what seems to the user like a simple customer record is actually spread across the Customers, CustomerPhones, CustomerEmails, CustomerAddresses, and CustomerContacts tables.

In some cases, it may be better to restrict the database's flexibility somewhat to gain speed and simplicity. For example, if you allow the customers to have only two phone numbers, one email address, and one contact, you cut the number of tables that make up the customer's information from five to two. The database won't be as infinitely flexible and it won't be quite as completely normalized, but it will be easier to use.

Usually it's also best not to store the same data in multiple ways because that can lead to modification anomalies. For example, you don't really need a Balance field in a customer's record if you can recalculate the balance by adding up all of the customer's credits and debits.

However, suppose you're running an Internet service that allows customers to download music so a typical customer makes dozens or even hundreds of purchases a month. After a year or two, adding up all of a customer's credits and debits could be time consuming. In this case, you might be better off adding a Balance field to the customer's record and exercising a little extra caution when updating the account.

Don't Squeeze in Everything

Just because you're using a database doesn't mean every piece of data that the system uses must be squeezed in there somewhere. Databases provide tools for storing and retrieving some strange pieces of data such as audio, video, images — just about anything you can cram into a computer file. That doesn't mean you should go crazy and store every file on your computer within the database.

For example, suppose an application must locate and play thousands of audio files. You could store all of them in the database or you could place the files in a directory tree somewhere and then store the locations of those files in the database. That makes the database simpler, smaller, and possibly more efficient because it doesn't need to store all of those files. It also makes it a lot easier to update the files. Instead of loading a new file into the database, you can simply replace the file on the disk.

This technique can also be useful for managing large amounts of shared data such as Web pages. You don't need to copy Wikipedia pages into your database (in fact, it would probably be a copyright violation). Instead you can store the URLs pointing to the pages you need. In this case you give up control of the data but you also don't have to store and maintain it yourself. If the data is updated, you'll see the new data the next time you visit a URL.

There are only a couple of drawbacks to this technique. First, you lose the ability to search inside any data that is not stored inside the database. I don't know of any databases that let you search inside video, audio, or jpeg data, however, so you probably shouldn't lose much sleep over giving up an ability that you don't have anyway. I wouldn't move textual data outside the database in this way, however, unless you're sure you'll never want to search inside it.

Second, you give up some of the security provided by the database. For example, you lose the database's record-locking features so you may have trouble allowing multiple concurrent users to update the data.

Try It Out   **First Normal Form**

Suppose you're building a database of amusing commercials (see www.veryfunnyads.com and giesbers.net/video for some good ones). The Commercials table includes the fields Name, Product, Description, Length, Video (the commercial), and Still (a representative frame to remind you what the commercial is about).

Figure out which of these fields should remain in the database and which might be moved outside into the file system:

1.   To figure out which fields should remain in the database, identify those that you might want to search. Include fields with simple values (such as numbers and short strings) that are easy to store in a database but that would not make a very big file on the disk.

2.   To figure out which fields might be moved outside of the database into the file system, identify the fields that contain large chunks of non-searchable data.

How It Works

1.   In this database, you might want to search the Name, Product, Description, and Length fields.

2.   You cannot search the Video or Still fields whether you want to or not so you might as well move them into the file system. The Video field will contain particularly large amounts of data so moving it outside of the database might even make the database more efficient.

Summary

Though the focus of this book and your database design efforts is on databases, a database rarely lives in total isolation. Usually someone writes a program to interact with it. Often the database is just a backend for a complicated user interface.

To get the most out of your database, you need to consider it in its environment. In particular, you should think about the applications and programmers who will interact with it. Often a few relatively small changes to the design can make life easier for everyone who works with the database.

In this chapter you learned to:

❏   Plan ahead and document everything.

❏   Convert domains into tables to help user interface programmers and to make maintaining domain information easier.

❏   Keep tables well-focused and make each perform a single task.

❏   Use some redundancy and denormalized tables to improve performance.

The last several chapters dealt with database design techniques and considerations. Those chapters explained general techniques for building a data model and then modifying it to make it more efficient.

The next chapter switches from general discussion to more specific techniques. It summarizes some of the methods described in the previous chapters and explains some common database design patterns that you may find useful in providing specific data features.

Before you move on to Chapter 9, however, use the following exercises to test your understanding of the material covered in this chapter. You can find the solutions to these exercises in Appendix A.

Exercises

1. Suppose you sell ocean cruises. Customers first decide what kind of Ship they want to travel on: Luxury Liner, Schooner, or Tuna Boat. Depending on that choice, they may select different classes of cabins. Luxury Liners provide 1st through 5th class. Schooners have 1st and 2nd class (basically a single or a double), and Tuna Boats have a single class (which they playfully call 1st Class) where you share a single large bunkroom with the rest of the crew.

   You could validate the Trips record's Ship and Cabin fields by using a table-level check constraint but, because you're a team player, you would rather build a foreign key constraint so the user interface can read the allowed values from the tables.

   Build such a table and display its data. Explain how this table will be used in the foreign key constraint.

2. Figure 8-4 shows a relational diagram showing the relationships between students, the classes they are taking, and the departments that hold the classes. For each table in this diagram, tell which of the three types of table it is: object, link, or lookup.

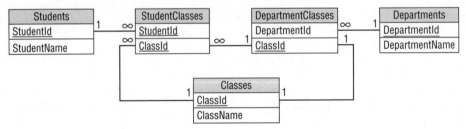

Figure 8-4

3. The following table stores information about checkers matches. Explain why it lacks focus and how you would fix it.

Player1	Player1Rank	Player2	Player2Rank	MatchTime
Smith	10	Jones	3	1:00
Marks	9	Lars	4	1:00
Aft	8	Cook	5	2:00
Mauren	7	Juno	6	2:00

4. Assume you have a large database that tracks how closely airplanes are to their scheduled departure and landing times. It tracks these values by plane (which is associated with a particular airline) and airport. It also records the weather at the starting and landing airports.

    Which of the following values should you store in a redundant variable and which should you calculate as needed?

    a. Average minutes late for an airline at a particular airport.

    b. Average minutes late for all airlines at a particular airport.

    c. Average minutes late for an airline across the country.

    d. Average minutes late for all airlines across the entire country.

    Assume that you need these numbers quickly several times per day.

Common Design Patterns

The previous chapters described general techniques for building database designs. For example, Chapter 5 explained how to build semantic object models and entity-relationship diagrams for a database, and how to convert those models into relational designs. Chapter 7 explained how to transform those designs to normalize the database.

This chapter takes a different approach. It focuses on data design scenarios and describes methods for building them in a relational model.

In this chapter you learn techniques for:

- ❏ Providing different kinds of associations between objects.
- ❏ Storing data hierarchies and networks.
- ❏ Handling time-related data.
- ❏ Logging user actions.

This chapter does not provide designs for specific situations such as order tracking or employee payroll. Appendix B, "Sample Database Designs," contains those sorts of examples.

This chapter focuses on a more detailed level to give you the techniques you need to build the pieces that make up a design. You can use these techniques as the beginning of a database design toolbox that you can apply to your problems.

The following sections group these patterns into three broad categories: associations, temporal data, and logging and locking.

Associations

Association patterns represent relationships among various data objects. For example, an association can represent the relationship between a rugby team and its opponents during matches.

The following sections describe different kinds of associations.

Many-to-Many Associations

It's easy to represent a many-to-many association in an ER diagram. For example, a Student can be enrolled in many Courses and a Course includes many Students, so there is a many-to-many relationship between Students and Courses. Figure 9-1 shows an ER diagram modeling this situation.

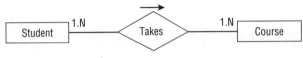

Figure 9-1

Unfortunately relational databases cannot handle many-to-many relationships directly. To build this kind of relationship in a relational database, you need to add an association table to represent the relationship between students and courses. Simply create a table called StudentCourses and give it fields StudentId and CourseId. Figure 9-2 shows this structure.

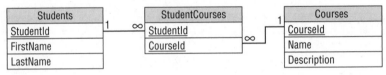

Figure 9-2

To list all of the courses for a particular student, find the StudentCourses records with that Student Id. Then use each of those records' CourseId values to find the corresponding Courses records.

To list all of the students enrolled in a particular course, find the StudentCourses records with that CourseId. Then use each of those records' StudentId values to find the corresponding Students records.

Multiple Many-to-Many Associations

Sometimes a many-to-many relationship contains extra associated data. For example, the previous section explained how to track students and their current course enrollments. Suppose you also want to track student enrollments over time. In other words, you want to know each student's enrollments for each year and semester. In this case, you really need to make multiple many-to-many associations between students and courses. You need whole sets of these associations to handle each school semester.

Fortunately this requires only a small change to the previous solution. The StudentCourses table shown in Figure 9-2 can already represent the relationship of students to courses. The only thing missing is a way to add more records to this table to store information for different years and semesters.

The solution is to add Year and Semester fields to the StudentCourses table. Figure 9-3 shows the new model.

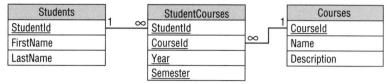

Figure 9-3

Now the StudentCourses table can store multiple sets of records representing different years and semesters.

If you need to store extra information about each semester, you could make a new Semesters table to hold that information. Then you could add the Year and Semester fields to this new table and use them as a foreign key in the StudentCourses table.

Try It Out Many-to-Many Relations

Suppose you're coordinating a week-long tour called "Junk Yards of the Napa Valley." Each day, the participants can sign up for several tours of different junk yards. They can also sign up for dinner at a fine restaurant or winery.

Build a relational model to record this information.

1. Build Participants, Tours, and Restaurants tables.

2. Study the relationships between Participants and Tours, and between Participants and Restaurants. Determine whether they are many-to-many or some other kind of relationship.

3. Build a relationship table to represent each many-to-many relationship. Be sure to include enough fields to distinguish among similar combinations of the involved tables. (For example, Bill really liked the trip to Annette's Scrap and Salvage on Tuesday so he took that tour again on Thursday.) Your model needs a ParticipantTours table and a ParticipantRestaurants table. To distinguish among repeats such as Bill's, add a Date field to each table.

How It Works

1. There's no real trick in Step 1. Just be sure to give each table an ID field so it's easy to refer to its records.

2. To understand Step 2, remember that each participant can go on many tours and each tour can have many participants so the Participants/Tours relationship is many-to-many. During the week, each participant can eat at several restaurants and each restaurant can feed many participants, so the Participants/Restaurants relationship is also many-to-many.

3. To model the two many-to-many relationships, the model needs a ParticipantTours table and a ParticipantRestaurants table. To distinguish among repeats (a customer takes the same tour twice or visits the same restaurant twice), add a Date field to each table.

Figure 9-4 shows the final relational model.

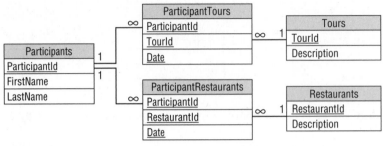

Figure 9-4

Multiple-Object Associations

A multiple-object association is one where many different kinds of objects are collectively associated to each other. For example, making a movie requires a whole horde of people including a director, a bunch of actors, and a huge number of crew members. You could model the situation with the ER diagram shown in Figure 9-5.

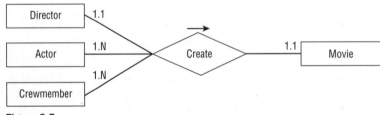

Figure 9-5

If this collection of people always worked as a team, this situation would be easy to implement in a relational model. You would assign all of the people a TeamId and then build a Movies table with a TeamId field to tell who worked on that movie.

Unfortunately, this idea doesn't quite work because all of these people can work on any number of movies in any combination.

You can solve this problem by thinking of the complex multi-object relationship as a combination of simpler relationships. In this case, you can model the situation as a one-to-one Director/Movie relationship, a many-to-many Actor/Movie relationship, and a many-to-many Crewmember/Movie relationship.

Figure 9-6 shows the new ER diagram.

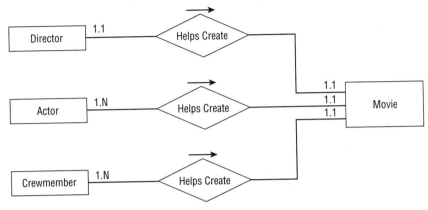

Figure 9-6

You can convert this simpler diagram into a relational model as shown in Figure 9-7.

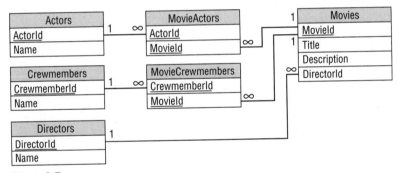

Figure 9-7

Notice that this model uses two association tables to represent the two many-to-many relationships. The relationship between Directors and Movies doesn't require an association table because this is a simpler one-to-one relationship.

Try It Out   Building Multiple-Object Associations

Consider another aspect of the "Junk Yards of the Napa Valley" tours. You have multiple tour guides and multiple vehicles. A Trip represents a specific instance of a tour by a guide, vehicle, and a group of participants.

Build a relational model to hold this data.

1.   Build Guides, Vehicles, Tours, Participants, and Trips tables.

2.   Study the relationships between Trips and Guides, Vehicles, Tours, and Participants. Determine whether they are many-to-many or some other kind of relationship.

3.   Build an ER diagram to show these relationships.

4.   Build a relationship table to represent each many-to-many relationship.

5.   Draw the relational model.

How It Works

1.   There's no real trick in this. Just be sure to give each table an ID field so it's easy to refer to its records.

2.   Each guide can lead several trips but each trip has a single guide, so Guides/Trips is a one-to-many relationship.

   Each vehicle can go on many trips but each trip has a single vehicle, so Vehicles/Trips is a one-to-many relationship.

   A tour represents a destination. A destination can be the target of many trips but each trip visits only one destination, so Tours/Trips is a one-to-many relationship.

   Finally, each participant can go on many trips and each trip can have many participants, so Participants/Trips is a many-to-many relationship.

3.   Figure 9-8 shows these relationships in an ER diagram.

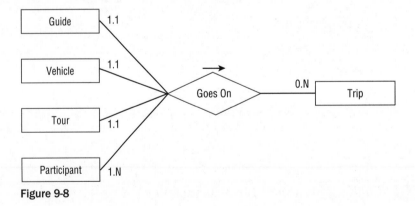

Figure 9-8

4.   This model has only one many-to-many relationship: Participants/Trips. To handle it, the model needs a ParticipantsTrips table.

   Figure 9-9 shows the final relational model.

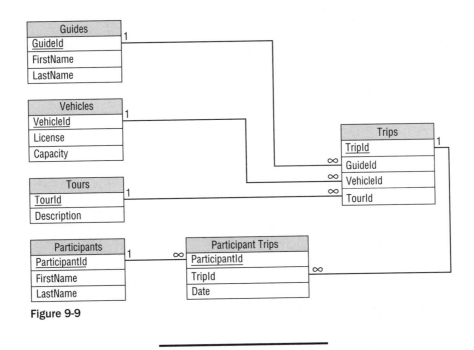

Figure 9-9

Repeated Attribute Associations

Some entities have multiple fields that represent either the same kind of data or a very similar kind of data. For example, it is common for orders and other documents to allow you to specify a daytime phone number and an evening phone number. Other contact-related records may allow you to specify even more phone numbers for such things as cell phone, FAX, pager, and others.

Figure 9-10 shows a semantic object model for a PERSON class that allows any number of Phone attributes.

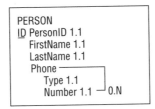

Figure 9-10

To allow any number of a repeated attributes in a relational model, build a new table to contain the repeated values. Use the original table's primary key to link the new records back to the original table.

Figure 9-11 shows how to do this for the PERSON class shown in Figure 9-10.

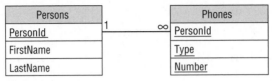

Figure 9-11

Because the Phones table's primary key includes all of the table's fields, the combination of PersonId/Type/Number must be unique. That means a particular person can only use a phone number for a particular purpose once. That makes sense. It would be silly to list the same phone number as a work number twice for the same person. However, a person could have the same number for multiple purposes (daytime and evening number are the same cell phone) or have multiple phone numbers for the same purpose (office and receptionist numbers for work phone).

You can use the primary keys and other keys to enforce other kinds of uniqueness. For example, to prevent someone from using the same number for different purposes, make PersonId/Number a unique key. To prevent someone from providing more than one number for the same purpose (for example, two cell phone numbers), make PersonId/Type a unique key.

For another example, suppose you want to add multiple email addresses to the Persons table. Allow each person to have any number of phone numbers and email addresses of any type, but don't allow duplicate phone numbers or email addresses. (For example, you cannot use the same phone number for Home and Work numbers.)

Just as you created a Phones table, you would create an Emails table with Type and Address fields, plus a PersonId field to link it back to the Persons table. To prevent an email address from being duplicated for a particular person, include those fields in the table's primary key. Figure 9-12 shows the new relational model.

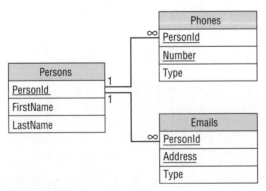

Figure 9-12

Reflexive Associations

A *relflexive* or *recursive* association is one in which an object refers to an object of the same class. You can use recursive associations to model a variety of different situations ranging from simple one-to-one relationships to complicated networks of association.

The following sections describe different kinds of reflexive associations.

One-to-One Reflexive Associations

As you can probably guess, in a one-to-one reflexive association an object refers to another single object of the same class. For example, consider the Person class's Spouse field. A Person can be married to exactly one other person (at least in much of the world) so this is a one-to-one relationship. Figure 9-13 shows an ER diagram representing this relationship.

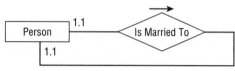

Figure 9-13

Figure 9-14 shows a relational model for this relationship.

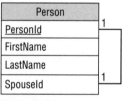

Figure 9-14

Unfortunately this design does not require that two spouses be married to each other. For example, Ann could be married to Bob and Bob could be married to Cindy. That might make an interesting television show, but it would make a confusing database.

Another approach would be to create a Marriage table to represent a marriage. That table would give the IDs of the spouses. Figure 9-15 shows this design.

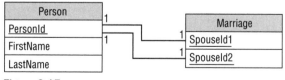

Figure 9-15

In this design the Person table refers to itself indirectly.

For another example, suppose you're making a database that tracks competitive rock-paper-scissors matches (see http://www.usarps.com). You need to associate multiple competitors with each other to show who faced off in the big arena. You also want to record who won and what the winning moves were.

You would start by making a Competitors table with fields Name and CompetitorId.

Next you would make a CompetitorMatches table to link Competitors. This table would contain CompetitorId1 and CompetitorId2 fields, and corresponding FinalMove1 and FinalMove2 fields to record the contestants' final moves. To distinguish among different matches between the same two competitors, the table would also include Date and Time fields.

Figure 9-16 shows the relational model.

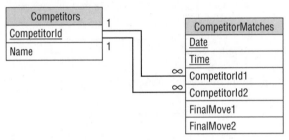

Figure 9-16

One-to-Many Reflexive Associations

Typically employees have managers. Each employee is managed by one manager and a manager can manage any number of employees, so there is a one-to-many relationship between managers and employees.

But a manager is just another employee, so this actually defines a one-to-many relationship between employees and employees. Figure 9-17 shows an ER diagram for this situation.

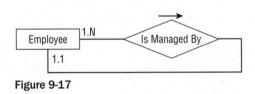

Figure 9-17

Figure 9-18 shows a relational model that handles this situation.

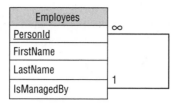

Figure 9-18

Hierarchical Data

Hierarchical data takes the form of tree-like structures. Every object in the hierarchy has a "parent" object of the same type. For example, a corporate organizational chart is a hierarchical data structure that shows which employee reports to which other employee. Figure 9-19 shows the org chart for a fictional company.

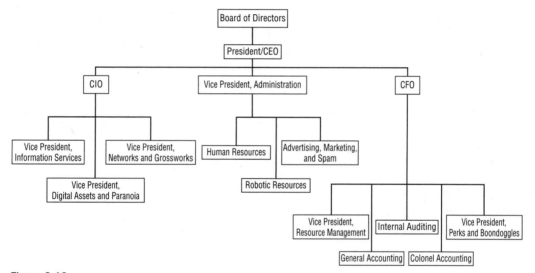

Figure 9-19

Hierarchical data actually is an instance of a one-to-many reflexive association as described in the previous section. Generally people think of the "Is Managed By" relationship as being relatively flat, so managers supervise front-line employees but no one needs to manage the managers. In that case, the hierarchy is very short.

An org chart represents the infinitesimally different concept of "Reports To." I guess this is more palatable to managers who don't mind reporting to someone even if they don't need help managing their own work. (Although I've known a few managers who could have used some serious help in that respect.)

The "Reports To" hierarchy may be much deeper (physically, not necessarily intellectually) than the "Manages" hierarchy but you can still model it in the same way. Figure 9-20 shows an `Employee` class that can model both hierarchies simultaneously.

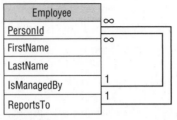

Figure 9-20

Notice that the relationships used to implement a hierarchy are "upward-pointing." In other words, each object contains a reference to an object higher up in the hierarchy. This is necessary because each object has a single "parent" in the hierarchy but may have many "children." Though you can list an object's parent in a single field, you cannot list all of its children in a single field.

Try It Out   Working with Hierarchical Data

The following table contains information about a corporate org chart.

PersonId	Title	ReportsTo
1	Mgr. Pie and Food Gags	9
2	Dir. Puns and Knock-Knock Jokes	6
3	Dir. Physical Humor	9
4	Mgr. Pratfalls	3
5	President	null
6	VP Ambiguity	5
7	Dir. Riddles	6
8	Dir. Sight Gags	3
9	VP Schtik	5

Use this data to reconstruct the org chart graphically.

1. Find the record that represents the root node.
2. For each node on the bottom level of the tree so far (initially this is just the root node), find all of the records that have that node as a parent (ReportsTo). Attach them below their parent. For example, the first time around you would find the people who report to President. Their records have ReportsTo equal to President's PersonId: 5. These people are VP Ambiguity and VP Schtik. Attach them below President.
3. Repeat until you have processed every record.

How It Works

1. The root node is the one that has no parent. In the table, it's the one where ReportsTo is null: President.

2. Draw the root node.

   a. Find the people who report to President. Their records have ReportsTo equal to President's PersonId: 5. These people are VP Ambiguity and VP Schtik. Attach them below President.

   b. Find the people who report to VP Ambiguity. They are Dir. Puns and Knock-Knock Jokes and Dir. Riddles. Draw them below VP Ambiguity.

   c. Find the people who report to VP Schtik. They are Mgr. Pie and Food Gags and Dir. Physical Humor. Draw them below VP Schtik.

   d. Find the people who report to Dir. Puns and Knock-Knock Jokes. There are none so Dir. Puns and Knock-Knock Jokes is a leaf node.

   e. Find the people who report to Dir. Riddles. There are none so Dir. Riddles is a leaf node.

   f. Find the people who report to Mgr. Pie and Food Gags. There are none so Mgr. Pie and Food Gags is a leaf node.

   g. Find the people who report to Dir. Physical Humor. They are Mgr. Pratfalls and Dir. Sight Gags. Draw them below Dir. Physical Humor.

   h. Find the people who report to Mgr. Pratfalls. There are none so Mgr. Pratfalls is a leaf node.

   i. Find the people who report to Dir. Sight Gags. There are none so Dir. Sight Gags is a leaf node.

   At this point, every record is represented on the tree so we're done.

3. Figure 9-21 shows the finished org chart.

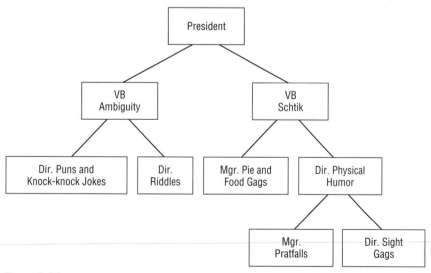

Figure 9-21

Network Data

A network contains objects that are linked in an arbitrary fashion. References in one object point to one or more other objects.

For example, Figure 9-22 shows a street network. Each circle represents a node in the network. An arrow represents a link between two nodes. The numbers give the approximate driving time across a link. Notice the one-way streets with arrows pointing in only one direction.

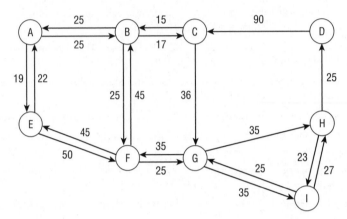

Figure 9-22

An object cannot use simple fields to refer to an arbitrary number of other objects, so this situation requires an intermediate table describing the links between objects.

Figure 9-23 shows an ER diagram describing the network's Node object. Notice that the Connects To relationship has a LinkTime attribute that stores the time needed to cross the link.

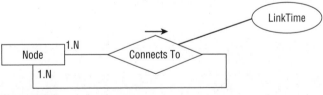

Figure 9-23

The section "Many-to-Many Associations" earlier in this chapter showed how to build a relational model for many-to-many relationships. That method just needs a small twist to make it work for a many-to-many reflexive relationship.

Instead of creating two tables to represent the related objects, just create a single Nodes table. Then create an intermediary table to represent the association between two nodes. That object represents the network link and holds the LinkTime data.

Figure 9-24 shows this design. In addition to a NodeId, the Nodes table contains X and Y coordinates for drawing the node.

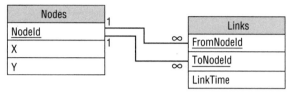

Figure 9-24

Note that you need to use some care when you try to use this data to build a network in a program. One natural approach is to start with a node, follow its links to new nodes, and then repeat the process, following those nodes' links.

Unfortunately if the network contains loops, the program will start running around in circles like a dog chasing its tail and it will never finish.

A better approach is to select all of the Nodes records and make program objects to represent them. Then select all of the Links records. For each Links record, find the objects representing the "from" node and the "to" node and connect them. This method is fast, requires only two queries, and best of all, eventually stops.

For a concrete example, consider the small network shown in Figure 9-25. The numbers next to links show the links' times.

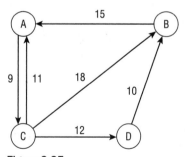

Figure 9-25

Start by making a Nodes table with fields NodeId, X, and Y. The following table shows the Nodes table's values. The X and Y fields are blank here because we're not really going to draw the network, but a real program would fill them in.

NodeId	X	Y
A		
B		
C		
D		

Next make a Links table with fields FromNode and ToNode, plus a LinkTime field. Looking at Figure 9-25, you see which nodes are connected to which others and what their LinkTime values should be. The following table shows the Links table's data.

FromNode	ToNode	LinkTime
A	C	9
B	A	15
C	A	11
C	B	18
C	D	12
D	B	10

Temporal Data

As its name implies, temporal data involves time. For example, suppose you sell produce and the prices vary greatly from month to month (tomatoes are expensive in the winter, while pumpkins are practically worthless on November 1). To keep a complete record of your sales, you not only need to track orders but also the prices at the time each order was placed.

The following sections describe a few time-related database design issues.

(For some more in-depth discussion of some of these issues, you can download the free eBook "Developing Time-Oriented Database Applications in SQL" at http://www.cs.arizona.edu/people/rts/ tdbbook.pdf.)

Effective Dates

One simple way to track an object that changes over time is to add fields to the object giving its valid dates. Those fields give the object's effective or valid dates.

Figure 9-26 shows a relational model for temporal produce orders or orders for any other products with prices that change over time.

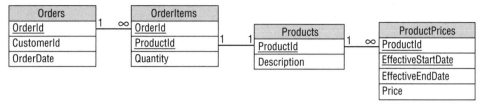

Figure 9-26

The Orders table contains an OrderId field and a Date, in addition to other order information such as CustomerId. The OrderId field provides the link to the OrderItems table.

Each OrderItems record represents one line item in an order. Its ProductId field provides a link to the Products table, which describes the product purchased on this line item. The Quantity field tells the number of items purchased.

The ProductPrices table has a ProductId field that refers back to the Products table. The Price field gives the product's price. The EffectiveStartDate and EffectiveEndDate fields tell when that price was in effect.

To reproduce an order, you would follow these steps:

1. Look up the order in the Orders table and get its OrderId. Record the OrderDate.

2. Find the OrderItems records with that OrderId. For each of those records, record the Quantity and ProductId. Then:

   a. Find the Products record with that ProductId. Use this record to get the item's description.

   b. Find the ProductPrices record with that ProductId and where EffectiveStartDate < = OrderDate < = EffectiveEndDate. Use this record to get the item's price at the time the order was placed.

The result is a *snapshot* of how the order looked at the time it was placed. By digging through all of these tables, you should be able to reproduce every order as it appeared when it was entered into the system.

Suppose you want to store one address for each employee but you want to track addresses over time. You don't want to track any other employee data temporally.

To build a relational model to hold this information, start by creating a basic Employees table that holds EmployeeId, FirstName, LastName, and other fields as usual.

Next design an Addresses table to hold the employee addresses. Create Street, City, State, and Zip fields as usual. Include an EmployeeId field to link back to the Employees record and EffectiveStartDate and EffectiveEndDate fields to track temporal data.

Figure 9-27 shows the resulting relational model.

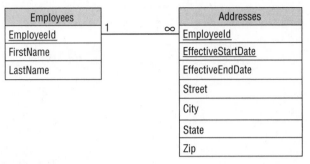

Figure 9-27

Deleted Objects

When you delete a record, the information that the record used to hold is gone forever. If you delete an employee's records, you lose all of the information about that employee including the fact that he was fired for selling your company's secrets to the competition. Because the employee's records were deleted, he could potentially get a job in another part of the company and resume spying with no one the wiser.

Similarly when you modify a record, its previous values are lost. Sometimes that doesn't matter but other times it might be worthwhile to keep the old values around for historical purposes. For example, it might be nice to know that an employee's salary was increased by only 0.25% last year so you might consider a bigger increase this year.

One way to keep all of this data is to never, ever delete or modify records. Instead you use effective dates to "end" the old record. If you're modifying the record rather than deleting it, you would then create a new record with effective dates starting now.

For example, suppose you hired Hubert Phreen on 4/1/2006 for a salary of $45,000. On his first anniversary, you increased his salary to $46,000 and on his second you increased it to $53,000. He then grew spoiled and lazy so he hasn't gotten a raise since. The following table shows the records this scenario would generate in the EmployeeSalaries table. Using this data, you can tell what Hubert's current salary is and what it was at any past point in time.

Employee	Salary	EffectiveStartDate	EffectiveEndDate
Hubert Phreen	$45,000	4/1/2006	4/1/2007
Hubert Phreen	$46,000	4/1/2007	4/1/2008
Hubert Phreen	$53,000	4/1/2008	1/1/3000

(To really be correct, you need to make one of the effective dates be exclusive. For example, you might decide that a record is valid starting on the effective start date up through but not including the effective end date. For example, Hubert's salary was $46,000 from April 1, 2007 through March 31, 2008. Then on April 1, 2008 his salary increased to $53,000.)

Deciding What to Temporalize

If you decide to use effective dates instead of deleting or modifying records, you will end up with a bigger database. Depending on how often these sorts of changes occur, it might be a *much* bigger database.

Disk space is relatively inexpensive these days (as little as $0.22 or so per GB and dropping every year) so that may not be a big issue. If the database is really huge, however, you may want to be selective in what tables you make temporal.

For example, in the model shown in Figure 9-26, only the ProductPrices table has effective dates. That would make sense for that example if you don't allow changes to orders after they are created.

That greatly reduces the amount of data that you will have to duplicate to record changes.

Before you rush out and add effective dates to everything in sight, carefully consider what data is worth saving in this manner.

Be sure to decide which tables to make temporal as early as possible because retrofitting effective date fields can be very difficult, particularly for any programs that access the data. Any queries that request data from tables with effective dates must be parameterized to get the right data. If you add effective date fields after you start development, you need to modify all of those queries and that gives you extra chances to make mistakes and insert bugs in the system.

This is definitely a case where you want thorough planning before you start to build.

Logging and Locking

Two techniques that I've found useful in a number of database applications are audit trails and turnkey records. Audit trails let you log changes to key pieces of data. Turnkey records let you easily control access to groups of related records.

Audit Trails

Many databases contain sensitive data, and it is important to make sure that the data is safe at all times. Though you cannot always prevent a user from incorrectly viewing or modifying the data, you can make a record showing who made a modification. Later, if it turns out that the change was unauthorized, you can hunt down the perpetrator and wreak a terrible vengeance.

> For example, in 2007 State Department contractors "inappropriately reviewed" the passport files of then Senator and presidential candidate Barack Obama. The offenders were probably just curious, but it violated the department's privacy rules so two people were fired and one reprimanded.

One way to provide a record of significant actions is to make an *audit trail* table. This table has fields Action, Employee, and Date to record what was done, who did it, and when it happened. For some applications, this information can be non-specific, for example, recording only that a record was modified and by whom. In other applications, it might record the fields that were modified and the old and new values.

A similar technique works well with the effective dates described in the section "Temporal Data" earlier in this chapter. If you never delete or update records, you can add a CreatedBy field to a table that you want to audit and fill in the name of the user who created the record. Later if someone modifies the record, you will be able to see who made the modification in the new version of the record.

You may still want a separate AuditEvents table, however, to record actions other than creating, deleting, and modifying records. For example, you might want to keep track of who views records (as in the State Department passport case), generates or prints reports, sends emails, or prints letters. You might even want to record user log in and log out times.

Turnkey Records

When a user needs to modify a record, the database locks that record so other users can't see an inconsistent view of the data. This prevents others from seeing a half-completed operation.

Relational databases also provide transactions that allow one user to perform a series of actions atomically — as if they were a single operation. This effectively locks all of the records involved in those actions until the transaction is complete.

Though these features work well, their record-locking behaviors can lead to a couple of problems.

First, most databases won't tell you who has a record locked. If someone is in the middle of editing a record in the Employees table, you won't be able to edit that record. Unfortunately the database also won't tell you that Frank has the record locked so you can't go down the hall and ask him to release it. Or worse, you'll discover that Frank left his computer locked and went home for an early weekend so you're stuck until Monday. In that case, it will require database administrator powers and an act of Congress to unlock the record so you can get some work done.

A second issue is that a complicated series of locks adds to the database's load.

One technique I've found useful for addressing these problems is to use turnkey records to control access to a group of tables.

Suppose normalization has spread a work order's data across several tables holding basic information, addresses, phone numbers, email addresses, and other stuff. Now suppose the system is designed to assign work orders to users for processing. It would be nice to lock a work order's data while a user is working on it so others can't blunder in and make conflicting changes. Unfortunately, it's wasteful to lock all of those records.

To use a turnkey record, add a LockedBy field to a table that is central to the work order. This is probably the table that contains the work order's basic information.

Now to "reserve" the work order for use by a particular user, the program sets this record's LockedBy field to the user's name. That token means that this user has permission to mess with all of the work order's records in all of its tables without actually locking anything. Because the user's name is in the database, other parts of the program can tell that the record is locked and by whom. The program can even allow an administrator with appropriate privileges to clear that field so you can fix the work order after Frank has gone home.

The one drawback to this method is that if Frank's computer crashes while he has the work order reserved, then it remains locked. To recover, you'll need to add an option in the program to clear those sorts of zombie reservations.

A similar technique gives most of the same benefits while removing the problems that come with a LockedBy field. Suppose you assign each work order to a particular person who then works on it, and no one else ever works on that order.

To handle this case, add an AssignedTo field to the order. Some agent (either human or automated) sets the AssignedTo field and after that the field doesn't need to be changed. In that case, if Frank's computer crashes, his record is still assigned to him after he reboots. Because Frank is still the one who should work on the job, you don't need to clear this field. (Although in practice there will always be a situation where someone needs to foist a job off on someone else for some weird reason, so you should allow some way for an administrator to step in and fix it if necessary.)

Summary

This chapter described some common patterns that you can use to solve particular database design problems. For example, if you need to build a database that includes many-to-many relationships, you can use the pattern described in the section "Many-to-Many Associations" to implement that part of your relational database design.

In this chapter you learned to model:

❑ Many-to-many relationships and multiple-object associations

❑ Repeated attribute associations

❑ Reflexive or recursive associations

❑ Temporal data

❑ Logging and locking

The next chapter does the opposite of this one. It describes common mistakes people make when designing databases and explains ways to avoid those mistakes.

Before you move on to Chapter 10, however, use the following exercises to test your understanding of the material covered in this chapter. You can find the solutions to these exercises in Appendix A.

Exercises

1. Parcheesi is a board game for two to four players. Make an ER diagram to record information about Parcheesi matches.

2. Build a relational model to record information about Parcheesi matches. Be sure to include a way to tell who finished first through fourth.

3. Chess enthusiasts often like to walk through the moves of past matches to study how the play developed. They even give names to the most famous of these matches. For example, the "Immortal Game" was played on June 21, 1851 by Adolf Anderssen and Lionel Kieseritzky (see http://en.wikipedia.org/wiki/Immortalgame).

    The following text shows the first six moves in the Immortal Game:

    ```
    e4 e5 f4 exf4 Bc4 Qh4+?! Kf1 b5?! Bxb5 Nf6 Nf3 Qh6
    ```

(If someone showed me this string and I wasn't thinking about chess at the time I'm not sure whether I would guess it was an assembly program, encrypted data, or some new variant of Leet. See http://en.wikipedia.org/wiki/Leet.)

Of course, a database shouldn't store multiple pieces of information in a single field, so the stream of move data should be broken up and stored in separate fields. In chess terms, a *ply* is when one player moves a piece and a *move* is when both players complete a ply.

Figure 9-28 shows a semantic object model for a CHESS_MATCH class that stores the move information as a series of Move attributes, each containing two Ply attributes. The Movement field holds the actual move information (Qh4+?!) and MoveName is something like "The Sierpinski Gambit" or "The Hilbert Defense." Commentary is where everyone else pretends they know what the player had in mind when he made the move.

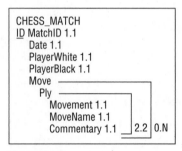

Figure 9-28

Draw an ER diagram to show the relationships between the Player, Match, Move, and Ply entity sets.

4. Build a relational model to represent chess relationships by using the tables Players, Matches, Moves, and Plies. How can you represent the one-to-two relationship between Moves and Plies within the tables' fields? How would you implement this in the database?

5. Consider the relational model you built for Exercise 4. The Moves table doesn't contain any data of its own except for MoveNumber. Build a new relational model that eliminates the Moves table. (Hint: collapse its data into the Plies table.) How does the new model affect the one-to-two relationship between Moves and Plies?

6. Suppose you are modeling a network of pipes and you want to record each pipe's diameter. Design a relational model that can hold this kind of pipe network data.

7. Suppose you run a wine and cheese shop. Wine seems to get more expensive the longer it sits on your shelves, but most cheeses don't last forever. Build a relational model to store cheese inventory information that includes the date by which it must be sold. Assume that each batch of cheese gets a separate sell-by date.

8. Modify the design you made for Exercise 7 assuming each *type* of cheese has the same shelf-life.

Common Design Pitfalls

Chapter 9 described some common patterns that you may want to use while designing a database. This chapter takes an opposite approach: it describes some common pitfalls that you don't want to fall into while designing a database. If you see one of these situations starting to sprout in your design, stop and rethink the situation so you can avoid a potential problem as soon as possible.

In this chapter you learn to avoid problems with:

- ❏ Normalization and denormalization.
- ❏ Lack of planning and standards.
- ❏ Mishmash and catchall tables.
- ❏ Performance anxiety.

The following sections describe some of the most common and troublesome problems that can infect a database design.

Lack of Preparation

I've nagged about this in earlier chapters but it's time to nag again. Database design is often one of the first steps in development. It's only natural for developers to want to rush ahead and get some serious coding done. That gives them something to show management to prove that they aren't *only* playing computerized mahjong and reading friends' MySpace pages. It's also more fun than working on plans, designs, use cases, documentation, and all the other things that you need to do before you can roll up your sleeves and get to work.

Before you start cranking out tables and code, you need to do your homework. Some of the things you need to do before you start wiring up the database include:

- ❏ Make sure you understand the problem.
- ❏ Write requirements documents to state the problem.
- ❏ Build use cases to see if you have solved the problem.

❑   Design a solution.

❑   Test the design to see if it satisfies the use cases.

❑   Document everything.

Remember, the time you spend on up-front design almost always pays dividends down the road.

Poor Documentation

This is part of preparation but is so important and under-appreciated that deserves its own section. Many developers think of documentation as busy work or a chore to keep managers who have no real talents off their backs while they build elegant data structures of intricate beauty and complexity.

I confess that occasionally that's a handy attitude, but the real purpose of documentation is to keep everyone on the project focused on the same goals. The documentation should tell people where the project is headed. It should spell out the project's design decisions so everyone knows how the pieces will fit together.

If the documentation is weak, different people will make different and often contradicting assumptions. Eventually those assumptions will collide and you'll have to resolve the conflict. That will require developers to go back and fix work that they made under the wrong assumptions. That leads to more work, more errors, and copious bickering over whose fault it was.

The real fault was poor documentation.

Poor Naming Standards

In a sense, naming standards are part of documentation. When done properly, an object's name should give you a lot of information about the object. For example, if I tell you to build an Employees table, you probably know a lot about that table without even being told. You know that it will need name, address, phone, email, and Social Security Number information (in the United States, at least). In most companies, it will also need an employee ID, hire date, title, department, salary, and payroll information (deductions, bank account for automatic deposit, and so forth). Somehow it should probably link to a manager and possibly to projects. You got all of that from the single word "Employees."

Now suppose I told you to build a People table but I really want to use the table to hold employee data. You'd probably only put about half of the necessary fields in this table. You'd get the name and address stuff right, but you'd completely miss the business-related fields.

The problems become worse when you start working with multiple related tables and fields. For example, suppose you use employee IDs to link a bunch of tables together but one table calls the linking field EmpNo, another calls it EmployeeId, and a third calls it Purchaser.

This may seem like a small inconvenience and in isolation it is, but together a lot of little inconveniences can add up to a real headache. Inconsistent naming makes developers think harder about names than the things they represent and that makes them less productive and less accurate.

I have worked on projects where poor naming conventions made small changes take days instead of hours because developers had to jump back and forth through the code to figure out what was happening. Inconsistent naming by itself is unlikely to sink a project, but it is enough to nudge an already leaky ship toward the rocky shoals.

Write down names for fields that will be used in more than one table and stick to them so the same concept gets the same name everywhere. Then use those names consistently. Consistency is more important than following particular arcane formulae to generate names, although I will mention two useful conventions for naming database objects such as tables and fields.

First, don't use keywords such as TABLE, DROP, and INDEX. Though these may make sense for your application and they may be allowed by the database, they can make programming confusing. If one of these words really fits well for your project, try adding something to make it even more descriptive. For example, if your database will hold seating assignments and it really makes sense to have a field named Table, try naming it TableNumber or AssignedTable instead.

Second, don't put special characters such as spaces in table or field names even if the database allows it. Although there are ways to use these sorts of names, it makes working with the database a lot more confusing and remember, the point of good naming conventions is to reduce confusion.

For some more information on naming conventions, see some of these links:

- ❏ http://en.wikipedia.org/wiki/Identifier_naming_convention
- ❏ http://standards.iso.org/ittf/PubliclyAvailableStandards/ c035347_ISO_IEC_11179-5_2005(E).zip
- ❏ http://www.gorillatraining.com/en-us/library/ms229002.aspx
- ❏ http://vyaskn.tripod.com/object_naming.htm

Picking good names for tables is like a vocabulary test. You need to think of a word or short phrase that sums up as many of the features in the related items as possible so someone else who looks at your table's name will immediately understand the characteristics that you're trying to record. The following table shows some examples.

A table that holds:	Should be called:
Magazines, newspapers, and comic books	Periodicals
Things that your company sells, including physical items and services	Products
People who work in your restaurant, including servers, bussers, cooks, and greeters	Employees
Things that cost you money, such as groceries, gasoline, and fencing lessons	Expenses
Things that you pay for but that are for work purposes, such as stationery, stamps, and phone calls	BusinessExpenses

Thinking Too Small

Too often developers design a perfectly reasonable database only to discover during the final stages of the project that it cannot handle the load that's dumped on it. Make some calculations, estimate the database's storage and transaction loads, calculate the likely network traffic, and then multiply by five. For some applications, such as online Web applications that can have enormous spikes in load over just a few hours, you might want to multiply by ten or more.

Be sure you use a realistic model of the users' computers and networks. It's fairly common in software development to give the programmers building a system great big, shiny, powerful computers so they can be more productive. (It takes a lot of horsepower to play those interactive role-playing games quickly so you can get back to work.)

Unfortunately, customers often cannot afford to buy new computers for every user. (Five developers times $3,000 is $15,000. That's not exactly pocket money, but it's nothing compared to $2,000 times 200 users for a total of $400,000.) Make sure your calculations are based on the hardware that the users will really have, not on the dream machine that you are using.

If you don't think your architecture can handle that load, you should probably rethink things a bit. You may be able to buy a more powerful server, buy more disk space, move to a faster network, or split the data across multiple servers. If those tricks don't work, you might need to consider a three-tier architecture with different middle-tier objects running on separate computers. You might need to think about moving some of the more intense calculations out of database code and moving them into code running on separate servers. You might need to redesign the database to use turnkey records. You might even need to split the database into disjoint pieces that can run in different computers.

Solving these problems may be difficult, but you should at least plan ahead and be prepared to face them. A sure way to ruin customer goodwill is to get the customers all excited, release the database, and then tell them they can't use it for four months while you rethink its performance problems.

Not Planning for Change

As you design the database, look for places that might need to change in the future. You don't need to build features that may never be needed, but you don't want to narrow the design so those features cannot be implemented later.

In particular, look for exceptions in the data. Customers often think in terms of paper forms, and those are easy to modify. It's easy to cross out headings and scribble in the margins of a paper form. It's a lot harder to do that in a computerized system.

Whenever you see two or more things that have a lot in common, ask the customers if those are enough or whether you'll sometimes need to add more. Listen for words such as "except," "sometimes," and "usually." Those words often hint at changes yet to come.

For example, suppose a customer says, "This field holds the renter's front binding tension, unless he's goofy-footed." Here the word "unless" tells you that this one field may not be good enough to hold all of the data. You'd better find out what "goofy-footed" means and change the database accordingly.

For another example, suppose the customer says, "The order form must hold two addresses, one for shipping and one for billing. Unless, of course, we're billing a split order." This says that two address fields (or groups of fields) isn't enough. At this point you probably need to pull the address data into a new table so you can accommodate any number of addresses, including the ones the customer hasn't remembered yet.

For a third example, suppose you're building a coaching tool for youth soccer teams. Figure 10-1 shows your initial design.

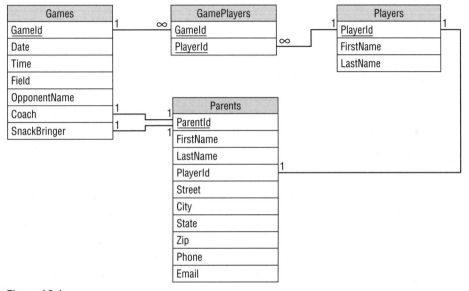

Figure 10-1

Let's review this design and identify any pieces that seem like they might change later.

It's often useful to look at fields that allow a single value and ask yourself if they might need to change later. In this design, there are several such fields. It's also particularly useful to look at one-to-one relationships and this design contains some of those, too.

First, do we need to change the one-to-many relationship between Games and GamePlayers to a many-to-many relationship? Probably not. If the group of players is the same in any two games, that's more or less coincidence rather than a more formal arrangement such as an "A team" and a "B team." (Although I've known some frighteningly serious youth soccer coaches. Seriously scary individuals with clipboards yelling at the tops of their lungs at four-year-olds.)

The many-to-one relationship between GamePlayers and Players, together with the Games/GamePlayers relationship, helps model the many-to-many relationship between Games and Players, so it probably shouldn't change.

What about the one-to-one relationship between Parents and Players? This link implies that a parent can have only one player and that may not be a good assumption. What if a parent has two players on the same team? For the younger age brackets, you won't see players of different ages on the same team, but you will find twins on the same team.

This relationship also implies that each player has a single parent (which is unlikely until cloning techniques become more practical). You could add information about a second parent (in fact, that's a very common approach) but if a player's parents are separated and remarried, you might need up to four parents and sometimes you might need to contact any subset of them to figure out if a player will be at a game. It might make the most sense to just allow a player to have any number of parents and not ask too many questions. (And don't even think about requiring players to have the same last names as their parents! The combinations, including hyphenated last names, are too numerous to contemplate.)

The first one-to-one relationship between Games and Parents means that one parent will be coach for that game. Is that a reasonable assumption? Will you ever need to worry about multiple coaches or assistant coaches? For a youth league, it's probably good enough to assume there is only one main coach and not worry about any others, so I wouldn't change that. But this is a good question to ask.

By far the most important piece of information in this database tells who is bringing a game's snacks. The second one-to-one relationship between Games and Parents means one parent will bring snacks for the game. Is that a reasonable assumption? In my experience, there has always been only one snack-bringer per game. As in the case with the coach, you can probably at least assume there is a main snack-bringer and if someone else wants to bring extra cupcakes for a player's birthday we just won't worry about it. But again, a good question.

One final place to look for these kinds of changes is in the fields within a table. In this design, the field that begs for multiple values is Phone. Lots of people have multiple phones and sometimes you may need to call several to track someone down. (Such as the all-important snack bringer!) I would split the Phone field off into a new table to allow parents to have any number of phone numbers.

Figure 10-2 shows the new and improved design.

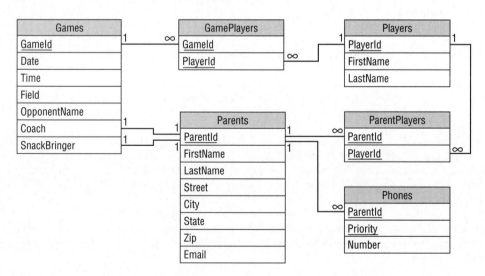

Figure 10-2

Again, you don't need to use psychic powers to build all of the features that the customer will need in the next 15 years, but keep your eyes open during requirements gathering and try not to close off opportunities for later change.

Too Much Normalization

Taken to extremes, too much normalization can lead to a database that scatters related data all over the place for little additional benefit. It can make the design confusing and can slow performance.

When you normalize, think about what a change will cost and what benefits it will provide. Think about how the data will be accessed. If data is only read and written through stored procedures or middle-tier code, that code can help play a role in keeping the data consistent and may allow you to get away with slightly less normalization in the database's tables. Putting every table in Fifth Normal Form or Domain/Key Normal Form isn't always necessary to keep the data safe.

I once worked on a project where a certain database developer (who coincidentally had just taken a class in database normalization) wanted to split every data value out into a separate table. For example, a customer record would contain little more than a CustomerId. Then a Values table would hold the actual data in its three fields Id, ValueName, and ValueData. To look up a customer's name, you would search the Values table for a record with Id equal to the customer's ID and ValueName equal to "Name." In some bizarre otherworldly sense, this table is very normalized and it lets you do some amazing things. For example, you could decide to add a new EarSize field to the customer data without changing the tables at all. However, that design doesn't reflect the structure of the data so it would be next to impossible to use.

Insufficient Normalization

Though too much normalization can make the database slower than necessary, poor performance is rarely the reason a software project fails. Much more common reasons for failure are designs that are too complex and confusing to build, and designs that don't do what they're supposed to do. A database that doesn't ensure the data's integrity definitely doesn't do what it's supposed to do.

Normalization is one of the most powerful tools you have for protecting the data against errors. If the database refuses to allow you to make a mistake, you won't have trouble with bad data later. Adding an extra level of indirection to gather data from a separate table adds only milliseconds to most queries. It's very hard to justify allowing inconsistent data to enter the database to save one or two seconds per user per day.

This doesn't mean you need to put every table in Fifth Normal Form, but there's no excuse for tables that are not in at least Third Normal Form. It's way too easy to normalize tables to that level for anyone to claim that it's not necessary.

If the code needs to parse data from a single field (Hobbies = "sail boarding, skydiving, knitting"), break it into multiple fields or split its values into a new table. If a table contains fields with very similar names (JanPayment, FebPayment, MarPayment), pull the data into a new table. If two rows might contain identical values, figure out what makes them logically different and add that explicitly to the table so you can make a primary key. If some fields' values don't depend on the entire key, consider spreading the record across multiple tables.

Insufficient Testing

This problem is closely related to "Thinking too Small" and "Too Much Normalization." Some developers perform little or no testing before releasing a database into the wild. They run through a few tests to check correctness (the better ones go through all of the use cases) and assume that everything will work in the field. Then when customers try to use it under realistic conditions, the whole thing falls apart. They discover bugs that the testers missed and the performance is unacceptable.

Be sure to test the database and any attached applications thoroughly. Fully testing every nook and cranny of a system takes a lot of work, but it's necessary. You need to be sure you exercise every piece of code, every table, and every constraint. You also need to perform load testing to see if the database can handle the expected load.

If you don't find all of the bugs and bottlenecks, sooner or later the user will, guaranteed!

> *It's also pretty safe to assume that every non-trivial application contains at least some bugs no matter how much testing you perform. In that case, you cannot find every bug so you may be temped not to even try. The goal isn't really to catch every bug, but to find enough of them and to find the most likely to occur so the probability of the users finding a bug is very small. The bugs will still be hiding in there, but if you only get one or two user complaints per year, you're doing pretty well.*

Performance Anxiety

Many developers focus so heavily on performance that they needlessly complicate things. They make a simple solution complicated and harder to build and maintain all in the name of speed. They denormalize tables to avoid using any more tables than necessary and they build business rules into the database so they don't need to use stored procedures or other code to implement them separately.

Modern hardware and software is pretty fast, however. Often these CPU-pinching measures save only milliseconds on a one-second query. Think hard about whether a convoluted design will really save all that much time before you make things so complicated that you can't build, debug, and maintain the application. If you're not sure, either make some tests and find out or go with the simpler version and change it later if absolutely necessary. Usually performance is acceptable, but a database that contains contradictory data is not.

> *I once worked on a huge database application where a simple change to the data might require five or more minutes of recalculation. After about three days digging through horribly convoluted code and database structure, I found the problem. The original developers had used a bunch of tricks to perform calculations in some sneaky ways to save a little bit of time here and there. Then they had done something really silly that made them perform the same calculations again and again more than a hundred thousand times. They were so busy worrying about tripping over the blades of grass that they wandered blindly into a patch of poison ivy. I managed to speed things up a little, but a lot of their time-saving tricks were so buried in the underlying design that there wasn't much we could do without a total rewrite.*

The moral is, you don't need to be stupid about design and ignore obvious chances to improve performance, but don't be so focused on the little things that they cloud the grander design.

First, make it work. Then make it work fast.

Mishmash Tables

Sometimes it's tempting to build tables that contain unrelated values. The classic example is a Domain-Values table that contains allowed values for fields in tables scattered throughout the database. For example, suppose the State, Brand, and Medium fields take values from lists. State can take values CA, CT, NV, and so forth; Brand can take values MixAll, Thumb Master, and Pheidaux; and Medium can take values Oil, Acrylic, Pastel, and Crayon. You could build a DomainValues table with fields Table-Name, FieldName, and Value. Then it would hold records such as TableName = Artwork, FieldName = Medium, Value = Crayon. You would use this magic table to validate foreign keys in all of the other tables.

This approach will work, but it's more of a headache than it's worth. The table is filled with unrelated values and that can be confusing. It might seem that having one table rather than several would simplify the database design, but this single table does so many things that it can be hard to keep track of them all. Just think about drawing the database design's ER diagram with this single table connected to dozens of other tables.

Tying this table to a whole bunch of others can make it a chokepoint for the entire system. It can also lead to unnecessary redundancy if multiple tables contain fields that have the same domains.

It's better to use separate tables for each of the domains that you need. In this example, just build separate States, Brands, and Media tables. Though this requires more tables, the pieces of the design are simpler, smaller, and easier to understand.

Remember the rule that one table should do one clearly defined thing and nothing else. Although this kind of mishmash table has an easily defined purpose, it does not do just one thing.

| Try It Out | Mishmash Bash |

Consider the following mishmash DomainValues table.

Table	Field	Value
Customers	State	CO
Customers	State	KS
Customers	State	WY
Employees	State	CO
Employees	State	KS
Employees	State	WY
OrderItems	Size	Large

Table	Field	Value
OrderItems	Size	Medium
OrderItems	Size	Small
Orders	ShippingMethod	Overnight
Orders	ShippingMethod	Priority
Orders	ShippingMethod	Snail Mail

How could you avoid building this mishmash table? What tables would use the new domain tables? To find out:

1. Figure out which records represent similar items.

2. Move similar records into smaller validation tables.

3. Define foreign keys to use the new tables for validation.

How It Works

1. Figure out which records represent similar items.

   This table contains domain values for four tables (Employees, Customers, OrderItems, and Orders) so you might think that you need four domain tables. However, the table really only holds domain values for three kinds of fields: states, sizes, and shipping methods. Those define the groups of similar items so you only need three new domain tables.

2. Move similar records into smaller validation tables.

   The States table contains the following data:

State
CO
KS
WY

   The Size table contains the following data:

Size
Large
Medium
Small

Finally, the ShippingMethod table contains the following data:

ShippingMethod
Overnight
Priority
Snail Mail

3. Define foreign keys to use the new tables for validation.

Instead of making every table validate domains against the mishmash table, the database now uses the following foreign key constraints:

- ❑ Customers.State = States.State
- ❑ Employees.State = States.State
- ❑ OrderItems.Size = Sizes.Size
- ❑ Orders.ShippingMethod = ShippingMethods.ShippingMethod

Not Enforcing Constraints

When you design a table, you should write down the domains and other constraints for every field. Most database designers can handle that, but it's surprising how often those restrictions don't make it into the actual database.

When you start building the database, go through the list of field constraints and check them off as you implement them. Often these are as simple as making a field required or writing field-level check constraints for a field.

You can rely on middle-tier objects and user interface code to enforce some of these, but the database is the final authority, so why not take advantage of its capabilities? You might want to allow the middle-tier to verify that a flyball team's number of dogs is no more than 3 because it's a possibly changing business rule. It seems unlikely that a team would ever include –1 dogs, however, so let the database enforce that rule at least.

Databases can also often verify field formats. For example, some databases can verify that a phone number string has the format ###-###-####. You may want the user interface to validate this type of format, too, but there's no reason not to let the database do whatever it can to ensure that garbage doesn't slip into the data.

The database is pretty good at enforcing these simple rules. Let it do its job so it can feel appreciated.

Obsession with IDs

ID numbers are nice. They are relatively small and efficient, and it's easy to ensure that they are always unique. However, they don't have any real meaning. You can probably recite your name, address, and phone number easily enough, but do you remember your employee ID, utility company account number, and driver's license number? Unless you have a better memory than mine (which is likely, I have a pretty poor memory) or someone took a shortcut when they defined their keys (in some states, your driver's license number is the same as your Social Security Number), you probably don't remember all of these.

It's okay to have some tables with keys that are not artificial IDs, particularly if the data provides a nice unique key readymade for you. Books have ISBNs (International Standard Book Numbers) that uniquely identify them so, if you're tracking books, use ISBN instead of creating a new meaningless number. Products often have SKU (Stock-Keeping Unit) or product numbers that are just as useful as an artificial number. Even keys that include multiple fields can be perfectly fine and give acceptable performance.

Three obvious times when you really do need to create an artificial primary key are:

❑   You might need to change the value of the natural key (you shouldn't change primary key values and some databases won't even let you).

❑   The natural key doesn't guarantee uniqueness.

❑   Adding an automatically generated surrogate key makes integration with other systems easier.

Before you create a new key field, ask yourself whether it's really necessary.

Try It Out   **IDs Undone**

Consider the following tables.

❑   Customers with fields FirstName, LastName, Street, and so on.

❑   ChessMatches with fields Date, WhitePlayerId, and BlackPlayerId.

❑   Books with fields Title, Author, Year, Pages, Price, and Publisher.

❑   InventoryItems with fields Name, Vendor, Description, and QuantityInStock.

❑   WeatherReadings with fields Date, Time, Temperature, and Humidity.

To figure out which of these probably needs an artificial primary key:

1.   Look for a natural key.

2.   Decide whether you will ever need to change the key's value.

3.   Decide whether the key guarantees uniqueness.

4.   Use the results from steps 1 through 4 to decide which tables need artificial IDs.

How It Works

1. Look for a natural key.

    ❑ **Customers with fields FirstName, LastName, Street, and so on:** FirstName/LastName is a natural key.

    ❑ **ChessMatches with fields Date, WhitePlayerId, and BlackPlayerId:** Date/WhitePlayerId /BlackPlayerId is a natural key.

    ❑ **Books with fields Title, Author, Year, Pages, Price, and Publisher:** Title/Author is a natural key.

    ❑ **InventoryItems with fields Name, Vendor, Description, and QuantityInStock:** Name/Vendor is a natural key.

    ❑ **WeatherReadings with fields Date, Time, Temperature, and Humidity:** Date/Time is a natural key.

2. Decide whether you will ever need to change the key's value.

    ❑ **Customers with fields FirstName, LastName, Street, and so on:** Depending on your application, you may need to change FirstName or LastName values. For example, when some friends of mine got married they decided to change both of their last names to something completely different. This means FirstName/LastName may not make a good primary key.

    ❑ **ChessMatches with fields Date, WhitePlayerId, and BlackPlayerId:** The application should never need to change Date/WhitePlayerId/BlackPlayerId after the data for a match is entered.

    ❑ **Books with fields Title, Author, Year, Pages, Price, and Publisher:** The application should never need to change Title/Author after the data for a book is entered.

    ❑ **InventoryItems with fields Name, Vendor, Description, and QuantityInStock:** There's some chance that a vendor will rename a product. In that case, Name/Vendor might not make a good primary key, although you could also treat the renamed product as a new product instead.

    ❑ **WeatherReadings with fields Date, Time, Temperature, and Humidity:** The application should never need to change Date/Time after the weather data for a reading is entered.

3. Decide whether the key guarantees uniqueness.

    ❑ **Customers with fields FirstName, LastName, Street, and so on:** FirstName/LastName is probably not enough to guarantee uniqueness. There are just too many John Smiths and Maria Garcias out there.

    ❑ **ChessMatches with fields Date, WhitePlayerId, and BlackPlayerId:** Unless you allow two players to play more than one match at the same time (which is possible), Date/WhitePlayerId/BlackPlayerId is unique.

❏ **Books with fields Title, Author, Year, Pages, Price, and Publisher:** It's extremely unlikely that the same author (or two authors with the same name) would publish two books with the same title but Title/Author does not absolutely guarantee uniqueness. You could make the key more unique by adding Year, but it's still not an absolute guarantee.

❏ **InventoryItems with fields Name, Vendor, Description, and QuantityInStock:** It's very unlikely that a particular vendor will have more than one product with the same name (you might not want to do business with such a confused vendor) so Name/Vendor guarantees uniqueness.

❏ **WeatherReadings with fields Date, Time, Temperature, and Humidity:** Unless you take more than one reading at the same time, Date/Time guarantees uniqueness.

4. Use the results from steps 1 through 4 to decide which tables need artificial IDs.

❏ **Customers with fields FirstName, LastName, Street, and so on:** A customer's First-Name/LastName value may change and these fields don't guarantee uniqueness, so this table really needs an ID field.

❏ **ChessMatches with fields Date, WhitePlayerId, and BlackPlayerId:** Date/WhitePlayerId/BlackPlayerId is a fine primary key.

❏ **Books with fields Title, Author, Year, Pages, Price, and Publisher:** It is unlikely that you would have trouble with Title/Author/Year as a primary key but it's easy enough to use the book's ISBN code to remove all doubt. Adding that data will make it a lot easier to integrate with other systems, such as online bookstores.

❏ **InventoryItems with fields Name, Vendor, Description, and QuantityInStock:** Name/Vendor is unlikely to cause trouble but there is a chance. Most products have part numbers, SKUs, UPCs (Universal Product Codes — those values that go with the barcode), or other ID values that make excellent primary keys, so I would add one of those.

❏ **WeatherReadings with fields Date, Time, Temperature, and Humidity:** The combination Date/Time guarantees uniqueness and you shouldn't need to change those values later, so this table shouldn't need an artificial key.

Not Defining Natural Keys

Closely related to Obsession with IDs is not defining natural keys. A natural key is a key that you might actually use to search the data. If a table is only there to provide detail for another table, then an ID makes a reasonable link between the two, but if you will be searching a table for natural values such as names or phone numbers, those may make good keys.

For example, suppose the Phones table uses CustomerId to link back to Customers records. Typically to look up a phone number, you will look up the customer's record and then look at its related phone records. It's unlikely that you will know a customer's phone number and need to look up the customer, so you probably don't need to define a key on the phone number table's PhoneNumber field.

In contrast, suppose the Customers table has a CustomerId for a primary key and contains basic customer information such as name and address. What are the chances that you'll need to look up customers by ID? Unless the ID is something special (such as phone number if you're running a phone company), that number is meaningless to mere mortals, so you're more likely to look a customer up by name. You can make that faster by making the name a key. It can't be the primary key because it doesn't guarantee uniqueness and you might need to change a customer's name, but making it a non-primary key will make searches by customer name faster. If that's the search you perform the most, this key is a worthwhile addition to the database.

You might also consider making other fields keys, too. For example, you might want to be able to list customers by city or ZIP Code to prepare mass mailings (postal spam). In that case, making City and ZipCode keys might also be useful if you perform those searches often.

Summary

This chapter described some common mistakes that people make while designing databases. I admit some of these ideas seem a bit wishy-washy for a book about a computer-related subject, but they're pretty important. If you don't pay attention to the ideas described in this chapter, you may end up redis-covering the importance of proper planning, documentation, and testing by painful experience.

Some of these lessons I've learned the hard way, some by studying others' mistakes, and some through research. Take my word for it when I say it's a lot easier (and sometimes humorous) to learn about these issues here instead of through firsthand experience.

In this chapter, you learned the importance of:

❑   Advanced preparation through thorough requirements gathering.

❑   Good design practices such as using naming conventions and making a design before building the database.

❑   Anticipating changes and increased database load.

❑   Using the database's tools to ensure that values are within their allowed domains.

❑   Avoiding artificial keys if they are unnecessary and making natural keys even if they cannot be a primary key.

This chapter ends the book's main discussion of general database design topics. The next few chapters explain some practical database implementation issues, paying extra attention to the Microsoft Access and MySQL database management systems.

Before you move on to Chapter 11, however, use the following exercises to test your understanding of the material covered in this chapter. You can find the solutions to these exercises in Appendix A.

Exercises

1. Suppose your client runs a ski rental shop and he's the most dreaded of all clients: one who thinks he knows something about databases. He has designed a Customers table that looks like this:

Name	Address	City	Zip	Phone1	Phone2	Stuff
Sue Rank	2832 Shush Ln. #2090	Boiler	72010	704-291-2039		Downhill, Snowboarding
Mark Bosc	276 1st Ave	East Fork	72013	704-829-1928	606-872-3982	X-country

The Stuff field contains a list of Downhill, X-country, Snowboarding, and Telemark. Your client plans to get the customer's state from the Zip value when he's sending out mailings.

Your client wants you to build Orders and other tables to go with this one.

For this exercise, explain to your client what's wrong with this table, paying particular attention to the ideas covered in this chapter.

2. Suppose you're building a system to track rentals for a company that owns two Blu-ray rental stores and plans to open a third next year. What special considerations do you need to ponder that might not be as important if the client were, for example, a well-established party rental store. (They rent chairs, punch bowls, big tents, and other stuff for large parties.)

3. What's wrong with an Addresses table that includes these fields:

- ❑ CustomerId
- ❑ StreetName
- ❑ StreetNumber
- ❑ StreetPrefix
- ❑ StreetSuffix
- ❑ StreetPreDirectional
- ❑ StreetPostDirectional
- ❑ ApartmentOrSuite
- ❑ Floor
- ❑ City
- ❑ Neighborhood
- ❑ State
- ❑ Zip
- ❑ PlusFour

The Zip and PlusFour fields hold detailed ZIP Code data. For example, if a customer's ZIP+4 is 02536-2918, the Zip field would hold 02536 and the PlusFour field would hold 2918.

4. Consider the relational design shown in Figure 10-3.

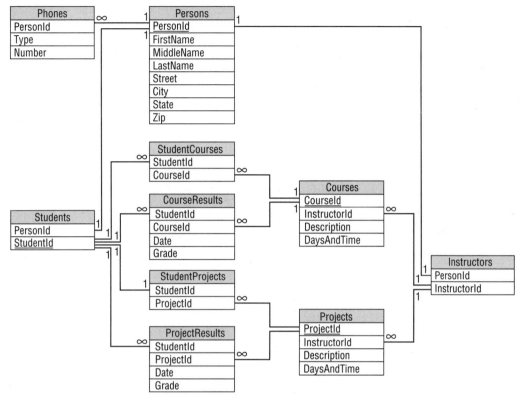

Figure 10-3

List the database constraints that you would place on the fields in this model and explain how you would implement each of those constraints. (Feel free to add new tables if necessary.)

Part III
A Detailed Case Study

Chapter 11: User Needs and Requirements

Chapter 12: Building a Data Model

Chapter 13: Extracting Business Rules

Chapter 14: Normalization and Refinement

The chapters in the next part of the book walk through a fictitious case study for The Pampered Pet, a pet supply store. These chapters work through the steps for building the company a new database from requirements gathering to implementation.

Chapter 11 begins the development process by gathering user requirements. It walks through the project's initial steps, including meeting the customers, picking the customers' brains, and examining the database's performance, security, and data integrity needs. It finishes by developing use cases and requirements documents.

Chapter 12 uses the requirements gathered in Chapter 11 to build initial data models. It builds semantic object models and entity-relationship models to satisfy the project's requirements and makes some improvements on the initial models.

Chapter 13 converts the models built in Chapter 12 into a relational model.

As you work through these chapters, you may find it useful to build an example of your own. Pick some other business, fictitious or otherwise, and work through the corresponding phases of database design and development as you read along.

User Needs
and Requirements

The first step in designing and building a database is gathering user requirements. You cannot build a database to solve the users' needs unless you understand those needs. This chapter walks you through the process for The Pampered Pet.

In this chapter you see examples of:

❏   Identifying user requirements.

❏   Determining what the database's main entities are.

❏   Defining use cases to verify that requirements have been met.

The scenarios described here do not necessarily present the most efficient possible outcome. Ideally your customers know exactly what they need and give you their full cooperation while spelling out the requirements in crystal-clear detail. Things don't always go that way, however (in fact, I've never seen it happen that way), so neither do the steps described here.

Perhaps you'll get lucky and things will go more smoothly than some of the discussions described here, but you should realize that at least sometimes people skills are as important as database design skills during this phase.

Meet the Customers

Requirements gathering for this project begins with a series of meetings in The Pampered Pet's back room (where they hold pet training courses, so it smells a bit funny). Occasionally customers have an agenda for these introductory meetings but, as often as not they won't have been through the process of building a database before, so it'll be up to you to keep things moving in the proper direction.

The initial meetings with The Pampered Pet are mostly to introduce you and the customers so you can get to know each other. For this example, four key players attend the first meeting:

❑ Bill Wye "The Pet Store Guy," the founder and owner of The Pampered Pet. Bill is the one who decided the company needed a complete database. He's the Executive Champion. Because this is a fairly small company and he's at the very top of the food chain, there will be no serious disputes over whether the project should go forward, although his help might be needed to keep unenthusiastic participants pulling in the right direction.

❑ Alicia Myth, the store's manager. Alicia has been working at the store since it was opened and knows just about everything there is to know about the business. She spends more time keeping things organized and running than anyone else at the store and knows more about the day-to-day business than anyone else, even Bill.

❑ Charlie "Ice" Walker is a trainer specializing in aggressive dogs. He also works shifts at the store and knows a lot about day-to-day operations. He doesn't care as much about selling as he does about training. He has a very "whatever" attitude about the new database system.

❑ Sveta Clark is a dog and exotic bird trainer who also works at the store about half the time. Sveta isn't convinced that the store needs a new computerized system and just wants to be left alone to do her job the way she always has. She's definitely more comfortable with animals than people.

During the first meeting, you realize that Bill isn't going to play much of a role in this project. He's the one who initiated the whole thing, and he can help keep things moving if they get bogged down, but he's not going to be directly involved on a daily basis. (He's too busy with his classic car collection.)

Charlie and Sveta are not particularly enthusiastic about the whole thing, but with Alicia's encouragement and an occasional nudge from Bill, they'll cooperate. Unfortunately Alicia's time will be largely taken up by running the store, so Charlie and Sveta will be your Customer Representatives. Alicia will be around to make critical decisions, break ties, and generally look menacing if Charlie and Sveta become difficult.

The purpose of the initial meeting is mostly to let you and the customers meet and get comfortable with each other. There's a chance that you'll get some serious work done, but it's more likely that this meeting will stay at a fairly high level.

A couple of questions that you should try to address right away are:

❑ What do the customers expect to get from the new system?

❑ Why do they think they need a new database system?

❑ Does this system enhance or replace an existing system?

❑ Are there other systems with which this one must interact?

These are big-picture executive-level questions that Bill can answer and because he probably won't be present at the more detailed meetings still to come, he should answer them now. In the ensuing discussion, during which Alicia talks more than anyone else, you realize that Bill doesn't really know what he'll get out of the database. Though Bill made the final decision, it was Alicia who thought a new database system would help.

Alicia thinks the new system can help better track inventory (there have been times when they've run out of products without realizing it). She also hopes it can streamline payroll (it currently takes quite a while for her to track everyone's hours) and she believes that it can help the company figure out how to reach new customers and better market their training courses.

There is no existing system and no other systems with which this one must interact. The current process is manual and uses paper order forms, paper shift assignments, and paper timesheets.

You should address these issues as soon as possible to give the customers the right expectations. A new database can help with inventory tracking and streamline payroll. It will also help identify which customers take which courses, but it's not really a marketing tool. It will tell you about existing customers but not about people who have never interacted with the company. Alicia seems a little disappointed, but she still sees some worthwhile benefits and is ready to get started.

After the initial meeting, where you and the key players get to know each other a bit, you begin a series of meetings where you try to pick Charlie's and Sveta's brains to define the project's requirements.

Pick the Customers' Brains

Sometimes customers have already prepared requirements documents before they bring in database designers and other developers, but often gathering requirements is part of the development process. In this project, that means locking Charlie and Sveta in a room and picking their brains.

This is where you pull out your prepared list of questions (described in the "Bring a List of Questions" section in Chapter 4). The following sections run through a series of sample questions and give the answers that Charlie and Sveta give.

Determining What the System Should Do

Charlie says he doesn't know what the system should do and Sveta doesn't care. For goals, they basically repeat what Bill and Alicia said during the kickoff meeting.

This could be a problem. If these two really won't join the team, they won't be much help and right now they're all you've got. You could ask Alicia to have a word with them, but it would be better if they enlist semi-voluntarily.

Rather than making waves right away, you decide to make some educated guesses and see if you can get Charlie and Sveta more interested in the project.

Instead of starting with basic system features, you decide to jump to something that Charlie and Sveta might find more interesting: training course information. You quickly sketch out a form that displays course information including the general description, dates, locations, and the instructor. You draw a little smiley face picture for the guide's picture and write Charlie's name beneath.

Training is the real reason why Charlie and Sveta work here and it's what they love, so this gets their attention. They start giving you useful information about what's involved in defining a course: general description (which includes the type of animal: dog, cat, bird, fish), locations, times, dates, price, and maximum number of participants.

You let Charlie and Alicia brainstorm and tell stories about courses they've run and funny pets they've met so they can build some enthusiasm. Before lunch you snap their pictures with your camera phone. Then during lunch you email the pictures to yourself and paste them into the quickly assembled form shown in Figure 11-1. A quick mockup makes the application seem more real to customers.

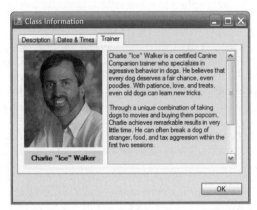

Figure 11-1

This may seem like a somewhat silly exercise, but a little glitz and showmanship can go a long way toward uniting a project team. A simple mockup such as this one shows the customers something tangible early on that they can understand. Database models and relational designs are your eventual goal, but they are too abstract to generate much excitement with all but the nerdliest customers. Putting a customer's face on a mockup will almost certainly grab and hold their attention.

After lunch, you present your mockup and let Charlie and Sveta suggest improvements. That may be as far as you get during this session. Before the next session, you build an improved mockup with Sveta's picture so she doesn't feel left out and to show that you listened to their suggestions and made appropriate changes.

The following list describes a few things to consider when you build this kind of mockup:

❑ **Decide what tool you want to use**. Use a tool that you find comfortable. I used Visual Basic to build the form shown in Figure 11-1 (you can download the free Express Edition at www.microsoft.com/express/vb) but you should use whatever tool you find comfortable. If you've programmed before, you can use a programming tool. If you like building Web pages, build one. If you are experienced with Microsoft Word or some other word processor, use it. Use drawing tools or even paper and colored markers. Whatever is easiest for you.

❑ **Put an image or graphic on the form**. Graphics make a form more interesting, so add some graphics to your mockup. Use familiar images such as the customers' pictures, company logos, or relevant clipart (a dog leaping to catch a disc or a cat stalking a mouse would work for The Pampered Pet). You can add interest with a special font for the company's name and with colors. Don't go overboard, though. You want the graphics to tie the form to the customer, not to distract from the form's purpose.

❏ **Add details that will be meaningful to the customer**. Use terms and concepts that are familiar to the customer. Use the customer's company name and logo. This doesn't have to be perfect (the lawyers will eventually tell you that you're not using exactly the right shade of blue anyway) and the information doesn't have to be perfectly correct. Just use anything that the customers will find familiar and comfortable so they can see how this project connects with their situation.

On one project for the Minnesota Department of Transportation, I gave the login form the shape of the state of Minnesota. When they first saw the demo project, they were amazed. They had never seen shaped forms before.

Determining How the Project Should Look

In later sessions with Charlie and Sveta, you can start defining what the finished project will look like. Sketch out screens or let them do it for you. These don't need to be perfect. The goal is to figure out what data the system must contain to provide those screens, not to do the user interface designer's job.

After this step, you should have a rough list of forms that the application should contain. In this case, they might include:

❏ **Login:** Log in with user name and password.

❏ **Orders:** Write up sales orders for customers.

❏ **Inventory:** View inventory levels.

❏ **Courses:** Create and edit courses.

❏ **Employees:** Enter and edit employee information. Employees include salespeople and trainers.

❏ **Shifts:** Assign work shifts.

❏ **Customers:** Information about customers, particularly courses they're taking.

You should sketch out these forms to make them easier for the customers to understand. The sketches not only help customers visualize the forms and help them remember what information should be on them, but they also help you understand what data they should contain.

The program also needs the following reports:

❏ **Weekly Work Schedule:** Displays the work shifts for the week.

❏ **Course Schedule:** Displays courses scheduled during a user-entered period of time.

❏ **Course Roster:** Prints a course roster for a trainer to use during a course.

❏ **Reorder Items:** Lists items that need to be reordered.

❏ **Sales Stats:** Lists employees sorted by amount of sales.

❏ **Item Sales:** Lists high and low selling items.

❏ **List Customers:** Displays a list of customers selected by as yet unknown criteria. (This sort of feature is very useful to customers. Fortunately most databases will allow the user to perform ad hoc queries so they can invent new reports long after the application has been built.)

Determining What Data Is Needed for the User Interface

Review the form sketches and figure out where the data should come from for the forms. For example, Figure 11-2 shows a customer order form mocked up in Microsoft Word.

Customer Order   4/1/10

Sold By: Sveta Clark

Items:

Description	Price Each	Quantity	Total Price
Doggy Diet food, senior	$34.95	1	$34.95
Squeaky toy	$2.99	3	$8.97
Misc. mouse, small	$1.99	4	$7.96
Class: Mouse Socialization, 4/1/10 – 4/29/10	$79.50	1	$79.50

Subtotal	$131.38
Tax	$6.57
Shipping	$0.00
Grand Total	$137.95

Purchased By:

Name: Robert Terwilliger
Street: 1265 Petlover Ln
          Apt. 12
City: Menagerie
State: WI   ZIP: 72827

Email: Phone:

Ship To:

☑ Same As Above
Name:
Street:

City:
State: ZIP:

Figure 11-2

At this point, you don't need to figure out exactly where every piece of data will be stored in the database. You just need to discover what data is needed on the form. (Although at this point, you can probably guess that there will be a Customers table for information such as Name and Street that doesn't change with every order, an Orders table to hold order-specific information such as the date and shipping information, and an OrderItems table to hold information about the items that make up the order.)

The following list shows the main types of data needed for each of the forms identified in the previous section.

- ❑ **Login:** User name and password. The program will use the database's integrated security so this data doesn't need to be stored in the database.

- ❑ **Order:** Customer data (name, address), order data (date, shipping address), order items (item, quantity), employees (sold by).

- ❑ **Inventory:** Inventory item data (UPC, description, buy price, sell price, quantity in stock, quantity to require reorder, reorder amount, vendor information).

- ❑ **Course:** Course information (description, trainer, price, dates, times, location, animal type), customer information.

- ❑ **Employee:** Employee information (name, address, Social Security number, skills).

- ❑ **Shift:** Employee, work shifts (date, time).

- ❑ **Customer:** Customer data (name, address, shipping address, orders, courses, email for newsletter).

Determining Where the Data Should Come From

You can start making a list of the entity sets that will take part in the new system as soon as you have a decent understanding of how the system will work. Be sure you don't grow emotionally attached to this very first design, however, because things are likely to change as you learn more.

For now, you can assume there will be entity sets corresponding to the forms listed in the previous section. You don't need to include a table for login information because the program will use the database's security features to log in. It will prompt for a user name and password, and try to connect to the database using them. If the connection fails, the program doesn't let the user do anything else.

The initial list of entities includes Order, Inventory, Course, Employee, Shift, and Customer.

At this point, you may realize that an order may include any number of items, so you know that you will need a separate OrderItem entity to handle the one-to-many relationship.

Determining How the Pieces of Data Are Related

Think about how these entities are related. The forms that you sketched out show relationships among pieces of data so they can help. For example, the order form shown in Figure 11-2 contains information about the customer, the order, and the order items, so those entities must be related.

The following list describes relationships defined by the initial forms:

- ❑ **Order:** Relates customer data, order data, order items, and employees. Some order items may be training courses, so it also relates course data.

- ❑ **Inventory:** This entity is fairly self-contained. Other entities such as Order refer to it but it doesn't need to refer to others.

- ❑ **Course:** Relates basic course information, trainer information, and customer information.

- ❑ **Employee:** This entity is fairly self-contained. Other entities such as Course refer to it but it doesn't refer to others.

❑   **Shift:** Relates work shifts and employee data.

❑   **Customer:** This entity is fairly self-contained. Other entities such as Order and Course refer to it but it doesn't refer to others.

Reports also define relationships among pieces of data. The following list shows where data comes from for the previously defined reports:

❑   **Weekly Work Schedule:** Relates employees and shifts.

❑   **Course Schedule:** Relates basic course information and trainers. This report doesn't need to list customer information.

❑   **Course Roster:** Relates basic course information, trainers, and customers.

❑   **Reorder Items:** This report only uses inventory data.

❑   **Sales Stats:** Relates inventory and employees.

❑   **Item Sales:** This report only uses inventory data.

❑   **List Customers:** Because the selection criteria for these reports are not yet defined, you can't know exactly which entities might be involved. However, you can make some guesses. Users will probably want to search for customers based on the items they purchased and courses they took. It's conceivable that they would want to search for customers who purchased items from a particular employee (perhaps so they can apologize) but most of the reports seem to relate customer, order, inventory, and course data.

Try It Out   Where's the Data?

Having a general idea of what data is required to build a report is very different from actually building the report. Often when you try to identify the fields needed to build a report, you will find holes in your understanding of the project. To fill in some of those holes, follow these steps for the Sales Stats and Item Sales reports:

1.   Determine exactly where the data comes from.

2.   Decide whether it seems likely that the database can build these reports quickly enough to satisfy the users.

How It Works

1.   Determine exactly where the data comes from.

To generate the Sales Stats report, you need to figure out how much each employee sold during a certain period of time. For each employee in the Employees table, you need to find the corresponding Orders items with dates within the desired time period. You will then need to look up the corresponding order items, calculate their total prices, and add up the results.

To generate the Item Sales report, you need to figure out how many of each type of item was sold during a particular time period. To get at this data by date, you'll need to search the Orders table for orders placed during the time period. For each order, you'll look up the order's items and add up the number of each item sold.

2. Decide whether it seems likely that the database can build these reports quickly enough to satisfy the users.

   If a user wants to look at Sales Stats or Item Sales figures for the past month, these queries shouldn't be a problem. They will probably involve a reasonable number of records so the report will run quickly.

   If the user wants to look at data for the last year, this might take slightly longer but should still be reasonable for The Pampered Pet. If the store were a large chain, these reports could take much longer. (Wal-Mart has almost 2 million employees worldwide, but they probably keep their data spread out on a bunch of different databases and only look at summaries on a global scale.)

In each of these cases, the report will probably run reasonably quickly if it doesn't cover too big a time span. Once you realize this, you might want to inform the customers so they can decide how important these reports are. You may also want to tell them that reports covering longer time periods (for example, the previous year or year-to-date) will take longer than reports covering the previous month.

Determining Performance Needs

The system must be fast enough to be usable by an employee working with a customer. This is a typical case of "fast enough is fast enough." Unfortunately "fast enough" isn't a verifiable quantity. You need to write down an explicit definition of what "fast enough" means so you can tell if you're meeting your goal.

For an interactive application, a good rule of thumb is a 5-second response. If the application takes longer than 5 seconds to respond to a request, users grow impatient. (They check their email, wander off to get coffee, bump into each other in the break room and start to chat, and pretty soon the 10-second response takes 30 minutes.)

So the goal of the system will be to respond to interactive requests within 5 seconds 90 percent of the time. Reports that are run daily should finish within 5 minutes and reports run less often can take as long as 15 minutes. (These are very generous limits for this application and should be easy to achieve, but they should be acceptable for most applications.)

Though this is an important application, it does not need 24/7 support. The data is fairly important, however, particularly the data concerning future events such as orders that you have not yet delivered, customer enrollment in courses, and future work shifts. Because the system doesn't need to run 24 hours a day, it can be shut down nightly for backups (and to save a little electricity). A manual system (using pens, notebooks, sales slips, manual credit forms, and so forth) should be in place in case of a power failure or in case the system crashes for some other reason.

Have you ever been in a store during a power failure or computer system crash and they couldn't process credit cards or even take cash? Not long ago my local McDonald's was closed most of a day because their computers were down. You'd think they could make and sell hamburgers for cash without a computer. During a recent power failure, my local grocery store had emergency power for its registers and computers so, while they were frantically moving cheese and salads into refrigerated trucks, they could still sell everything else.

Determining Security Needs

At first, Charlie and Sveta don't see any need for extra levels of security. You point out that things such as setting prices, reordering inventory, and assigning work shifts can only be performed by Alicia (the store manager) so the system needs at least two classes of users: general employees and managers.

It will probably also be useful to have a third class of user to perform system administration tasks, although Alicia may perform that role as well.

The general employees will make and fulfill orders. Managers (Alicia) will set prices, run reports, and assign work shifts. System administrators will change system parameters, define reports, and perform backups.

Charlie and Sveta probably won't like the idea of an audit trail keeping track of their every move, but most of what they do (making orders) should include their user names anyway in the Sold By field so perhaps audit trails may not be necessary.

This is a place where you should look for future modifications. As long as Alicia makes all of the system-wide changes (changing prices and assigning work shifts), you probably don't need audit trails. Orders hold a user name in the Sold By field so you know who created an order. If the system doesn't allow users to change orders after they are placed, there aren't too many opportunities for Charlie and Sveta to cause serious damage so any other changes are Bill's or Alicia's fault.

However, if the store ever gets another manager, it might be handy to record who makes what changes.

Only Bill can really decide whether audit trails are necessary. They're not too hard to implement, so let's include them in this design.

Determining Data Integrity Needs

To really address this issue, you need to start making a list of the fields that belong to each of the database entities. For example, the following table gives the data types and constraints for the fields in the Order entity.

Field	Req'd?	Data Type	Domain
Date	Yes	String	Any date.
FirstName	Note 1	String	Any first name. Not validated.
LastName	Note 1	String	Any first name. Not validated.
Street	Note 1	String	Any street name and number. Not validated.
City	Note 1	String	Any city name. Not validated?
State	Note 1	String	Foreign key to States table.
Zip	Note 1	String	Valid ZIP Code. Not validated?

Field	Req'd?	Data Type	Domain
Email	No	String	Valid email address. If provided, send the customer a monthly email newsletter.
HomePhone	Note 2	String	Valid 10-digit phone number.
CellPhone	Note 2	String	Valid 10-digit phone number.
SameAsAbove	Yes	Boolean	If unchecked, and we're shipping, then the Ship To fields are required.
ShipToFirstName	Note 3	String	Any first name. Not validated.
ShipToLastName	Note 3	String	Any first name. Not validated.
ShipToStreet	Note 3	String	Any street name and number. Not validated.
ShipToCity	Note 3	String	Any city name. Not validated?
ShipToState	Note 3	String	Foreign key to States table.
ShipToZip	Note 3	String	Valid ZIP Code. Not validated?
SoldBy	Yes	Reference	Reference to employee information.
Description	Yes	String	Foreign key to Inventory table.
PriceEach	Yes	Currency	Taken from Inventory table.
Quantity	Yes	Integer	> 0.
TotalPrice	Yes	Currency	Calculated from PriceEach and Quantity.
Subtotal	Yes	Currency	Calculated from the Items.
Tax	Yes	Currency	Calculated from the Subtotal.
Shipping	Yes	Currency	> = 0.
GrandTotal	Yes	Currency	Subtotal + Tax + Shipping.

❑ Note 1 — This field is required if the customer is signing up for a course or if we're shipping products to the customer.

❑ Note 2 — If the customer is signing up for a course or if we're shipping products to the customer, at least one of the HomePhone and CellPhone fields is required.

❑ Note 3 — This field is required if we are shipping products to the customer and SameAsAbove is false.

The customer contact fields (FirstName, LastName, Street, City, State, and Zip) are only required if we are shipping the order to the customer or if the customer is enrolled in a course. If we are shipping, either the Same As Above check box must be checked or the user must fill in the Ship To address fields.

Try It Out   **Inventory**

Build a table similar to the previous one for the InventoryItem entity.

1.   List the fields.
2.   Determine which are required.
3.   Determine their data types.
4.   Determine their domain requirements.

How It Works

The following table describes the fields in the InventoryItem entity.

Field	Req'd?	Data Type	Domain
UPC	Yes	String	Valid UPC values.
Description	Yes	String	Any description.
BuyPrice	No	Currency	> 0.
SellPrice	Yes	Currency	> 0.
QuantityInStock	Yes	Integer	> = 0.
StockLocation	Yes	String	Where the item is stored when not on display.
ShelfLocation	Yes	String	Where the item is stored when on display.
ReorderWhen	No	Integer	> 0. If null, don't reorder automatically.
ReorderAmount	No	Integer	> = 0. If null, someone must specify the amount.
Vendor	No	Reference	Vendor information (name, address, and so on).

The UPC, Description, SellPrice, and QuantityInStock fields are required. The BuyPrice and Vendor will be filled in after the first purchase. When the database first goes into use, however, those values may not be known so they cannot be required.

The Vendor field contains a bunch of data such as name, address, and phone number so it is a reference to another entity that we need to add to the model.

Write Use Cases

One of the most important parts of identifying customer requirements is writing use cases. These help drive the database toward its final goals and help keep developers on track. They let you test whether the project is moving closer to completion and they let you verify that you have met your goals after you're finished.

The following list shows use cases for The Pampered Pet database:

- ❑ Login
    - ❑ Log in successfully
    - ❑ Log in unsuccessfully
- ❑ Orders
    - ❑ Create a new order for a new customer (see "Create a customer record")
    - ❑ Create a new order for an existing customer
    - ❑ Modify a pending order
    - ❑ Cancel a pending order
    - ❑ Fulfill an order (ship the items)
- ❑ Inventory
    - ❑ View all inventory
    - ❑ View low inventory
    - ❑ View excess inventory
    - ❑ Add an item to inventory
    - ❑ Remove an item from inventory
    - ❑ Modify an item in inventory
    - ❑ Reorder low inventory
    - ❑ List best and worst selling items in the last week, month, quarter, and year
- ❑ Courses
    - ❑ Create a course
    - ❑ Modify a course
    - ❑ Delete a course
    - ❑ Display and print a list of current and future courses
    - ❑ Select a course and display its information
    - ❑ Enroll a customer in a course
    - ❑ Remove a customer from a course
    - ❑ "Delete" a course after is has been completed by marking it as inactive
    - ❑ Print a flyer about a course
    - ❑ Print a course roster

❑ Employees

    ❑ Create a new employee

    ❑ Modify an employee

    ❑ "Delete" an employee by marking it as inactive

    ❑ List employees and sales for the last week, month, quarter, and year sorted by sales

    ❑ Verify that sensitive information (salary, Social Security number, and so on) are visible only to manager and administrator

❑ Shifts

    ❑ Assign work shifts for a week

    ❑ Display and print work shifts for a week

    ❑ Copy shifts from one week to a new week for all employees

    ❑ Copy shifts from one week to a new week for one employee

    ❑ Modify work shifts

    ❑ Swap two employees' shifts

    ❑ Verify that no one can modify work shifts for past weeks

❑ Customers — Information about customers, particularly courses they're taking.

    ❑ Create a customer record

    ❑ Modify a customer record

    ❑ Print or email general customer mailing

    ❑ Print or email customer mailing based on criteria (for example, customers who took or are taking a particular course)

    ❑ Display and print customers selected by ad hoc criteria

    ❑ "Delete" a customer record by marking it as inactive

Note that it's important to write use cases *before* you build the database. Developers who build use cases after the fact tend to slant the tests toward what the application *can actually do* rather than what it *should do*. (Sort of like the politician who predicts prosperity if he's elected and then after a year of recession says, "See, I told you there were tough times ahead!")

Try It Out   What's the Use?

Each use case must be specified in enough detail that someone can try it out and decide whether the database or project has passed the test. Ideally the instructions should be simple enough that less experienced developers or even users can try them out while the more experienced developers concentrate on making excuses and fixing the problems that the use cases uncover.

Write out a detailed description for the use case "Display and print customers selected by ad hoc criteria." Give the use case these sections:

1. Goals.
2. Summary.
3. Actors.
4. Normal Flow.
5. Alternative Flow.

Refer to Chapter 4 for more information on use cases if necessary.

How It Works

1. Goals.

   Allow the user to display and print customer lists using ad hoc criteria.

2. Summary.

   Allow the user to enter criteria to select customers. Display a list of the selected customers. Let the user print the list. Let the user jump from a customer in the list to that customer's detailed information.

3. Actors.

   Only the Manager and Administrator should be able to use this feature.

4. Normal Flow.

   Here's where the bulk of the test case begins. The following steps test the normal flow:

   a. User selects Reports ⇨ List Customers from menu.

   b. Customer List screen appears.

   c. User selects fields (Zip, TotalPurchases, LastPurchaseDate) and operators ($<, >, > =$) from combo boxes. User clicks List button.

   d. The screen displays a list of the selected customers.

   e. User selects Data ⇨ Details from the menu to display a dialog where the user can check the fields that should be displayed in the list. The list clears after new selections are made. The user can click List again to rebuild the list.

   f. The user double-clicks a customer's entry to open that customer's detailed information.

   g. The user selects File ⇨ Print from the menu to print the list with the selected fields. (Test lists containing 1, 2, and 3 pages.)

5. Alternative Flow.

These steps test unusual or exceptional circumstances. The following steps test unusual conditions:

a. Criteria select no customers.

b. User enters no criteria (should select all customers).

c. User selects no fields for the list (should make empty list). (Question: Always include customer name?)

d. User tries to print empty list (should refuse).

Write the Requirements Document

The requirements document is the first blueprint detailing the project's scope. It sets the tone for future development and guides developers as the project progresses, so it's a very important document.

Unfortunately, it's also fairly long. This chapter identified about a half dozen main tables (later chapters will define more) and around 50 use cases, so a reasonable requirements document would probably take 50 to 75 pages. To save space, a full requirements document for The Pampered Pet database isn't included here.

Fifty or so pages is about the minimum I've seen on a formal project. I've worked on some projects with requirements documents with around 500 pages stored in multiple ring binders.

Before wrapping up, however, this section shows two key pieces of the requirements document: the mission statement and the executive overview.

The mission statement is a *very* brief declaration of the project's overall purpose. Sometimes it is the only part of the requirements document that upper management reads, so it needs to be written for "big picture" executives. (Insert your own joke about "big picture" executives here.) Ideally it should include at least a little content so the executives can discuss the project in the clubhouse after a hard round of golf.

The mission statement for The Pampered Pet database might read:

> **The Pampered Pet Database will allow management to better track and understand its customers, orders, and inventory. It will provide streamlined administration of currently manual processes such as work shift assignment to allow key personal to dedicate additional time to more productive uses. Its data-tracking capabilities will allow management to better identify customer purchasing trends so the company can position itself to take best advantage of emerging industry trends. The database will truly allow The Pampered Pet to move aggressively into 21st century data management and forecasting.**

Seriously, this mission statement in all of its polysyllabic splendor isn't quite as silly as it sounds. It gives your executive champion some useful information and buzzwords that can be used to fight for resources if necessary and to defend the project from possible outside interference.

For more hands-on managers such as Bill Wye, you should also provide an executive summary. This gives him a little more information if he needs it or he's just curious while not flooding him with so many details that his eyes glaze over. It explains what and why but not how.

The following bulleted list makes a concise executive summary that identifies the project's key points.

The Pampered Pet Database will allow management to better:

❑   **Track customer orders and fulfillment**

❑   **Identify customers with particular purchasing histories**

❑   **Identify customers with a history of taking training courses**

❑   **Streamline work shift assignment**

❑   **Identify products that are hot**

❑   **Identify products that are under-performing**

❑   **Identify salespeople who are over- or under-performing**

Demand Feedback

It's important to get feedback at every stage of development. Remember, the longer a mistake is in the system, the harder it is to fix. Mistakes made during requirements gathering can throw the whole effort out of whack.

Unfortunately customers, particularly those who know the most about their business, are often very busy and may not feel they have time to look over the requirements documents thoroughly and provide feedback. Because this feedback is so important, you may need to push on them a bit. In this example, that means pestering Alicia mercilessly until she makes time to review the plan so far. When she has a chance to look things over thoroughly, she finds the following mistakes:

❑   Some inventory items such as live food (crickets, mealworms, feeder guppies) and pet feed have expiration dates. That means:

     ❑   The InventoryItem entity needs a new ExpirationDate field.

     ❑   The system needs a new Expiring Inventory report.

❑   Employees don't always show up for their shifts on time and sometimes leave early, particularly if business is slow. That means the work shift data is not enough to determine the hours that an employee actually worked. That in turn means the database needs a new TimeEntry entity.

❑   The system should have a report that shows how much money each employee earned for the store during a particular week, month, quarter, or year.

❑   The system should print payroll checks and record the date on which they were printed.

❑   Alicia mentions that they may want to provide direct deposit at some point.

This may seem like a lot of changes but it's really not so bad. The basic database structure is close to correct. The only real changes are one new field, one new entity, and a couple of reports. This chapter won't make these changes but the following chapter will include them.

Summary

Any project begins with requirements gathering. If you don't have a good understanding of the customers' needs, you have little chance of building an effective solution for the customers' problems.

This chapter described the requirements gathering phase for The Pampered Pet database project. In this chapter, you saw examples of:

❑   Meeting with customers to identify requirements.

❑   Building a mockup to increase customer understanding, buy-in, and enthusiasm.

❑   Defining the database's main entities and their relationships.

❑   Determining data integrity requirements for entities.

❑   Defining and writing use cases.

After you gather requirements information, you're ready for the next stage of design and development: building a data model. The following chapter describes this phase for The Pampered Pet database project.

Before you move on to Chapter 12, however, use the following exercises to test your understanding of the material covered in this chapter. You can find the solutions to these exercises in Appendix A.

Exercises

1.   Make a table showing the data integrity needs for the Course entity. Note any special requirements and conditions, which fields are required, and any relationships with other entities.

2.   Make a table showing the data integrity needs for the Employee entity. Note any special requirements and conditions, which fields are required, and any relationships with other entities.

3.   Make a table showing the data integrity needs for the Shift entity. Note any special requirements and conditions, which fields are required, and any relationships with other entities.

4.   Make a table showing the data integrity needs for the Customer entity. Note any special requirements and conditions, which fields are required, and any relationships with other entities.

5.   Make a table showing the data integrity needs for the TimeEntry entity. Note any special requirements and conditions, which fields are required, and any relationships with other entities.

6.   Make a table showing the data integrity needs for the Vendor entity. Note any special requirements and conditions, which fields are required, and any relationships with other entities.

Building a Data Model

The previous chapter described requirements gathering for The Pampered Pet database project. It took the basic requirements and used them to build the fundamental entities that will take part in the database's operations.

This chapter builds more formal data models describing those entities. Semantic object models emphasize the entities' fields and entity-relationship diagrams emphasize the relationships among them.

In this chapter you see examples of:

❑ Converting requirements entities into semantic objects.

❑ Splitting off repeated data into new objects.

❑ Converting requirements entities and semantic objects into entity-relationship diagrams.

❑ Converting semantic object models and entity-relationship diagrams into relational models.

Semantic Object Modeling

Semantic object models have the advantage that they are relatively close in structure to the kinds of entity definitions that you typically get out of requirements gathering. They focus on the attributes that objects have. That is the same type of information that you get by studying the customer's needs and user interface mockups, and then figuring out where those mockups will get their data.

Building an Initial Semantic Object Model

To build a semantic object model, review the tables showing data integrity needs that were presented in the section "Determining Data Integrity Needs" in Chapter 11. The chapter's text showed the data needed by the Order and InventoryItem entities. The exercises built tables showing the data needed by the Course, Employee, Shift, Customer, TimeEntry, and Vendor entities. Chapter 11 also discussed the relationships among those entities.

To convert the data requirements tables in Chapter 11 into semantic objects, simply convert the entity's pieces of data into attributes. Then add object attributes to represent relationships with other object classes.

For example, the following table summarizes the Course entity's fields given in Chapter 11.

Field	Req'd?	Data Type	Domain
Title	Yes	String	Any string.
Description	Yes	String	Any string.
MaximumParticipants	Yes	Integer	> 0
Price	Yes	Currency	> 0
AnimalType	Yes	String	One of Cat, Dog, Bird, and so on.
Dates	Yes	String	List of dates.
Time	Yes	Time	Between 8am and 11pm.
Location	Yes	String	One of Room 1, Room 2, yard, arena, and so on.
Trainer	No	Reference	The Employee teaching the course.
Students	No	Reference	Customers table.

This entity has two relationships, one to the employee teaching the course (Trainer) and a second to the customers taking the course (Students). Figure 12-1 shows the corresponding semantic object class.

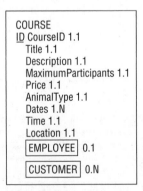

Figure 12-1

Try It Out   A Little Class

Define a semantic EMPLOYEE class.

1.   Write down the data requirements for the Employee entity.

2.   Convert the entity's fields into attributes.

3.   Add object attributes to represent relationships between Employee and other entities.

How It Works

1.   The following table shows the data requirements for the Employee entity identified in Chapter 11.

Field	Req'd?	Data Type	Domain
FirstName	Yes	String	Any first name.
LastName	Yes	String	Any last name.
Street	Yes	String	Any street name and number. Not validated.
City	Yes	String	Any city name. Not validated?
State	Yes	String	Foreign key to States table.
Zip	Yes	String	Valid ZIP Code. Not validated?
Email	No	String	Valid email address. If provided, send the customer a monthly email newsletter.
HomePhone	No	String	Valid 10-digit phone number.
CellPhone	No	String	Valid 10-digit phone number.
SocialSecurityNumber	Yes	String	Valid Social Security number.
Specialties	No	String	Zero or more of: Dog, Cat, Horse, Bird, Fish, and so on.

2.   The FirstName, LastName, Street, City, State, Zip, Email, HomePhone, CellPhone, SocialSecurityNumber, and Specialties fields all turn into attributes in the EMPLOYEE class.

3.   The Employee entity is related to the entities Course (an employee teaches courses), Shift (an employee is assigned to work a shift), and Time Entry (an employee actually works sometimes). Figure 12-2 shows the initial model for the EMPLOYEE class.

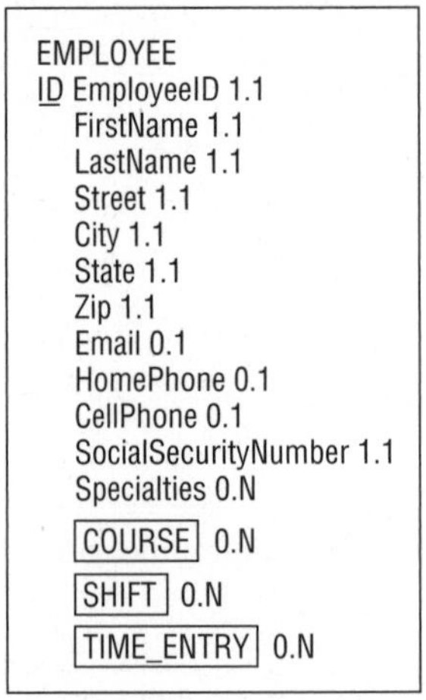

```
EMPLOYEE
ID EmployeeID 1.1
    FirstName 1.1
    LastName 1.1
    Street 1.1
    City 1.1
    State 1.1
    Zip 1.1
    Email 0.1
    HomePhone 0.1
    CellPhone 0.1
    SocialSecurityNumber 1.1
    Specialties 0.N

    COURSE   0.N
    SHIFT  0.N
    TIME_ENTRY   0.N
```

Figure 12-2

Improving the Semantic Object Model

Figure 12-3 shows a first attempt at building a semantic object model for the major entities identified so far.

Notice that the relationships in Figure 12-3 are two-way. If object A is related to object B, then object B is related to object A. For example, in this model the EMPLOYEE class contains an object attribute referring to COURSE and the COURSE class contains an object attribute referring to EMPLOYEE.

A quick look at Figure 12-3 uncovers several problems. First, the ORDER class contains two addresses, the customer's address and a shipping address. They are the same kind of data, so they should be represented by a repeating multi-valued attribute.

This model doesn't acknowledge the relationship between orders and customers. A customer places an order, but there's no link between the ORDER and CUSTOMER classes. The model should be changed to make that relationship explicit.

Furthermore, one of the addresses contained in the ORDER class is actually the customer's address. That address is already represented in the CUSTOMER class, so it's not needed in ORDER.

The ORDER class's second address is the shipping address. It probably makes sense to leave that address in the ORDER class rather than moving it into CUSTOMER because it tells where that particular order should be shipped. If this address is missing, the order should be shipped to the customer's address.

Because ORDER and CUSTOMER both contain addresses, it makes sense to create a new ADDRESS class to hold address data for both of those classes.

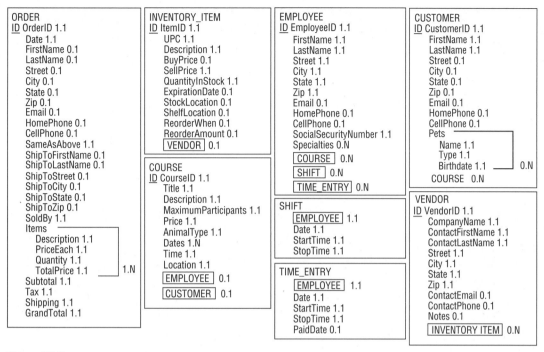

Figure 12-3

Figure 12-3 also shows that the CUSTOMER, EMPLOYEE, and VENDOR classes share several attributes in common. They all include name, address, email, and phone information. This makes intuitive sense because customers, employees, and vendors are all types of people.

To recognize the relationship among customers, employees, and vendors, it makes sense to build a PERSON parent class that holds name, address, email, and phone information. The CUSTOMER, EMPLOYEE, and VENDOR classes then become subclasses of the PERSON class.

Finally, the phone information in the CUSTOMER, EMPLOYEE, and VENDOR classes is not exactly identical. The CUSTOMER and EMPLOYEE classes include both home and cell numbers, whereas the VENDOR class has only a single contact phone number. That makes sense (most vendors don't want you calling their employees at home), but it's easy to generalize the model slightly and allow the PERSON class to hold any number of phone numbers of various kinds. A VENDOR object may never need a home phone number, but it doesn't hurt to allow the possibility.

Figure 12-4 shows the improved model.

Note that some of these steps used to improve the model actually make the database more normalized. Many people think of normalization as a step that occurs after the data model is complete, but it really occurs throughout the data modeling process. As you see parts of the database that need to be normalized (and with experience you'll see them earlier and earlier), go ahead and fix them even if the model isn't complete yet.

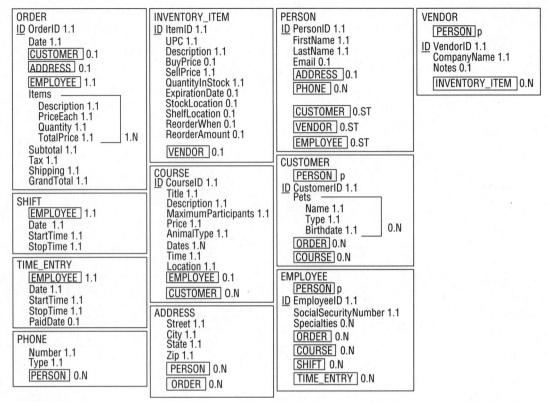

Figure 12-4

Entity-Relationship Modeling

Though semantic object models are fairly easy to build from lists of the database's main objects and their properties, they have the disadvantage that their structure doesn't closely match that of a relational database. Though the objects typically map into relational tables, the semantic object model doesn't emphasize the relationships among the entities. It also allows data arrangements that don't fit the relational model, such as attributes that are repeated any number of times within the same entity.

An entity-relationship model has a structure that's closer to the one used by relational databases, so it makes some sense to convert the semantic object model into a set of ER diagrams.

Building an ER Diagram

To start converting the semantic object model into ER diagrams, consider a particular semantic class and build a corresponding entity set. Connect it to other entity sets representing the class's object attributes.

Finally, consider the class's group attributes. If a group attribute is repeated, you should probably move it into a new entity connected to the original one. If a group attribute occurs only once, you might still think about moving the data into a new entity to either allow repetition later or to make similar data uniform across other entities. If a Student class contains a single Address group attribute, it might be worth moving the Address data into a new table that holds address data for all kinds of entities (Instructor, Employee, and so forth).

For example, the ORDER class shown in Figure 12-4 is one of the more complicated classes, having relationships with three other classes: CUSTOMER, ADDRESS, and EMPLOYEE. To start building the ER diagram, you would create an Order entity set and connect it to Customer, Address, and Employee sets.

The ORDER class has one repeating group attribute: Items. Move that data into a new InventoryItem entity set and connect it to the Order entity.

For each of the relationships, think about how many of each type of entity could be associated with a single instance of the other entity type. For example, the Order entity is related to the Customer entity. A single Order must have exactly one Customer, so the Customer end of the relationship gets cardinality 1.1. Looking at the relationship from the other end, a single Customer might have 1 or more Orders, so the Order end of the relationship gets cardinality 1.N.

Similarly, you can find the cardinalities for the Order/Employee, Order/Address, and Order/InventoryItem relationships.

Figure 12-5 shows the ER diagram for the Order entity and its relationships.

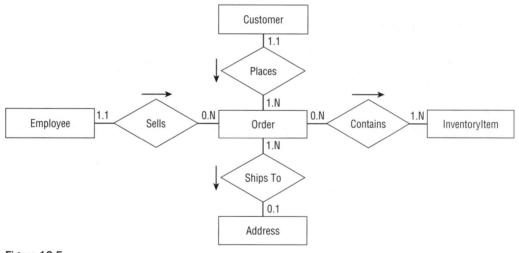

Figure 12-5

Try It Out **A Matter of Course**

Make an ER diagram representing the COURSE class shown in Figure 12-4.

1. Make a Course entity set.

2. Make entity sets corresponding to the COURSE class's object attributes and connect them to the Course entity.

3. Consider any group attributes and decide whether to move them into new entities.

How It Works

1. Simply create a rectangle to hold the new Course entity.

2. The COURSE class has object references to EMPLOYEE and CUSTOMER, so you should create Employee and Customer entities and connect them to Course.

3. The COURSE class doesn't have any group attributes, so you don't need to move them into new entities. Figure 12-6 shows an ER diagram for the Course entity and its relationships.

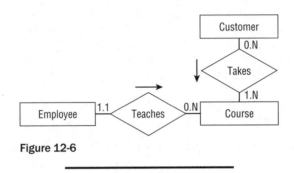

Figure 12-6

Building a Combined ER Diagram

After you build separate ER diagrams for each of the classes defined by the semantic object model, you can combine them into one big diagram. The individual diagrams are enough to let you understand the entities' relationships on a local level but a combined diagram can help show larger patterns of relationship.

Sometimes it can be tricky arranging the entities so their relationships don't overlap and are easy to read. In that case, it is sometimes useful to leave parts of the model out and show them in a separate diagram.

Figure 12-7 shows the combined ER diagram for the bottom-level classes modeled in Figure 12-4. To keep things a bit simpler, the diagram displays the Customer, Employee, and Vendor entities but does not show the fact that they are subclasses of the Person parent class.

The diagram shown in Figure 12-7 uses more descriptive and business-oriented terms wherever possible. For example, from a purely theoretical perspective, you could say that an Employee "has a" Shift, "has a" TimeEntry, and "has a" Course. That would be more uniform but would make the diagram much harder to read.

> *The phrase "Customer Owns Pet" is a bit tricky where I live in Boulder, Colorado. Here people decided that pet owners would be more responsible and caring if they were called "guardians" instead of "owners," so all of the city documents were changed appropriately. My tax dollars hard at work! I suppose for cities such as Boulder, San Francisco, Berkeley, and others we'll have to make a special edition of the book that changes the "Owns" relationship to "Is The Responsible And Caring Guardian Of."*

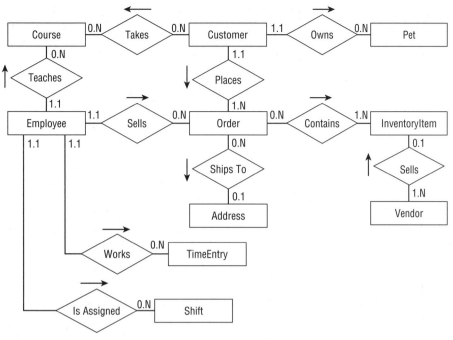

Figure 12-7

Figure 12-8 shows the inheritance hierarchy containing the Person, Customer, Employee, and Vendor classes. You could squeeze this onto the diagram shown in Figure 12-7, but it would make the result more complicated. (I think this part of the model is easier to understand in two pieces.)

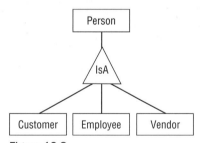

Figure 12-8

Figure 12-9 shows the entities representing the last remaining classes shown in Figure 12-4. This figure shows the relationship between the Person parent class and the Address and Phone entities. (You could easily add this to Figure 12-8 but to me the two seem logically separate. One shows inheritance and the other shows entity relationships.)

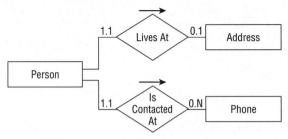

Figure 12-9

Improving the Entity-Relationship Diagram

If you look closely at Figure 12-7, you'll find two many-to-many relationships. First, a Customer may take many Courses while a Course may have many Customers enrolled. Second, an Order may contain many InventoryItems and an InventoryItem can be part of many Orders.

Entity-relationship diagrams have no trouble modeling many-to-many relationships, but a relational model cannot. To see why not, consider the relationship between Customer and Course. To build this relationship in a relational model, one of the tables must contain information linking it to the other.

To link a single Customer record to many Course records, you would need to list many Course IDs in the Customer record. Because a customer might take any number of courses, that would require the Customer record to contain an indefinite number of fields, and that's not allowed in a relational model.

Now suppose you try to make a single Course record hold information linking it to several Customer records. That would require the Course record to contain an indefinite number of fields, and that's not allowed in a relational model.

The way out of this dilemma is to create an intermediate entity to represent the combination of a particular customer and a particular course. Then you can connect the Customer and Course entities to the new one with one-to-many relationships, which can be represented in a relational model.

Figure 12-10 shows this new piece of the entity-relationship puzzle. Now a Customer is associated with any number of CustomerCourse entities, each of which is associated with a single Course. Similarly, a Course is associated with any number of CustomerCourse entities, each of which is associated with a single Customer.

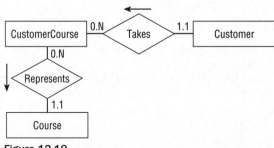

Figure 12-10

Try It Out   Broken Relationships

Restructure the other many-to-many relationship shown in Figure 12-7 between Order and InventoryItem so it doesn't require a many-to-many relationship.

1.   Create a new intermediate entity.

2.   Associate the new entity with the old ones.

How It Works

1.   To connect the Order and InventoryItems entity sets, create a new OrderItem entity set.

2.   Connect the Order and InventoryItems entity sets with the new one.

One order can contain one or more items so the OrderItem end of the Order/OrderItem relationship has cardinality 1.N. One OrderItem is associated with exactly one Order so the Order end of this relation has cardinality 1.1.

One inventory item can be used in zero or more orders, so it may be represented by many OrderItems. That means the OrderItem end of the InventoryItem/OrderItem relationship has cardinality 0.N. A single order item represents a particular inventory item, so the InventoryItem end of this relationship has cardinality 1.1.

Figure 12-11 shows an ER diagram representing the Order/OrderItem/InventoryItem relationships.

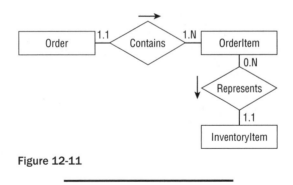

Figure 12-11

Figure 12-12 shows the new larger ER diagram from Figure 12-7 with the many-to-many relationships replaced by intermediate tables.

The changes to remove the many-to-many relationships are another step that normalizes part of the database. They remove the need for repeated columns in tables by replacing them with intermediate tables. The entity-relationship model can represent many-to-many relationships, so you don't really need to remove them at this stage. Instead you could wait and remove them when you build the relational model in the next step. However, the diagram shown in Figure 12-7 makes these relationships easy to see, so this is a reasonable time to straighten them out and it will make building the relational model easier in the following chapter.

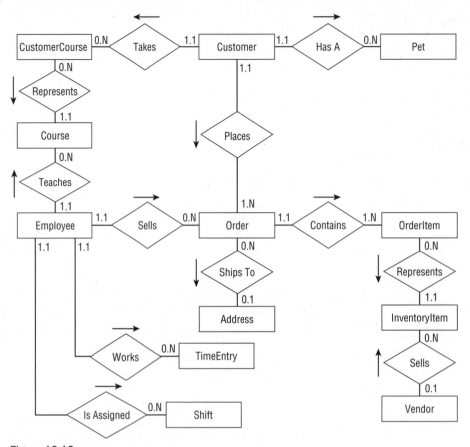

Figure 12-12

Relational Modeling

The semantic object model made it easy to study the classes that will make up the database and allowed some normalization. The entity-relationship model emphasized the entities' relationships and made it easy to remove many-to-many associations.

Now it's time to use what you've learned by building the semantic object and entity-relationship models to create a relational model.

Start by making a table for each of the models' classes and entity sets. Look at the final ER diagrams shown in Figures 12-8, 12-9, and 12-12, and make tables for the entities drawn in rectangles. The following list shows the tables that you need to create:

❑   CustomerCourses

❑   Customers

❑   Pets

- ❏ Courses
- ❏ Employees
- ❏ Orders
- ❏ OrderItems
- ❏ Addresses
- ❏ InventoryItems
- ❏ TimeEntries
- ❏ Shifts
- ❏ Vendors
- ❏ Persons
- ❏ Phones

Refer to the semantic object model in Figure 12-4 to find the basic fields that each table needs.

Next consider the tables that are directly related in the ER diagrams. Figure 12-12 contains several one-to-many relationships. To implement those in the relational model, you need one of the related tables to include a field that leads back to a field in the other table. The table at the "one" end of the one-to-many relationship cannot hold an unknown number of fields linking to the "many" records, so the fields must work the other way around.

In the table on the "one" side of the relationships, identify the primary key fields. Remember, to qualify as a primary key, the fields must guarantee uniqueness so no two records in the table can have exactly the same primary key values.

Because those fields will be used as the record's primary key, they should not be values that you will want to modify later. For example, a combined FirstName/LastName key is a bit risky because people do occasionally change their names.

The key values will also be contained in the table on the "many" side of the relationship, so it's better if the key doesn't include a lot of data. The FirstName/LastName pair might be a moderately long text string. Though it won't hurt database performance too much if you use such a key, it's easier to work with a single field key.

If the table on the "one" side of the relationship doesn't contain an easy-to-use natural key, add one. Name it after the table and add "Id" at the end.

For example, consider the relationship between the Address and Order entities. Figure 12-12 shows that this is a one-to-many relationship with the Address entity on the "one" side. That entity contains Street, City, State, and Zip attributes. Even if you allow only a single customer per street address, using those fields as the primary key would be a risky because you might need to change them later. For example, an employee might misspell the customer's street name when creating the customer's record. Even worse, a customer might move to a new address. In both of those cases, it would be seriously annoying to have to delete the customer's record and create a new one just to update the address. (Although I have an Internet service provider that cannot seem to figure out how to change a customer's email address without closing the account and opening a new one. I'd send them a copy of this book if I thought they'd read it.)

Because this table has no natural primary key, add an AddressId field to it and use that to link the tables together.

Now add an AddressId field to the "many" side of the relationship. In this example, that means adding a new field to the Orders table.

Finally, draw the link between the two tables, place a 1 next to the "one" end of the relationship, and a ∞ next to the "many" end.

Figure 12-13 shows the resulting relational model for these two tables. Note that this version considers only those two tables. In the more complete model, these tables will need additional ID fields to link them to other tables.

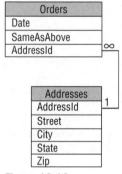

Figure 12-13

Try It Out   Identifying IDs

Figure out what fields to add to represent the relationship between the Orders and OrderItems tables.

1. Identify the "one" side of the one-to-many relationship. Find or create a primary key for that table.

2. Give the table representing the "many" side of the relationship fields to refer to the first table's primary key.

3. Draw the tables and the new link. Include the information about the relationship between Orders and Addresses shown in Figure 12-13.

How It Works

1. The Orders table represents the "one" side of this one-to-many relationship because one order can include many OrderItems. There is no natural primary key in an Order entity (if the same customer placed another order on the same date, it could have exactly the same values), so add a new OrderId field to the Orders table.

   A single order can have many order items, so OrderId isn't enough to uniquely identify the records in the OrderItems table. Add a SequenceNumber field to the primary key to uniquely identify the records. This field also lets you display the items for an order in sorted order. The record with SequenceNumber = 1 comes first, the records with SequenceNumber = 2 comes next, and so forth. Displaying the items in the same order in which they were originally entered is generally comforting to the users.

2.   The OrderItems table represents the "many" side of the one-to-many relationship. Give it an OrderId field that refers back to the Orders table's OrderId field. Notice that the OrderItems table's primary key includes both the OrderId and SequenceNumber fields but the Orders table refers only to the OrderId field. A program listing an order's items would use the OrderId value to fetch all of the related OrderItems records and then would use the SequenceNumber field to sort them.

3.   Figure 12-14 shows a relational diagram that includes the previous relationship between Orders and Addresses shown in Figure 12-13 plus the new relationship between Orders and OrderItems.

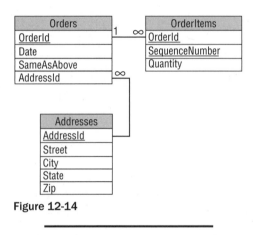

Figure 12-14

Putting It All Together

Continue examining the relationships shown in the ER diagram in Figure 12-12. Find or create a primary key in the table on the "one" side of the relationship and add a corresponding field in the table on the "many" side.

You can make arranging the tables easier if you place them in roughly the same arrangement that the corresponding entities occupied in the entity-relationship diagram. (Figures 12-13 and 12-14 show the Addresses table below the Orders table because the Address entity is below the Order entity in Figure 12-12.)

You'll probably need to move the tables around a little because they won't be the same size as the rectangles in the ER diagram, but starting with that arrangement should make drawing relationships between the tables easier.

Figure 12-15 shows the resulting relational model.

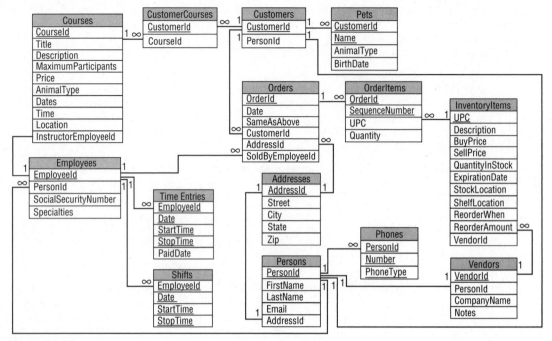

Figure 12-15

As a quick check, examine each relational link. The end touching a primary key field should have cardinality 1. The field's name should be the table's name plus "Id." The exception to this naming convention is in the InventoryItems table, which includes the natural primary key field UPC.

The end of a link touching the foreign key field on the "many" side of the relationship should have the same name as the ID field and should have cardinality 1 (for a one-to-one relationship) or ∞ (for a one-to-many relationship).

Note that the two intermediate tables used to represent many-to-many relationships, CustomerCourses and OrderItems, contain little more than keys linking to the two tables that they connect. For example, the CustomerCourses table contains only a CustomerId field linking to the Customers table and a CourseId field linking to the Courses table.

The OrderItems table includes its two linking ID fields plus the SequenceNumber field to make the primary key unique and to allow sorting. It also contains a Quantity field to indicate the number of that type of item included in the order (for example, 3 pencils).

Summary

This chapter explains the data modeling steps for The Pampered Pet database project. It showed how to build a semantic object model and how to convert that into an entity-relationship model. Along the way, it showed how to improve the models by normalizing parts of them.

In this chapter, you saw examples of:

- ❏ Building semantic objects.
- ❏ Moving repeated semantic group attributes and some other group attributes into new classes.
- ❏ Converting a semantic object model into an entity-relationship model.
- ❏ Representing many-to-many relationships with two one-to-many relationships.
- ❏ Improving models by normalizing parts of them.
- ❏ Converting semantic object models and ER diagrams into a relational model.
- ❏ Adding ID fields to tables.
- ❏ Converting entity relationships into relational links.

Not all projects use both semantic object models and entity-relationship models. Many developers prefer one or the other and don't bother with the extra work of creating two models. Some even jump straight to a relational model. Each of these types of models has its strengths and weaknesses, however, so it's often useful to work through all three kinds.

Figure 12-15 shows a pretty reasonable relational model for The Pampered Pet database, but it's still not perfect. If you look closely, you may be able to identify a few places where the tables are not well normalized. (Can you spot the tables that are not even in First Normal Form?)

Chapter 13 shows how to improve the model by isolating business rules that are likely to change in the future. Chapter 14 further normalizes the database and puts the finishing touches on it.

Before you move on to Chapter 13, however, use the following exercises to test your understanding of the material covered in this chapter. You can find the solutions to these exercises in Appendix A.

Exercises

Consider the entity-relationship diagram shown in Figure 12-12 and think about possible changes that The Pampered Pet might later want to make to the database. Easy changes include adding or removing non-identifier fields from an entity. Harder changes would require adding or removing entities or changing the relationships among them. For each of the following changes, explain how you would make the change and how hard it would be.

1. The Pampered Pet opens a café that serves snacks for pets and their owners. How would you handle the new food items for sale?

2. Management decides that only certain employees with special training can teach courses. How would you model this new type of employee?

3. The Pampered Pet opens a new store. Management wants to track customers company-wide but wants to track sales by store. How would you handle that?

4. New courses are offered offsite. How would you store the addresses of these offsite courses?

5. The Pampered Pet offers free clinics and outings such as dog and llama hikes. How would you store information about these freebies?

6. You need to allow more than one address on an order. How would you store the new addresses?

7. You need to store a phone number for each order. How would you store these phone numbers?

8. Management decides they want to track the department that sold each item. How would you track item departments?

9. Management decides to track customer addresses as they change over time. How would you remember old addresses?

10. The Pampered Pet starts holding sales and offering discounts to employees. Where do you store the discount information?

11. Figure 12-16 shows an ER diagram for a Robot Wars competition (see www.marcthorpe.com/ robot.html). A competitor builds one or more robots either alone or with others (so robots can have one or more builders). Each robot can fight in any number of matches (if it survives) and a match involves several robots. Finally, each match has a single winner (the last robot survivor). Unfortunately, the design shown in Figure 12-16 includes two many-to-many relationships. Draw a new ER diagram that replaces those relationships with one-to-many relationships.

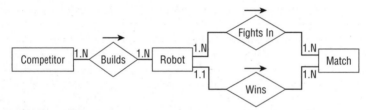

Figure 12-16

12. Build a relational model for the solution you built for Exercise 11.

Extracting Business Rules

The previous chapters have built up a basic design for The Pampered Pet database. They gathered customer requirements, built a semantic object model and entity-relationship diagrams, and converted those into a relational model.

This chapter further refines the design by identifying business rules in the relational model and isolating them so they will be easy to modify in the future if necessary.

In this chapter you see examples that:

❑   Identify required fields and other field-level constraints that are unlikely to change.

❑   Identify sanity checks that are also unlikely to change.

❑   Identify business rules that are more complicated or likely to change in the future.

Identifying Business Rules

The text and exercises in Chapter 11 listed the fields required for the initial database design. For each field, that chapter gave the field's data type, whether the field is required, and its domain. That information describes most of the project's business rules.

Domain information usually includes simple "sanity check" constraints. These are conditions that basically verify the "laws of physics" for the database. For example, an item's cost cannot be less than $0.00. Exercise 5 in Chapter 12 discussed free clinics and outings, so it's possible that an item might be free, but it's hard to imagine The Pampered Pet's management charging less than nothing for a product.

Other sanity check conditions include field data types and whether a field is required. It may also include simple pattern validation. For example, the database might require a phone number to have a 10-digit format, as in 602-827-1298.

Because these sanity checks will never change, they can be coded directly into the database by setting field conditions (data type and required) and check constraints.

Primary key information is also built into the database. For example, making the InventoryItems table's primary key be its UPC field ensures that every record has a non-null UPC value and that every record has a unique UPC value.

Other domain information is either more complicated or more likely to change over time. Those conditions should be isolated as much as possible to make them easier to change in the future.

The following sections describe the constraints on each of the tables defined in the relational model shown in Figure 12-15. They explain which of those constraints can be built into the database and which should be isolated as business rules.

Courses

The Courses table's required fields include: CourseId (the primary key), Title, Description, MaximumParticipants, Price, AnimalType, Dates, Time, and Location. The InstructorEmployeeId is not required and only gets filled in after an employee is assigned to teach the course. The required fields can be built into the database.

Sanity checks include:

❑   MaximumParticipants $> = 0$ and MaximumParticipants < 100.

❑   Price > 0.

❑   Dates no earlier than the current date.

❑   Time between 8am and 11pm.

The sanity checks can be built into the database as field-level check constraints.

This table has two fields that take values from enumerated lists:

❑   AnimalType comes from the list Cat, Dog, Bird, and so on.

❑   Location comes from the list Room 1, Room 2, Back Yard, arena, and so on.

If you coded the lists of choices allowed for AnimalType and Location into field-level check constraints, you would have to make non-trivial changes if the allowed values changed. To make the design more flexible, the choices should be placed in lookup tables AnimalTypes and Locations. Then the fields in the Courses table can refer to those values as foreign key constraints.

This table contains one slightly more complicated validation:

❑   Price > 0. The price must be at least 0. Management has not said it could be equal to 0 but that's a change they could make in the future.

This rule could be implemented in the user interface or in middle-tier code that fetches and updates course data.

It's tempting to make this a field-level check constraint. After all, it would be relatively easy to do so and the change isn't inevitable. However, suppose the company offers free clinics for a while and then decides to no longer offer them. At that point, there would be old course entries with Price = 0 and you could not change the field-level check constraint back to Price > 0 because it would contradict existing data.

The management will get the most flexibility for this constraint if it is kept separate from the database's structure. It could be implemented in middle-tier routines that fetch and update Courses data.

Figure 13-1 shows the Courses table with its new lookup tables. The lookup tables are drawn with dashed rectangles so the main tables stand out from them. This figure omits all of the other tables and their relationships.

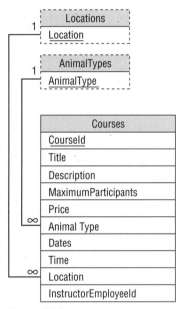

Figure 13-1

Try It Out   Address Constraints

Identify the various kinds of constraints on the Addresses table and determine which should be implemented in the database and which should be provided elsewhere as business rules.

1. Identify the primary key and the required fields.
2. Identify sanity checks that will never change.
3. Create lookup tables for fields with a fixed set of allowed values.
4. Identify more complicated business rules and rules that may change in the future.

How It Works

1. The Addresses table's required fields are: AddressId (the primary key), Street, City, State, Zip. All of these fields should be marked as required in the database.

2. In the United States at least, the Zip value must always have the form 12345 or 12345-6789. Verifying the format could be implemented as a simple field-level check constraint.

3. The State field's values must be one of the standard state abbreviations. Those abbreviations should be added to a States table and then this field can refer to it as a foreign key.

4. The relationship between City, State, and Zip is complex. It probably doesn't make a lot of sense to validate every possible combination because that would require a huge lookup table. It's unlikely that The Pampered Pet will do business in every state, so most of that data would never be used. (The United States Postal Service FAQ at `www.maponics.com/ZIP_Code_Maps/ZIP_Code_FAQ/zip_code_faq.html` says there are roughly 45,000 ZIP Codes and there are approximately 25,000 ZIP Code changes every month. There's no way I would want to try to keep up with that!)

An alternative would be to build a CityStateZips lookup table to hold the nearby City/State/Zip combinations and then warn the user if a record has a set of values that is not in the list. This way if the user misspells a local town or enters a Zip value that doesn't match that town, the program will let the user fix it. In contrast, if a customer wants an order shipped a thousand miles away, the program warns that it doesn't know about this City/State/Zip combination but lets the user enter it anyway.

Database constraints are unyielding. A value is either allowed or it isn't. By itself, the database won't ask the user "Are you sure?" and then accept a suspicious value. That means this constraint cannot be implemented in the database. It must be implemented in a middle-tier routine or in the user interface.

Figure 13-2 shows the Addresses table with its States lookup table and the pseudo-lookup CityStateZip table. Both are drawn in dashed rectangles to indicate that they are lookup tables. The relationship between the Addresses table and the CityStateZips table is also dashed because it is implemented in a middle-tier routine or the user interface rather than inside the database.

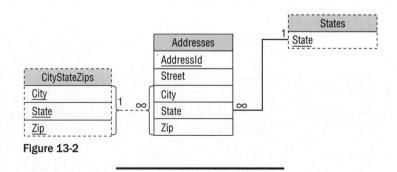

Figure 13-2

CustomerCourses

This table is an intermediate table representing the many-to-many relationship between the Courses and Customers tables. It contains only two fields, CustomerId and CourseId. Both of these are required because they are part of the table's primary key. They are also used as foreign key constraints matching values in the Courses and Customers tables. That's about as constrained as a field can get, so there isn't much more to do with this table.

Customers

The version of the Customers table shown in Figure 12-15 contains only two fields. CustomerId is the primary key. PersonId is used in a foreign key constraint matching values in the Persons table so it's completely constrained.

Pets

The Pets table's CustomerId and Name fields form the primary key. Its other fields, AnimalType and BirthDate, are also required, so they should be flagged as required, in the database.

It wouldn't hurt to put a sanity check constraint on the BirthDate field to verify that new dates are not after the current date. Some pets live a really long time, so it's hard to set a safe lower limit on BirthDate. (Macaws can live 65 or more years and aggressive little yippy dogs live practically forever — at least that seems to be the case with my neighbor's dogs.)

The AnimalType field can only take a value from a list of allowed values, so those values should be placed in a lookup table. The design already calls for an AnimalTypes lookup table (see the section about the Courses table earlier in this chapter), so this table can refer to that one.

Employees

The Employees table's primary key is its EmployeeId field. The PersonId and SocialSecurityNumber fields are also required.

The SocialSecurityNumber field must have a format similar to 123-45-6789. That pattern can be verified by a field-level check constraint.

PersonId is a foreign key constraint referring to the Persons table, so it is completely constrained.

Orders

The Orders table's primary key is OrderId. The Date, SameAsAbove, CustomerId, and SoldByEmployeeId fields are also required.

CustomerId is a foreign key constraint referring to the Customers table, so it is constrained. Similarly, SoldByEmployeeId is a foreign key constraint referring to the Employees table so it also is constrained.

The AddressId field is optional. It is a foreign key constraint referring to the Addresses table, so if it is present it is completely constrained. (This field is fairly confusing. If the SameAsAbove field has value True, the customer wants the order shipped to the customer's address. If the SameAsAbove is False and AddressId is present, the customer wants the order shipped to that address. If SameAsAbove is False and AddressId is null, the customer is picking up the order and doesn't want it shipped. All of this must be implemented in the user interface but doesn't affect the database design.)

OrderItems

Like the CustomerCourses table, this table is an intermediate table used to implement a many-to-many relationship.

This table's OrderId and SequenceNumber fields make up the primary key. The UPC and Quantity fields are also required.

UPC is used as a foreign key constraint referring to the InventoryItems table, so it is completely constrained.

For sanity checking, a field-level check constraint should also verify that Quantity > 0.

InventoryItems

This table's UPC field is its primary key. The Description, SellPrice, QuantityInStock, StockLocation, and ShelfLocation fields are also required.

Sanity checks include:

- ❑ If present, BuyPrice > = $0.00.
- ❑ SellPrice > = $0.00.
- ❑ QuantityInStock > = 0.
- ❑ If present, ExpirationDate > January 1, 2008 (or some other date guaranteed to be earlier than the oldest expiration date in current inventory when you build the database).
- ❑ On new records, if present, ExpirationDate > the current date.
- ❑ If present, ReorderWhen > 0. (If null, reorder only occurs manually.)
- ❑ If present, ReorderAmount > = 0. (If null, someone must specify the amount.)

VendorId is a foreign key constraint referring to the Vendors table so, if its value is not null, the value is completely constrained.

The StockLocation and ShelfLocation fields can only take certain values, so those values should be moved into the lookup tables StockLocations and ShelfLocations.

TimeEntries

This table's EmployeeId, Date, StartTime, and StopTime fields make up its primary key.

EmployeeId is a foreign key constraint referring to the Employees table, so it is completely constrained.

The table should also contain the following field-level sanity check constraints:

- ❑ Date > = some early date such as the date the database is put into use.
- ❑ StartTime > = 6am.

❑   StopTime $< = 11$pm.

❑   If present, PaidDate $> =$ Date.

Shifts

The Shifts table is similar to the TimeEntries table except it doesn't have a PaidDate field. Its EmployeeId, Date, StartTime, and StopTime fields make up its primary key.

EmployeeId is a foreign key constraint referring to the Employees table, so it is completely constrained.

The table should also contain the following field-level sanity check constraints:

❑   Date $> =$ some early date such as the date the database is put into use.

❑   StartTime $> = 6$am.

❑   StopTime $< = 11$pm.

Persons

This table's PersonId is its primary key. The FirstName and LastName fields are also required.

Email should have a valid email format. Unfortunately it's pretty hard to define valid email formats, so this should be considered a more complicated business rule. Validation should be provided by a middle-tier routine that saves Persons records, a stored procedure, or user interface code. Then if management decides to change the way this field is validated, you can make the change reasonably easily.

This table's AddressId field is a foreign key constraint referring to the Addresses table so, if it is present, it is completely constrained.

Phones

This table's primary key includes all of its fields: PersonId, Number, and PhoneType.

PersonId is also a foreign key constraint referring to the Persons table, so it is completely constrained.

Number should have a valid phone number format such as 987-6543 or 202-123-4567. This won't change (unless the store starts accepting international orders), so it can be checked in a field-level check constraint.

PhoneType must be one of several values such as Home, Cell, or Work. Those values should be moved into a PhoneTypes lookup table so this field can refer to it as a foreign key constraint.

Vendors

The Vendors table's primary key is its VendorId field. The PersonId and CompanyName fields are also required.

PersonId is a foreign key constraint referring to the Persons table, so it is completely constrained.

The Notes field is completely unconstrained and optional.

Drawing a New Relational Model

Figure 13-3 shows the new relational model.

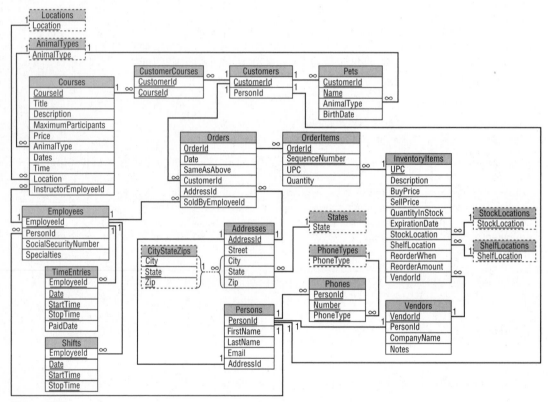

Figure 13-3

Summary

This chapter showed how to classify table constraints in The Pampered Pet database. It showed how to:

❑   Identify the primary key and the required fields (to implement in the database).

❑   Identify sanity checks that will never change (to implement in the database).

❑   Create lookup tables for fields with a fixed set of allowed values.

❑   Identify more complicated business rules and rules that may change in the future.

After identifying these constraints and adding lookup tables, this chapter showed a new relational design for the database.

Even at this point, however, the database isn't perfect. The following chapter makes a few final changes to make the database more flexible and robust.

Before you move on to Chapter 14, however, use the following exercises to test your understanding of the material covered in this chapter. You can find the solutions to these exercises in Appendix A.

Exercises

For these exercises, consider the relational model for a Robot Wars competition shown in Figure 13-4 (see the exercises at the end of Chapter 12 and www.marcthorpe.com/robot.html). Use your own judgment while working through the exercises.

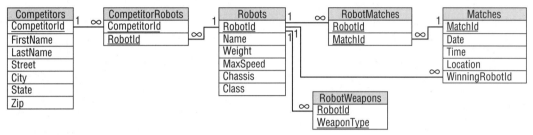

Figure 13-4

1. Identify the tables' primary keys and required fields.

2. Identify the tables' sanity checks that will never change.

3. Define lookup tables for fields with a fixed set of allowed values.

4. I can think of three somewhat more complicated business rules that should be implemented, but in general it would be hard to identify more complicated business rules without knowing more about the competition. See if you can think of the three I thought of and make up some others. What sorts of things would make interesting business rules that should not be built into the database?

5. Draw a new relational model showing the new tables.

Normalization and Refinement

Chapters 11 through 13 walked through the steps of designing a preliminary database for The Pampered Pet. They showed how to gather requirements, build semantic object and entity-relationship models, and convert those into a relational model. Chapter 13 showed how to identify rules that should be built into the database and more complex or changeable rules that should be isolated as business rules.

Even after all of this work, the database isn't perfect. This chapter puts the finishing touches on the database by normalizing it appropriately.

In this chapter you see examples of:

❑ Improving the design to make the database more flexible.

❑ Identifying tables that are insufficiently normalized.

❑ Normalizing tables to prevent data anomalies.

❑ Not normalizing where normalization would be more trouble than it's worth.

Improving Flexibility

Figure 14-1 shows the relational design built in Chapter 13.

This design is fairly reasonable, and I've seen worse designs in working databases, but it can use a couple of improvements. Later sections in this chapter discuss normalization, but first there's a big flaw to fix.

If you think about the design long enough and you walk through the use cases, you'll notice that there's a problem with the course data. Currently the design allows many customers to take a course and it allows a course to hold many customers. However, the design allows only one instance of any given course. If you run a Puppy Socialization course in April, you cannot run the same course again in May because the course's dates would have already passed.

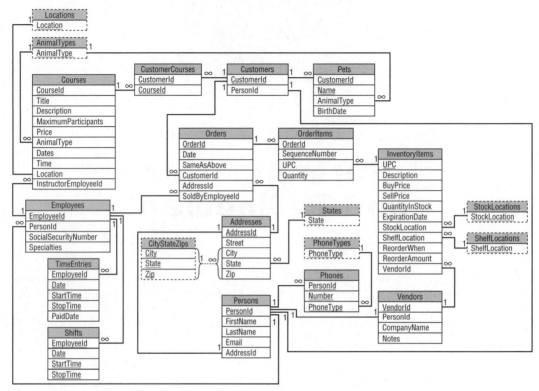

Figure 14-1

Furthermore, the same customer couldn't take both the April and May courses (some dogs are slow learners) because that would require identical records in the CustomerCourses table.

Instead you would need to make a completely new Courses record for the May course. That wouldn't be the end of the world, and some applications would do exactly that, but now the table contains multiple records that really represent different offerings of the same thing. You can tell that there's a problem because the records would have so many duplicated fields: Title, Description, Price, and AnimalType. The fields that would change between offerings are MaximumParticipants, Dates, Time, Location, and InstructorEmployeeId.

The customers taking the course would also change (except for those who fail the first time and retake the course), so the course offering would need some kind of new ID value to link it to the CustomerCourses table.

The database needs a new type of object to represent a course offering. The course offerings will link to a Courses record that provides all of their shared data.

One course can have many offerings, but an offering corresponds to only one course, so this is a one-to-many relationship, and you can add it to the database the way you always build a one-to-many relationship. First, add an ID field to the "one" table. Then refer to the ID field in the "many" table as a foreign key.

Now the CustomerCourses table should link to the new CourseOfferings table instead of the Courses table (because the customer takes an offering of a course not the abstract course description).

Figure 14-2 shows the design with the new table added.

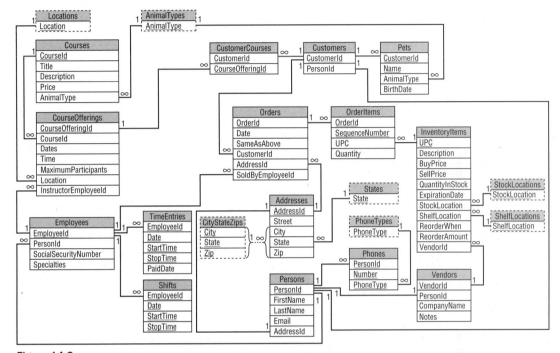

Figure 14-2

Verifying First Normal Form

The previous chapters were pretty careful about building their tables so they're almost certainly in 1NF, right? Not always. With some experience and attention to detail, you should be able to build tables in 1NF almost all of the time and 3NF most of the time, but occasionally a few normalization bugs slip through.

Recall the rules for 1NF:

1. Each column must have a unique name.

2. The order of the rows and columns doesn't matter.

3. Each column must have a single data type.

4. No two rows can contain identical values. (The table has a unique primary key.)

5. Each column must contain a single value.

You can easily verify the first four rules. For example, the Courses table's columns all have different names, the order of rows and columns doesn't matter, each column in the Courses table has a single data type, and the CourseId field is the primary key so no two records can have the same CourseId value and therefore, they are different.

The rule that usually catches people is rule 5: Each column must contain a single value. Sometimes the data in a field contains more than one logical piece of data. In that case, the field should be broken into pieces.

If you know how many pieces there will be, you can use multiple fields in the same table. For example, if you have a Name field that should be broken into FirstName and LastName, you know there are only two pieces to the field and you can just replace it with two new fields.

If the field's data could contain any number of values, you should move the values into a new table and link back to the original table. For example, suppose the Customers table contains a Children field that lists the customer's children's names separated by commas. In that case you can't just add a bunch of Child fields to the Customers table. Instead you need to add a Cus-tomerChildren table that uses CustomerId to find the Customer associated with a particular record.

If you look carefully at each of the fields shown in Figure 14-2, you'll find a couple that might contain multiple data values. You can ignore simple compound values such as the Pets table's BirthDate field and the Phones table's Number field. Though you can think of a birth date as containing a day, month, and year, The Pampered Pet will probably never need to look at those values separately. I suppose someone might want to make a list of all pets born on the 13th of every month, but that would be pretty strange. Similarly, unless the requirements call for you to be able to list customers in a given area code, it isn't worth breaking up the phone number field.

The first field that truly holds more than one value is the CourseOfferings table's Dates field. This single field is supposed to hold a list of the dates when a course offering takes place. For example, a particular offering might occur every Wednesday for six weeks.

If every course is only offered on a weekly schedule, such as every Wednesday, you could encode that in a single field by simply giving the day of the week. If there might be exceptions (for example, six Mondays, skipping Labor Day), that system doesn't work as well.

To solve this problem, you can break the Dates field into pieces. If The Pampered Pet doesn't require every course to have the same number of sessions, you need to move the values into a new CourseOffer-ingDates table that refers back to its course offering.

Figure 14-3 shows the design with the new CourseOfferingDates table.

One hint that a field might contain multiple values is that its name is plural. If the field represents a number, such as the CourseOfferings table's MaximumParticipants field, it probably represents a single value. If the field represents a group of values, however, it should probably be broken apart.

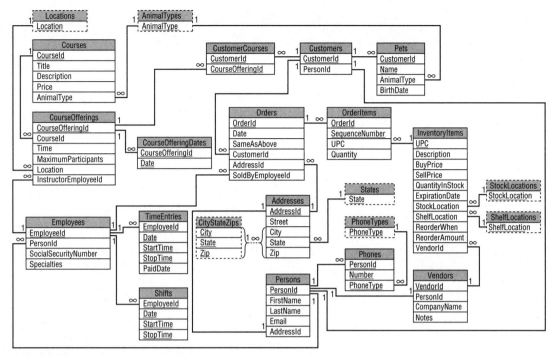

Figure 14-3

Try It Out   Normal

There's one other table in Figure 14-3 that isn't in 1NF. Find and fix it.

1. Look for fields that don't represent a single value.

2. Decide whether the field contains a fixed, known number of values or an unknown number of values. If the field contains a fixed number of values, split it into the required number of fields. If the field contains an unknown number of values, move the values into a new table.

3. Perform other modifications to the design if this change requires them. (Hint: In this case, you'll need to create a new lookup table.)

How It Works

1. All of the fields shown in Figure 14-3 represent a single value except the Employees table's Specialties field. This field lists the employee's areas of expertise. They might include animal types, products, problems, and so forth. A typical value might be, "Cat, Dog, Parasites." (This is also the only field in Figure 14-3 that has a plural name other than MaximumParticipants, which represents a single number.)

2. The Specialties field could contain any number of values so it cannot be broken into new fields within the Employees table. Instead the model needs a new Specialties table that refers back to Employees. The new table will have fields EmployeeId and Specialty.

3. The new table's Specialty field can contain only specific values, such as Cat, Dog, and Penguin, so the model should validate the field by making it a foreign key that refers to a lookup table. In this case, the new table should be called Specialties and will have a single field Specialty. Figure 14-4 shows the new design.

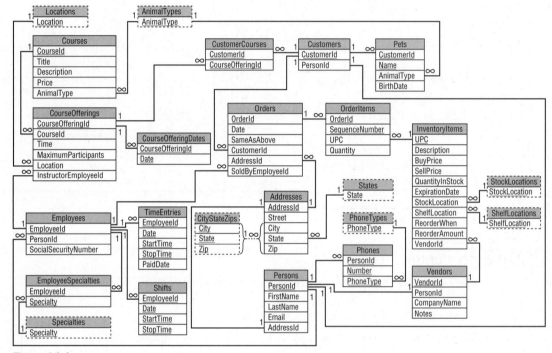

Figure 14-4

Verifying Second Normal Form

Recall the rules for 2NF:

1. The table is in 1NF.

2. All of the non-key fields depend on all of the key fields.

Many of the tables have a one-field primary key, so every other field must depend on the entire primary key. In the intermediate tables representing many-to-many relationships and the lookup tables, every field is part of the primary key, so rule 2 doesn't apply.

The only tables remaining to consider are Pets, OrderItems, and TimeEntries.

Pets

The Pets table's primary key contains the combination CustomerId/Name. Its other fields are AnimalType and BirthDate. AnimalType depends on both CustomerId and Name because you need to know both CustomerId and Name to deduce the pet's AnimalType.

Another way to think of this is to notice that if you know the CustomerId alone, you cannot guess the pet's AnimalType because the customer might have a cat and a fish. Similarly, if you know the pet's Name, you cannot determine the AnimalType because different customers might have different kinds of pets with the same name. You can use similar arguments to show that BirthDate depends on both CustomerId and Name.

A third way to look at this, which may be less intuitive but which is easy to apply mechanically, is to ask yourself whether the database could contain any record with the same CustomerId, a different Name, and a different AnimalType. If CustomerId alone determines animal type, then every record with the same CustomerId must have the same AnimalType.

In this case, the database could hold a record with the same CustomerId, a different Name, and a different AnimalType (someone could own a fish named Phred and a dog named Pheidaux) so you know that AnimalType depends on CustomerId.

Similarly, you can ask whether another record could have the same Name, different CustomerId, and different AnimalType. I have a dog named Snortimer and I've met two other people with cats named Snortimer, so that situation is possible. That means AnimalType also depends on CustomerId.

You can use similar arguments to show that BirthDate depends on both CustomerId and Name.

(This all assumes a customer doesn't give multiple pets the same name. There's a silly Sandra Boynton song named "Fifteen Animals" about a guy who has 15 pets all named Bob, except his turtle, which he named Simon James Alexander Ragsdale III. For this customer, you'll probably have to assign the pets serial numbers or something: Bob-1, Bob-2, Bob-3, and so forth.)

Try It Out   **OrderItems**

Verify that the OrderItems table is in 2NF. For each of the table's primary keys (OrderId and SequenceNumber) and each of the non-key fields (UPC and Quantity), see if another record could have a different value for the key field and a different value for the non-key field. Consider all four combinations:

1. OrderId and UPC
2. OrderId and Quantity
3. SequenceNumber and UPC
4. SequenceNumber and Quantity

How It Works

1. Could there be two records with the same SequenceNumber, different OrderId, and different UPC? Yes. Two orders could contain different items listed first. Then the OrderItems records will

have the same SequenceNumber (because the items are listed first), different OrderId (because they're two separate orders), and different UPC (because the orders are for different things).

2. Could there be two records with the same SequenceNumber, different OrderId, and different Quantity? Yes. Two orders could contain different quantities of the same item. For example, one customer could order one toy mouse and a second customer could order two toy mice. Then the OrderItem records will have the same SequenceNumber (because they are the first items for each order), different OrderId (because they are different orders), and different Quantity (because the first customer ordered one toy mouse and the second customer ordered two).

3. Could there be two records with the same OrderId, different SequenceNumber, and different UPC? Yes. Suppose an order contains two different items. Then the OrderItems records will have the same OrderId (because they're part of the same order), different SequenceNumber (because they're different line items in the order), and different UPC (because the two items are different).

4. Could there be two records with the same OrderId, different SequenceNumber, and different Quantity? Yes. Suppose an order contains two items with different quantities (for example, one hamster wheel and two rawhide bones). Then the OrderItems table will contain two records for this order with the same OrderId, different SequenceNumber (1 and 2), and different Quantity (1 and 2).

Because the table can hold all of these combinations, all of the non-key fields depend on every primary key field, so the table is in 2NF.

TimeEntries

The TimeEntries table's primary key includes the fields EmployeeId, Date, StartTime, and StopTime. Its only remaining field is PaidDate. To see that PaidDate depends on all of the primary key fields, ask yourself whether you could deduce the PaidDate value if you are missing one of the key values.

If EmployeeId is missing, another employee might have worked the same shift and may or may not be paid.

If Date is missing, the employee might have worked similar hours on another date and may or may not have been paid.

The StartTime and StopTime fields are a bit trickier. If StartTime is missing, the table could contain another record for the same employee on this date with the same StopTime but a different StartTime. However, the business rules require that this table cannot have two records for the same employee on the same date with overlapping times, so this record would not be allowed.

Does that mean the PaidDate field doesn't depend on StopTime, so the table isn't in 2NF? Not really. Though the table isn't allowed to hold a record with overlapping times, the table's structure doesn't prevent it; a business rule does.

To see this in another way, consider the wrestling match schedule described in the "Second Normal Form (2NF)" section of Chapter 7. The following table shows part of a schedule of matches. The table's primary key is the Time/Wrestler combination.

Time	Wrestler	Class	Rank
1:30	Annette Cart	Pro	3
2:00	Sydney Dart	Amateur	1
3:45	Annette Cart	Pro	3

The problem with this table is that Class and Rank depend only on Wrestler and not on Time. Annette Cart is ranked 3rd professionally no matter when she wrestles. That makes the table vulnerable to data anomalies. For example, if you change the first entry's Class to Amateur, it contradicts the third entry.

Now consider again the TimeEntries table. Because of the "no overlapping time" business rule, this table cannot hold two records with the same EmployeeId, Date, and StopTime. It cannot hold two records that correspond to the two wrestling schedule records for Annette Cart and that means it cannot suffer from the same kind of modification anomaly as the wrestling schedule table.

Similarly, the table is safe from update anomalies because you cannot add two records with the same EmployeeId, Date, and StopTime.

Verifying Third Normal Form

Recall the rules for 3NF:

1. The table is in 2NF.
2. It contains no transitive dependencies.

A *transitive dependency* is when one non-key field's value depends on another non-key field's value. It takes a bit more work to find transitive dependencies than it does to detect other errors.

Because transitive dependencies occur when two non-key fields are related, you only need to consider tables that have at least two non-key fields. In this example, those tables are Courses, CourseOfferings, Pets, Orders, OrderItems, InventoryItems, Employees, Vendors, Addresses, and Persons.

Most of these tables are easy to check. For example, consider OrderItems. Its non-key fields are UPC and Quantity. Are these fields related? Of course not. The type of item a customer is buying does not determine the number of items bought or vice versa. (If the store has only one Jack Russell Terrier, you can only buy one, but that's an inventory issue, not a database design issue. Of course Jack Russells are so energetic it might be insane to buy more than one but again, that's not a database design issue.)

In the Courses table, the Title, Description, Price, and AnimalType fields don't depend on each other. If the business requirements stated that all Dog courses had the same price, then things would be different, but in this example there are no such restrictions.

The Orders table might give you pause because the CustomerId might be related in some sense to the AddressId. Remember that an Orders record has an AddressId field only if the customer wants the order shipped to an address other than the customer's usual address, however, so the relationship is not really there. If the order included the customer's home address every time, there would be a relationship between the CustomerId and the AddressId.

The Addresses table also contains the standard weird relationship between City, State, and Zip. Chapter 13 already considered this relationship (see the section "Try It Out, Address Constraints") and decided to live with a lookup table for local addresses rather than building an enormous lookup table for every City/State/Zip combination.

The last tricky table is CourseOfferings. The maximum number of participants for a course is determined by the location where it is taught. For example, the store's back conference room can only hold 20 people so that's the maximum size for any course taught there.

This transitive dependency means that any course in a particular location will have the same MaximumParticipants value. To remove this dependency, you should create a new table that lists the MaximumParticipants value for each location and then remove MaximumParticipants from the CourseOfferings table. However, the design already contains a Locations lookup table that holds location names. You can use that table if you add the MaximumParticipants field to it.

Note that it's not always a good idea to combine tables in this manner. In this case, however, the new version of the table holds data for a single, clearly defined purpose: to describe locations. Because the table's fields both fit this purpose, it makes sense to put them in the same table.

Figure 14-5 shows the new design. The new version of the Locations table is no longer simply a lookup table, so it's not drawn with a dashed rectangle in Figure 14-5.

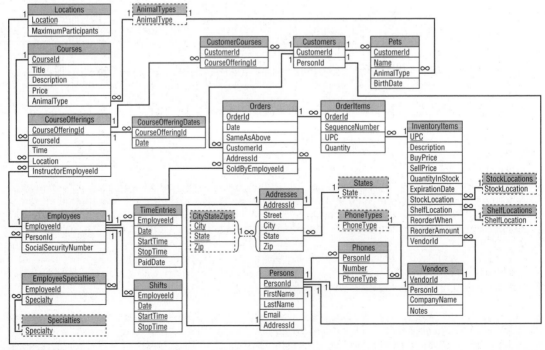

Figure 14-5

Notice that the Locations table acts as a lookup table for the CourseOfferings table's Location field. The Locations table is not only a lookup table, however, so it's not drawn with a dashed rectangle. You could remove the pure lookup tables from the database and the database would still function, although you would need to implement some field-level check constraints. If you removed the Locations table, you would lose all of the MaximumParticipants data.

Note that the business rules could have indicated that different courses using a particular location might be able to have different numbers of participants. For example, a seminar on piranha feeding takes less room than a hands-on elephant training workshop, so more people will fit in the room. You could model that situation by making the Locations table use Location and AnimalType as its primary key, but this example seems complicated enough already.

Summary

This chapter refined The Pampered Pet database to increase its flexibility. It also normalized the database's tables to make the database more resistant to data anomalies.

This chapter showed examples of:

❑ Increasing the database's flexibility by allowing multiple offerings of a particular course.

❑ Putting the CourseOfferings table into 1NF by moving course dates into a new CourseOffering-Dates table.

❑ Putting the Employees table into 1NF by moving employee specialty information into a new EmployeeSpecialties table.

❑ Putting the CourseOfferings table into 3NF by moving information about the maximum number of participants at a location into a new Locations table.

(Of course you may have seen these problems earlier and been muttering under your breath about how silly the design was for the last few chapters, but sometimes these problems sneak through to the bitter end.)

At this point, the database is in pretty good shape and you should be able to build it with some confidence that it can successfully fend off some serious data anomalies.

However, Figure 14-5 doesn't show the complete picture. It shows the table structures and lookup tables, but it doesn't show the many additional constraints that were identified in Chapters 11 and 13. Those must be implemented as field- and table-level check constraints.

The following chapters show how to build this database in the Access and MySQL relational database management systems. They show how to build the tables shown in Figure 14-5 and how to provide the necessary check constraints to really make the database robust.

Before you move on to Chapter 15, however, use the following exercises to test your under-standing of the material covered in this chapter. You can find the solutions to these exercises in Appendix A.

Exercises

For these exercises, consider the following aquarium show schedule. The show times with asterisks match with the shows with asterisks. For example, the 11:15 show in Sherman's Lagoon is "Sherm's Shark Show" and the 1:15 show is "Meet the Rays." (Yeah, I think it's a strange way to list shows, too, but I saw a real schedule very similar to this one recently.)

Show	Venue	Seating	Times
Sherm's Shark Show / Meet the Rays*	Sherman's Lagoon	375	11:15, 1:15*, 3:00, 6:00*
Deb's Daring Dolphins / The Walter Walrus Comedy Hour*	Peet Amphitheater	300	11:00, 12:00, 2:00*, 5:27*, 6:30
Flamingo Follies / Wonderful Waterfowl*	Ngorongoro Wash	413	2:00, 3:00*

1. Explain why this table isn't in 1NF. Make a relational design that uses one table in 1NF. Show the data in the new table.

2. Explain why the solution to Exercise 1 isn't in 2NF. Make a relational design that fixes it. Show the data in the new tables.

3. Explain why the solution to Exercise 2 isn't in 3NF. Make a relational design that fixes it. Show the data in the new tables.

4. If you made the fewest changes possible while converting the original table into 1NF, 2NF, and 3NF, the new tables probably use show name, time, and venue name as primary keys. That bodes ill if you need to change a show's name (Pete Penguin holds out for equal billing in The Walter Walrus Comedy Hour), a time, or a venue's name (the Trustees decide to sell naming rights and change the name of "Peet Amphitheater" to "Pampered Pet Cove").

   Modify the design to make those kinds of changes easier. Show the data in the new tables.

Part IV

Implementing Databases (with Examples in Access and MySQL)

The chapters earlier in this book explained how to design a database. They showed how to gather requirements, build data models, convert those models into relational designs, and refine those designs for a particular database example. They showed you how to prepare to build a database but they didn't actually build one.

The chapters in this part of the book show how to actually build a database using two database management systems. Chapter 15 explains how to build a database with Microsoft Access. Chapter 16 explains how to build a database with MySQL.

Microsoft Access

The chapters earlier in this book explained how to design a database. This chapter explains how to build a database in Microsoft Access. In this chapter you learn how to:

❑   Create tables.

❑   Create foreign key constraints graphically.

❑   Create check constraints that validate data.

(The examples in this chapter were tested in Microsoft Access 2007 with Service Pack 1.)

Understanding Access

One disadvantage of Access is that, unlike MySQL described in the next chapter, it's not free. However, you can download a 60-day free trial version as part of Microsoft Office Professional at office.microsoft.com/en-us/access/default.aspx.

A second disadvantage to Access is that it is not really intended to support many users accessing the database simultaneously. It doesn't provide separate user accounts with different passwords, and it doesn't provide the same levels of record and field locking that are provided by some database management systems.

One advantage to Access is that it is ubiquitous. Many Windows users have Access installed as part of Microsoft Office. It's possible that you have Access installed and don't even know it.

The database drivers needed for programs to interact with Access databases are also very common. Because programming environments such as Microsoft Visual Studio (which includes Visual Basic and C#) come with Access drivers, it's easy to write programs in those languages that work with Access databases even if you don't have Access installed.

Another advantage to Access is that Access databases come in simple files that are easy to distribute with an application. Though some other database products can produce database files, most normally use a database engine that contains all of the databases on the system. For example, SQL Server and MySQL run a server process that controls all of the databases on the system.

In contrast, an Access database file is self-contained. You can simply copy the database file to another computer to give that computer a copy of the database. You can also back up a database by simply copying the database file somewhere safe.

Access is more than simply a relational database management system. In addition to providing a backend database, Access also provides a complete development environment. The development environment not only lets you design and build the database, but it also lets you write code to interact with the database and build Access forms that display and modify the data. With Access you can build a database and a user interface, too.

Getting Started

When you first start Access, it displays the Getting Started screen shown in Figure 15-1.

Figure 15-1

To create a new database, click the Blank Database template at the top, enter the name of the database file that you want to create on the right, and click Create. This builds the file that will contain the database.

After you create the database, Access displays a new table in the Datasheet view as shown in Figure 15-2. This editor lets you define a table by entering data. To add new rows and columns to the table, simply type into the cells.

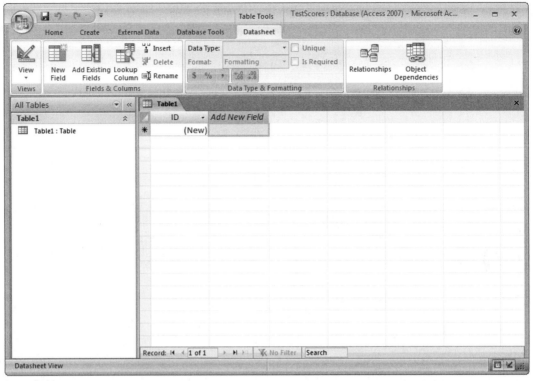

Figure 15-2

When you type values into the Datasheet view's columns, Access tries to guess the data types of the columns. For example, if you enter a number, it assumes the column is a long integer.

To get more control over the table's column definitions, expand the View dropdown (in the upper left) and select the Design view. Figure 15-3 shows the Students table in Design view.

Enter the names of the table's fields in the left column and select the fields' data types in the right column. When you have a field selected, the tabs at the bottom give you additional options. For example, in Figure 15-3 the default ID field's options let you change the field's size.

Some of the fields, such as Text Align, apply to Access forms and not to the database itself.

Figure 15-4 shows a more complete Students table. In this figure, the name of the ID field has been changed to StudentId. The FirstName and LastName fields are 40-character text fields that are required and that do not allow zero-length strings.

This table's primary key is the StudentId field. To change the primary key, click to the left of the field's name to select it and then click the Primary Key button (next to the View button at the top of the program). To use multiple fields as the primary key, click-and-drag or Shift+click to select the fields you want and then click the Primary Key button.

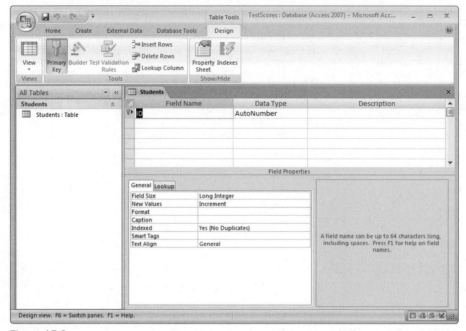

Figure 15-3

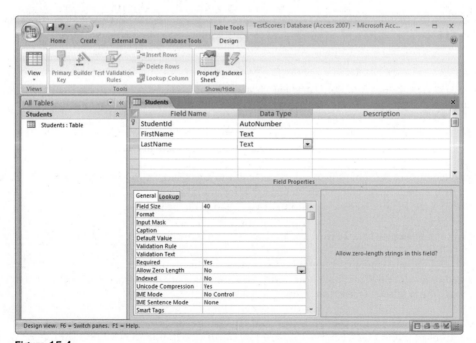

Figure 15-4

Try It Out   **Build a Test Scores Database**

Access is easy to use with a little practice. Get some by building a test scores database.

1. Create the database. Start Access. Click the Blank Database template, enter the database name **TestScoresDB.accdb**, and click the Create button.

2. Make the Students table: Click the View button and select Design. When Access asks you what to name the new table, enter the name **Students**.

Change the default first field's name from ID to **StudentId**. Leave its other properties alone. This field is an AutoNumber field, which means the database automatically creates new values for it when you add a new record to the table.

Add FirstName and LastName fields. Set their Data Types to Text. In the properties tab at the bottom, set Field Size = 40, Required = Yes, and Allow Zero Length = No.

Save the database.

3. Make the TestScores table: Select the Create tab and click Table to make a second table. Click the View button and select Design. When Access asks you what to name the new table, enter the name **TestScores**.

Change the default first field's name from ID to **StudentId**. Later this field will be a foreign key referring to the StudentId field in the Students table so this cannot be an AutoNumber field (you don't want the database to automatically create these values). Change the field's Data Type to Number. Then in the properties tab at the bottom, set Required = Yes.

Create a new TestNumber field. Set its Data Type to Number. In the properties tab, set Required = Yes.

Create a third field named **Score**. Set its Data Type to Number. In the properties tab, set Required = Yes.

Now in the main column list, click-and-drag to the left of the field names (in the little column that holds the primary key symbol) to select the StudentId and TestNumber fields. Then click the Primary Key button to make those fields the table's primary key.

Save the database.

4. Add some data to the tables: In the list of tables on the left, double-click the Students table to open the table in Datasheet view. Click the empty FirstName cell and enter the name **Ben**. Notice when you do this, Access automatically sets the record's StudentId field to 1 because this is an AutoNumber field.

Try to click the table's blank second row. Notice that Access displays a message telling you that you must enter a LastName value.

Click the record's LastName cell and enter **Franklin**. Now Access will let you click the empty second row.

Add another record for Thomas Edison.

Now double-click the TestScores table to open it in Datasheet view. Create a record with values StudentId = 1, TestNumber = 1, and Score = 99.

Then try to create a second record with values StudentId = 1, TestNumber = 1, and Score = 100. When you try to move to a new record, Access will tell you that this would create a duplicate primary key entry (two records with the same StudentId and TestNumber). Change the Test-Number to 2 and move to a new record.

Create some more records so the data looks like Figure 15-5. Then save the database.

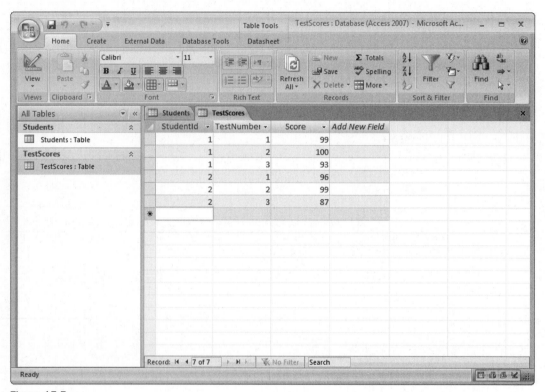

Figure 15-5

How It Works

1. Create the database.

When you create the database, Access makes the database file. Initially it contains no tables.

2. Make the Students table.

Access initially displays a new empty form in Datasheet view. Usually I switch to Design view to get better control over column definitions.

3. Make the TestScores table.

4. Add some data to the tables.

   In this example, the database doesn't have any foreign key constraints so you can enter values that don't make sense. For example, you can enter TestScores records for StudentId 3 even though there's no such student in the Students table. The following section explains how to add constraints to prevent this.

Defining Relationships

Before you define the relationships between tables, close all of the tables' views. You can open the relationship editor with the tables open, but they will cause problems later when you try to define relationships.

Next click the Database Tool tab at the top of the application and then click the Relationships button shown in the upper left of Figure 15-6.

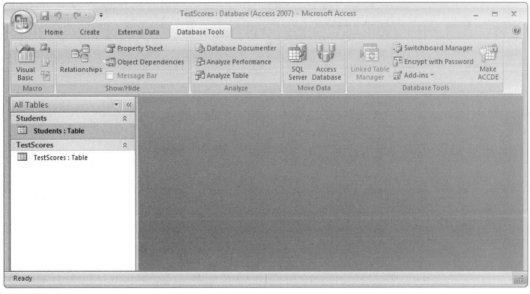

Figure 15-6

In the dialog shown in Figure 15-7, select the tables that you want in the relationship diagram and click Add. Then click Close to close the dialog.

Figure 15-7

Figure 15-8 shows the relationship editor displaying the two tables.

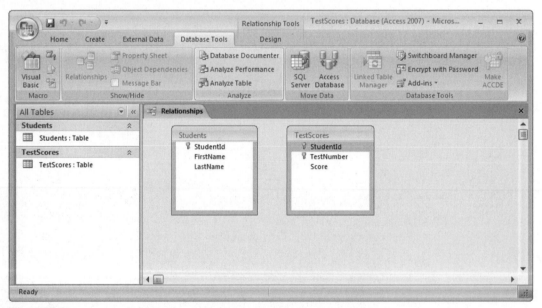

Figure 15-8

To create a foreign key relationship between the two tables, click the Students table's StudentId field and drag it onto the TestScores table's StudentId column. In the dialog shown in Figure 15-9, check the Enforce Referential Integrity box to make the database validate foreign key constraints.

If you don't click the right field or you drop it on the wrong field, use the field dropdowns in Figure 15-9 to select the right fields.

You can use other rows in the field list to add other fields to the relationship. For example, if you wanted to relate the Addresses table's City, State, and Zip fields to the City, State, and Zip fields in a CityStateZips table, you would add those fields here.

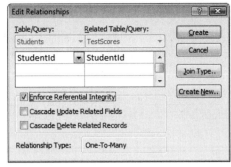

Figure 15-9

If you check the Cascade Update Related Fields box, the database automatically copies changes to related fields. For example, if you change a StudentId value in the Students table, the database automatically updates the corresponding StudentId values in the TestScores table.

If you check the Cascade Delete Related Records box, the database automatically deletes related records containing that field. For example, if you delete a particular StudentId value in the Students table, the database automatically deletes any records with that StudentId in the TestScores table.

After you have chosen the relationship's properties, click the Create button. Figure 15-10 shows the relationship editor displaying the new relationship. If you checked the Enforce Referential Integrity box, the diagram shows the link's cardinalities.

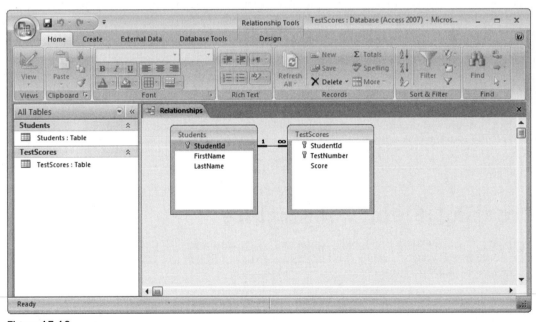

Figure 15-10

Building Relationships

Foreign key constraints are crucial to validating data in relational databases. In this Try It Out, you add two constraints, one linking the Students table's StudentId field with the TestScores table's StudentId field, and one linking the Students table's State field with a new States table's State field.

1. Create the Students/TestScores relationship: Open the database you created for the previous Try It Out and close any table editors that might be open. Select the Database Tools tab and click the Relationships button.

   In the Show Table dialog, select the Students and TestScores tables. Click Add and then click Close.

   Click the Students table's StudentId field and drag it onto the TestScores table's StudentId field. In the Edit Relationships dialog, verify that the StudentId fields are selected, check the Enforce Referential Integrity box, and click Create.

2. Add address fields to the Students table: Right-click the Students table and select Design View. Below the LastName field, add new fields Street (Text length 40), City (Text length 40), State (Text length 2), and Zip (Text length 5).

   Save the database and close the table's Design view.

3. Add a States table: Select the Create tab and click Table. Switch to Design view and name the new table **States**.

   Rename the default ID field **States**. Change it to a length 2 Text field. Save the database.

4. Create a Students/States relationship.

   Close any open table views. If the relationship editor is not open, select the Database Tools tab and click the Relationships button to open it.

   Right-click the relationship editor and select Show Table. Select the States table, click Add, and then click Close.

   Drag the Students table's State field onto the States table's State field. In the Edit Relationships dialog, verify that the State fields are selected, check the Enforce Referential Integrity box, and click Create.

   Resize and rearrange the tables if you like to ensure that the relationship links don't run under any of the tables. Figure 15-11 shows the result.

Creating Field Constraints

To add a field-level constraint, open a table in Design view and click the field. In the property tab at the bottom, the Validation Rule entry contains the constraint that you want to execute when the field is created or modified.

The validation rule should be a series of tests combined with logical operators such as And, Not, and Or. For example, the validation rule "> = 1 And < = 5" checks whether the field's value lies between 1 and 5.

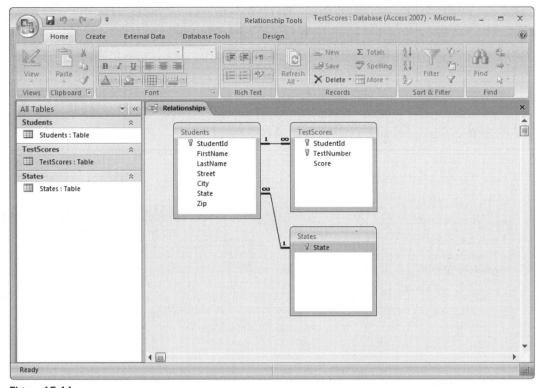

Figure 15-11

If you select the Validation Rule property and click the ellipsis on the right, the Expression Builder shown in Figure 15-12 appears. You can click its buttons and the entries in the lists at the bottom to add pieces to the test.

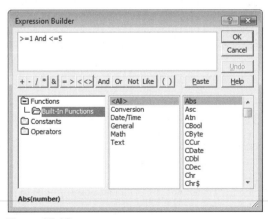

Figure 15-12

A field's Validation Rule property gives an expression to validate the field's value. The Validation Text property gives the text that Access displays if you try to set a field to an invalid value.

Figure 15-13 shows the TestScores table in Design view with the TestNumber field selected. The Validation Rule property is set to ">= 1 And <= 5" and the Validation Text property is set to "TestNumber must be between 1 and 5."

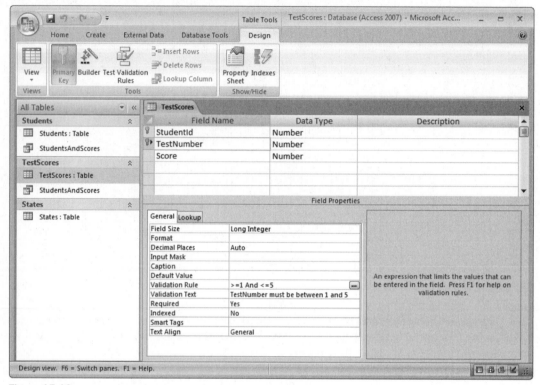

Figure 15-13

Figure 15-14 shows the message Access displayed when I tried to change a TestNumber value to 0.

Creating Table Constraints

Access also lets you define table-level constraints. At this level, you can refer to all of the fields in a record, not just a single field. For example, suppose your Relativistic Embroidery class has five tests. All are graded on a 0- to 100-point scale except the final, which has a 10-point bonus question. ("Discuss parallels between Fabric Grin Through and Randall-Sundrum Brane Cosmology.")

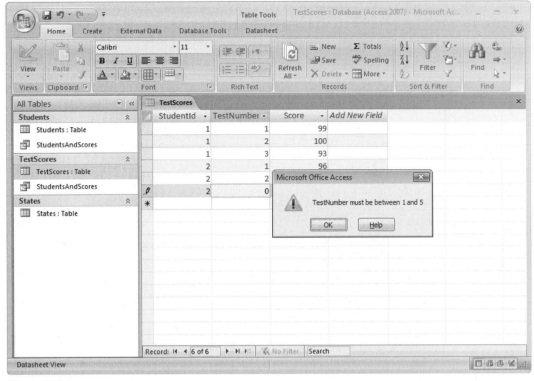

Figure 15-14

The following constraint verifies that a TestScores record has a Score value up to 100, unless the Test-Number value is 5, in which case the Score can be as large as 110.

```
([Score]<=100) Or (([TestNumber]=5) And ([Score]<=110))
```

The database should also require that Score be at least zero. You could add that condition to this constraint or, to avoid making this rule more complex than it already is, you could give the Score field the field constraint ">= 0" as described in the previous section.

To make a table-level constraint, open the table in Design view. Select the Design tab and click the Property Sheet tool on the upper right.

Figure 15-15 shows the Design tab with the Property Sheet command highlighted (next to the Indexes command). The Property Sheet window appears on the right side of the form.

Enter the constraint in the Property Sheet window's Validation Rule field. Enter the message that you want Access to display when the rule is violated in the Validation Text field.

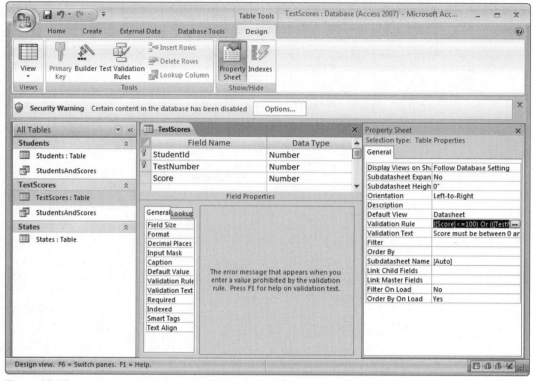

Figure 15-15

If you click the ellipsis next to the Validation Rule field, the Expression Builder shown in Figure 15-16 appears. This Expression Builder is similar to the one shown in Figure 15-12 for field-level constraints except now it provides an expression category containing the table's fields. Double-click a field to add it to the validation rule.

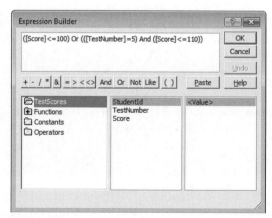

Figure 15-16

Creating Queries

This book isn't really about Access so it doesn't go into great detail about creating forms, views, charts, and reports. See the Access documentation and the Web for more information on those topics. (There are approximately seven zillion Web pages dealing with Access. A quick Google while I wrote this showed an estimated 682,000 pages containing the exact phrase ''Microsoft Access Database'' so there's plenty of information out there.)

However, I do want to cover queries at least in passing because they're useful and they also apply to other database products, not just Access. Chapter 17 has more to say about queries.

A query is a SELECT statement that selects values from one or more tables. Optionally you can select only records that match certain conditions and you can group or sort the results. The SELECT statement is one of the more complicated SQL statements so it's not covered thoroughly here. However, Access provides some nifty tools that make building queries easier and those *are* covered here.

To create a query, select the Create tab and click either the Query Wizard or the Query Design tool on the upper right. Figure 15-17 shows the Create tab with the Query Wizard tool highlighted.

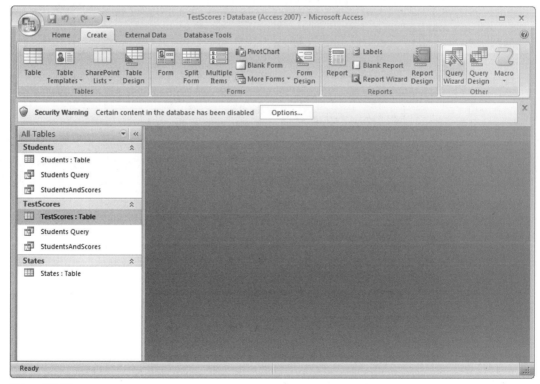

Figure 15-17

Figure 15-18 shows the first page of the Query Wizard. For this example, select the Simple Query Wizard and click OK.

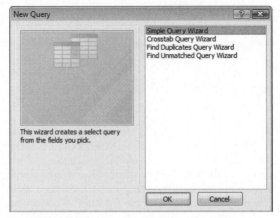

Figure 15-18

Figure 15-19 shows the Query Wizard's second page. Use the Tables/Queries dropdown to select a table. Then select a field and use the > button to move it into the Selected Fields list on the right. This list shows which fields will be selected in the query's result. For example, if you want a list of student names, select the FirstName and LastName fields.

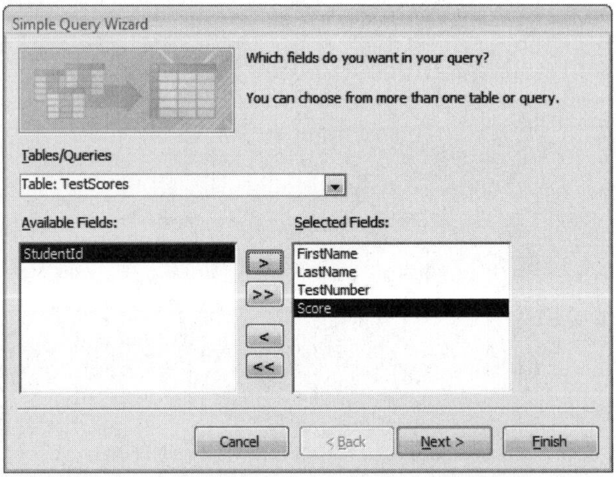

Figure 15-19

After you select the fields you want from the tables, click the Next button to display the page shown in Figure 15-20. Pick Detail to see all of the data in the fields you selected. Pick Summary to make the query display sums, averages, minimums, and other combined values. For this example, pick Detail and click Next.

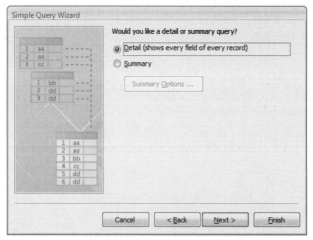

Figure 15-20

Figure 15-21 shows the Query Wizard's final page. Give the query a meaningful name. Then select the first option (Open the query to view information) to run the query now or select the second option (Modify the query design) if you want to change the query in Design view. For now, pick the first option and click Finish.

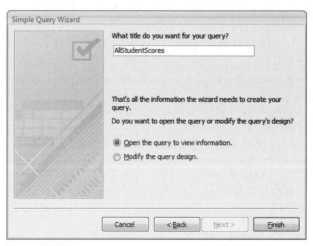

Figure 15-21

Figure 15-22 shows the query's results. Notice that it shows the values in the four fields selected in Figure 15-19.

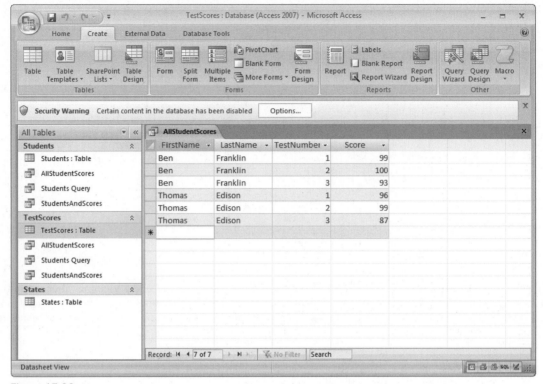

Figure 15-22

To change the query, select the Home tab, click the Views dropdown, and select Design View. The following section explains how to edit a query in Design view.

Query Design View

Figure 15-23 shows the query built in the previous section opened in Design view. You can make changes to the query's column in the grid at the bottom. To delete a column, click just above the column and press the Delete key. You can click and drag fields from the tables above onto the grid to add a field to the query. In Figure 15-23, I removed the LastName field and then dragged it back onto the query in the leftmost position.

To sort by a field, click the field's Sort entry and use the dropdown to select Ascending, Descending, or (not sorted). In Figure 15-23, the query sorts its results by the LastName field's values in ascending order.

To select only some records, add a condition to a field's Criteria cell. In Figure 15-23, the query selects only records where the Score field's value is at least 95.

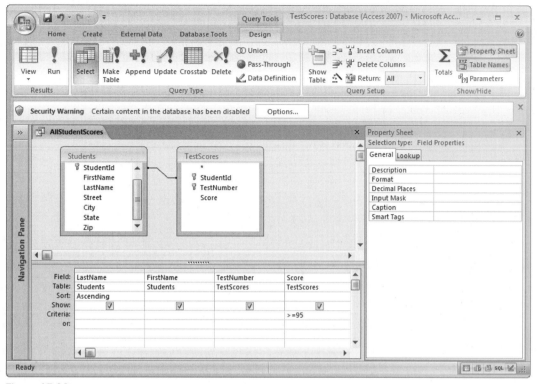

Figure 15-23

To run the query, click the Run button in the upper left of Figure 15-23. Figure 15-24 shows the results. Compare this to the results shown in Figure 15-22. This display shows the last name first, then sorts the results by last name, and only shows records with Score > = 95.

Try It Out   Make a Query

Create a query to select students whose addresses are in CA.

1. Add records to the States table. In the list of tables on the left, double-click the States table. In the table's Datasheet view, add some state abbreviations. Be sure to include CA.

2. Add address information to the Students table: In the list of tables on the left, double-click the Students table. In the table's Datasheet view, add some address information for the students. You can add more students if you like. Try giving a student a State that isn't listed in the States table and verify that the database won't let you. (If it does let you, then you didn't correctly make the foreign key constraint between the Students table and the States table in the previous Try It Out, "Building Relationships.")

Be sure you give at least one student the State CA.

3. Use the Query Wizard to build a basic query: Select the Create tab and click the Query Wizard tool. Use a Simple Query Wizard to select the Students table's FirstName, LastName, and State fields, and the TestScores table's TestNumber and Score fields. Pick the Detail query and name the query **CA Students**.

4. Modify the query to select only students in CA: In the grid at the bottom of the Query Design view, find the State field's column. In its Criteria cell, type = **'CA'**. Note the straight quotes surrounding the value CA.

5. Click the Run command and verify that the records displayed all have State value CA.

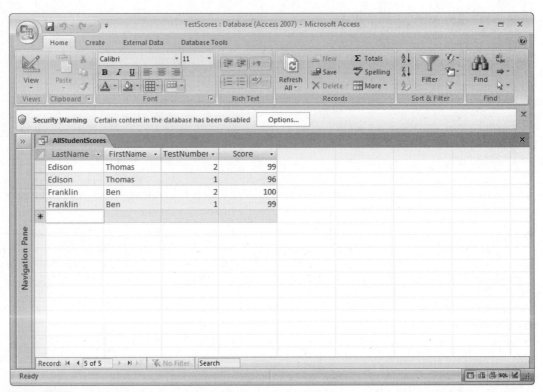

Figure 15-24

SQL View

The Query Wizard and the Query Design view let you build and modify queries relatively quickly and easily but some people prefer the control they can get by just typing out a SQL SELECT statement by hand. (Some of these people also prefer the extra control they get driving manual instead of automatic.)

To manually edit a query, open it, select the Design tab, click the View dropdown, and select SQL View. Figure 15-25 shows the SQL view showing the same query designed in Figure 15-23 and executed in Figure 15-24.

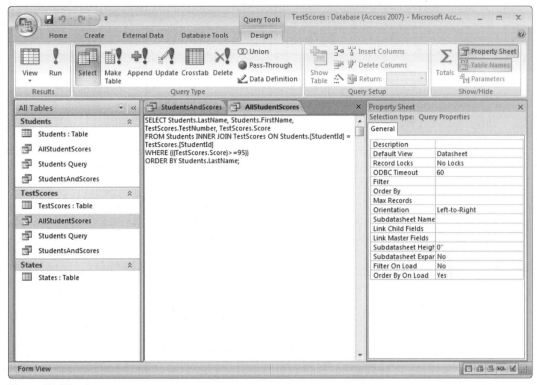

Figure 15-25

The following code shows the SQL statement, reformatted a bit to make it easier to read:

```
SELECT Students.LastName, Students.FirstName, TestScores.TestNumber,
    TestScores.Score
FROM Students
INNER JOIN TestScores ON Students.[StudentId] = TestScores.[StudentId]
WHERE (((TestScores.Score)>=95))
ORDER BY Students.LastName;
```

Scary isn't it? Don't worry, it's not that bad if you take it a piece at a time.

The SELECT clause on the first two lines tells the database which fields you want to see. The FROM clause tells it to look for those fields in the Students table.

The INNER JOIN statement tells the database to also look at records in the TestScores table where the Students record's StudentId value matches the TestScores record's StudentId value. In other words, match up records in the two tables that have the same StudentId values.

The WHERE clause tells the database to select only records where the Score value is at least 95. (I don't know why the Query Wizard and Query Design view got carried away and added all of those parentheses. I think they treat parentheses like beer at a picnic, figuring it's better to have extra rather than not enough.)

Finally, the ORDER BY clause tells the database to sort the results by the LastName field's values.

Here's a slightly simplified version that works just as well but without some of the redundant table names and parentheses:

```
SELECT LastName, FirstName, TestNumber, Score
FROM Students
INNER JOIN TestScores ON Students.StudentId = TestScores.StudentId
WHERE Score >=95
ORDER BY LastName;
```

Chapter 17 has a bit more to say about SQL but if you're brave, you can modify this statement to produce other results. For example, to select tests where students failed, you could change the WHERE clause to WHERE Score < 60.

For more complicated queries, you can use the Query Wizard and the Query Design view, and then use the SQL view to see how the query works.

Summary

This chapter showed how to use Microsoft Access to build a database. It explained how to:

❑   Create tables and define fields.

❑   Set a table's primary key.

❑   Define foreign key relationships and view them graphically.

❑   Create field-level constraints to validate field values separately.

❑   Create table-level constraints to validate a record's fields together.

The next chapter explains how to use the MySQL database management system to build databases much as this chapter explained how to build them with Access.

Before you move on to Chapter 16, however, use the following exercises to test your understanding of the material covered in this chapter. You can find the solutions to these exercises in Appendix A.

Exercises

These exercises all involve the same database, which you create in Exercise 1.

1.   Use Access to create an AquariumDB database containing the three tables ShowTimes, Shows, and Venues that were designed for Exercise 4 of Chapter 14. The following table shows the field types for the three tables.

Table	Field	Data Type
ShowTimes	ShowId	Number (Long Integer)
ShowTimes	Time	Date/Time
Shows	ShowId	AutoNumber (Long Integer)
Shows	ShowName	Text (45)
Shows	VenueId	Number (Long Integer)
Venues	VenueId	AutoNumber (Long Integer)
Venues	VenueName	Text (45)
Venues	Seating	Number (Integer)

2.   Use the Relationships editor to define foreign key constraints as shown in Figure 15-26.

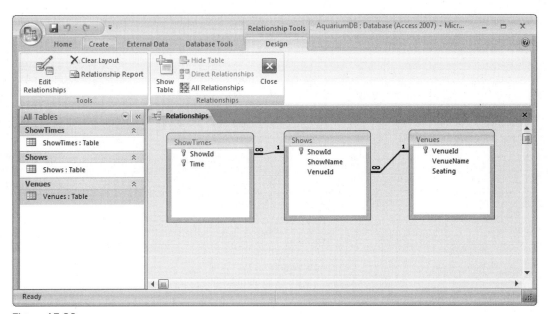

Figure 15-26

3.   Use the tables' Datasheet views to add values matching the data shown in Figure 15-27. (Access won't let you set values in AutoNumber fields, so don't worry if the ID values don't match those shown in Figure 15-27 as long as they make the correct relational links.)

ShowTimes	
11:15	1
3:00	1
1:15	2
6:00	2
11:00	3
12:00	3
6:30	3
2:00	4
5:27	4
2:00	5
3:00	6

Shows		
1	Sherm's Shark Show	1
2	Meet the Rays	1
3	Deb's Daring Dolphins	2
4	The Walter Walrus Comedy Hour	2
5	Flamingo Follies	3
6	Wonderful Waterfowl	3

Venues		
1	Sherman's Lagoon	375
2	Peet Amphitheater	300
3	Ngorongoro Wash	413

Figure 15-27

Try adding some duplicate primary key values and some data that doesn't satisfy the foreign key constraints. (For example, a ShowTimes record with ShowId = 100.)

4. Create a field-level constraint to check that the Venues table's Seating value is between 10 and 1000 (a sanity constraint). Add appropriate Validation Text for the field. Try to modify records so they violate the constraint.

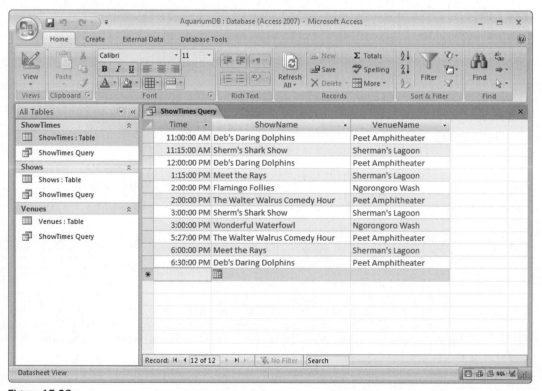

Figure 15-28

Create a field-level constraint to check that the ShowTimes table's Time value is between 9:00am and 9:00pm. (Tip: In Access, you must surround times with hash marks as in #16:30:00#.) Add appropriate Validation Text for the field. Try to modify records so they violate the constraint.

5. Use the Query Wizard to build a query that displays the data shown in Figure 15-28. Be sure to sort the results by time and then by show name.

MySQL

MySQL is a database engine designed to be used as a backend for a separate user interface. The user interface might be a Web page that uses Java, JavaScript, ASP, ASP.NET, or some other scripting technology to interact with the database. Alternatively the user interface might be a desktop application built in a high-level programming language such as Visual Basic, C#, or C++.

This chapter explains how to use MySQL to design and build a relational database. In this chapter you learn how to:

- ❑ Create tables.
- ❑ Create foreign key constraints.
- ❑ Create entity-relationship diagrams.
- ❑ Create triggers that validate data.
- ❑ Export scripts that build a database.

Installing MySQL

One of MySQL's greatest strengths is its price: $0. That makes it a very popular database with those trying to build an application or Web site on a budget. It has its roots in Linux computers so it's also very popular with those who use the various flavors of Linux.

A couple of feature-enhanced (in other words, not free) versions are also available. They provide extra support for teams of developers and enterprise applications. They're not really necessary for the examples shown here so they're not covered in this book. After you work through the examples and exercises in this chapter, you can decide whether you should look into these enhanced versions.

MySQL itself is a database engine, not a sophisticated development tool such as Microsoft Access. Though it is functional, you will probably find MySQL easier to use if you also install some of its graphical user interface (GUI) tools. You'll probably also want to download at least some of the documentation (you can also view it online).

The MySQL Workbench is a particularly useful tool that lets you design a database, draw pretty pictures of it, and create a script that can actually build it. Most of this chapter explains how to use MySQL Workbench, so you will need to install it to get the most out of this chapter.

The following list shows where you can download these important MySQL tools.

❑ `dev.mysql.com/downloads/mysql/5.0.html` — Here you can download MySQL itself. You need this if you want to use MySQL (for example, if you want to follow along with the examples and exercises in this chapter). I tested the code in this chapter using MySQL version 5.0.51b for 32-bit Windows XP.

❑ `dev.mysql.com/doc/workbench/en/index.html` — Here you can learn more about MySQL Workbench.

❑ `dev.mysql.com/downloads/workbench/5.0.html` — Here you can download MySQL Workbench. I highly recommend that you get this tool. (You can build a database by typing SQL commands into the Command Line Client or writing scripts for the Client to execute, but it's hard. Like flint knapping and butter churning, it's a lost art that is mostly dragged out once a year for Pioneer Days festivals.) For this chapter I used version 5.0.21 OSS Revision 3111. ("OSS" stands for "Community Edition." I don't know why. Perhaps it really stands for "Obscure Something Silly." All part of the Linux heritage.)

❑ `dev.mysql.com/downloads/gui-tools/5.0.html` — Here you can download additional MySQL GUI tools. These include a graphical administrator and a query browser that are easier to use than the Command Line Client.

❑ `dev.mysql.com/doc` — Here you can view or download MySQL documentation. Either bookmark this page if you have an always-on fast Internet connection or download the documentation for your version of MySQL.

Download and install MySQL, MySQL Workbench, and any other tools you want. I found the installations pleasantly quick and painless.

MySQL is an Open Source project, and it is constantly undergoing modifications and improvements. As you use some of the tools described in this chapter, you will probably encounter an occasional bug. To avoid losing a lot of work, be sure to save your work often and take everything with a grain of salt. After all, this is a free tool, and even with a few bugs you're getting a lot more than you paid for.

Using MySQL Command Line Client

MySQL is a database engine that doesn't really have a user interface of its own. Fortunately it comes with a selection of tools that you can use to manipulate the database so you don't have to write a program to perform the simplest tasks.

MySQL's natural habitat is the Linux operating system, and that has given some of its tools a command-line orientation. For example, Figure 16-1 shows one of the most important MySQL tools: the Command Line Client.

If, like me, you've become addicted to the point-and-click convenience of a windowing operating system such as one of the flavors of the Microsoft or Macintosh operating systems, you may find the MySQL

Command Line Client a bit disconcerting. It is a primitive text-based tool. You type a command, the Client executes it, and then it displays the result. If you look at Figure 16-1, you can see the commands and results for this session.

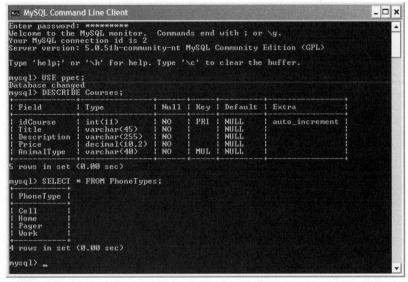

Figure 16-1

When the Client first started, it prompted for the database's password. You can see the asterisks it displayed as I entered the password.

The Client displays the mysql> prompt after which you can enter a command. The first command in Figure 16-1, USE ppet, tells the Client to use the database named ppet, the database for The Pampered Pet project.

Note that the commands are case-insensitive so USE ppet, use PPET, and use ppet all do the same thing. I usually type command words such as USE in ALL CAPS so they stand out.

The next command, DESCRIBE Courses, tells the Client to show information about the Courses table. The response shows the table's fields, their data types, whether each allows null values, whether they are used in keys, their default values, and extra information. This information is useful but displayed in a primitive ASCII table.

(The first applications in the Paleolithic era painted their results on the sides of caves using this kind of ASCII table output. Later, during the Neolithic era, special characters that draw lines were used to make the result prettier. Only fairly recently during the Renaissance did windowing operating systems bring us such features as dropdown menus, combo boxes, Ctrl+triple-clicking to select multiple paragraphs, and bugs that can crash the entire operating system instead of just the window that the program is using.)

The last command shown in Figure 16-1, SELECT * FROM PhoneTypes, makes the Client select and display all of the records in the PhoneTypes table. In this example, the table contained four records holding the values Cell, Home, Pager, and Work.

Notice that all of the commands end with a semicolon. Some of the commands can be quite long so the Client lets you continue them across multiple lines. The semicolon lets it know when you're done and tells it to execute the command.

Some of the commands that the Command Line Client understands are instructions to the Client itself. These make it do such things as connecting to a different host, selecting a different database on a host, and executing a SQL script (which is covered further in the following section).

One of the most important commands displays help (notice that in Figure 16-1 the first thing the Client does after accepting the password is tell you how to find help).

Other commands that you can send to the Client are SQL (Structured Query Language) commands. These are industry-standard commands for building, modifying, and controlling relational databases. The command SELECT * FROM PhoneTypes shown in Figure 16-1 is a SQL command. (Chapter 17 describes SQL in greater detail.)

Try It Out   **Using the Command Line Client**

After you install MySQL, give the Command Line Client a try. The following steps walk you through some simple database actions.

1. Start the Command Line Client: Assuming you used a typical installation in Windows, open the Start menu and select All Programs ⇨ MySQL ⇨ MySQL Server 5.0 ⇨ MySQL Command Line Client. When it prompts you for the database's password, enter the password you used when you installed MySQL.

2. List the available databases: Enter the command **SHOW DATABASES;**. (Remember to end each command with a semicolon and press Enter.) The Client should list the available databases running in MySQL.

3. Select the mysql database: Enter the command **USE mysql;**. This makes the Client use the database named mysql.

4. List the database's tables: Enter the command **SHOW TABLES;**. This makes the Client list the tables in the mysql database.

5. Select some data: Most of the mysql database's tables will be empty, but the user table should hold one record for the root user that was created when you installed MySQL. Enter the command **SELECT user, password FROM user;**. The Client should list a single record showing the user name root and that user's password. You won't be able to read the password because it is encrypted.

6. Create a new database: enter the command **CREATE DATABASE testdb;**. To select the new database, enter the command **USE testdb;**. If you execute the **SHOW TABLES** command now, you should find that the new database contains no tables.

7. Create a table by using a SQL CREATE TABLE statement. This is a long, potentially complex statement that can span several lines. For this example, enter the command:

```
CREATE TABLE People (
  FirstName VARCHAR(40) NOT NULL,
  LastName VARCHAR(40) NOT NULL,
  PRIMARY KEY (FirstName, LastName)
);
```

8. Make some data. Enter the following two commands one after the other:

```
INSERT INTO People VALUES("Assam", "Lembek");
INSERT INTO People VALUES("Nedlim", "Popo");
```

Then press the up arrow and press Enter to try to add the second record again. The database should throw a fit and say, "Duplicate entry `Nedlim-Popo´ for key 1." It won't allow this entry because there is already a record that has the same primary key value.

9. Select some data: To select all of the rows in the table, enter the command SELECT * FROM People;.

10. Drop a table: enter the command **DROP TABLE People;**. This immediately removes the table and all of its data without any warning or confirmation. To see that the table is gone, enter the command **SHOW TABLES;**.

11. Drop a database: enter the command **DROP DATABASE testdb;**.

12. Enter the command **EXIT;**.

How It Works

The CREATE TABLE command, repeated here, warrants a little discussion:

```
CREATE TABLE People (
   FirstName VARCHAR(40) NOT NULL,
   LastName VARCHAR(40) NOT NULL,
   PRIMARY KEY (FirstName, LastName)
);
```

This command makes a table named People with two fields FirstName and LastName. Both fields are 40-character variable-length text fields, and both are required (neither allows null values). The table's primary key is the FirstName/LastName pair.

Now if you execute the SHOW TABLES statement, you should see the new table. To learn about the table's structure, enter the command DESCRIBE People.

The SELECT statement is quite complex and has many variations. The following table lists a few variations that you can try.

Command	Result
SELECT * FROM People	Selects all fields in all records.
SELECT * FROM People WHERE LastName = 'Lembek'	Selects all fields from records where LastName is Lembek.
SELECT * FROM People ORDER BY LastName DESC	Selects all fields from all records and sorts the results by LastName in descending order.

The DROP TABLE command is dangerous because it instantly deletes all of the data in a table without any warning. The data is gone forever, and there's no way to get it back other than typing it all in again.

The DROP DATABASE testdb command is even more dangerous than DROP TABLE because it deletes the entire database including all of its tables and all of the data they contain immediately without any confirmation. All of the data is permanently gone with no apologies or do-overs. If you're not careful, working with the Command Line Client can be harsh and brutal!

Executing SQL Scripts

The following text shows all of the commands described in the previous Try It Out steps:

```
SHOW DATABASES;
USE mysql;
SHOW TABLES;
SELECT user, password FROM user;
CREATE DATABASE testdb;
USE testdb;
SHOW TABLES;
CREATE TABLE People (
   FirstName VARCHAR(40) NOT NULL,
   LastName VARCHAR(40) NOT NULL,
   PRIMARY KEY (FirstName, LastName)
);
SHOW TABLES;
INSERT INTO People VALUES("Assam", "Lembek");
INSERT INTO People VALUES("Nedlim", "Popo");
INSERT INTO People VALUES("Nedlim", "Popo");
SELECT * FROM People;
SELECT * FROM People
WHERE LastName='Lembek';
SELECT * FROM People
ORDER BY LastName DESC;
DROP TABLE People;
SHOW TABLES;
DROP DATABASE testdb;
SHOW DATABASES;
```

A series of commands such as this that is contained in a file is called a *script*. By convention, scripts such as this one that contain SQL statements have a .sql extension. For example, this script might be in the file tests.sql.

If you open a script in a text editor, you can select the commands and press Ctrl+V to copy them to the Clipboard. Then you can right-click the MySQL Command Line Client and select Paste to make the Client execute them all at once. This is an easy way to execute a series of commands more than once without typing them all over again.

In fact, the Command Line Client provides a SOURCE command that executes a script to make working with scripts even easier. The command SOURCE C:\Scripts\testdb.sql makes the Client execute the script contained in the file C:\Scripts\testdb.sql. (This script file is available for download on the book's Web site.)

Scripts make working with the Command Line Client a lot easier and safer than typing them in by hand because they let you study the commands and check for mistakes before you execute them. For example, you can make darned sure that you don't have a DROP TABLE or DROP DATABASE statement where you don't want it.

This technique also lets you test the commands a few at a time. For example, you can start with a script that creates a database and makes a table. Then you can write another script to create a second table and insert records into it.

After you have each script debugged, you can glue them together in one huge master script if you like. Alternatively you can leave each script in a separate file so you can execute them separately, or you can make a master script that uses the SOURCE command to invoke the individual scripts.

Writing scripts by hand and testing them can be somewhat tedious. Two MySQL tools that can make the process a bit easier are MySQL Query Browser and MySQL Workbench.

Using MySQL Query Browser

MySQL Query Browser is a MySQL GUI tool that lets you interactively write and execute queries. If you install the MySQL GUI tools with default settings in Windows, you can open the Start menu and select All Programs ⇨ MySQL ⇨ MySQL Query Browser to see the login form shown in Figure 16-2. Enter the root password that you specified when you installed MySQL. In the Default Schema field, you can enter the name of the database that you want to use initially. ("Schema" is MySQL-ese for "database.")

Figure 16-2

Figure 16-3 shows the Query Browser after it opens. On the right you can see the Schemata window listing the installed databases. Click the little triangle to the left of an entry in this window to expand that entry. In Figure 16-3, the ppet database is expanded to show its tables and the courses table is expanded to show its fields. By using this window, you can learn about the database's basic structure.

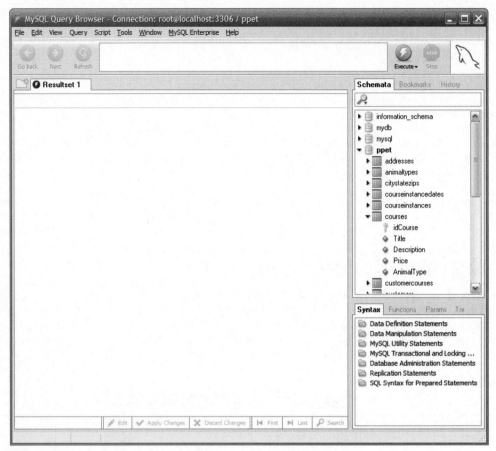

Figure 16-3

Executing Queries

One of the simpler features of the Query Browser is letting you enter and execute queries. You can enter an SQL query in the large text box at the top of the Query Browser. If you double-click a table in the Schemata window, the program enters a query to select all of the records from this table for you.

When this query area contains a query, you can click the Execute button to run the query and see what data is in the database. Figure 16-4 shows the Query Browser after I double-clicked the some_people database's People table to build a default query and then clicked Execute. (I also rearranged the result area's columns a bit to fit all of the values on the form.)

Editing Data

After you execute a query, you can use the result grid to edit the database. Click the Edit button on the bottom of the Query Browser to start editing. Double-click a cell to change its value or double-click the row below the last row to create a new record. Right-click a row and select Delete Row(s) to remove a row.

Figure 16-4

Figure 16-5 shows the Query Browser editing the People table with its context menu open so you can see some of the other tools that you can use to edit data. You can't tell in the book, but the Query Browser uses color to show changes. Modified fields are shown in dark blue, new records are shown in green, and deleted records are shown in red.

If you click the Discard Changes button, the Query Browser throws out any changes, additions, or deletions that you made in the editing grid.

If you click the Apply Changes button, the Query Browser tries to save your changes and additions to the database. If there are any errors (for example, a text field is too long or a required field is missing), the Query Browser tells you.

Figure 16-6 shows the program after trying to add two records with the same primary key values. The row that didn't get added is shown in red with white text and the error is described at the bottom of the Query Browser. If you click the Execute button again, you'll see the latest data from the database so you can tell which changes made it into the data and which didn't.

Creating and Modifying Databases

In addition to executing queries, the Query Browser can create databases and modify their structures. If you right-click a database in the Schemata window, the context menu shown in Figure 16-7 appears.

Figure 16-5

Use the Drop Schema command to drop a database. Use the Copy CREATE Statement to Clipboard command to copy a CREATE DATABASE command to the Clipboard so you can paste it into a script. Use Create New Schema to make a new database. Use the Create New Table command to add a new table to a database.

If you right-click a table in the Schemata window, you see a slightly different set of commands. The Edit Table command lets you change the fields in the table. The Drop Table command removes the table from the database. The Copy CREATE Statement to Clipboard command copies an SQL statement as before but this time it's a CREATE TABLE statement.

If you right-click a table and selected Edit Table, the Query Browser displays the MySQL Table Editor that lets you design the table. Figure 16-8 shows the editor displaying a more complete version of the People table.

Double-click in the field definition area to change the table's basic structure. For example, if you double-click the City field's Datatype column, you can change the field's type to VARCHAR(50) or some other type.

To define a foreign key, select the Foreign Keys tab as shown at the bottom of Figure 16-8. Click the plus sign at the bottom left to add a new foreign key. In the dialog that appears (not shown in Figure 16-8), enter a name for the new key. Select the table that the key references in the Ref. Table dropdown. Then use the Column and Reference Column area if necessary to specify the columns in the two tables that should match.

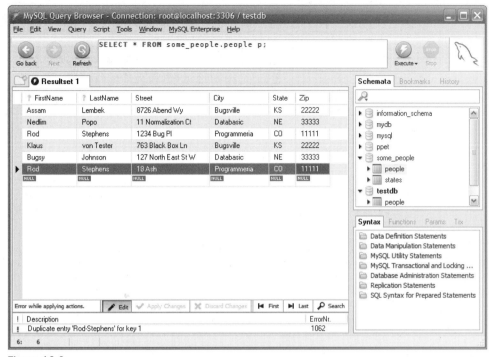

Figure 16-6

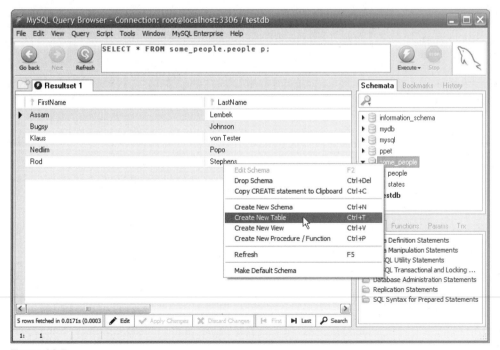

Figure 16-7

When you're done making changes to the table's structure, click Apply Changes (at the bottom in Figure 16-8) to make the Table Editor try to apply the changes you specified.

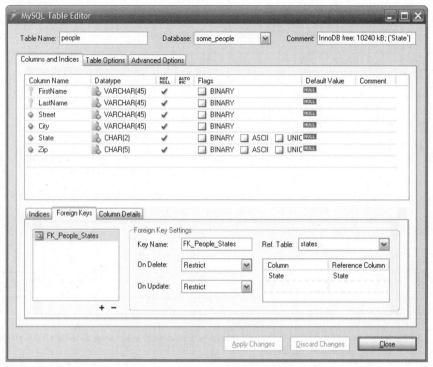

Figure 16-8

Note that you can also use the Query Browser while the Table Editor is open. For example, you can drop the original table from the database if you need to make changes to it that would conflict with the data it currently contains.

Try It Out   **Build a Database**

The Query Browser provides tools you can use to build a complete database. Take a few minutes to practice by building a small test database.

1.   Create a new database. Right-click in the Schemata window and select Create New Schema. Name the new database **some_people**.

2.   Add a States table and give it some data. Right-click the some_people database and select Create New Table. In the Table Name text box, enter **States**. Double-click the cell below the Column Name header and enter the field name **state**. In the Datatype column, enter **CHAR(2)**. Be careful not to add an extra closing parenthesis. (The Table Editor tries to be helpful and adds one for you so don't add another one. Usually clicking Apply Changes, clicking Execute on the following dialog, reading the error message, figuring out what it means, and removing the extra parenthesis

takes a lot more of my time than I would save by not typing that extra parenthesis. But I appreciate the thought.) The data type CHAR(2) means a two-character fixed-length string. Click the Apply Changes button and then the Close button.

To add data to the table, return to the Query Browser, expand the some_people database, and double-click the new table. This makes the Query Browser put a SQL SELECT statement in the text box at the top to select the records from the States table. Click the Execute button to run the query and return an empty list (because the table holds no data yet).

Click the Edit button at the bottom of the program. Then double-click the empty cell below the State field in the result grid. Type the value CO and press Enter. Repeat this process, double-clicking below the last value and adding a new one, until you have added several records as shown in Figure 16-9.

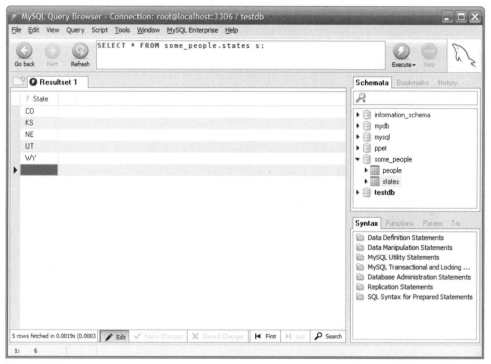

Figure 16-9

When you have finished adding the records, click the Apply Changes button at the bottom of the program to add the new values to the database.

3.   Add a People table and give it a foreign key constraint referring to the States table. Right-click the some_people database and select Create New Table. Use the Table Editor to create fields **FirstName**, **LastName**, **Street**, **City**, **State**, and **Zip**. Use the field properties shown in Figure 16-10. (Be careful when you enter the data types. The Query Browser doesn't validate those so if you misspell a data type as CHA(2), for example, it won't tell you until you try to apply the changes.)

Initially the table will use its first field as its primary key. To make it use both the FirstName and LastName fields instead, select the Indices tab as shown in Figure 16-10. Click and drag the Last-Name field into the Index Columns area on the lower right.

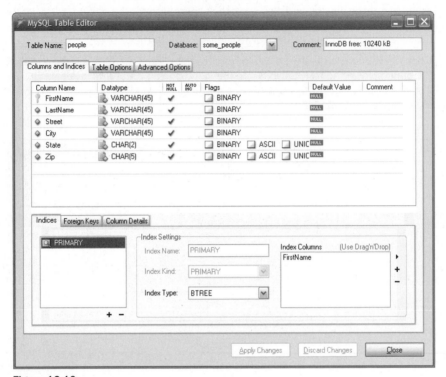

Figure 16-10

To create the foreign key constraint, select the Foreign Keys tab and click the plus sign. In the dialog that appears, name the new key `FK_People_States`. Open the Ref. Table dropdown and select States. The Table Editor will correctly select the State field for both tables so you don't have to make any changes here.

Click the Apply Changes button to create the new People table. Then click the Close button.

4.   Add some data to the People table. Try to violate the foreign key constraint. Double-click the table in the Schemata window to copy a query for that table into the query area. Then click the Execute button to display the empty results. Double-click the cells below the header fields and enter some data. When you have finished entering data, click the Apply Changes button.

Figure 16-11 shows the Query Browser after trying to add new People records. The last record for Joe Kerr violated its foreign key constraint because the States table doesn't contain the State value AZ. The Query Browser didn't add that record and flagged the error.

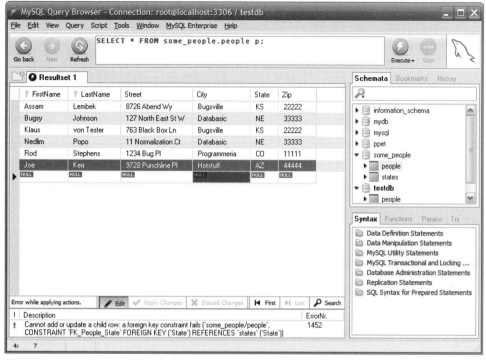

Figure 16-11

Using Scripts

In addition to building databases and executing queries, the Query Browser can execute scripts. This makes writing and executing a complex series of commands even easier than using the Command Line Client's source command.

To create a blank script, open the File menu and select New Script Tab. To load an existing script file, open the File menu and select Open Script.

After you write or load a script, click the Execute button to run it. Figure 16-12 shows the Query Browser after executing a script. The program displays the error message at the bottom because the script tried to create two records with the same primary key values. If you double-click the error message, the program moves the cursor to the line that caused the error.

By using the Query Browser's script editor, you can write and debug scripts relatively quickly.

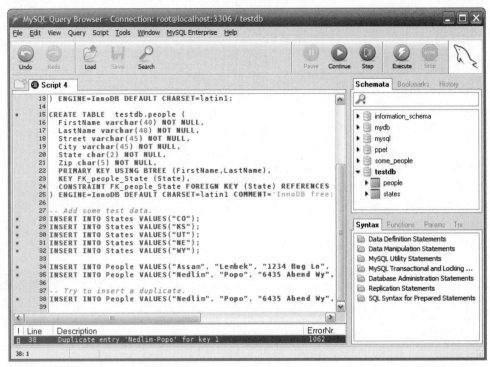

Figure 16-12

Try It Out   Writing a Script

MySQL Query Browser makes editing and running scripts easy. The following steps walk you through loading and running a simple script.

1.   Start MySQL Query Browser. Assuming you used a typical installation in Windows, open the Start menu and select All Programs ⇨ MySQL ⇨ MySQL Query Browser. When it prompts you for the database's password, enter the password you used when you installed MySQL.

2.   Make and execute a new script to create a database. In MySQL Query Browser, open the File menu and select New Script Tab. Enter the following code (don't worry about it if you can't easily type the special characters ö, ç, and so forth):

```
DROP DATABASE IF EXISTS PoliticianDB;
CREATE DATABASE PoliticianDB;

USE PoliticianDB;

CREATE TABLE Politicians (
  Country VARCHAR(45) NOT NULL,
  FirstName VARCHAR(45) NOT NULL,
  LastName VARCHAR(45) NOT NULL,
```

```
    PRIMARY KEY (Country)
);

INSERT INTO Politicians VALUES("Germany", "Horst", "Köhler");
INSERT INTO Politicians VALUES("France", "François", "Fillon");
INSERT INTO Politicians VALUES("Italy", "Romano", "Prodi");
INSERT INTO Politicians VALUES("Spain", "José Luis Rodríguez", "Zapatero");
```

Use the File menu's Save command to save the script with a reasonable name. Then click the Execute button to run this script. This creates the PoliticianDB database, adds the Politicians table, and inserts some values into it.

3. Execute a query against the newly created table and modify the data. In the Schemata window, double-click the Politicians table. The Query Browser should create a query tab with the following query at the top:

```
SELECT * FROM politiciandb.politicians p;
```

(Once in a while, the Query Browser decides it has better things to do than listen to you so it doesn't create this tab or it doesn't create the proper query. At those times, I've had some luck opening another database, selecting a table in it, and then double-clicking the Politicians table again. If it really won't behave, you can type the query into a query tab yourself. Remember, this is a free tool!)

Click the Execute button to run the query. You should see four records.

Click the Edit button at the bottom to enter editing mode. Then double-click the Italy entry and change it to Italia. Click the Apply Changes button to accept the change.

Change the query to this:

```
SELECT * FROM politiciandb.politicians
WHERE Country < 'M'
ORDER BY FirstName;
```

Click the Execute button to run the new query. You should see only three records (Spain comes after the letter M so it's not listed) and they should be sorted by the politicians' first names.

In the Schemata window, right-click the new database and select Drop Schema to remove the new database.

Getting Syntax Help

One very nice feature of the Query Browser is its integrated help for SQL syntax. To get help, expand the folders in the Syntax window on the lower right of Figure 16-12. Then double-click an item to see help for that entry. Figure 16-13 shows the Query Browser displaying help for the CREATE TABLE statement.

This integrated help is particularly useful when you are editing a script.

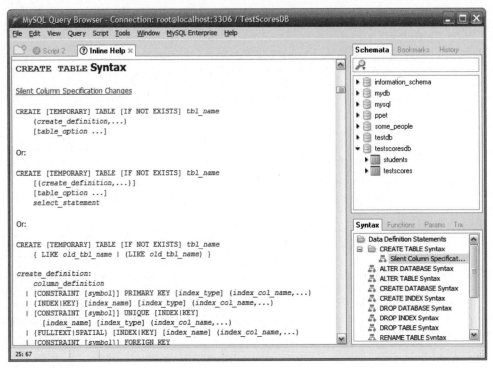

Figure 16-13

Using MySQL Workbench

Query Browser is a great tool for building a database, exploring its tables, executing queries, and writing scripts, but it doesn't provide any tool for visualizing the structure of the database. By examining each table separately, you can figure out which tables are related to others through foreign key constraints, but the process is slow and tedious.

That's where MySQL Workbench comes in. It allows you to build and view an Extended Entity-Relationship diagram (EER diagram) showing the database's relational structure.

Loading Scripts

MySQL Workbench can load an existing database's structure from a creation script (a script that builds the database with CREATE commands). It can also load structure from a running database. Unfortunately only the commercial versions of Workbench will load from a running database so, if you're using the free version, you need to work from a creation script.

If you don't have a creation script, the Query Browser can help you build one. Right-click an object in the Query Browser's Schemata window and select Copy CREATE Statement to Clipboard. Then paste the result into a script file.

For a big database, this can be time-consuming, and you'll need to arrange the commands in the script so tables are created in a valid order. For example, suppose the Addresses table's State field refers to the States table's State field as a foreign key. In that case, you'll need to create the States table before you create the Addresses table (so Addresses has something to reference).

To load a creation script, open the File menu's Import submenu and select Reverse Engineer MySQL Create Script. Select the script file that you want to load and click Next. The program loads the file and checks that it's not complete gibberish. Click the Next and Finish buttons to move through the rest of the dialog's pages.

Figure 16-14 shows Workbench with The Pampered Pets database loaded. The Catalog window on the right is similar to the Schemata window displayed by the Query Browser except it displays only a single database.

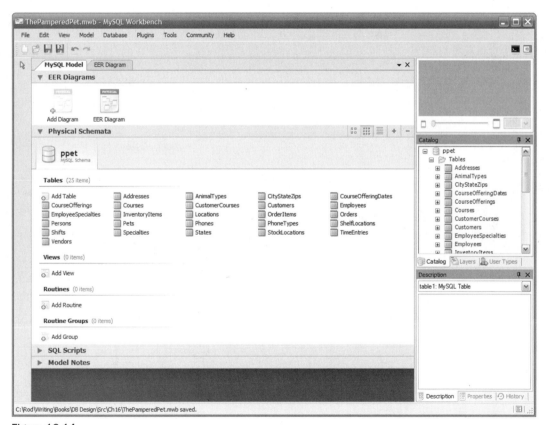

Figure 16-14

Creating EER Diagrams

One the most useful features of Workbench is that it lets you build and edit EER diagrams. You can build them from scratch or you can let Workbench do some of the work for you.

The final page of the script loading dialog includes a checkbox labeled Autoplace Objects in New Diagram. If you check this box before clicking the Finish button, Workbench creates a new EER diagram for the database and drops its tables in default locations on it.

If you don't create an autoplace diagram when you load the creation script, you can make one later by selecting the Model menu's command Create Diagram from Catalog Objects.

The automatically generated diagrams aren't perfect. Tables sometimes overlap slightly and links showing relationships between tables often run underneath other tables, but it's a start. From there you can drag tables into new positions to try to make the diagram look nicer.

Figure 16-15 shows Workbench displaying a hand-made EER diagram for The Pampered Pet database. The key in the upper right shows the part of the diagram that is visible in the main window. The slider and combo box below the key area lets you adjust the diagram's scale.

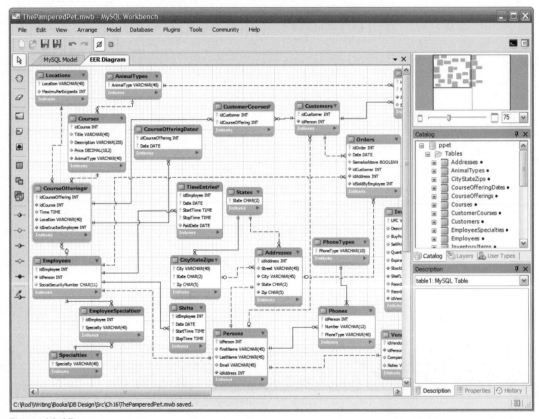

Figure 16-15

Solid links indicate an identifying relationship where a child table cannot be identified without its parent. For example, it doesn't make much sense to look up a particular TimeEntries record by itself — normally you would look up the TimeEntries records that go with a particular Employees record.

Dashed links indicate a non-identifying relationship.

Symbols on the links indicate the cardinality of the objects at each end. The three cardinality symbols are:

❏ **Circle** — Means 0.

❏ **Tick mark** — Means 1.

❏ **Crow's foot** (looks like a little teepee or something) — Means "many."

For example, take a look at the link between the Employees and TimeEntries entities in Figure 16-15. The Employees end of the link is marked by two tick marks so its cardinality is 1 to 1. In other words, exactly one Employees entity participates in this relationship. The TimeEntries end of the link is marked with a circle and crow's foot. That means the relationship involves zero or more TimeEntries entities. All that makes sense: a single employee is associated with any number of time entries (including zero), and a time entry is associated with exactly one employee.

By using the tools on the left edge of the program shown in Figure 16-15, you can annotate an EER diagram with text or pictures. You can also add tables and relationships. If you double-click or right-click and select the appropriate Edit command, you can edit a table or relationship.

Some changes you can only perform using the EER diagram editor. For example, a relational database only represents one-to-many relationships. If you want to build a one-to-one relationship such as the one between the Employees and Persons table shown in Figure 16-15, you need to edit that link manually.

That link should also be an identifying relationship because you wouldn't normally look up a Persons record without going through the corresponding Employees record. To make that change, you would need to delete the non-identifying link and use the tools on the left to make a new one-to-one identifying relationship (it's the third tool from the bottom).

The diagramming tool can also represent many-to-many relationships (the second-to-last tool on the left), which the database cannot represent directly.

Editing Databases

Workbench has many of the same table creation and editing features as Query Browser. To create a new table, select the Model tab and in the Tables area double-click the Add Table item. Figure 16-16 shows Workbench creating a new table.

Enter the table's name and then use the other tabs in the table editing area to define the table. For example, use the Columns, Indexes, and Foreign Keys tabs to define the table's columns, non-primary key indexes, and foreign keys.

The Inserts tab allows you to add data to the table. Click the Open Editor button on the tab to display the dialog shown in Figure 16-17. Use the grid to enter data and click OK.

When you export the database creation script (described in the section "Exporting Scripts" later in this chapter), Workbench adds INSERT statements to the script to create this data. For the data shown in Figure 16-17, it adds the following statements:

```
INSERT INTO 'TestScores' ('idStudent','TestNumber','Score') VALUES (1, 1, 97);
INSERT INTO 'TestScores' ('idStudent','TestNumber','Score') VALUES (1, 2, 91);
INSERT INTO 'TestScores' ('idStudent','TestNumber','Score') VALUES (1, 3, 87);
```

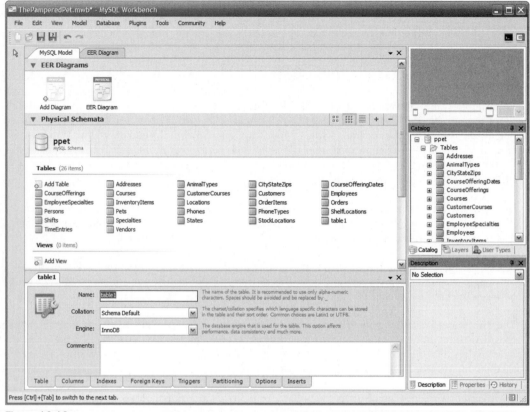

Figure 16-16

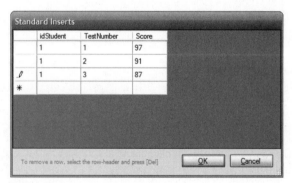

Figure 16-17

Defining Triggers

MySQL databases don't perform check constraints, at least not in the current version. It does, however, execute triggers. A *trigger* is a piece of database code that is automatically executed when certain events occur. For example, you can define a routine to run before a record is updated or after a record is deleted.

Though MySQL doesn't have check constraints, you can use triggers to perform checks when a record is created or updated. You can type CREATE TRIGGER statements into database creation scripts or you can let MySQL Workbench do it for you.

To create a trigger, edit the table that should contain it, select the Triggers tab, and type the statements to create the trigger. The following code shows how you could create triggers to run before records are added or updated in a test score database. This example tries to ensure that the TestScores table's TestNumber value is between 1 and 5 and its Score value is between 0 and 100:

```
-- Trigger DDL Statements
USE TestScoresDB;
DELIMITER //

CREATE TRIGGER TestScores_BeforeInsert BEFORE INSERT ON TestScores
  FOR EACH ROW BEGIN
    IF NEW.TestNumber < 1 THEN
        -- Cause an error.
        SET NEW.idStudent = null;

    ELSEIF NEW.TestNumber > 5 THEN
        -- Cause an error.
        SET NEW.idStudent = null;
    ELSEIF NEW.Score < 0 THEN
        -- Cause an error.
        SET NEW.idStudent = null;
    ELSEIF NEW.Score > 100 THEN
        -- Cause an error.
        SET NEW.idStudent = null;
    END IF;

  END;
//

CREATE TRIGGER TestScores_BeforeUpdate BEFORE UPDATE ON TestScores
  FOR EACH ROW BEGIN
    IF NOT(NEW.TestNumber BETWEEN 1 AND 5) THEN
        -- Reset the value.
        SET NEW.TestNumber = OLD.TestNumber;
    ELSEIF NOT (NEW.Score BETWEEN 0 AND 100) THEN
        -- Reset the value.

        SET NEW.Score = OLD.Score;
    END IF;
  END;
//
```

Normally a script uses a semicolon to delimit statements. Because a trigger contains database code (it's basically a little script), it may contain semicolons so the database cannot use a semicolon to tell when the trigger's definition is complete. The DELIMITER statement tells the database what to use for the statement delimiter while the trigger is defined.

The first trigger executes before a new record is added to the TestScores table. For each row about to be added, the trigger checks the new value in its TestNumber field. If the new value is less than 1 or greater than 5, the trigger would like to raise some sort of error to tell the database not to accept the new record. Unfortunately MySQL doesn't have a command to raise an error so the trigger does the next best thing: it does something illegal. In this case, it sets the idStudent field's value to null. The idStudent field is required so setting the value to null causes an error and the database refuses to add the new record.

Next the trigger checks the new Score value. If the new value is less than 0 or greater than 100, the trigger again sets idStudent to null to cause an error.

The second trigger executes before a record is updated. The documentation says causing an error makes the update fail, but in my tests the database seems to reset the invalid field to a default value and accept the change, so this trigger doesn't use the same trick as the previous one. Instead, if a new TestNumber or Score value is out of bounds, the trigger resets it to the old value that it had before the update began.

The two triggers demonstrate different styles of checking their values. The first uses inequalities and the second uses the BETWEEN statement.

Unfortunately there seem to be a few bugs in the Workbench's trigger code. If you check the Generate DROP TABLE Statements check box while exporting the database creation script, the program also creates DROP TRIGGER statements that contain syntax errors. If you don't check this box, the program generates a script that contains an empty statement where it would have tried to create the DROP TRIGGER statement and that causes an error.

The easiest solution I've found is to create the DROP TRIGGER statements and remove them from the script. You can then add correct ones before the trigger's DELIMITER statement if you like. The correct statements for this example are:

```
DROP TRIGGER IF EXISTS TestScores_BeforeInsert;
DROP TRIGGER IF EXISTS TestScores_BeforeUpdate;
```

Exporting Scripts

After you have modified the database, defined foreign keys, added triggers, and so forth, Workbench can generate a database creation script. Open the File menu's Export submenu and select Forward Engineer SQL CREATE Script to display the dialog shown in Figure 16-18.

Select the items that you want in the database creation script and click Next to move to the page shown in Figure 16-19.

If you want the script to include only some tables, triggers, or other objects, click the corresponding Detailed Selection button and make your selections.

After you make your selections, click Finish to make Workbench generate the database creation script. The result isn't perfect (have I mentioned that this is a free tool?), but it's a pretty good start and at least defines the database's tables and foreign keys. You can load the script into MySQL Script Browser to test and debug it.

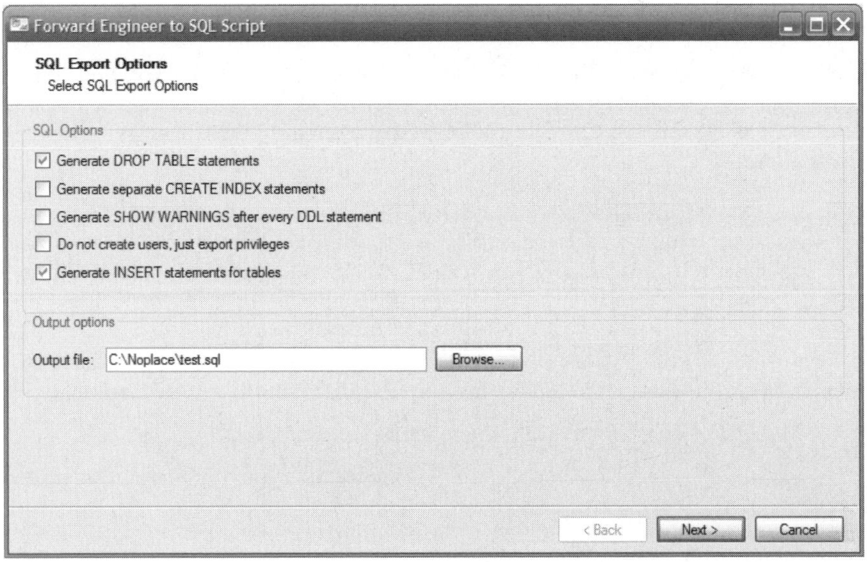

Figure 16-18

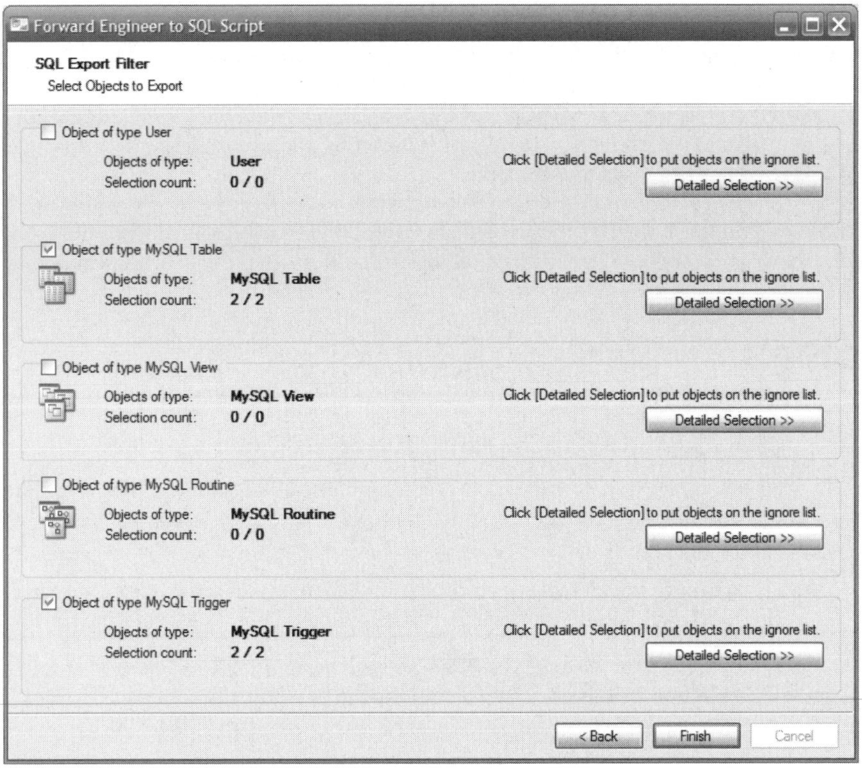

Figure 16-19

Summary

This chapter showed how to use the MySQL Query Browser and MySQL Workbench tools. They have a few rough edges, but overall they are very useful. They let you create and modify databases for MySQL databases more easily than you can with the MySQL Command Line Client. Workbench also lets you draw EER diagrams.

This chapter explained how to:

❑   Use MySQL Query Browser to create tables, define their columns, and give them foreign key constraints.

❑   Use MySQL Workbench to create and modify tables and EER diagrams.

❑   Use MySQL Workbench to modify links in EER diagrams to specify cardinality.

❑   Use MySQL Workbench to create triggers that validate data.

❑   Use MySQL Workbench to export database creation scripts containing triggers and INSERT statements.

This chapter completes your introduction to database design and construction. Using the techniques described up to this point in the book, you can design and implement a flexible, robust database in Access or MySQL.

Database programming is an enormous topic, however, and there's much more to study. The next part of the book explains some more advanced database design and development topics.

This chapter used scripts to create MySQL databases and insert data into them, but it didn't really explain how those scripts worked. The following chapter provides a lot more detail by introducing SQL, the database language used to write those scripts.

Before you move on to Chapter 17, however, use the following exercises to test your understanding of the material covered in this chapter. You can find the solutions to these exercises in Appendix A.

Exercises

1.   Use MySQL Workbench to create the database shown in Figure 16-20.

Add insert and update triggers to ensure that the TestNumber is between 1 and 10 and that the test scores are between 0 and 100. Also give each table some INSERT statements on the Inserts tab.

Be sure to save your Workbench project and then export a database creation script. Load the script in MySQL Query Browser, fix the trigger errors, and execute the script.

2.   Use MySQL Workbench to create the database designed in Exercise 4 of Chapter 14 and shown in Figure 16-21.

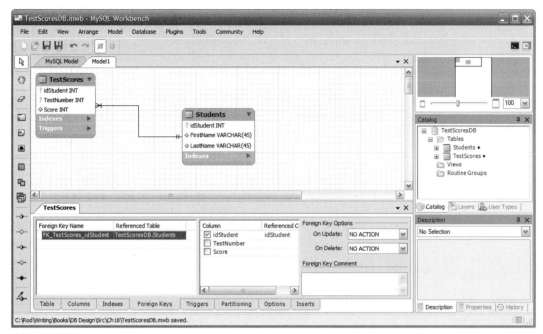

Figure 16-20

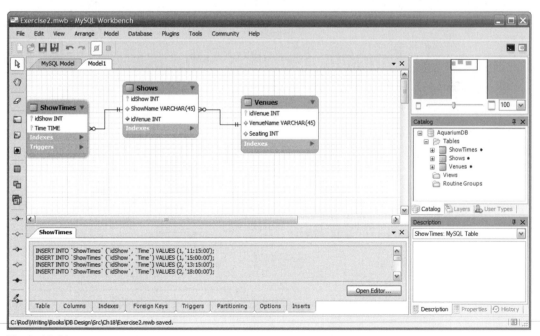

Figure 16-21

Add insert and update triggers to ensure that show times are between 9:00am and 9:00pm. (Tip: In scripts and insert statements, write times in 24-hour notation surrounded by straight single quotes. For example, the time '14:15:00' is 2:00pm.)

Give each table INSERT statements matching the data shown in Figure 16-22.

ShowTimes		Shows			Venues		
11:15	1	1	Sherm's Shark Show	101	101	Sherman's Lagoon	375
3:00	1	2	Meet the Rays	101	102	Peet Amphitheater	300
1:15	2	3	Deb's Daring Dolphins	102	103	Ngorongoro Wash	413
6:00	2	4	The Walter Walrus Comedy Hour	102			
11:00	3	5	Flamingo Follies	103			
12:00	3	6	Wonderful Waterfowl	103			
6:30	3						
2:00	4						
5:27	4						
2:00	5						
3:00	6						

Figure 16-22

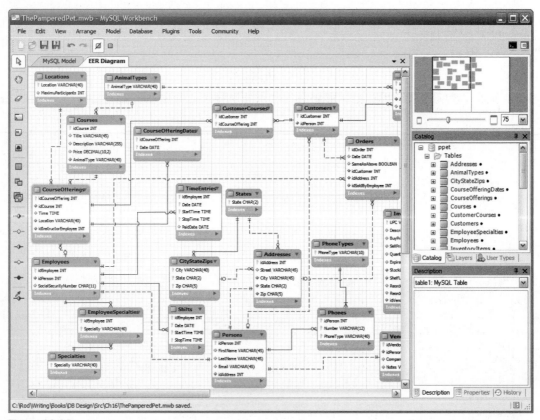

Figure 16-23

Save your Workbench project and then export a database creation script. Load the script in MySQL Query Browser, fix the trigger errors, and execute the script.

3. Use MySQL Workbench to create The Pampered Pet database designed in Chapter 14 and shown in Figure 16-23.

Save your Workbench project and then export a database creation script. Load the script in MySQL Query Browser and execute the script.

Part V
Advanced Topics

Chapter 17: Introduction to SQL

Chapter 18: Building Databases with SQL Scripts

Chapter 19: Database Maintenance

Chapter 20: Database Security

The chapters in the next part of the book deal with more advanced topics. Though they are not strictly necessary for designing a database, they are very important for database practitioners. You can design a database without understanding these topics but it's unlikely that you will do a good job implementing the database without at least some awareness of them.

Chapter 17 provides an introduction to SQL (Structured Query Language). Chapter 18 explains how to use SQL to make scripts that create, populate, and otherwise manipulate databases. Chapter 19 discusses database maintenance issues and Chapter 20 describes database security.

Although these chapters don't cover every last detail of these topics, they should provide you enough background to let you build a database competently.

Introduction to SQL

Eventually you (or someone else) must actually build the database that you've designed. Also at some point, someone will probably want to actually use the database you've spent so much time designing.

SQL (pronounced "sequel") includes commands that let you build, modify, and manipulate a database. Chances are SQL will be used either directly or behind the scenes to create and use the database. Even tools such as MySQL, Access, and SQL Server that let you interactively build a database also allow you to use SQL.

SQL is also directly useful for creating and initializing a database. In fact, it's so useful that it's the topic of the next chapter.

SQL is such an important part of database development that your education as a database designer is sadly lacking if you don't at least understand the basics. (The other developers will rightfully mock you if you don't chuckle when you see a tee-shirt that says, "SELECT * FROM People WHERE NOT Clue IS null.")

In this chapter you learn how to use SQL to:

- ❏   Create and delete tables.
- ❏   Insert data into tables.
- ❏   Select data from the database using various criteria and sort the results.
- ❏   Modify data in the database.
- ❏   Delete records.

Background

SQL, which stands for Structure Query Language, was developed by IBM in the mid-1970s. It is an English-like command language for building and manipulating relational databases.

From a small but ambitious beginning, SQL has grown into a large language containing around 70 commands with hundreds of variations. Because SQL has grown so large, this chapter cannot possibly cover it all. Instead this chapter gives a brief introduction to SQL and then describes some of the most useful SQL commands in greater detail. Even then, this chapter doesn't have room to cover most of the more interesting commands completely. The SELECT statement alone includes so many variations that you could practically write a book about just that one command.

Finding More Information

SQL is intuitive enough that, once you master the basics, you should be able to get pretty far on your own. The Internet is practically clogged with Web sites that are chock full of SQL goodness in the form of tutorials, references, FAQs, question and answer forums, and discussion groups.

In fact, I'll start you off with a small list of Web sites right now. The following list shows a few Web sites that provide SQL tutorials:

- ❑ www.sql-tutorial.net/
- ❑ www.w3schools.com/sql
- ❑ www.sql.org/
- ❑ sqlcourse.com/

For help on specific issues, you should find a few SQL forums where you can ask questions. A huge number of developers work with databases and SQL so there are lots of forums out there. IT Toolbox alone (www.ITToolbox.com) has more than a dozen SQL or database-related forums.

These tutorials can help you get started using some of the more common SQL statements but they aren't designed as references. If you need more information about a particular command, you should look for a SQL reference. The following links lead to references for different versions of SQL.

- ❑ **Microsoft Transact-SQL:** msdn.microsoft.com/en-us/library/ms189826.aspx
- ❑ **PostgreSQL:** www.postgresql.org/docs/8.1/interactive/sql-commands.html
- ❑ **Oracle SQL:** www.adp-gmbh.ch/ora/sql/
- ❑ **MySQL:** dev.mysql.com/doc/refman/5.0/en/index.html

Each of these pages provides simple navigation to look up specific SQL commands.

Note, however, that these Web pages deal with specific versions of SQL (Transact-SQL, PostgreSQL, Oracle SQL, and MySQL). Though the basics of any version of SQL are fairly standard, there are some differences between the different flavors. In fact, this is such an important issue that it deserves its own section.

Standards

Although all relational databases support SQL, different databases may provide slightly different implementations of SQL. In fact, this is such an important point that I'll say it again in a box.

> **Different databases provide slightly different implementations of SQL.**

Both the International Organization for Standardization (ISO) and the American National Standards Institute (ANSI) have standards for the SQL language and most database products follow those standards pretty faithfully. However, different database products also add extra features to make certain chores easier. Those extras can make your life easier but only if you are aware of which features are standard and which are not and you use the extra features with caution.

(I don't know why the International Organization for Standardization is abbreviated ISO instead of IOS. Possibly it's a French thing. Or perhaps that's just the way it is, like when NIST, formerly the "National Institute of Standards and Technology," decided that NIST no longer stands for anything and is just a name.)

For example, in the Transact-SQL language used by SQL Server, the special values @@TOTAL_ERRORS, @@TOTAL_READS, and @@TOTAL_WRITES return the total number of disk write errors, disk reads, and disk writes respectively since SQL Server was last started. Other relational databases don't provide those, although they may have their own special values that return similar statistics.

If you use them haphazardly, it may be very hard to rebuild your database or the applications that use it if you are forced to move to a new kind of database. For that matter, extra features can make it hard for you to reuse tools and techniques that you develop in your next database project.

(In one project I worked on, we didn't know which database engine we would be using for almost a year. Management had two database vendors bidding against each other so they kept changing their minds to keep the pressure on the vendors. They didn't finally pick one until development was almost complete.)

Fortunately most flavors of SQL are 90+ percent identical. You can guard against troublesome changes in the future by keeping the non-standard features in a single place as much as possible.

Usually the places where SQL implementations differ the most is in system-level chores such as database management and searching meta-data. For example, different databases might provide different tools for searching through lists of tables, creating new databases, learning about the number of reads and writes that the database performed, examining errors, and optimizing queries.

Basic Syntax

As is mentioned earlier in this chapter, SQL is an English-like language. It includes command words such as CREATE, INSERT, UPDATE, and DELETE.

SQL is case-insensitive. That means it doesn't care whether you spell the DELETE keyword as DELETE, delete, Delete, or DeLeTe.

SQL also doesn't care about the capitalization of database objects such as table and field names. If a database has a table containing people from the Administrative Data Organization, SQL doesn't care whether you spell the table's name ADOPEOPLE, AdoPeople, or aDOPEople.

To make the code easier to read, however, most developers write SQL command words in ALL CAPS and they write database object names using whatever capitalization they used when building the database. For example, I prefer Mixed Case for table and field names.

A final SQL feature that makes commands easier to read is that SQL ignores whitespace. That means it ignores spaces, tabs, line feeds, and other "spacing" characters so you can use those characters to break long commands across multiple lines or to align related statements in columns.

For example, the following code shows a typical SELECT command as I would write it.

```
SELECT FirstName, LastName, Clue,
       Street, City, State, Zip
FROM People
WHERE NOT Clue IS NULL
ORDER BY Clue, LastName, FirstName
```

This command selects name and address information from the records in the People table where the record's Clue field has a value that is not null. (Basically it selects people who have a clue, normally a pretty small data set.) It sorts the results by Clue, LastName, and FirstName.

This command places the different SQL clauses on separate lines to make them easier to read. It also places the person's name and address on separate lines and indents the address fields so they line up with the FirstName field. That makes it easier to pick out the SELECT, FROM, WHERE, and ORDER BY clauses.

Command Overview

SQL commands are typically grouped into four categories: Data Definition Language (DDL), Data Manipulation Language (DML), Data Control Language (DCL), and Transaction Control Language (TCL).

Note that some commands have several variations. For example, in Transact-SQL the ALTER command has the versions ALTER DATABASE, ALTER FUNCTION, ALTER PROCEDURE, ALTER TABLE, ALTER TRIGGER, and ALTER VIEW. The following tables just provide an overview of the main function (ALTER) so you know where to look if you need one of these.

DDL commands define the database's structure. The following table briefly describes the most commonly used DDL commands.

Command	Purpose
ALTER	Modifies a database object such as a table, stored procedure, or view. The most important variation is ALTER TABLE, which lets you change a column definition or table constraint.
CREATE	Creates objects such as tables, indexes, views, stored procedures, and triggers. In some versions of SQL, this also creates databases, users, and other high-level database objects. Two of the most important variations are CREATE TABLE and CREATE INDEX.
DROP	Deletes database objects such as tables, functions, procedures, triggers, and views. Two of the most important variations are DROP TABLE and DROP INDEX.

DML commands manipulate data. They let you perform the CRUD operations: Create, Read, Update, and Delete. (Where athletes "talk smack," database developers "talk CRUD.") The following table summarizes the most common DML commands. Generally developers think of only the CRUD commands INSERT, SELECT, UPDATE, and DELETE as DML commands but this table includes cursor commands because they are used to select records.

Command	Purpose
CLOSE	Closes a cursor.
DECLARE	Declares a cursor that a program can use to fetch and process records a few at a time instead of all at once.
DELETE	Deletes records from a table.
FETCH	Uses a cursor to fetch rows.
INSERT	Inserts new rows into a table. A variation lets you insert the result of a query into a table.
SELECT	Selects data from the database, possibly saving the result into a table.
TRUNCATE	Deletes all of the records from a table as a group without logging individual record deletions. It also removes empty space from the table while DELETE may leave empty space to hold data later. (Some consider TRUNCATE a DDL command, possibly because it removes empty space from the table. Or possibly just to be contrary. Or perhaps I'm the contrary one.)
UPDATE	Changes the values in a record.

DCL commands allow you control access to data. Depending on the database, you may be able to control user privileges at the database, table, or field level. The following table summarizes the two most common DCL commands.

Command	Purpose
GRANT	Grants privileges to a user.
REVOKE	Revokes privileges from a user.

TCL commands let you use transactions. A transaction is a set of commands that should be executed atomically as a single unit so either every command is executed or none of the commands are executed.

For example, suppose you want to transfer money from one account to another. It would be bad if the system crashed after you had subtracted money from the first account but before you added it to the other. If you put the two commands in a transaction, the database guarantees that either both happen or neither happens.

The following table summarizes the most common TCL commands.

Command	Purpose
BEGIN	Starts a transaction. Operations performed before the next COMMIT or ROLLBACK statement are part of the transaction.
COMMIT	Closes a transaction, accepting its results.
ROLLBACK	Rewinds a transaction's commands back to the beginning of the transaction or to a savepoint defined within the transaction.
SAVE	Creates a savepoint within a transaction. (Transact-SQL calls this command SAVE TRANSACTION whereas PostgreSQL calls it SAVEPOINT.)

The following sections describe the most commonly used commands in greater detail.

CREATE TABLE

The CREATE TABLE statement builds a database table. The basic syntax for creating a table is:

```
CREATE TABLE table_name (parameters)
```

Here `table_name` is the name you want to give to the new table and `parameters` is a series of statements that define the table's columns. Optionally `parameters` can include column-level and table-level constraints.

A column definition includes the column's name, its data type, and optional extras such as a default value or the keywords NULL or NOT NULL to indicate whether the column should allow null values.

A particularly useful option that you can add to the CREATE TABLE statement is IF NOT EXISTS. This clause makes the statement create the new table only if it doesn't already exist.

For example, the following statement creates a Students table with three fields. Notice how the code uses whitespace to make the data types and NOT NULL clauses align so they are easier to read:

```
CREATE TABLE IF NOT EXISTS Students (
    idStudent    INT           NOT NULL    AUTO_INCREMENT,
    FirstName    VARCHAR(45)    NOT NULL,
    LastName     VARCHAR(45)    NOT NULL,
    PRIMARY KEY (idStudent)
)
```

The idStudent field is an integer (INT) that is required (NOT NULL). The database automatically generates values for this field by adding one to the value it last generated (AUTO_INCREMENT).

The FirstName and LastName fields are required variable-length strings up to 45 characters long.

The table's primary key is the idStudent field.

A key part of a column's definitions is the data type. The following list summarizes the most common SQL data types:

- ❑ **BLOB:** A Binary Large Object. This is any chunk of binary data such as a JPEG file, audio file, video file, or Word document. The database knows nothing about the internal structure of this data so, for example, if the BLOB contains a Word document the database cannot search its contents.

- ❑ **BOOLEAN:** A true or false value.

- ❑ **CHAR:** A fixed-length string. Use this for strings that always have the same length such as two-letter state abbreviations or five-digit ZIP Codes.

- ❑ **DATE:** A month, date, and year such as February 29, 2012.

- ❑ **DATETIME:** A date and time such as 12:34pm February 29, 2012.

- ❑ **DECIMAL(p, s):** A fixed-point number where p (precision) gives the total number of digits and s (scale) gives the number of digits to the right of the decimal. For example, DECIMAL(6, 2) holds numbers of the form 1234.56.

- ❑ **INT:** An integer value.

- ❑ **NUMBER:** A floating point number.

- ❑ **TIME:** A time without a date such as 3:14am.

- ❑ **TIMESTAMP:** A date and time.

- ❑ **VARCHAR:** A variable-length string. Use this for strings of unknown lengths such as names and street addresses.

Specific database products often provide extra data types and aliases for these types. They also sometimes use these names for different purposes. For example, in different databases the INT data type might use 32 or 64 bits, and the database may provide other data types such as SMALLINT, TINYINT, BIGINT, and so forth to hold integers of different sizes.

Most databases can handle the basic data types but before you make specific assumptions (for example, that INT means 32-bit integer), check the documentation for the database product you are using.

The following code builds a frankly hacked together table with the sole purpose of demonstrating most of the common data types. Notice that this command uses the combined FirstName and LastName fields as the table's primary key:

```
CREATE TABLE IF NOT EXISTS MishmashTable (
    FirstName                VARCHAR(40)     NOT NULL,
    LastName                 VARCHAR(40)     NOT NULL,
    Age                      INT             NULL,
    Birthdate                DATE            NULL,
    AppointmentDateTime      DATETIME        NULL,
    PreferredTime            TIME            NULL,
    TimeAppointmentCreated   TIMESTAMP       NULL,
    Salary                   DECIMAL(8,2)    NULL,
    IncludeInvoice           BOOLEAN         NULL,
    Street                   VARCHAR(40)     NULL,
    City                     VARCHAR(40)     NULL,
```

```
State                   CHAR(2)         NULL,
Zip                     CHAR(5)         NULL,
PRIMARY KEY (FirstName, LastName) )
```

Try It Out   **Create a Table**

The CREATE TABLE statement can be quite complicated. You need to specify the fields' names, data types, default values, and whether they allow null values. You need to specify the table's primary key and indexes, and foreign key constraints.

Try writing a CREATE TABLE statement to make an inventory items table.

1. Give the new table the following fields:

Name	Type	Required?
UPC	String up to 40 characters	Yes
Description	String up to 45 characters	Yes
BuyPrice	Number of the form 12345678.90.	No
SellPrice	Number of the form 12345678.90.	Yes
QuantityinStock	Integer	Yes
ExpirationDate	Date	No
StockLocation	String up to 40 characters	No
ShelfLocation	String up to 40 characters	No
ReorderWhen	Integer	No
ReorderAmount	Integer	No
idVendor	Integer	No

To create the table, enter the following code:

```
CREATE TABLE IF NOT EXISTS InventoryItems (
    UPC             VARCHAR(40)     NOT NULL,
    Description     VARCHAR(45)     NOT NULL,
    BuyPrice        DECIMAL(10,2)   NULL,
    SellPrice       DECIMAL(10,2)   NOT NULL,
    QuantityinStock INT             NOT NULL,
    ExpirationDate  DATE            NULL,
    StockLocation   VARCHAR(40)     NULL,
    ShelfLocation   VARCHAR(40)     NULL,
    ReorderWhen     INT             NULL,
    ReorderAmount   INT             NULL,
    idVendor        INT             NULL
)
```

2. Make the table's primary key be the UPC field with the following line:

```
PRIMARY KEY (UPC)
```

3. Some of the fields are used in foreign key constraints. Make indexes for those fields. Set their DELETE and UPDATE actions to NO ACTION. The fields are:

Local Field	Foreign Table	Foreign Field
idVendor	Vendors	idVendor
StockLocation	StockLocations	StockLocation
ShelfLocation	ShelfLocations	ShelfLocation

Use the following code:

```
INDEX FK_InventoryItems_idVendor       (idVendor      ASC),
INDEX FK_InventoryItems_StockLocation (StockLocation ASC),
INDEX FK_InventoryItems_ShelfLocation (ShelfLocation ASC),
```

4. Make foreign key constraints for the fields listed in step 3. Set their DELETE and UPDATE actions to NO ACTION. (That prevents the database from deleting or modifying a record in the foreign table if the value is needed by one of these constraints.) The following code defines these constraints:

```
CONSTRAINT FK_InventoryItems_idVendor
  FOREIGN KEY (idVendor )
  REFERENCES Vendors (idVendor )
  ON DELETE NO ACTION
  ON UPDATE NO ACTION,

CONSTRAINT FK_InventoryItems_StockLocation
  FOREIGN KEY (StockLocation )
  REFERENCES StockLocations (StockLocation )
  ON DELETE NO ACTION
  ON UPDATE NO ACTION,

CONSTRAINT FK_InventoryItems_ShelfLocation
  FOREIGN KEY (ShelfLocation )
  REFERENCES ShelfLocations (ShelfLocation )
  ON DELETE NO ACTION
  ON UPDATE NO ACTION
```

How It Works

1. Give the new table the following fields.

   The main part of the CREATE TABLE statement defines the fields, their data types, default values if any, and whether they are required. The following code shows the basic statement:

```
CREATE TABLE IF NOT EXISTS InventoryItems (
  UPC              VARCHAR(40)    NOT NULL,
```

```
        Description        VARCHAR(45)      NOT NULL,
        BuyPrice           DECIMAL(10,2)    NULL,
        SellPrice          DECIMAL(10,2)    NOT NULL,
        QuantityinStock    INT              NOT NULL,
        ExpirationDate     DATE             NULL,
        StockLocation      VARCHAR(40)      NULL,
        ShelfLocation      VARCHAR(40)      NULL,
        ReorderWhen        INT              NULL,
        ReorderAmount      INT              NULL,
        idVendor           INT              NULL
    )
```

2. Make the table's primary key be the UPC field.

To define the primary key, you simply add a PRIMARY KEY clause to the statement like this:

```
    PRIMARY KEY (UPC),
```

3. Make indexes for fields used in foreign key constraints.

Creating indexes for fields used in foreign key constraints is not mandatory but it makes matching up the related values in the two tables faster. By default, MySQL Workbench creates indexes for fields used in foreign keys.

Use the INDEX clause to define these indexes. Give them names that tell what table they are used in (InventoryItems), what fields they contain, and the fact that they are used in foreign key constraints. The following lines of code create the indexes:

```
    INDEX FK_InventoryItems_idVendor       (idVendor       ASC),
    INDEX FK_InventoryItems_StockLocation (StockLocation ASC),
    INDEX FK_InventoryItems_ShelfLocation (ShelfLocation ASC),
```

4. Make foreign key constraints for the fields listed in step 3.

Use the CONSTRAINT clause to define the constraints. Give the constraints names that indicate the table, fields, and the fact that these are foreign key constraints. The following code defines these constraints:

```
    CONSTRAINT FK_InventoryItems_idVendor
      FOREIGN KEY (idVendor )
      REFERENCES Vendors (idVendor )
      ON DELETE NO ACTION
      ON UPDATE NO ACTION,

    CONSTRAINT FK_InventoryItems_StockLocation
      FOREIGN KEY (StockLocation )
      REFERENCES StockLocations (StockLocation )
      ON DELETE NO ACTION
      ON UPDATE NO ACTION,

    CONSTRAINT FK_InventoryItems_ShelfLocation
      FOREIGN KEY (ShelfLocation )
      REFERENCES ShelfLocations (ShelfLocation )
```

```
ON DELETE NO ACTION
ON UPDATE NO ACTION
```

The following code shows the complete CREATE TABLE statement:

```
CREATE TABLE IF NOT EXISTS InventoryItems (
  UPC             VARCHAR(40)    NOT NULL,
  Description     VARCHAR(45)    NOT NULL,
  BuyPrice        DECIMAL(10,2)  NULL,
  SellPrice       DECIMAL(10,2)  NOT NULL,
  QuantityinStock INT            NOT NULL,
  ExpirationDate  DATE           NULL,
  StockLocation   VARCHAR(40)    NULL,
  ShelfLocation   VARCHAR(40)    NULL,
  ReorderWhen     INT            NULL,
  ReorderAmount   INT            NULL,
  idVendor        INT            NULL,

  PRIMARY KEY (UPC),

  INDEX FK_InventoryItems_idVendor       (idVendor      ASC),
  INDEX FK_InventoryItems_StockLocation (StockLocation ASC),
  INDEX FK_InventoryItems_ShelfLocation (ShelfLocation ASC),

  CONSTRAINT FK_InventoryItems_idVendor
    FOREIGN KEY (idVendor )
    REFERENCES Vendors (idVendor )
    ON DELETE NO ACTION
    ON UPDATE NO ACTION,

  CONSTRAINT FK_InventoryItems_StockLocation
    FOREIGN KEY (StockLocation )
    REFERENCES StockLocations (StockLocation )
    ON DELETE NO ACTION
    ON UPDATE NO ACTION,

  CONSTRAINT FK_InventoryItems_ShelfLocation
    FOREIGN KEY (ShelfLocation )
    REFERENCES ShelfLocations (ShelfLocation )
    ON DELETE NO ACTION
    ON UPDATE NO ACTION
)
```

The following chapter has more to say about using the CREATE TABLE statement to build databases.

CREATE INDEX

The previous CREATE TABLE example uses INDEX clauses to define indexes for the table as it is being created. The CREATE INDEX statement adds an index to a table after the table has been created.

For example, the following statement adds an index named `IDX_Persons_Names` to the Persons table. This index makes it easier to search the table by the records' combined FirstName/LastName fields:

```
CREATE INDEX IDX_Persons_Names ON Persons (FirstName, LastName)
```

You could use a `CREATE INDEX` statement to add an index to a table if you didn't realize you would need one or just forgot to do it earlier, but there's also a strategic reason to do it this way. Relational databases use complicated self-balancing trees to provide indexes. When you add or delete a record, the database must perform a non-trivial amount of work to update its index structures. If you add the records in sorted order, as is often the case when you first populate the database, this can mean even more work than usual because the tree structures tend to have trouble with sorted values.

When you create an index after the table is populated, the database must perform a fair amount of work to build the index tree, but it has a big advantage that it doesn't when indexing records one at a time: it knows how many records are in the table. Instead of resizing the index tree as it is built one record at a time, the database can build a big empty tree and then fill it with data.

Some databases may not use this information effectively but some may be able to fill the table and then add an index more quickly than they can fill the table if the index is created first. Note that the difference is small so you probably shouldn't worry about creating the indexes separately unless you are loading a lot of records.

DROP

The `DROP` statement removes an object from the database. For example, the following statement removes the index named IDX_Persons_Names from the Persons table in a MySQL database:

```
DROP INDEX IDX_Persons_Names ON Persons
```

The following statement shows the Transact-SQL language version of the previous command:

```
DROP INDEX Persons.IDX_Persons_Names
```

The other most useful `DROP` statement is `DROP TABLE`. You can add the `IF EXISTS` clause to the basic command to make the database ignore the command if the table does not already exist. That makes it easier to write scripts that drop tables before creating them. (If you don't add `IF EXISTS` and you try to drop a table that doesn't exist, the script will crash.)

The following command removes the Persons table from the database:

```
DROP TABLE IF EXISTS Persons
```

Note that `DROP TABLE` is instant, immediate, and irrevocable. The database doesn't give you any warning or make you confirm the deletion. It instantly destroys the table and all of the data it contains. You cannot undo this command so be really, really, *really* sure you want to do it before you execute a `DROP TABLE` command.

INSERT

The INSERT statement adds data to a table in the database. This command has several variations. For the following examples, assume the Persons table was created with the following command:

```
CREATE TABLE IF NOT EXISTS Persons (
    idPerson       INT           NOT NULL    AUTO_INCREMENT,
    FirstName      VARCHAR(45)   NOT NULL    DEFAULT '<missing>',
    LastName       VARCHAR(45)   NOT NULL    DEFAULT '<none>',
    State          VARCHAR(10)   NULL,
    PRIMARY KEY (idPerson)
)
```

The simplest form of the INSERT statement lists the values to be inserted in the new record after the VALUES keyword. The values must have the correct data types and must be listed in the same order as the fields in the table.

The following command inserts a new record in the Persons table:

```
INSERT INTO Persons VALUES (1, "Rod", "Stephens", "CO")
```

Some databases will not let you specify values for AUTO INCREMENT fields such as idPerson in this example. If you specify the value null for such a field, the database automatically generates a value for you. (Although some databases won't even let you specify null. In that case, you must use a more complicated version of INSERT that lists the fields.)

If you replace a value with the keyword DEFAULT, the database uses that field's default value if it has one.

When it executes the following command, the database automatically generates an idPerson value, the FirstName value defaults to <missing>, the LastName value is set to Markup, and the State value is set to null:

```
INSERT INTO Persons VALUES (null, DEFAULT, "Markup", null)
```

The next form of INSERT statement explicitly lists the fields that it will initialize. The values in the VALUES clause must match those listed earlier and they must be in the correct order. Listing the fields that you are going to enter lets you omit some fields or change the order in which they are given.

The following statement creates a new Persons record. It explicitly sets the FirstName field to Snortimer and the State field to Confusion. The database automatically generates a new idPerson value and the LastName value gets its default value <none>:

```
INSERT INTO Persons (FirstName, State) VALUES ("Snortimer", "Confusion")
```

The final version of INSERT INTO described here gets the values that it will insert from a SELECT statement (described in the next section) that pulls values from a table.

The following example inserts values into the SmartPersons table's LastName and FirstName fields. It gets the values from a query that selects FirstName and LastName values from the Persons table where the corresponding record's State value is not Confusion:

```
INSERT INTO SmartPersons (LastName, FirstName)
    SELECT LastName, FirstName FROM Persons
    WHERE State <> 'Confusion'
```

Unlike the previous INSERT statements, this version may insert many records in the table if the query returns a lot of data.

SELECT

The SELECT command retrieves data from the database. This is one of the most often used and complex SQL commands. The basic syntax is:

```
SELECT select_clause
FROM from_clause
[ WHERE where_clause ]
[ GROUP BY group_by_clause ]
[ ORDER BY order_by_clause [ ASC | DESC ] ]
```

The parts in square brackets are optional and the vertical bar between ASC and DESC means you can include one or the other of those keywords.

The following sections describe these main clauses in more detail.

SELECT Clause

The SELECT clause specifies the fields that you want the query to return.

If a field's name is unambiguous given the tables selected by the FROM clause (described in the next section), you can simply list the field's name as in FirstName.

If more than one of the tables listed in the FROM clause have a field with the same name, you must put the table's name in front of the field's name as in Persons.FirstName.

The special value * tells the database that you want to select all of the available fields. If the query includes more than one table in the FROM clause and you want all of the fields from a specific table, you can include the table's name before the asterisk as in Persons.*.

The following query returns all of the fields for all of the records in the Persons table:

```
SELECT * FROM Persons
```

Optionally you can give a field an alias by following it with the keyword AS and the alias that you want it to have. When the query returns, it acts as if that field's name is whatever you used as an alias. This is useful for such things as differentiating among fields with the same name in different tables, for creating a new field name that a program can use for nicer display (for example, changing the `CustName` field to `Customer Name`), or for creating a name for a calculated column.

A particularly useful option you can add to the `SELECT` clause is `DISTINCT`. This makes the database return only one copy of each set of values that are selected.

For example, suppose the Orders table contains customer first and last names. The following MySQL query selects the `FirstName` and `LastName` values from the table, concatenates them into a single field with a space in between, and gives that calculated field the alias Name. The `DISTINCT` keyword means the query will only return one of each Name result even if a single customer has many records in the table.

```
SELECT DISTINCT CONCAT(FirstName, " ", LastName) AS Name FROM Orders
```

The following code shows the Transact-SQL equivalent of this statement:

```
SELECT DISTINCT FirstName + " " + LastName AS Name FROM Orders
```

FROM Clause

The `FROM` clause lists the tables from which the database should pull data. Normally if the query pulls data from more than one table, the query either uses a `JOIN` or a `WHERE` clause to indicate how the records in the tables are related.

For example, the following statement selects information from the Orders and OrderItems tables. It matches records from the two using a `WHERE` clause. That clause tells the database to associate Orders records with OrderItems records that have the same OrderId value.

```
SELECT * FROM Orders, OrderItems
WHERE Orders.OrderId = OrderItems.OrderId
```

Several different kinds of `JOIN` clauses perform roughly the same function as the previous `WHERE` clause. They differ in how the database handles records in one table that have no corresponding records in the second table.

For example, suppose the Courses table contains the names of college courses and holds the values in the following table.

CourseId	CourseName
CS 120	Database Design
CS 245	The Customer: A Necessary Evil
D? = h@p	Introduction to Cryptography

Furthermore, suppose the Enrollments table contains the following information about students taking classes.

FirstName	LastName	CourseId
Guinevere	Conkle	CS 120
Guinevere	Conkle	CS 101
Heron	Stroh	CS 120
Heron	Stroh	CS 245
Maxene	Quinn	CS 245

Now consider the following query:

```
SELECT * FROM Enrollments, Courses
WHERE Courses.CourseId = Enrollments.CourseId
```

This may seem like a simple enough query that selects enrollment information plus each student's class name. For example, one of the records returned would be:

FirstName	LastName	CourseId	CourseId	CourseName
Guinevere	Conkle	CS 120	CS 120	Database Design

(Note that the result contains two CourseId values, one from each table.)

The way in which the kinds of JOIN clause differ is in the way they handle missing values. If you look again at the tables, you'll see that no students are currently enrolled in Introduction to Cryptography. You'll also find that Heron Stroh is enrolled in CS 245, which has no record in the Courses table.

The following query that uses a WHERE clause discards any records in one table that have no corresponding records in the second table:

```
SELECT * FROM Enrollments, Courses
WHERE Courses.CourseId = Enrollments.CourseId
```

The following statement uses the INNER JOIN clause to produce the same result:

```
SELECT * FROM Enrollments INNER JOIN Courses
   ON  (Courses.CourseId = Enrollments.CourseId)
```

The following table shows the results of these two queries.

FirstName	LastName	CourseId	CourseId	CourseName
Guinevere	Conkle	CS 120	CS 120	Database Design
Heron	Stroh	CS 120	CS 120	Database Design
Maxene	Quinn	CS 245	CS 245	The Customer: A Necessary Evil
Heron	Stroh	CS 245	CS 245	The Customer: A Necessary Evil

The following statement selects the same records except it uses the LEFT JOIN clause to favor the table listed to the left of the clause in the query (Orders). If a record appears in that table, it is listed in the result even if there is no corresponding record in the other table.

```
SELECT * FROM Orders LEFT JOIN OrderItems
    ON (Orders.OrderId = OrderItems.OrderId)
```

The following table shows the result of this query. Notice that the results include a record for Guinevere Conkle's CS 101 enrollment even though CS 101 is not listed in the Courses table. In that record, the fields that should have come from the Courses table have null values.

FirstName	LastName	CourseId	CourseId	CourseName
Guinevere	Conkle	CS 120	CS 120	Database Design
Heron	Stroh	CS 120	CS 120	Database Design
Maxene	Quinn	CS 245	CS 245	The Customer: A Necessary Evil
Guinevere	Conkle	CS 101	NULL	NULL
Heron	Stroh	CS 245	CS 245	The Customer: A Necessary Evil

Similarly the RIGHT JOIN clause makes the query favor the table to the right of the clause so it includes all of the records in that table even if there are no corresponding records in the other table. The following query demonstrates the RIGHT JOIN clause:

```
SELECT * FROM Orders RIGHT JOIN OrderItems
    ON (Orders.OrderId = OrderItems.OrderId)
```

The following table shows the result of this query. This time there is a special record for the Introduction to Cryptography course even though no student is enrolled in it.

FirstName	LastName	CourseId	CourseId	CourseName
Guinevere	Conkle	CS 120	CS 120	Database Design
Heron	Stroh	CS 120	CS 120	Database Design
Maxene	Quinn	CS 245	CS 245	The Customer: A Necessary Evil
Heron	Stroh	CS 245	CS 245	The Customer: A Necessary Evil
NULL	NULL	NULL	D? = h@p	Introduction to Cryptography

Both the left and right joins are called *outer joins* because they include records that are outside of the "natural" records that include values from both tables.

Many databases, including MySQL and Access, don't provide a join to select all records from both tables like a combined left and right join. You can achieve a similar result by using the UNION keyword to combine the results of a left and right join. The following query uses the UNION clause:

```
SELECT * FROM Courses LEFT JOIN Enrollments
  ON Courses.CourseId=Enrollments.CourseId
UNION
SELECT * FROM Courses RIGHT JOIN Enrollments
  ON Courses.CourseId=Enrollments.CourseId
```

The following table shows the results.

FirstName	LastName	CourseId	CourseId	CourseName
Guinevere	Conkle	CS 120	CS 120	Database Design
Heron	Stroh	CS 120	CS 120	Database Design
Maxene	Quinn	CS 245	CS 245	The Customer: A Necessary Evil
Guinevere	Conkle	CS 101	NULL	NULL
Heron	Stroh	CS 245	CS 245	The Customer: A Necessary Evil
NULL	NULL	NULL	D? = h@p	Introduction to Cryptography

WHERE Clause

The WHERE clause provides a filter to select only certain records in the tables. It can compare the values in the tables to constants, expressions, or other values in the tables. You can use parentheses and logical operators such as AND, NOT, and OR to build complicated selection expressions.

For example, the following query selects records from the Enrollments and Courses tables where the CourseId values match and the CourseId is alphabetically less than CS 200 (upper division classes begin with CS 200):

```
SELECT * FROM Enrollments, Courses
WHERE Enrollments.CourseId = Courses.CourseId
  AND Courses.CourseId < 'CS 200'
```

The following table shows the result.

FirstName	LastName	CourseId	CourseId	CourseName
Guinevere	Conkle	CS 120	CS 120	Database Design
Heron	Stroh	CS 120	CS 120	Database Design

GROUP BY Clause

If you include an aggregate function such as AVERAGE or SUM in the SELECT clause, the GROUP BY clause tells the database which fields to look at to determine whether values should be combined.

For example, the following query selects the CustomerId field from the CreditsAndDebits table. It also selects the sum of the Amount field values. The GROUP BY clause makes the query combine values that have matching CustomerId values for calculating the sums. The result is a list of every CustomerId and the corresponding current total balance (calculated by adding up all of the customer's credits and debits).

```
SELECT CustomerId, SUM(Amount) AS Balance
FROM CreditsAndDebits
GROUP BY CustomerId
```

ORDER BY Clause

The ORDER BY clause gives a list of fields that the database should use to sort the results. The optional keyword DESC after a field makes the database sort that field's values in descending order. (The default order is ascending. You can explicitly include the ASC keyword if you want to make the order obvious.)

The following query selects the CustomerId field and the total of the Amount values for each CustomerId from the CreditsAndDebits table. It sorts the results in descending order of the total amount so you can see who has the largest balance first.

```
SELECT CustomerId, SUM(Amount) AS Balance
FROM CreditsAndDebits
GROUP BY CustomerId
ORDER BY Amount DESC
```

The following query selects the distinct first and last name combinations from the Enrollments table and orders the results by LastName and then by FirstName. (For example, if two students have the same last name Zappa, then Dweezil comes before Moon Unit.)

```
SELECT DISTINCT LastName, FirstName
FROM Enrollments
ORDER BY LastName, FirstName
```

Try It Out   Be Selective

Though the SELECT statement has many variations, the basic ideas are reasonably intuitive so a little practice will go a long way toward learning how to write SELECT statements.

Suppose the Authors table has fields AuthorId, FirstName, and LastName. Suppose also that the Books table has fields AuthorId, Title, ISBN (International Standard Book Number), MSRP (Manufacturer's Suggested Retail Price), Year, and Pages. Write a query to select book titles, prices, and author names. Concatenate the authors' first and last names and give the result the alias Author. Select only books where MSRP is less than $10.00. Sort the results by price in ascending order.

1.   Write the SELECT clause. The following code shows the SELECT clause:

```
SELECT MSRP, Title, CONCAT(FirstName, " ", LastName) AS Author
```

2.   Write a FROM clause to select an inner join using the Authors and Books tables. The following code shows the FROM clause:

```
                FROM Books INNER JOIN Authors
                   ON (Books.AuthorId = Authors.AuthorId)
```

3. Write a WHERE clause to select records where MSRP < $10.00. The following code shows the WHERE clause:

    ```
    WHERE MSRP < 10
    ```

4. Write an ORDER BY clause to sort the results by MSRP in ascending order:

    ```
    ORDER BY MSRP
    ```

How It Works

The basic SELECT clause includes the Books table's Title and MSRP fields. It also concatenates the Authors table's FirstName and LastName fields with a space in between.

The FROM clause selects an inner join using the Authors and Books tables. This query uses the tables' AuthorId fields to match corresponding records.

The WHERE clause adds a further condition on the selected records, requiring that the MSRP value be less than 10.

The ORDER BY clause sorts the results by MSRP. The default order for ORDER BY clauses is ascending so the statement doesn't need to explicitly include the ASC keyword.

The following code shows the complete query.

```
SELECT MSRP, Title, CONCAT(FirstName, " ", LastName) AS Author
FROM Books INNER JOIN Authors
   ON (Books.AuthorId = Authors.AuthorId)
WHERE MSRP < 10
ORDER BY MSRP
```

UPDATE

The UPDATE statement changes the values in one or more records' fields. The basic syntax is:

```
UPDATE table SET field = new_value
WHERE where_clause
```

For example, the following statement fixes a typo in the Books table. It changes the Title field's value to "The Portable Door" in any records that currently have Title "The Potable Door."

```
UPDATE Books SET Title = "The Portable Door"
WHERE Title = "The Potable Door"
```

The WHERE clause is extremely important in an UPDATE statement. If you forget the WHERE clause, the update affects every record in the table! In the previous example, the statement would change the title of every book to "The Portable Door," probably not what you intended. The effects of the UPDATE statement are immediate and irreversible so forgetting the WHERE clause can be disastrous. (In fact, some developers have suggested that an UPDATE statement without a WHERE clause should generate an error unless you take special action to say "yes, I'm really, really sure.")

Try It Out   **Updates**

Suppose the Sales table includes the fields EmployeeId, Year, Month (which holds three-letter month abbreviations), TotalSales (the number of light sabers sold), and Salary. Write an update statement that gives a $100 bonus to employees who made their sales quota of 10 light sabers sold during the month of August 2008.

1. Write the UPDATE statement including the table name and the SET clause:

```
UPDATE Sales
SET Salary = Salary + 100
```

2. Write the WHERE clause to select the records that should be updated:

```
WHERE TotalSales >= 10
   AND Month="AUG"
   AND Year=2008
```

How It Works

The UPDATE clause will affect the Sales table. You need to add $100 to the Salary field for certain records. To do that, the clause sets the Salary value to $100 plus the current Salary value.

The WHERE clause has three parts that require the number of light sabers sold to be at least 10, the month to be AUG, and the year to be 2008.

The following code shows the complete UPDATE statement.

```
UPDATE Sales
SET Salary = Salary + 100
WHERE TotalSales >= 10
   AND Month="AUG"
   AND Year=2008
```

DELETE

The DELETE statement removes records from a table. The basic syntax is:

```
DELETE FROM table
WHERE where_clause
```

For example, the following statement removes all records from the Books table where the AuthorId is 7:

```
DELETE FROM Books
WHERE AuthorId = 7
```

As is the case with UPDATE, the WHERE clause is very important in a DELETE statement. If you forget the WHERE clause, the DELETE statement removes every record from the table mercilessly and without remorse.

Summary

SQL is a powerful tool. The SQL commands described in this chapter let you perform basic database operations such as determining the database's structure and contents. This chapter explained how to:

❑ Use the CREATE TABLE statement to create a table with a primary key, indexes, and foreign key constraints.

❑ Use INSERT statements to add data to a table.

❑ Use SELECT statements to select data from one or more tables, satisfying specific conditions, and sort the result.

❑ Use the UPDATE statement to modify the data in a table.

❑ Use the DELETE statement to remove records from a table.

SQL statements let you perform simple tasks with a database such as creating a new table or inserting a record. By combining many SQL statements into a script, you can perform elaborate procedures such as creating and initializing a database from scratch. Chapter 18 explains this topic in greater detail. It describes the benefits of using scripts to create databases and discusses some of the issues that you should understand before writing those scripts.

Before you move on to Chapter 18, however, use the following exercises to test your understanding of the material covered in this chapter. You can find the solutions to these exercises in Appendix A.

Exercises

1. Write SQL statements to create the three tables shown in Figure 17-1. Include the primary keys, foreign key constraints, and indexes on the fields used in those constraints.

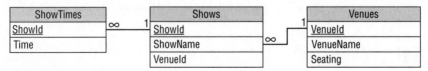

Figure 17-1

2. Write a series of SQL statements to insert the data shown in Figure 17-2.

ShowTimes	
11:15	1
3:00	1
1:15	2
6:00	2
11:00	3
12:00	3
6:30	3
2:00	4
5:27	4
2:00	5
3:00	6

Shows		
1	Sherm's Shark Show	101
2	Meet the Rays	101
3	Deb's Daring Dolphins	102
4	The Walter Walrus Comedy Hour	102
5	Flamingo Follies	103
6	Wonderful Waterfowl	103

Venues		
101	Sherman's Lagoon	375
102	Peet Amphitheater	300
103	Ngorongoro Wash	413

Figure 17-2

Hint: Use 24-hour clock times as in 14:00 for 2:00pm.

3. Management has decided that no two shows should start fewer than 15 minutes apart. Write SQL statements to change the 2:00 Flamingo Follies show to 2:15 and the 3:00 Sherm's Shark Show to 3:15.

    Hint: Include both the ShowTimes and Shows tables in the UPDATE clause. Then use a WHERE clause to select the correct record by Time and ShowName.

4. Write a SQL statement to select data from the tables and produce the following result.

Show	Time	Location
Deb's Daring Dolphins	11:00am	Peet Amphitheater
Sherm's Shark Show	11:15am	Sherman's Lagoon
Deb's Daring Dolphins	12:00pm	Peet Amphitheater
Meet the Rays	1:15pm	Sherman's Lagoon
The Walter Walrus Comedy Hour	2:00pm	Peet Amphitheater
Flamingo Follies	2:15pm	Ngorongoro Wash
Wonderful Waterfowl	3:00pm	Ngorongoro Wash
Sherm's Shark Show	3:15pm	Sherman's Lagoon
The Walter Walrus Comedy Hour	5:27pm	Peet Amphitheater
Meet the Rays	6:00pm	Sherman's Lagoon
Deb's Daring Dolphins	6:30pm	Peet Amphitheater

Hints:

❑   Sort the results by Show and then Time.

❑   In MySQL at least, "SHOW" is a keyword so you cannot simply use "AS Show" to give the ShowName field the alias Show because that would confuse MySQL. Instead put quotes around the word Show wherever you need it as in AS "Show" and ORDER BY "Show".

❑ To format the times as in 6:30pm in MySQL, use the DATE_FORMAT function. To make the times line up nicely on the right, use the LPAD function to pad them on the left with spaces. The following code shows how:

```
LPAD(DATE_FORMAT(Time, "%l:%i %p"), 8, " ")
```

❑ Unfortunately when you pad the times, the ORDER BY statement treats the result as a string rather than a time. That means, for example, " 3:00pm" comes alphabetically before "11:00am" because " 3:00pm" begins with a space. To fix this, use the TIME function to convert the times as strings back into times in the ORDER BY clause. For example, if you use the alias Time for the result of this field, then the ORDER BY clause should contain the following:

```
TIME(Time)
```

5. Write a SQL statement to select data from the tables and produce the following result.

Time	Show	Location
11:00am	Deb's Daring Dolphins	Peet Amphitheater
11:15am	Sherm's Shark Show	Sherman's Lagoon
12:00pm	Deb's Daring Dolphins	Peet Amphitheater
1:15pm	Meet the Rays	Sherman's Lagoon
2:00pm	The Walter Walrus Comedy Hour	Peet Amphitheater
2:15pm	Flamingo Follies	Ngorongoro Wash
3:00pm	Wonderful Waterfowl	Ngorongoro Wash
3:15pm	Sherm's Shark Show	Sherman's Lagoon
5:27pm	The Walter Walrus Comedy Hour	Peet Amphitheater
6:00pm	Meet the Rays	Sherman's Lagoon
6:30pm	Deb's Daring Dolphins	Peet Amphitheater

See Exercise 4 for hints.

Building Databases with SQL Scripts

The previous chapter provided an introduction to using SQL to create and manage databases. That chapter also hinted at techniques for using SQL scripts to make database maintenance easier.

This chapter goes a little further. It discusses some of the details that you need to take into account when you use scripts to manage a database.

In this chapter you learn how to:

❑   Know when scripts can be useful.

❑   Build tables in a valid order.

❑   Insert data into tables in a valid order.

❑   Drop tables in a valid order.

Why Bother with Scripts?

SQL statements let you create, populate, modify, and delete the tables in a database. In many database products, SQL statements even let you create and destroy the database itself. For example, MySQL's CREATE DATABASE and DROP DATABASE statements create and destroy databases.

If you put these SQL commands in a script, you can rerun that script whenever it's necessary. You can easily rebuild the database if it gets corrupted, make copies of the database on other computers, fill the tables with data to use when running tests, and reinitialize the data after the tests are finished.

Being able to reinitialize the data to a known state can also be very helpful in tracking down bugs. It's extremely hard to find a bug if it just pops up occasionally and then disappears again. If you can reinitialize the database and then make a bug happen by following a series of predictable steps, it's much easier to find and fix the problem.

Script Categories

Scripts that are useful for managing databases fall into at least four categories, described in the following sections.

Database Creation Scripts

Database creation scripts build the database's structure. They build the tables, primary keys, indexes, foreign key constraints, field and table check constraints, and all of the other structure that doesn't change as the data is modified.

Basic Initialization Scripts

Basic initialization scripts initialize basic data that is needed before the database can be useful. This includes system parameter tables, lookup tables, and other tables that hold data that changes only rarely when the database is in use.

For example, you might use one of these scripts to initialize a list of allowed states or regions, physical constants (the speed of light, Avogadro's number, Finagle's Variable Constant), or define data type conversion constants (how many centimeters in an inch, how many millimeters in an attoparsec, how many seconds in a microfortnight).

Data Initialization Scripts

These scripts place data in tables. These range from small scripts to initialize a few values to huge monster scripts that insert thousands of records into the database.

Often it's useful to have a separate subcategory for test scripts that fill the tables with data for use in specific tests. You would run a script to prepare the data and then run the test. If the test can be executed by SQL statements, the script might perform the test, too. Sometimes it may be useful to have a separate test initialization script for every use case defined by your requirement documents.

It's also often useful to have separate scripts to initialize different parts of the database. For example, you might have a script that creates users, another that creates orders, and a third that creates invoice and payment data.

You can build scripts that invoke smaller scripts to perform larger tasks. For example, you might make a test initialization script that calls the standard user initialization script and then inserts or updates specific records in other tables to prepare for the test that you are about to perform.

For example, the following MySQL script invokes three others. It creates a database, selects it, and then calls three other scripts that create a table, insert some data, and select the data. It then drops the database.

```
CREATE DATABASE MultipleScripts;

USE MultipleScripts;

SOURCE C:\Rod\DB Design\MultiScript1.sql
SOURCE C:\Rod\DB Design\MultiScript2.sql
```

```
SOURCE C:\Rod\DB Design\MultiScript3.sql

DROP DATABASE MultipleScripts;
```

It may not always be necessary to break the database scripts into little pieces, but on some projects it's even useful to have two separate scripts to create and initialize each table. Then if you change a table, it's easy to find the creation and initialization code for it. Higher-level scripts can then call those scripts to build and initialize the database.

Cleanup Scripts

Often it's easier to simply drop the database and re-create it than it is to clean up the mess left by a test, but occasionally it's useful to truncate or drop only some of the tables. For example, if the database contains a lot of data (millions of records), it may be easier and faster to repair changes made by tests than to rebuild the whole thing from scratch.

It's not always easy to undo changes made by a complex series of tests, particularly if you later make changes to the tests. In fact, it's often hard to even tell if you've successfully undone the changes. For those reasons, I usually prefer to rebuild the database from scratch when possible.

Saving Scripts

Just as any other piece of software does, scripts change during development, testing, and use. Also as is the case for other types of software, it's often useful to look back at previous versions of scripts. To ensure that those versions are available, always keep the old versions of scripts. Later if you discover a problem, you can compare the current and older versions to see what's changed.

One way to keep old scripts is to use version control software. Programs such as CVS (Concurrent Versions System, see www.nongnu.org/cvs) and VSS (Visual Source Safe, see msdn.microsoft.com/en-us/vs2005/aa718670.aspx) keep track of different versions of files. You can store your scripts in one of those systems and then update the files whenever you create a new version. Then you can always go back and see the older versions if you have a reason.

If you don't feel like using a formal version control system, you can invent your own in one of several ways. For example, you can put a version number in the script file names. You might make a script named MakeUsers.sql that fills the Users table. The file MakeUsers.sql would always contain the most current version and MakeUsers001.sql, MakeUsers002.sql, and so forth would contain older versions.

Another approach is to email scripts to yourself when you revise them. Later you can search through the emails sorted by date to see the older versions. To keep your normal email account uncluttered so you can easily find those offers for mortgage debt elimination, jobs as a rebate processor, and pleas for help in getting $10 million out of Nigeria (you get to keep $3 million for your trouble), create a separate email account to hold the scripts. You can use free email accounts on Gmail, Yahoo! Mail, or Hotmail if you don't want to use up your own mail space.

Ordering SQL Commands

One issue that you should consider when building scripts is that some commands must be executed in a particular order. For example, if the Races table for your cheese-rolling database (see www.cheese-rolling.co.uk) has a WinnerId field that refers to the Racers table's RacerId field as a foreign key, you must create the Racers table before you create the Races table. Clearly the Races table cannot refer to a field in a table that doesn't yet exist.

Usually you can create the tables in some order so none refers to another table that doesn't yet exist. (*Tip:* build lookup tables first.) If for some bizarre reason there is no such ordering, you can use an ALTER TABLE ADD FOREIGN KEY statement (or a similar statement in whatever version of SQL you are using) to create the foreign key constraints after you build all of the tables.

You may also be able to tell the database to turn off constraint checking while you build the tables. For example, the following MySQL script builds three tables that are mutually dependent. TableA refers to TableB, TableB refers to TableC, and TableC refers to TableA.

```
SET @OLD_UNIQUE_CHECKS=@@UNIQUE_CHECKS, UNIQUE_CHECKS=0;
SET @OLD_FOREIGN_KEY_CHECKS=@@FOREIGN_KEY_CHECKS, FOREIGN_KEY_CHECKS=0;
SET @OLD_SQL_MODE=@@SQL_MODE, SQL_MODE='TRADITIONAL';

CREATE DATABASE CycleDb;
USE CycleDb;

CREATE TABLE TableC (
   CType     VARCHAR(10)     NOT NULL,
   AType     VARCHAR(10)     NULL,

   PRIMARY KEY (CType),

   INDEX FK_CrefA (AType ASC),

   CONSTRAINT FK_CrefA
     FOREIGN KEY (AType)
     REFERENCES TableA (AType)
     ON DELETE NO ACTION
     ON UPDATE NO ACTION
);

CREATE TABLE TableB (
   BType     VARCHAR(10)     NOT NULL,
   CType     VARCHAR(10)     NULL,

   PRIMARY KEY (BType),

   INDEX FK_BrefC (CType ASC),

   CONSTRAINT FK_BrefC
     FOREIGN KEY (CType)
     REFERENCES TableC (CType)
     ON DELETE NO ACTION
     ON UPDATE NO ACTION
);

CREATE TABLE TableA (
   AType     VARCHAR(10)     NOT NULL,
   BType     VARCHAR(10)     NULL,

   PRIMARY KEY (AType),
```

```
    INDEX FK_ArefB (BType ASC),

    CONSTRAINT FK_ArefB
      FOREIGN KEY (BType)
      REFERENCES TableB (BType)
      ON DELETE NO ACTION
      ON UPDATE NO ACTION
);

INSERT INTO TableA VALUES("A value", "B value");
INSERT INTO TableB VALUES("B value", "C value");
INSERT INTO TableC VALUES("C value", "A value");

SET SQL_MODE=@OLD_SQL_MODE;
SET FOREIGN_KEY_CHECKS=@OLD_FOREIGN_KEY_CHECKS;
SET UNIQUE_CHECKS=@OLD_UNIQUE_CHECKS;

SELECT * FROM TableA;
SELECT * FROM TableB;
SELECT * FROM TableC;

DROP DATABASE CycleDb;
```

The first three statements tell the database not to check for unique key values, not to check foreign key constraints, and to use traditional SQL behavior (in short, give errors instead of warnings).

The script then creates the three interdependent tables and inserts some values in them. It then restores the original values for the SQL mode, foreign key checking, and unique key checking.

The script finishes by performing some queries and dropping the database.

Just as you may need to create tables in a particular order, you may need to insert values into the tables in a particular order. For example, you'll need to create the Racer's record for Nick Morris before you create the Races record for the 2007 cheese-rolling uphill race in the Boys Under 12 Years division (Nick won that race).

If you cannot find a legal ordering for the INSERT statements, you may be able to disable the database's checks just as you can while creating tables. The preceding script inserts records that depend on each other so there is no valid way to enter those values without disabling the error checking.

Finally, if you delete records or entire tables, you may need to do so in a particular order. After you've built your cheese-rolling database, you cannot remove Nick Morris's record from the Racers table before you remove the Races record that refers to him.

Try It Out   Ordering Tables

I haven't actually seen a real database with mutually dependent tables so I have always been able to put them in a valid order. (If you know of a real-world database that has mutually dependent tables, please email me at RodStephens@vb-helper.com. I'd love to hear about a real example.)

To hone your ordering skills, make a list showing a valid order for creating the tables in the design shown in Figure 18-1.

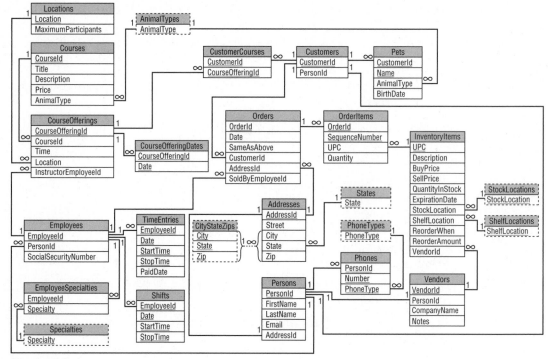

Figure 18-1

A list where some of the objects must come before others but not all of the relationships are known is called a *partial ordering*. Creating a full ordering that satisfies a partial ordering is called *extending the partial ordering*.

1. Define a partial ordering by making a list of the tables. Next to each table, make a *predecessor list* showing all of the other tables that must be defined *before* that one.

2. Use this list to build an output list giving the tables in a valid order.

    a. Look through the list you created in Step 1 and find any tables that have no predecessors.

    b. Put those tables in the output list.

    c. Remove those tables from any other table's predecessor list.

    d. Remove the outputted tables' rows from the list.

    e. Repeat this process until every table is in the output list or you find a group of mutually dependent tables.

How It Works

1. Define a partial ordering by making a list of the tables.

    If two tables are related by a one-to-many relationship, the table on the "many" side of the relationship depends on the table on the "one" side. For example, a CourseOfferings record refers to a Locations record (each course offering occurs at some location) so you must create the Locations table before you create the CourseOfferings table.

If two tables are related by a one-to-one relationship, you need to think a bit harder about which depends on the other. Normally such a relationship involves the primary key of only one of the tables. In that case, the non-primary key table depends on the primary key table. For example, the Addresses and Persons tables in Figure 18-1 have a one-to-one relationship. The relationship connects the Addresses table's primary key AddressId with the Persons table's non-primary key AddressId field, so the Persons table (non-primary key) depends on the Addresses table (primary key).

The following list shows the database's tables and their predecessors.

Table	Predecessors
Addresses	CityStateZips, States
AnimalTypes	
CityStateZips	
CourseOfferingDates	CourseOfferings
CourseOfferings	Locations, Courses, Employees
Courses	AnimalTypes
CustomerCourses	CourseOfferings, Customers
Customers	Persons
Employees	Persons
EmployeeSpecialties	Specialties, Employees
InventoryItems	StockLocations, ShelfLocations, Vendors
Locations	
OrderItems	Orders, InventoryItems
Orders	Customers, Employees, Addresses
Persons	Addresses
Pets	Customers, AnimalTypes
Phones	PhoneTypes, Persons
PhoneTypes	
ShelfLocations	
Shifts	Employees
Specialties	
States	
StockLocations	

Table	Predecessors
TimeEntries	Employees
Vendors	Persons

(Give yourself bonus points if you cringed a bit at this table and said to yourself, "Hey, that's not in 1NF because the second column doesn't hold a single value!")

2. Use this list to build an output list giving the tables in a valid order.

During the first pass through this list, the AnimalTypes, CityStateZips, Locations, PhoneTypes, ShelfLocations, Specialties, States, and StockLocations tables have no predecessors. You can immediately output those tables (so you can build them first in the database creation script) and remove them from the list.

After removing those tables from the list, the revised list has only two tables with no predecessors: Addresses and Courses. Output them and build them next in the database creation script.

After removing those tables from the list, the revised list has only one table with no predecessors: Persons. Output it and build it next in the database creation script.

At this point things seem pretty grim and you might wonder whether you will get stuck. Fortunately after removing the Persons table, the revised list contains several tables without predecessors: Customers, Employees, Phones, and Vendors. Output them and build them next in the database creation script.

After removing those tables from the list, the revised list contains lots of tables without predecessors: CourseOfferings, EmployeeSpecialties, InventoryItems, Orders, Pets, Shifts, and TimeEntries. You can build them next in the database creation script.

When you remove those tables from the list, the three remaining tables have no predecessors: CourseOfferingDates, CustomerCourses, and OrderItems. You can build those tables last when you create the database.

The complete ordering of the tables is: AnimalTypes, CityStateZips, Locations, PhoneTypes, ShelfLocations, Specialties, States, StockLocations, Addresses, Courses, Persons, Customers, Employees, Phones, Vendors, CourseOfferings, EmployeeSpecialties, InventoryItems, Orders, Pets, Shifts, TimeEntries, CourseOfferingDates, CustomerCourses, OrderItems.

Note that this is not the only possible complete ordering for these tables. Each time a group of tables had no predecessors, you could have created them in any order.

Summary

SQL scripts can make building and maintaining a database much easier than working manually with database tools such as MySQL or Access. They are particularly useful for repeatedly performing tasks such as initializing the database before performing a test.

This chapter explained:

- ❏ Why scripts are useful.
- ❏ Different categories of useful scripts such as database creation, basic initialization, data initialization, and cleanup.
- ❏ How to save different versions of scripts.
- ❏ How to create tables, insert data, remove data, and delete tables in a valid order.

Scripts are useful for maintaining databases. The following chapter discusses some of the typical maintenance chores that you should perform to keep a database in working order. Before you move on to Chapter 19, however, use the following exercises to test your understanding of the material covered in this chapter. You can find the solutions to these exercises in Appendix A.

Exercises

1. Consider the movie database design shown in Figure 18-2. A movie can have many actors and producers but only one director. Actors, producers, and directors are all persons and any person can hold any of those positions, sometimes simultaneously. (For example, in *Star Trek IV: The Voyage Home*, Leonard Nimoy is the director, an actor, and a writer. In *The Nutty Professor*, Eddie Murphy plays practically everyone.)

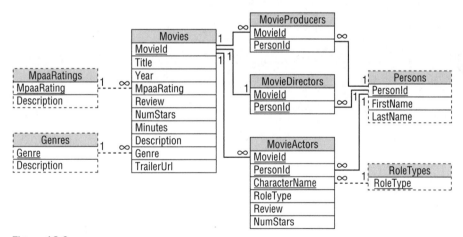

Figure 18-2

    Find an order in which you can create the database's tables so no table is created before another that depends on it.

2. Write a SQL script to build the movie database shown in Figure 18-2.

Database Maintenance

At this point, you've learned how to identify customer needs, design a database, refine the design, and implement the database interactively or by using scripts. Even after you start using the database, however, the work isn't done. You (or someone) must perform regular maintenance to keep the database healthy and efficient.

Like a high-performance sports car, the database needs regular maintenance to keep it running at peak efficiency. Just as the best engineering and construction in the world won't save your engine if you drive 100,000 miles without an oil change, your database design won't give you optimal performance if you don't give it regular tune-ups. (At least the database doesn't need collision insurance.)

This chapter describes some of the maintenance chores that must be performed to keep the database working smoothly. Unfortunately the details of performing these chores differ greatly in different databases so the exact steps you need to perform are not included here. Instead this chapter describes the issues that you should keep in mind when you design the database's maintenance schedule. You should consult the documentation for your particular database product to flesh out the details.

In this chapter you learn:

- ❏   What tasks are necessary to keep a database functional.
- ❏   How to schedule backups to safeguard data.
- ❏   What you can do to keep a database working efficiently.

Backups

Backups are one of the most important parts of database maintenance. Unfortunately they are also sometimes the most neglected part of a larger software effort. No database design can protect against system crashes, power failures, and the user accidentally deleting critical information. Without good backups, you could lose significant chunks of data.

(In one project, a ne'er-do-well tried to delete our entire code database. Fortunately he was stopped in time. We had backups anyway but we would probably have wasted an hour or so recovering the lost files. Unfortunately corporate policy didn't include burying him up to his neck in an ant hill.)

There are two main kinds of backups that many databases support: full and incremental.

A full backup makes a copy of everything in the database. Depending on the size of the database, this might take a lot of time and disk space. For a reasonably small database that is only used during business hours, you might have the computer automatically back up the database at midnight. Even if the backup takes several hours, the computer has little else to do in the middle of the night. It might slow down your SETI@home program (`setiathome.berkeley.edu`) so it may take a little longer to contact Starfleet but a full backup is the easiest and quickest to restore.

An incremental backup only records data that has changed since some earlier date. For example, you might back up all changes since the previous full backup. To restore an incremental backup, you need to first restore a full backup and then reapply the changes saved in the incremental backup.

Making an incremental backup is faster than making a full backup but restoring the data is harder. Because they are faster, incremental backups are useful for really big databases where it would take too long to make a full backup.

For example, suppose you have a really active database that records many thousands of transactions per day, such as a database that tracks keywords used in major news stories around the world (see `tenbyten.org/10x10.html` for an interesting display). Suppose that you need the database to be running at full speed 20 hours a day on weekdays but a full backup takes 12 hours. Then on Saturday morning you might make a full backup and on other days you would make an incremental backup.

Now suppose the database crashes and burns on a Thursday. To restore the database, you would restore the previous weekend's full backup and then apply the incremental backups for Monday, Tuesday, and Wednesday in order. That could take quite a while.

To make the process a bit faster, you could make a larger incremental backup halfway through the week. On Monday, Tuesday, Thursday, and Friday, you would make an incremental backup recording changes since the previous day. On Wednesday you would make an incremental backup to record all changes made since the previous Saturday full backup. Now to recover from a crash on Thursday, you only need to restore Saturday's full backup and then Wednesday's incremental backup. It will still take a while but it will be a bit faster and easier. Wednesday's incremental backup will also take longer than the daily backups but it will be a lot faster than a full backup.

Some databases allow you to perform backups while the database is in use. This is critical for databases that must be available most or all of the time. The backup will slow the database down so you still need to schedule backups for off-peak periods such as weekends or the middle of the night, but at least the database can keep running.

For example, my local grocery store's cash registers perform downloads, uploads, and backups in the middle of the night. If you stop in around midnight, the self-checkout machines usually run much slower than they do during the day. (I was there in the spirit of scientific inquiry, not because I was debugging software at midnight and needed a donut. Honest!)

One final note about backups. Backups are intended to protect you against unexpected damage to the database. That includes normal damage caused by logical disasters such as power glitches, the CIH virus (see en.wikipedia.org/wiki/CIH_virus), spilled soda, and EBCAK (Error Between Chair and Keyboard) problems, but it also includes physical calamities such as fire, tornado, and volcanic eruption. Your backups do you no good if they're stored next to the database's computer and you are hit by one of these. A full backup won't do you any good if the flash drive or DVD that holds it is sitting on top of the computer and a meteor reduces the whole thing to a pile of steel and plastic splinters.

To avoid this kind of problem, think about taking backups offsite. Of course, that creates a potential security issue if your data is sensitive (for example, credit card numbers, medical records, or salary information).

Try It Out   **Make a Backup Plan**

Suppose you have a really large database. A full backup takes around 10 hours, whereas an incremental backup takes about 1 hour per day of changes that you want to include in the backup. You are not allowed to make backups during the peak usage hours of 3:00am to 11:00pm weekdays, and 6:00am to 8:00pm on weekends.

Figure out what types of backups to perform on which days to make restoring the database as easy as possible.

1.   Figure out when you have time for a full backup.

2.   For each day after the full backup, make an incremental backup. Make the backup go back to the most complete previous backup it can reach given the time constraints.

How It Works

1.   Figure out when you have time for a full backup.

The following table shows the number of off-peak hours you have available for performing backups during each night of the week.

Night	Off-Peak Start	Off-Peak End	Off-Peak Hours
Monday	11:00pm	3:00am	4
Tuesday	11:00pm	3:00am	4
Wednesday	11:00pm	3:00am	4
Thursday	11:00pm	3:00am	4
Friday	11:00pm	6:00am	7
Saturday	8:00pm	6:00am	10
Sunday	8:00pm	3:00am	7

The only time when you have enough off-peak hours to perform a full backup is Saturday night.

2.   For each day after the full backup, make an incremental backup. Make the backup go back to the most complete previous backup it can reach given the time constraints.

On Sunday, Monday, Tuesday, and Wednesday nights, the incremental backup has at least 4 hours so it can save changes for up to the previous 4 days. All of these backups should record the changes since the full backup on Saturday night. If you need to restore one of these backups, you only need to apply the previous full backup and then one incremental backup.

On Thursday and Friday nights, you don't have time to go all the way back to the previous full backup. There is time, however, to record all changes since the Wednesday night incremental backup so you should do so. If you need to restore one of these backups, you will have to restore the last full backup, then the Wednesday night backup, and then this backup.

The following table shows the complete backup schedule.

Night	Backup Type
Monday	Incremental from last Saturday
Tuesday	Incremental from last Saturday
Wednesday	Incremental from last Saturday
Thursday	Incremental from last Wednesday
Friday	Incremental from last Wednesday
Saturday	Full
Sunday	Incremental from last Saturday

Don't forget to store copies of the backups offsite in a secure location.

Data Warehousing

Many database applications have two components: an online part that is used in day-to-day business and an offline "data warehousing" part that is used to generate reports and perform more in-depth analysis of the data.

The rules for a data warehouse are different than those for an online database. Often a data warehouse contains duplicated data, non-normalized tables, and special data structures that make building reports easier. Warehoused data is updated much less frequently than online data. In a data warehouse, flexibility in reporting is more important than speed.

For the purposes of this chapter, it's important that you be aware of your customers' data warehousing needs so you can plan for appropriate database maintenance. In some cases, that may be as simple as passing a copy of the most recent full backup to a data analyst. In others, it may mean writing and executing special data extraction routines periodically.

For example, as part of nightly maintenance (backups, cleaning up tables, and what have you), you might need to pull sales data into a separate table or database for later analysis.

This book isn't about data warehousing so this chapter doesn't say any more about it. For a more complete overview, see en.wikipedia.org/wiki/Data_warehouse. For more in-depth coverage, see a book about data warehousing such as *Professional Microsoft SQL Server Analysis Services 2008 with MDX* by Sivakumar Harinath, Robert Zare, Sethu Meenakshisundaram, and Matt Carroll (Wiley Publishing, Inc., 2008). (If you go to Amazon or your favorite book retailer and search for "data warehouse," you should find lots of relevant books.)

Repairing the Database

Although databases provide lots of safeguards to protect your data, databases sometimes become corrupted. They are particularly prone to index corruption because it can take a while to update a database's index structures. If the computer crashes while the database is in the middle of updating its index trees, the trees may contain garbage, invalid keys, and pointers leading to nowhere (similar to the Gravina Island Bridge, en.wikipedia.org/wiki/Gravina_Island_Bridge).

When an index becomes corrupted, the results you get from queries may become unpredictable. You may get the wrong records, records in the wrong order, or no records at all. The program using the database may even crash.

To ensure that your database works properly, you should periodically run its repair tools. That should clean up damaged records and indexes.

Compacting the Database

When you delete a record, many databases don't actually release the space that the record occupied. Some databases may be able to undelete the record in case you decide you want it later but most databases do this so they can reuse the space later for new records. If you add and then remove a lot of records, however, the database can become full of unused space.

The trees that databases typically use to store indexes are self-balancing. That ensures that they never grow too tall so searches are fast, but it also means that they contain extra unused space. They use that extra space to make adding new entries in the trees more efficient but, under some circumstances, the trees can contain a lot of unused space.

These days disk space is relatively cheap (as little as 18 cents per gigabyte) so the "wasted" space may not be much of an issue. Just pull the sock full of money out from under your bed and buy a bigger hard drive. Having some extra unused space in the database can even make adding and updating the database faster.

In some cases, however, parts of the database may become fragmented so the database may take longer to load records that are logically adjacent but that are scattered around the disk. In that case, you may get better performance if you compact and defragment the database. Look at your database product's instructions and notes to learn about good maintenance strategies.

Performance Tuning

Normally you don't need to worry too much about how the database executes a query. In fact, if you start fiddling around with the way queries are executed, you take on all sorts of unnecessary responsibility. It's kind of like being an air traffic controller: when everything works, no one notices that you're doing your job, but when something goes wrong everyone knows it was your fault.

Generally you shouldn't try to tell the database how to do its job, but often you can help it help itself. Some databases use a statistical analysis of the values in an index to help decide how to perform queries using that index. If the distribution of the values changes, you can sometimes help the database realize that the situation has changed. For example, the Transact-SQL statement UPDATE STATISTICS makes a SQL Server database update its statistics for a table or view, possibly leading to better performance in complex queries.

Often you can make queries more efficient by building good indexes. If you know that the users will be looking for records with specific values in a certain field, put an index on that field. For example, if you know that you will need to search customer records by LastName, make LastName an index.

If you have a lot of experience with query optimization, you may even be able to give the database a hint about how it should perform a particular query. For example, you may know that a GROUP BY query will work best if the database uses a hashing algorithm. In Transact-SQL you could use the OPTION (HASH GROUP) clause to give the database that hint (technet.microsoft.com/en-us/library/ms181714.aspx). Only *serious* SQL nerds (with IQs exceeding their weights in pounds) should even consider this level of meddling.

Some databases provide tools such as query analyzers or execution plan viewers so you can see exactly how the database will perform an operation. That not only lets you learn more about how queries are performed so you can aspire to write your own query hints, but it also lets you look for problems in your database design. For example, an execution plan may point out troublesome WHERE clauses that require executing a function many times, searches on fields that are not indexed, and nested loops that you might be able to remove by rewriting a query.

More expensive database products may also be able to perform other optimizations at a more physical level. For example, database replication allows several databases to contain the same information and remain synchronized. This can be useful if you perform more queries than updates. If one database is the master and the others are used as read-only copies, the copies can take some of the query burden from the main database.

Another advanced optimization technique is partitioning. A partitioned table stores different records in different locations, possibly on different hard disks or even different computers. If your typical queries normally divide the data along partition boundaries, the separate partitions can operate more or less independently. You may even be able to back up different partitions separately, improving performance.

In a variation on partitioning, you use multiple databases to handle different parts of the data. For example, you might have different databases to handle customers in different states or time zones. Because the databases operate independently, they are smaller and faster, and you can back them up separately. You can extract data into a data warehouse to perform queries that involve more than one database.

Try It Out   The Keys to Success

Not all indexes are created equal. You need to tailor a table's indexes and keys to help the database perform the queries that you expect to actually perform.

Suppose you have a Customers table that contains the usual sorts of fields: CustomerId, FirstName, LastName, Street, City, State, and Zip. It also includes some demographic information such as BirthDate, AnnualIncome, and Gender.

1. Decide which fields should be indexed to support normal database queries that must join Orders and OrderItems records to Customers records.

2. Decide which fields should be indexed to support typical customer queries where a customer wants information about an order.

3. Decide which fields should be indexed to support reporting queries such as "Find all orders placed by female customers between ages 15 and 25."

How It Works

1. Decide which fields should be indexed to support normal database queries that must join Orders and OrderItems records to Customers records.

   In a typical database, the Customers table's CustomerId field will link to the Orders table. The Orders table will have an OrderId field that links to the OrderItems table. CustomerId is the Customers table's primary key and OrderId is the Orders table's primary key. Relational databases automatically index the primary key (I have yet to meet one that doesn't) so you don't need to add any additional indexes to support this typical joining operation.

2. Decide which fields should be indexed to support typical customer queries where a customer wants information about an order.

   Depending on your business, customers *might* know (or be able to figure out) their customer IDs. For example, I can read the account number from my bank statements, utility bill, and telephone bill. But customers who walk into your store, phone you, or send you a flaming email typically don't know their customer IDs. You could force them to go dig through their trash looking for an old statement while you joke with the other customer service representatives ("I can hear him digging through the trash compactor! Snigger."), but that's not very customer-friendly.

   It would be better if you could look up customers given something they actually might know such as their name, address, or phone number. Name works very well (most customers over two years of age know their names), although the user interface must be prepared to handle duplicates. (So you can ask, "Are you the Zaphod Beeblebrox on Improbable Blvd or the one on Unlikely Terrace?") You probably also need to handle ambiguous first names for cases where it's not clear which member of the household opened the account or when someone goes by a nickname ("The name's George but everyone calls me Dubbya.").

   You may also want to consider spelling errors ("Is that Melllvar with three L's?). If you have a very large customer base, you might want to look into soundex (en.wikipedia.org/wiki/Soundex) and other algorithms for handling names phonetically.

   Even with these issues, the combination of LastName/FirstName is an excellent choice for a secondary index.

   Address and phone number also make good keys. Usually they are slightly less natural for customers but sometimes they may have special meaning that makes them more useful. For example, the phone number is critical for telephone companies so it might make sense to look up the records for the phone number that is giving the customer problems.

3. Decide which fields should be indexed to support reporting queries such as "Find all orders placed by female customers between ages 15 and 25."

   To really understand how this query works in all of its gruesome detail, you would probably need to look at the database's execution plan.

Does the database search for customers in the right age group and then look through their orders to find the ones for at least $100 and ordered by women? In that case, you might improve performance by indexing the BirthDate field.

Does the database select orders placed by women and then look through those to find the ones with the right total prices and birth date? In that case, you might improve performance by indexing the Gender field.

The best approach depends on exactly what your data looks like. Typically I recommend that you not try to optimize this type of query until you have tried it out with some real data and you know there is a problem. After all, there's a chance that the query will be fast enough without adding any extra indexes.

However, not knowing what's going on rarely prevents me from having an opinion so let me mention two points.

First, the Gender field would make a terrible index. It can only hold two values (assuming a typical distribution of customers) so using that field to select women doesn't really help the query narrow down its search much. The database will still need to wade through about half of its records to figure out which are interesting. Using BirthDate or total purchase price would probably narrow the search much more quickly so, if the database is stupid enough to filter using Gender first, you should probably change the query somehow to coerce it into doing something more sensible.

Second, this is a query for a data warehouse not for an online system. This is an off-line query used to study data after the fact so it probably doesn't need to execute in real time. It could be that your boss's, boss's, boss said, "I bet if we changed these hideous plaid golf shorts to pink, we could sell more to teenage girls" and you're stuck gathering data to justify this brilliant insight. This query probably won't take all that long to execute even without extra indexes and you can probably run it at night so it won't matter if it takes a few hours in any case. Adding extra indexes to a table makes inserting, updating, and deleting records in that table slower so it's better to just grit your teeth and take a few hours to run this sort of one-time query at midnight rather than slowing down typical database operations to satisfy this one query. (During the night management will have a brainwave and decide to focus on building a play stove painted in camouflage colors that transforms into a robot to sell more play kitchens to boys anyway and this issue will be forgotten.)

Summary

Designing and building a database is one thing, but keeping it running efficiently is another. Without proper maintenance, a database can become infected with bloated tables, inefficient indexes, and even corrupted data. This chapter explained that to get the most out of a database you must:

- ❏ Perform regular full and incremental backups.
- ❏ Extract data into a data warehouse to perform off-line queries.
- ❏ Repair damaged indexes.
- ❏ Build indexes to support the queries that you will actually perform.
- ❏ Optionally compact tables and index structures to remove unused space.

Unfortunately the exact details of performing these tasks are specific to different kinds of databases so this chapter cannot provide all of the details. The following chapter describes another topic that is database-specific: security. Though the precise details for providing security depends on the type of database you are using, the following chapter describes some of the general issues that you should take into account to keep your data secure.

Before you move on to Chapter 20, however, use the following exercises to test your understanding of the material covered in this chapter. You can find the solutions to these exercises in Appendix A.

Exercises

1. Suppose your database is big enough that it takes about 4 hours to perform a full backup and 2 hours to perform an incremental backup per day of changes that you want to include in the backup. Peak hours are 4:00am to 11:00pm on weekdays and 6:00am to 9:00pm on weekends. Design a backup schedule for the database that doesn't require any backup during peak hours.

2. Your business flourishes (a problem we all wish we had) so the database described in Exercise 1 grows and now takes 6 hours to perform a full backup and 3 hours per day of changes for an incremental backup. A large part of your success comes from increased sales in new time zones so your peak hours have grown to 3:00am to 12:00 midnight on weekdays and 5:00am to 10:00pm on weekends. Design a new backup schedule that doesn't require any backup during peak hours.

Database Security

Like database maintenance, database security is an important topic with details that vary from database to database. This chapter doesn't try to cover everything there is to know about database security. Instead it explains some of the general concepts that you should understand.

In this chapter you learn how to:

❑   Pick a reasonable level of security for the database.

❑   Choose good passwords.

❑   Give users necessary privileges.

❑   Promote a database's physical security.

The Right Level of Security

Database security can range from nonexistent to tighter than Fort Knox. You can allow any user or application to connect to a database or you can use encryption to prevent even the database itself from looking at data that it shouldn't see.

Though many people think more security is better, that's not always the case. Some databases can encrypt the data they contain so it's very hard for bad guys to peek at your data. Unfortunately it takes extra time to encrypt and decrypt data as you read and write it in the database, and that slows things down. For most applications, that level of security is overkill.

Although you may not need as much security as the White House or Pentagon, it does make sense to take advantage of whatever security features your database does provide. The following sections describe some of the security features that you should look for in a database product.

Rather than buying the most powerful security system money can buy, you should consider the needs of your application and the security features that are available. Then you can decide how tightly to lock things down.

Passwords

Passwords are the most obvious form of security in most applications. Different databases handle passwords differently and with different levels of safety. The following sections describe some of the password issues that you should consider when you build a database application.

Single-Password Databases

Different databases provide different kinds of password protection. At the weaker end of the spectrum, some databases provide only a single password for the entire database. A database may be protected by a password or not, but that's about it.

The single password provides access to the entire database. That means a bad guy who learns the password can get into the database. It also means that anyone who should use the database must share that password. One consequence of that is that you cannot easily tell which user makes which changes to the data.

In practice that often means the program that provides a user interface to the database knows the password and then it may provide its own extra layer of password protection. For example, the application might store user names and passwords (hopefully encrypted, not in their plain text form) in a table. When the user runs the program, it uses its hard-coded password to open the database and verifies the user's name and password in the table. It then decides whether to allow the user in (and decides what privileges the user deserves) or whether it should display a nasty message, shut itself down, send threatening email to the user's boss, and so forth.

There are a couple of reasons why this is a weak approach. First, the program must contain the password in some form so it can open the database. Even if you encrypt the password within the code, a determined hacker will be able to get it back out. At worst, a tenacious bit-monkey could examine the program's memory while it was executing and figure out what password the database used.

A second reason why this approach can be risky is that it relies on the correctness of the user interface. Every non-trivial program contains bugs so there's a chance that users will find some way to bypass the homemade security system and sneak in somewhere they shouldn't be.

Individual Passwords

More sophisticated databases give each user a separate password and that has several advantages over a single password database.

If the database logs activity, you can tell who logged into the database when. If there are problems, the log may help you narrow down who caused the problem and when. If the database logs every interaction with the database (or if your application does), you can tell exactly who messed up.

Another advantage to individual passwords is that the user interface program doesn't ever need to store a password. When the program starts, the user enters a user name and password and the program tries to use them to open the database. The database either opens or not and the program doesn't need to worry about why. Even a "seriously dope uberhacker with mad skillz" can't dig a password out of the application if the password isn't there.

Because the database takes care of password validation, you can focus on what the program is supposed to help the users do instead of worrying about whether you made a mistake in the password validation code.

If your database allows individual user passwords, use them. They provide a lot of benefits with relatively little extra work on your part.

Operating System Passwords

Some databases don't manage passwords very well. They may use little or no encryption, may not enforce any password standards (allowing weak passwords such as "12345" and "password"), and may even write passwords into log files where a hacker can find them relatively easily.

If your database can integrate its own security with the security provided by the operating system, make it do so. In any case, take advantage of the operating system's security. Make sure users pick good operating system passwords and don't share them. A hacker won't get a chance to attack your database if he can't even log in to the operating system.

Good Passwords

Picking good passwords is something of an art. You need to pick something obscure enough that an evil hacker (or your prankster coworkers) can't guess but that's also easy enough for you to remember. It's easy to become overloaded when you're expected to remember the database password in addition to your computer user name and password, bank PIN number, voice mail password, online banking password, PayPal password, eBay password, locker combination, anniversary, and children's names.

And you don't want to use the same password for all of these because then if someone ever steals your eBay password, they know all of your passwords.

Many companies have policies that require you to use certain characters in your password (must include letters, numbers, and a special character such as $ or #, and you need to type every other character with your left hand and your eyes crossed). They also force you to change your password so often it's pretty much guaranteed that you'll forget it. (I've never quite understood that. Do they assume that a hacker will guess your password and then say, "Whew! That was hard. I think I'll wait a month before I take advantage of this password and trash the database?" Okay, I know they're really worried about someone just prowling through the database unnoticed and they want to change the password to shut them out as quickly as possible. I'm not sure which is more common, an eavesdropper or someone who wreaks havoc as soon as they break in.)

So what do users do when faced with dozens of passwords that must pass complex checks? They write their passwords down where they are easy to find. They pick sequential passwords such as Secret1, Secret2, and so forth. They use names and dates that are easy to remember and guess. (Once as a security check I attacked our own password database to see how many passwords I could guess. By throwing names, dates, and common words at the database, I was able to guess more than half of the 300 or so passwords in just a few hours.)

It's much better to give the users a little extra training so they can figure out how to pick a really good password and then not require changes so often. For example, a series of unrelated words is a lot better than a single word but is usually just as memorable. The password beeR&Pizza%suckS is pretty easy to remember, tricky to guess, and what self-respecting hacker would ever want to type that? Replacing letters in the password with other symbols can further obscure the message. Replacing "z" with "2" and "e" with "3" turns this password into b33R&Pi22a%suckS. (Search the Web for "leet" to learn about a hacker wannabe language that uses this kind of substitution to make plain and simple text practically unintelligible. Or look at congressional legislation or a legal contract for some serious incomprehensibility.)

A technique that is particularly useful for touch-typists is to shift your fingers before typing. For example, if you type "Potatoe" (with the "optional" extra "e") with your fingers shifted one key to the right you get "pysypr" on a standard qwerty keyboard. Combine a few of these tricks and you can build a fairly tough password that's still reasonably easy to remember.

There are a few "don'ts" when it comes to making good passwords. Don't use names, dates, places, ID numbers (such as Social Security numbers or driver's licenses), or anything else that would be easy to guess or figure out by rummaging through your email or trash. In fact, don't use words at all, unless you do something to obscure them such as replacing letters with other symbols or keyboard shifting. A few words together, even if they're logically incompatible (such as "Politician" and "Honest" or "Inexpensive" and "Plumber") are easy to guess. Remember that modern computers are *really fast* so guessing a few million or even a few billion password combinations is child's play.

Privileges

Most relational databases allow you to restrict each user's access to specific tables and even columns within a table. Typically you would define groups such as Clerks or Managers and then grant permission for users in those groups to view certain data. You may also be able to grant exceptions for individual users. (You can perform similar feats of cleverness yourself in your application even if you're using a single password database but it's a lot more work.)

For example, suppose your Employees table contains columns holding three levels of data. Data available to anyone includes the employee's name, office number, phone number, and so forth. Data available only to managers includes the employee's salary and performance reviews. Data available to human resources includes the employee's next of kin, insurance information, school grades, and beneficiary name. You could get into serious trouble if some of that data were to slip out.

If you use the database's security features to prevent certain users from viewing sensitive data, you don't need to worry about the wrong people seeing the wrong data. If Ann is a non-manager employee, she will be able to view Bob's office and phone number so she can call him but the database won't let her view Bob's salary.

Some databases also provide row-level security that allows you to restrict access to particular rows in a table. For example, suppose a table contains government documents that are labeled with one of the security levels Public, Secret, Top Secret, and Illegal (you get thrown in jail if anyone finds those). When a program queries this table, it compares the user's privileges with the records' security labels and returns only those that the user should be able to see.

Some databases don't provide access control at such a refined level. They may let you restrict access to a table but not to particular columns or rows within a table. Fortunately you can provide similar behavior by using views.

A view is the result of a query. It looks a lot like a table but it may contain only some of the columns or records in one or more tables. If the database doesn't provide column-level security, you can deny access to the table and then create different views for the different groups of users. For the Employees table, you would create separate views that include public data, manager accessible data, and data that should be visible to human resources. Now you can grant access for the views to let users see the types of data they should be able to view.

The SQL GRANT and REVOKE statements let you give and withdraw privileges. It is generally safest to give users the fewest privileges possible to do their jobs. Then if an application contains a bug and accidentally tries to do something stupid, such as dropping a table or showing the user sensitive information, the database won't allow it.

Rather than remembering to remove every extraneous privilege from a new user, many database administrators revoke all privileges and then grant those that are needed. That way the administrator cannot forget to remove some critical privilege.

The following three MySQL scripts demonstrate user privileges. You can execute the first and third scripts in the MySQL Command Line Client. You need to start the Command Line Client in a special way (described shortly) to use the second script properly.

The following script prepares a test database for use:

```
CREATE DATABASE UserDb;
USE UserDb;

-- Create a table.
CREATE TABLE People (
   FirstName            VARCHAR(5)     NOT NULL,
   LastName             VARCHAR(40)    NOT NULL,
   Salary               DECIMAL(10,2)  NULL,
   PRIMARY KEY (LastName, FirstName)
);

-- Create a new user with an initial password.
-- Note that this password may appear in the logs.
CREATE USER Rod IDENTIFIED BY 'secret';

-- Revoke all privileges for the user.
REVOKE ALL PRIVILEGES, GRANT OPTION FROM Rod;

-- Grant privileges that the user really needs.
--GRANT INSERT ON UserDb.People TO Rod;
GRANT INSERT (FirstName, LastName, Salary) ON UserDb.People TO Rod;
GRANT SELECT (FirstName, LastName) ON UserDb.People TO Rod;
GRANT DELETE ON UserDb.People TO Rod;
```

This script creates the database UserDB and gives it a People table. It then creates a user named Rod, giving it the password "secret." (Yes, that is a terrible password. Don't do something like this in your database!)

Next the script drops all privileges including the GRANT privilege (which would allow the user to grant privileges to himself). It then grants privileges that allow the user to insert FirstName, LastName, and Salary values into the People table, select only the FirstName and LastName values, and delete records from the table.

Before you can execute the next script, you need to start the MySQL Command Line Client as the user Rod. To do that, start a command window (in Windows, open the Start menu, pick Run, type CMD, and press Enter). At the command prompt, change to the directory that contains the MySQL Command Line Client mysql.exe. (On my Windows XP system, it's at C:\Program Files\MySQL\MySQL Server 5.0\bin.) After you move to that directory, start the MySQL Command Line Client by executing this command:

```
mysql -u Rod -p
```

(You might need to use mysql --u Rod --p on Unix systems.)

Note that the user name is case-sensitive, so type Rod not rod or ROD. When prompted, enter the password "secret." The Command Line Client should run in the operating system command window and you should see the mysql prompt.

Now you can execute the following script to test the user's privileges:

```
USE UserDB;

-- Make some records.
INSERT INTO People VALUES('Annie', 'Lennox', 50000);
INSERT INTO People VALUES('Where', 'Waldo',  60000);
INSERT INTO People VALUES('Frank', 'Stein',  70000);

-- Select the records.
-- This fails because we don't have SELECT privilege on the Salary column.
SELECT * FROM People ORDER BY FirstName, LastName;

-- Select the records.
-- This works because we have SELECT privilege on FirstName and LastName.
SELECT FirstName, LastName FROM People ORDER BY FirstName, LastName;

-- Create a new table.
-- This fails because we don't have CREATE TABLE privileges.
CREATE TABLE MorePeople (
   FirstName            VARCHAR(5)    NOT NULL,
   LastName             VARCHAR(40)   NOT NULL,
   PRIMARY KEY (LastName, FirstName)
);

-- Delete the records.
DELETE FROM People;
```

This script sets UserDB as the default database and inserts some records into the People table. This works because the user Rod has privileges to insert FirstName, LastName, and Salary values into this table.

Next the script tries to select all of the fields in this table. That operation fails because Rod doesn't have privilege to select the Salary field. Even if the user-interface application managing this database contains a bug and tries to select salary data, the database won't let the user see the Salary field.

The script then tries to select the FirstName and LastName values from the People table. That works because Rod does have privileges to select those fields.

Next the script tries to create a table and fails because Rod doesn't have that privilege.

Finally the script deletes all of the records from the table. That works because Rod has that privilege.

After you test the user's privileges, you can close the Command Line Client by entering the command "exit." You can then close the operating system window by typing "exit" again.

Back in the original MySQL Command Line Client that created the database and the user, you can execute the third script to clean up:

```
DROP USER Rod;

DROP DATABASE UserDb;
```

The technique of removing all privileges and then granting only those that are absolutely necessary is very useful for preventing mistakes. In fact, many database administrators deny even the administrator accounts all of the dangerous privileges that they don't need on a daily basis (such as DROP TABLE and CREATE USER). The account still has the GRANT privilege so it can grant itself more power if necessary, but that takes an extra step so it's harder to accidentally make dangerous mistakes such as dropping critical tables.

A similar technique is for administrators to log in as a less powerful "mortal" user normally and only log in to an administrator account when they really need to do something special and potentially dangerous.

Try It Out   A Privileged Few

Consider the database design shown in Figure 20-1.

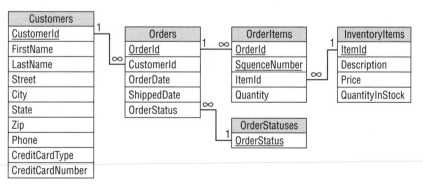

Figure 20-1

Many users need relatively few privileges to do their jobs. Write a SQL script that gives a shipping clerk enough privileges to fulfill orders in the database shown in Figure 20-1 by following these steps:

1. Make a permission table showing the CRUD (Create, Read, Update, and Delete) privileges that the user needs for the tables and their fields.

2. Deny all privileges.

3. Grant SELECT privileges for the fields in the Customers, Orders, OrderItems, and InventoryItems tables that the clerk needs to properly address a shipment.

4. Grant UPDATE privileges for the fields in the Customers, Orders, OrderItems, and InventoryItems tables that the clerk needs to properly record a shipment.

How It Works

1. Make a table showing the CRUD (Create, Read, Update, and Delete) privileges that the user needs for the tables and their fields.

   The following table lists the privileges that the user needs. The user might need Create or Delete privileges for tables and Read or Update privileges for fields.

Table or Field	Privileges
Customers	–
CustomerId	R
FirstName	R
LastName	R
Street	R
City	R
State	R
Zip	R
Phone	R
CreditCardType	–
CreditCardNumber	–
Orders	–
OrderId	R
CustomerId	R
OrderDate	R
ShippedDate	RU
OrderStatus	RU

Table or Field	Privileges
OrderItems	–
OrderId	R
SequenceNumber	R
ItemId	R
Quantity	R
InventoryItems	–
ItemId	R
Description	R
Price	–
QuantityInStock	RU
OrderStatuses	–
OrderStatus	R

2. Deny all privileges.

The following MySQL code creates a ShippingClerk user and revokes all privileges. (Again this is a terrible password. Don't use it.)

```
CREATE USER ShippingClerk IDENTIFIED BY 'secret';

-- Revoke all privileges for the user.
REVOKE ALL PRIVILEGES, GRANT OPTION FROM ShippingClerk;
```

3. Grant SELECT privileges for the fields in the Customers, Orders, OrderItems, and InventoryItems tables that the clerk needs to properly address a shipment.

To prepare and ship orders, the user must see all fields in the Orders, OrderItems, and InventoryItems tables. The clerk must also see the name and address information in the Customers table. The following MySQL statements grant privileges to select those fields:

```
GRANT SELECT ON ShippingDb.Orders TO ShippingClerk;
GRANT SELECT ON ShippingDb.OrderItems TO ShippingClerk;
GRANT SELECT ON ShippingDb.InventoryItems TO ShippingClerk;
GRANT SELECT (CustomerId, FirstName, LastName, Street, City, State,
    Zip, Phone) ON ShippingDb.Customers TO ShippingClerk;
```

Notice that the last statement grants privileges to select specific fields and doesn't let the clerk view the customer table's other fields such as CreditCardNumber.

4. Grant UPDATE privileges for the fields in the Customers, Orders, OrderItems, and InventoryItems tables that the clerk needs to properly record a shipment.

When shipping an order, the clerk must update the InventoryItems table's QuantityInStock field. The clerk must also update the Orders table's OrderStatus and ShippedDate fields. The following statements grant the necessary privileges:

```
GRANT UPDATE (QuantityinStock) ON ShippingDb.InventoryItems TO ShippingClerk;
GRANT UPDATE (OrderStatus, ShippedDate) ON ShippingDb.Orders TO ShippingClerk;
```

You can download scripts that demonstrate these privileges from the book's Web site. The script MakeShippingClerk.sql builds a test database and uses the previous code snippets to create the ShippingClerk with the correct privileges. The UseShippingClerk.sql script performs the tasks that the shipping clerk would perform while shipping an order. The DropShippingClerk.sql script deletes the ShippingClerk account and the test database.

Initial Configuration and Privileges

Databases (and many other software tools) often come preconfigured to make it easy for you to get started. Find out how the database is initially configured and modify the default settings to make the database more secure.

For example, databases often come with an administrator account that has a default user name and password. It is amazing how many people build a database and don't bother changing those default settings. Anyone who knows the defaults can not only open your database but can do so with administrator privileges so they can do anything they want to your data. Hackers are very aware of these default accounts and, not surprisingly, trying to open those accounts is often the first attack a hacker makes.

Too Much Security

Ironically one of the most common security problems I've seen in large applications is caused by too much security. The user interface application tries to restrict users so they cannot do things they're not supposed to do accidentally or otherwise. When it's done properly, that type of checking is quite important but if the system is too restrictive and too hard to change, the users will find ways to circumvent your security.

For example, suppose an application manages telephone accounts. Customer representatives can disconnect a customer for outstanding bills, answer customer questions, and reconnect service when payments are received. They can also reconnect service if the customer comes up with a really good sob story. ("My doggy Mr. Tiddles ate the bill. I sent it in anyway half chewed up, but the Post Office returned it for insufficient postage. It would have been a day late, but I was on a cruise and the ship crossed the International Date Line. I can pay now but it would be in a third party check written in Florins from a bank in a country that no longer exists. Etc.") At this point, the representative hands the customer to a shift supervisor who reconnects services for 15 days in self-defense just to shut the customer up.

Unfortunately a lot of customers have sob stories that are more believable than this one (it's hard to imagine one less believable) so the shift supervisors waste a lot of time approving service reconnections. To save time, the supervisor writes his user ID and password in huge letters on the whiteboard at the front of the room so every representative can approve reconnections without interrupting the supervisor's online shopping.

Your expression of amusement should change to one of horror when you learn that this is actually a true story. (Not the one about Mr. Tiddles, the one about the password on the whiteboard.) Everyone in the entire billing center could log on as a supervisor at any time to approve special actions without wasting the supervisor's time.

At this point, a reasonable security feature, making supervisors approve special reconnections, has completely backfired. Not only can anyone approve special reconnections, but they could log on as a supervisor and perform all sorts of other unauthorized actions without leaving any trace of who actually did them.

The moral is, restrict access to various database features appropriately but make it easy for the customers to change the settings. If the supervisors could have changed the program to allow representatives to approve special reconnections, this would never have been a problem.

Physical Security

Many system administrators spend a great deal of effort on software and network security and do nothing about physical security. It makes sense to focus on network attacks because an open Internet connection makes you potentially vulnerable to millions of would-be hackers and cybersnoops.

However, focusing exclusively on software security and ignoring physical security is like building a James Bond–caliber fortress and then leaving the screen door wide open. While an unsecured Internet connection does expose you to a huge number of potential hackers, you shouldn't completely ignore local villains.

Though most employees are honest and hardworking, there have been several spectacular cases where employees have stolen data. There have also been many cases where employees and contractors have lost data through carelessness.

In one case, a former Boeing employee was accused of stealing 320,000 files using a portable drive. Boeing estimated that the files could cause $5 billion to $15 billion in damages if they fell into the wrong hands. (See www.scmagazineus.com/Former-Boeing-employee-charged-in-data-theft/article/35228.)

I generally prefer to assume that people are basically honest but that doesn't mean you should make it easier for them to make bad decisions and silly mistakes.

Flash drives small enough to fit in a wallet hold several gigabytes of data. Portable USB drives that fit easily in a backpack or briefcase can hold up to 2 terabytes and larger drives will probably be available soon.

I'm not suggesting that you frisk employees before they leave for home but, if your database contains financial data, credit card numbers, and other proprietary secrets (such as numerological algorithms for picking lottery numbers), you should at least provide some supervision to discourage employees from walking out with the database.

Many powerful computers are also relatively small so, in some cases, it may be possible for someone to simply pick up your server and walk away with it. If the computer is too large to carry away, a few minutes with a screwdriver will allow just about anyone to remove the hard drive. Keeping your database server in a separate office that's accessible by an internal network provides some extra security.

Even if you lock the network down so Internet hackers can't find a seam to open, you should also consider outgoing connections. An employee can probably email data outside of your system or surf to a Web site that allows file uploading.

Laptop security is a particularly tricky issue these days. Laptops are designed for portability. If you didn't need that portability, you would probably buy a less expensive desktop computer so you must assume the laptop will go offsite. Laptop theft is a huge and growing problem so you should assume that any data you have on your laptop may be stolen. If you absolutely must store sensitive data on a laptop, encrypt it. Don't assume the laptop's operating system security will stop a thief from reading the hard disk. The Web contains lots of sites with advice for preventing laptop theft, so look around and adopt whatever measures you can.

I once worked at a company that didn't allow cameras or cell phones with cameras because they were afraid someone might steal their corporate secrets. However, they didn't prohibit flash drives, USB drives, laptops, MP3 players (which have drives that can hold computer files, see `news.cnet.com/Beware-the-pod-slurping-employee/2100-1029_3-6039926.html`), outgoing email, or Web surfing to sites where you could upload files. They had plugged one possible channel for misdeeds but had left lots of others open. (My theory is that management was a bit behind the times and wasn't familiar enough with the other methods to realize that they were a potential problem.)

This all begs the question of whether the company has any data worth stealing. In the time I worked there, I saw lots of company confidential material but nothing that had any real financial or strategic value. Before you start installing security cameras and metal detectors, you should ask yourself how likely it is that someone would want to steal your data and how expensive the loss would be. Then you can take appropriate measures to reduce the likelihood of loss.

Though ignoring physical security is a mistake, obsessing over it can make you paranoid. Not everyone is an undercover agent for your competition or looking to sell credit card numbers to drug dealers. Take reasonable measures but try not to go completely overboard unnecessarily.

Summary

Database security doesn't happen all by itself. Many databases provide sophisticated security features but it's up to you to take advantage of them. This chapter described some of the issues you should consider to protect your data against accidental and malicious damage. It explained how to:

❑ Decide on a reasonable level of security for the database.

❑ Restrict privileges so users cannot harm the database accidentally or intentionally.

❑ Protect the database physically.

The chapters in this book explain how to determine customers' data needs. They explain how to build data models to study those needs, how to use the models to form a design, and how to refine the design to make it more efficient. Finally, the chapters explain how to implement the database, and how to examine the database's maintenance and security needs.

Having studied these chapters, you are ready to design and build effective relational databases but there's a lot more to learn. Although I've tried to cover the most important topics of relational database design in some depth, database design is a huge topic and you can always learn more. You may want to increase your knowledge by surfing the Web or reading other database books that focus on different aspects of database design and development. In particular, you may want to seek out books that deal with specific issues for whichever database product you are using.

Before you leave these pages, however, use the following exercises to test your understanding of the material covered in this chapter. You can find the solutions to these exercises in Appendix A.

Exercises

For these exercises, consider the database design shown in Figure 20-1.

In the Try It Out earlier in this chapter, you determined the privileges needed by a shipping clerk for this database. These exercises consider other roles that users will play.

1. Build a permission table showing the privileges needed by an order entry clerk to create new orders. Write SQL statements to create an order entry clerk with the appropriate privileges.

2. Build a permission table showing the privileges needed by a customer service clerk who answers questions about users' accounts and orders. This clerk should be able to modify customer and order data, and should be able to cancel an order that has not yet shipped.

3. Build a permission table showing the privileges needed by an inventory manager who orders new inventory as needed. This person also changes an order's status from Back Ordered to Ordered when there is enough inventory to fulfill the order. The inventory manager also keeps the InventoryTable up-to-date and may need to add, remove, or modify records.

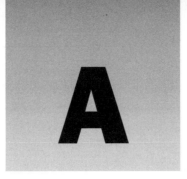

Exercise Solutions

Chapter 1

Exercise 1 Solution

The following list summarizes how the book provides (or doesn't) database goals:

❑ **CRUD:** This book doesn't let you easily CREATE information. You could write in new information but there isn't much room for that and that's not really its purpose. The book lets you READ information, although it's hard for you to find a particular piece of information (unless it is listed in the table of contents or the index). You can UPDATE information by crossing out the old information and entering the new. You can also highlight key ideas by underlining, by using a highlighter, and by putting bookmarks on key pages. Finally, you can DELETE data by crossing it out.

❑ **Retrieval:** The book's mission in life is to let you retrieve its data, although it can be hard to find specific pieces of information unless you have bookmarked them, or they are in the table of contents or the index.

❑ **Consistency:** I've tried hard to make the book's information consistent. If you start making changes, however, it will be extremely hard to ensure that you make related changes to other parts of the book.

❑ **Validity:** The book provides no data validation. If you write in new information, the book cannot validate your data. (If you write, ''Normalization rocks!'' the book cannot verify that it indeed rocks.)

❑ **Easy Error Correction:** Correcting one error is easy; simply cross out the incorrect data and write in the new data. Correcting systematic errors (for example, if I've methodically misspelled ''the'' as ''thue'' and the editors didn't catch it) would be difficult and time consuming.

❑ **Speed:** The book's structure will hopefully help you learn database design relatively efficiently but a lot relies on your reading ability.

❑ **Atomic Transactions:** The book doesn't really support transactions of any kind, much less atomic ones.

❑ **ACID:** Because it doesn't support transactions, the book doesn't provide ACID.

❑ **Persistence and Backups:** The book's information is non-volatile so you won't lose it if the book "crashes." If you lose the book or it is destroyed (my dog ate it), you can buy another one but you'll lose any updates you have written into it. You can buy a second copy and backup your notes into it but the chances of a tornado destroying your book are low and the consequences aren't all that earth-shattering, so I'm guessing you'll just take your chances.

❑ **Low Cost and Extensibility:** Let's face it, books are pretty expensive these days, although not as expensive as even a cheap computer. You can easily buy more copies of the book but that isn't really extending the amount of data. The closest thing you'll get to extensibility is buying a different database-related book or perhaps buying a notebook to improve your note taking.

❑ **Ease of Use:** This book is fairly easy to use. You've probably been using books for years and are familiar with its user interface.

❑ **Portability:** It's a fairly large book but you can reasonably carry it around. You can't read it remotely the way you can a computerized database, but you can carry it on a bus.

❑ **Security:** The book isn't password protected but it doesn't contain any top-secret material, so if it is lost or stolen you probably won't be as upset by the loss of its data as by the loss of the concert tickets that you were using as a bookmark. It'll also cost you a bit to buy a new copy if you can't borrow someone else's.

❑ **Sharing:** After you lose your copy, you could read over the shoulder of a friend and you could borrow someone else's book. Sharing isn't as easy as it would be for a computerized database, however, so you might just want to splurge and get a new copy.

❑ **Ability to Perform Complex Calculations:** Sorry, not in this edition.

Overall the book is a reasonably efficient read-only database with limited search and correction capabilities. As long as you don't need to make too many corrections, it's a pretty useful tool. The fact that instructional books have been around for a long time should indicate that they work pretty well.

Exercise 2 Solution

This book provides a table of contents to help you find information about general topics and an index to help you find more specific information if you know the name of the concept that you want to study.

Features that help you find information in less obvious ways include the introductory chapter that describes each chapter's concepts in more detail than the table of contents does, and references within the text.

Exercise 3 Solution

CRUD stands for the four fundamental database operations: Create (add new data), Read (retrieve data), Update (modify data), and Delete (remove data from the database).

Exercise 4 Solution

A chalkboard provides:

- ❏ **Create:** Use chalk to write on the board.
- ❏ **Read:** Look at the board.
- ❏ **Update:** Simply erase old data and write new data.
- ❏ **Delete:** Just erase the old data.

A chalkboard has the following advantages over a book:

- ❏ **CRUD:** It's easier to create, read, update, and delete data.
- ❏ **Retrieval:** Though a chalkboard doesn't provide an index, it usually contains much less data than a book so it's easier to find what you need.
- ❏ **Consistency:** Keeping the data consistent isn't trivial but again, because there's less data than in a book, you can find and correct any occurrences of a problem more easily.
- ❏ **Easy Error Correction:** Correcting one error is trivial; just erase and write in the new data. Correcting systematic errors is harder but a chalkboard contains a lot less data than a book so fixing all of the mistakes is easier.
- ❏ **Backups:** You can easily backup a chalkboard by taking a digital picture of it. (This is actually more important than it may seem in a research environment where chalkboard discussions can contain crucial data.)
- ❏ **Ease of Use:** A chalkboard is even easier to use than a book. Toddlers who can't read can still scribble on a chalkboard.
- ❏ **Security:** It's relatively hard to steal a chalkboard nailed to a wall.
- ❏ **Sharing:** Usually everyone in the room can see what's on a chalkboard at the same time. This is one of the main purposes of chalkboards.

A book has the following advantages over a chalkboard:

- ❏ **Persistence:** A chalkboard is less persistent. For example, someone brushing against the chalkboard may erase data. (I once had a professor who did that regularly and always ended the lecture with a stomach covered in chalk.)
- ❏ **Low Cost and Extensibility:** Typically books are cheaper than chalkboards, at least large ones.
- ❏ **Portability:** Books typically aren't nailed to a wall.

The following database properties are roughly equivalent for books and chalkboards:

- ❏ **Validity:** Neither provides features for validating new or modified data against other data in the database.
- ❏ **Speed:** Both are limited by your reading (and writing) speed.
- ❏ **Atomic Transactions:** Neither provides transactions.

❑ **ACID:** Neither provides transactions so neither provides ACID.

❑ **Ability to Perform Complex Calculations:** Neither can do this (unless you have some sort of fancy interactive computerized book or chalkboard).

In the final analysis, books contain a lot of information and are intended for use by one person, whereas chalkboards hold less information and are tools for group interaction. Which you use depends on which of these features you need.

Exercise 5 Solution

A recipe card file has the following advantages over a book:

❑ **CRUD:** It's easier to create, read, update, and delete data in a recipe file. Updating and deleting data is also more aesthetically pleasing. In a book, these changes require you to cross out old data and optionally write in new data in a place where it probably won't fit too well. In a recipe file, you can replace the card containing the old data with a completely new card.

❑ **Consistency:** Recipes tend to be self-contained so this usually isn't an issue.

❑ **Easy Error Correction:** Correcting one error in the recipe file is trivial; just replace the card that holds the error with one that is correct. Correcting systematic errors is harder but less likely to be a problem. (What are the odds that you'll mistakenly confuse metric and English units and mix up liters and tablespoons? Although NASA and Lockheed managed to mix metric and English to crash a $125 million Mars orbiter. See www.cnn.com/TECH/space/9909/30/mars.metric.)

❑ **Backups:** You could back up a recipe file fairly easily. In particular, it would be easy to make copies of any new or modified cards. I don't know if anyone (except perhaps Martha Stewart) does this.

❑ **Low Cost and Extensibility:** It's extremely cheap and easy to add a new card to a recipe file.

❑ **Security:** You could lose a recipe file but it will probably stay in your kitchen most of the time. Someone could break into your house and steal your recipes but you'd probably give copies to anyone who asked (except for your top-secret Death-by-Chocolate Brownies recipe).

A book has the following advantages over a recipe file:

❑ **Retrieval:** A recipe file's cards are sorted, essentially giving it an index, but a book also provides a table of contents. With this kind of recipe file, it would be hard to simultaneously sort cards alphabetically and group them by type (entrée, dessert, aperitif, midnight snack).

❑ **Persistence:** The structure of a recipe file is slightly less persistent than that of a book. If you drop your card file down the stairs, the cards will be all mixed up. (Although that may be a useful way to pick a random recipe if you can't decide what you want to eat.)

The following database properties are roughly equivalent for books and recipe files:

❑ **Validity:** Neither provides features for validating new or modified data against other data in the database.

❑ **Speed:** Both are limited by your reading (and writing) speed.

❑ **Atomic Transactions:** Neither provides transactions.

❑ **ACID:** Neither provides transactions so neither provides ACID.

- ❏ **Ease of Use:** Many people are less experienced with using a recipe file than a book but both are fairly simple. (Following the recipes will probably be harder than using the file, at least if you cook anything interesting.)

- ❏ **Portability:** Both books and recipe files are portable, although your recipe may never leave the kitchen.

- ❏ **Sharing:** Neither is easy to share.

- ❏ **Ability to Perform Complex Calculations:** Neither can do this. (Some computerized recipe books can adjust measurements for different number of servings but index cards cannot.)

Instructional books usually contain tutorial information and you are expected to read them in big chunks. A recipe file is intended for quick reference and you generally use specific recipes rather than reading a bunch of them. This is more like a dictionary and has many of the same features.

Exercise 6 Solution

ACID is an acronym describing four features that an effective transaction system should provide. ACID stands for Atomicity, Consistency, Isolation, and Durability.

- ❏ *Atomicity* means transactions are atomic. The operations in a transaction either all happen or none of them happen.

- ❏ *Consistency* means the transaction ensures that the database is in a consistent state before and after the transaction.

- ❏ *Isolation* means the transaction isolates the details of the transaction from everyone except the person making the transaction.

- ❏ *Durability* means that once a transaction is committed, it will not disappear later.

Exercise 7 Solution

If transaction 1 occurs first, Alice tries to transfer $150 to Bob and her balance drops below zero, which is prohibited.

If transaction 2 occurs first, Bob tries to transfer $150 to Cindy and his balance drops below zero, which is prohibited.

So transaction 3 must happen first: Cindy transfers $25 to Alice and $50 to Bob. Afterwards Alice has $125, Bob has $150, and Cindy has $25.

At this point, Alice and Bob have enough money to perform either transaction 1 or transaction 2.

If transaction 1 comes second, then Alice, Bob, and Cindy have $0, $275, and $25 respectively. (If he can, Bob should walk away at this point and quit while he's ahead.) Transaction 2 follows and the three end up with $0, $125, and $175.

If transaction 2 comes second, then Alice, Bob, and Cindy have $125, $0, and $175 respectively. Transaction 1 follows and the three end up with $0, $125, and $175.

So the allowed transaction orders are 3 – 1 – 2 and 3 – 2 – 1. Note that the final balances are the same in any case.

Exercise 8 Solution

If the data is centralized, it does not remain on your local computer. In particular, if your laptop is lost or stolen, you don't need to worry about your customers' credit card information because it is not on your laptop.

Be sure to use good security on the database so cyber-criminals can't break into it remotely.

Chapter 2

Exercise 1 Solution

Assuming the dogs are not inbred so they have the most genetic diversity, this is a tree so it could be stored in a hierarchical database. It would be a moderately small tree so it would fit easily in a small XML file.

You could also coerce the hierarchical data in a relational database if you wanted to be able to find dogs with certain characteristics such as dog show winners and flyball champions.

Exercise 2 Solution

This seems like a much bigger database than the one in Exercise 1 but it's still a tree. The tree has two main branches: one leading to descendants and one leading to ancestors. As long as you don't track other relationships such as uncles, cousins, and sisters-in-law, it's just another tree so you could still store it in a hierarchical database or an XML file. You could also use a relational database to allow more general queries.

Exercise 3 Solution

Application settings are easy to store in a flat file located in the user's directory hierarchy (for example, in My Documents or the user's `Documents and Settings\UserName\Local Settings` directory).

If you have a lot of settings and you want to access them by name as needed instead of reading the entire file all at once, you could store them in an INI file, again in a location specific to each user. You could also use the system registry's `HKEY_CURRENT_USER` hive.

I have written applications that stored this kind of information in a shared relational database. That made it centralized so it was easy for the system administrators to fix it when a user managed to make a window zero pixels wide or dragged a window completely off of the screen. It also meant that if you logged into the application from any computer you found your personal settings ready and waiting for you.

Exercise 4 Solution

This sounds like a very simple database whose major requirement is graphing so a spreadsheet can probably handle this. This does tie the application into a dead-end technology, however, and if the users decide that they want to store more complex data and perform sophisticated queries on it, you'll wish you'd chosen a relational database.

Exercise 5 Solution

A spreadsheet can also handle this requirement but there's the same risk that the users will later decide they need more features than a spreadsheet can handle.

Exercise 6 Solution

A spreadsheet will *still* work, with the same caveats. At this point, however, I would notice that the users are starting to add more and more features. I would want to explore the requirements more fully and make sure this is *really* their final request before committing to a spreadsheet. It would be better to move to a more complicated database model now than to have to rebuild everything from scratch in six months. (Or just as likely, have users complain about how the spreadsheet doesn't do all of the things they didn't tell you it was supposed to do.)

Exercise 7 Solution

This is a fairly simple tree so it will fit easily in a hierarchical database or XML file. It's such a small tree (relatively speaking) that it seems unlikely that you'll need to perform complex ad hoc queries.

Exercise 8 Solution

This needs to be some sort of relational database. They are great at handling large amounts of interconnected data and performing complex ad hoc queries.

Which flavor of relational database you should pick (regular, object-oriented, object-relational, object-relational mapping) depends largely on your development philosophy and environment.

Exercise 9 Solution

As in Exercise 8, this problem cries out for some kind of relational database. To make the boss happy, you could use an object-oriented database, object-relational database, or object-relational mapping. In several projects I've used an object-relational mapping approach planted on top of a relational database and it has always worked quite well.

Exercise 10 Solution

If the recipe book will be fairly small, you could just put each recipe on a separate page in a Microsoft Word document and use Word's search capability to find recipe names, part of meal, or main ingredient. (Fooled you, didn't I? That wasn't one of the main topics covered in this chapter! However, it would be a reasonable solution for such a simple application. Remember, the goal is to provide a useful solution with the minimum amount of work.)

Of the solutions that *are* described in this chapter, I would probably pick a relational database. It will provide better search capabilities than the simpler flat file, spreadsheet, or XML databases. Truly object-oriented databases are probably serious overkill for this project. (I would only pick one of them if I wanted practice with a particular new tool, for example, one that I knew was going to be used on a future project.)

Exercise 11 Solution

This one could require some serious sorting and searching so a relational database is your best bet. (You would use a separate table or two to define power decks.) Which flavor you should pick (regular, object-oriented, object-relational, object-relational mapping) depends largely on your development philosophy and environment.

Exercise 12 Solution

These collections could require some serious sorting, searching, and grouping so a relational database is your best bet. The statement "And anything else you might think of later." is a sure sign of a vague specification that will almost certainly require you to implement other queries later. A relational database's ability to perform ad hoc queries is just what you need.

Which flavor of relational database you should pick (regular, object-oriented, object-relational, object-relational mapping) depends largely on your development philosophy and environment.

To support those future unknown queries, you will need to be sure to include as much data as possible about every item in the database. If you don't record each DVD's Best Boy and Key Grip, you won't be able to search on them later.

Exercise 13 Solution

These databases will require some serious sorting, searching, and grouping so a relational database is in order. It will allow you to perform complex queries linking players and their teams.

Which flavor of relational database you should pick (regular, object-oriented, object-relational, object-relational mapping) depends largely on your development philosophy and environment.

Exercise 14 Solution

This situation lends itself naturally to a document-oriented database. I use a separate directory for each book with subdirectories for manuscript files, figure files, and planning files such as the schedule spreadsheet. It's simple and it works fairly well, although it is sometimes tricky to find some items. (For example, find all of the bitmap files containing figures that show image processing techniques. Or find all of the figures that contain pictures of people.)

Exercise 15 Solution

This data is so simple that it could conveniently be stored in just about any kind of database. If the application uses a database for some other purpose, you might consider adding this information to it because the database will be there anyway.

Otherwise you should use the simplest solution that makes sense. A plain old text file would work just fine.

Chapter 3

Exercise 1 Solution

This constraint means that all salespeople must have a salary or work on commission but they cannot have both a salary and receive commissions.

Exercise 2 Solution

In Figure A-1, lines connect the corresponding database terms.

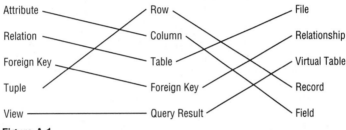

Figure A-1

Exercise 3 Solution

State/Abbr/Title is a superkey because no two rows in the table can have exactly the same values in those columns.

Exercise 4 Solution

Engraver/Year/Got is not a superkey because the table could hold two rows with the same values for those columns.

Exercise 5 Solution

The candidate keys are State, Abbrev, and Title. Each of these by itself guarantees uniqueness so it is a superkey. Each contains only one column so it is a minimal superkey and therefore a candidate key.

All of the other fields contain duplicates and any combination that doesn't have duplicates in the data shown (such as Engraver/Year) is just a coincidence (someone could engrave two coins in the same year). That means any superkey must include at least one of State, Abbrev, or Title to guarantee uniqueness so there can be no other candidate keys.

Exercise 6 Solution

The domains for the columns are:

- ❑ **State:** The names of the fifty U.S. states.
- ❑ **Abbrev:** The abbreviations of the fifty U.S. states.
- ❑ **Title:** Any text string that might describe a coin.
- ❑ **Engraver:** People's names.
- ❑ **Year:** A four-digit year. More precisely, 1999 through 2008.
- ❑ **Got:** "Yes" or "No."

Exercise 7 Solution

Room/FirstName/LastName and FirstName/LastName/Phone/CellPhone are the possible candidate keys.

CellPhone can uniquely identify a row if it is not null. If CellPhone is null, we know Phone is not null because all students must have either a room phone or a cell phone. But roommates share the same Phone value so we need FirstName and LastName to decide which is which. (Basically Phone/CellPhone gets you to the Room.)

Exercise 8 Solution

In this case, FirstName/LastName is not enough to distinguish between roommates. If their room has a phone, they might not have cell phones so there's no way to tell them apart in this table. In this case, the table has no candidate keys. That might be a good reason to add a unique column such as StudentId. (Or if the administration assigns rooms, just don't put two John Smiths in the same room. You don't have to tell them it's because of your poorly designed database!)

Exercise 9 Solution

The room numbers are even so you could use `Room Is Even` (don't worry about the syntax for checking that a value is even). You could also use some simple range checks such as `(Room > = 100) AND (Room < 300)` depending on what room numbers are actually allowed.

You might also notice that every Phone value has the same area code and exchange 202-237 so you could check for that.

Exercise 10 Solution

Every student must have a Phone or CellPhone value so you could check that `(Phone <> null) OR (CellPhone <> null)`.

Chapter 4

Exercise 1 Solution

In Figure A-2, lines connect the customer roles with their corresponding descriptions.

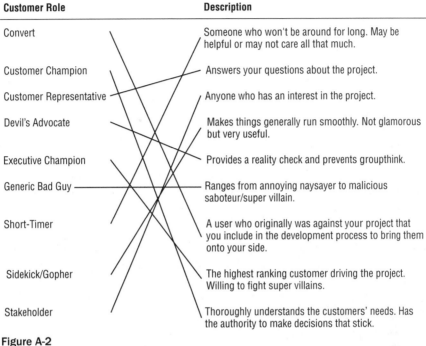

Customer Role	Description
Convert	Someone who won't be around for long. May be helpful or may not care all that much.
Customer Champion	Answers your questions about the project.
Customer Representative	Anyone who has an interest in the project.
Devil's Advocate	Makes things generally run smoothly. Not glamorous but very useful.
Executive Champion	Provides a reality check and prevents groupthink.
Generic Bad Guy	Ranges from annoying naysayer to malicious saboteur/super villain.
Short-Timer	A user who originally was against your project that you include in the development process to bring them onto your side.
Sidekick/Gopher	The highest ranking customer driving the project. Willing to fight super villains.
Stakeholder	Thoroughly understands the customers' needs. Has the authority to make decisions that stick.

Figure A-2

Exercise 2 Solution

A use case can cover any part of the customers' operation including big or little pieces of the whole process. In fact, it's easier to test a big scenario if you break it into smaller pieces. The answer that doesn't describe a use case is:

c. Should cover the customer's entire operation from start to finish.

Exercise 3 Solution

Brainstorming sessions should include everyone interested so the correct answer is:

d. All of the above.

Although technically Customer Representatives and the Devil's Advocate are also Stakeholders.

Exercise 4 Solution

The correct answer is:

b. Ask the customer why he thinks that.

You never know if the customer knows more than he's admitting and he may have very good reasons for suggesting that kind of database. Even if he's wrong, the reasons he gives will tell you more about the situation and may lead to other important insights.

Exercise 5 Solution

Whenever you don't understand something about the customers' operation you should ask someone so the correct answer is:

a. Ask someone what that's all about.

The answer you get may be as arbitrary as "that's just the way Mark likes to do it" but in this fictitious scenario the customers use the first date stamp to record when the order was received and the second to indicate that the order entry operator looked at the back of the order to check for notes and comments.

If you didn't ask, you might have incorrectly placed two date fields in the Orders table. Once the process is online, however, you won't need the second date because there is no "other side" of the order to check. (Looking at the back of your computer monitor won't tell you much.) All of the notes and comments will be in a text box at the bottom of the online form.

Exercise 6 Solution

The following table summarizes the fields' data requirements:

Field	Required?	Domain
Address 1	Yes	Valid street addresses or street names without numbers.
Address 2	No	Apartment, suite, floor, etc.
City	Yes	Valid cities.
State	Yes	Valid states.
ZIP Code	No	Five digit or ZIP+4 codes as in 12345 and 12345-6789.

The required fields are marked on the form with asterisks.

The form could use a foreign key validation for the City, checking against a table listing every city in the country. It would be a huge table and would probably contain errors so in many applications this might not be worth the effort. However, this application needs the city to look up the ZIP Code so if the City isn't legal the lookup will fail. (In fact, that may be the way to validate the data: see if you can look up the ZIP Code.)

The form could also verify that the ZIP Code is valid for the City, if the user enters both. Again the whole point is to look up a ZIP Code so it would be easy to check it against any value that the user entered.

Exercise 7 Solution

Backup policy is a data reliability issue more than a security issue so the correct answer is:

c. The frequency with which you need to perform backups.

Although the two issues are often closely related. For example, in many applications backups must be stored securely so sensitive data doesn't fall into the wrong hands.

Exercise 8 Solution

The correct answer is:

d. It depends (you need more information).

This is probably a priority 1 or 2 feature, depending on how serious Frank is and how soon he wants to add this feature. This doesn't sound too complicated (it would probably just require a few new fields in an inventory table or a new plant lookup table) so I would say if Frank is serious he should make this a priority 1 feature and add it to the database design. I would also make this data not required in case Frank doesn't have time to enter all of this information right away for every kind of plant.

Exercise 9 Solution

The answer to this one depends on the operating system you're using. I'm currently sitting at a computer running Windows XP so here's how my use case might read:

- ❑ **Goals:** Authorized users should be able to log in while unauthorized users should not.
- ❑ **Summary:** The user tries to enter a user name and password. If they are correct, the user is allowed access to the system.
- ❑ **Actors:**
  - ❑ The user — Tries to log in.
  - ❑ The operating system — Validates the user name and password and grants or denies access.
- ❑ **Pre-conditions:** No one is currently logged in to the system.
- ❑ **Post-conditions:** If the user enters a valid user name and password, the system is logged in and displays the user's desktop. If the user enters an invalid user name/password combination, the system remains logged out and the user cannot see the desktop or any of the data in the computer.
- ❑ **Normal Flow:** The user should try all of the possible combinations of blank, valid, and invalid user names and passwords and click OK. The following table lists the combinations and their

desired results. The tester should fill in the blank column with "Pass" or "Fail" to indicate whether each test gave the desired result.

Username	Password	Desired Result	Pass/Fail
Blank	Blank	No access	
Blank	Valid	No access	
Blank	Invalid	No access	
Valid	Blank	No access	
Valid	Valid	Access	
Valid	Valid for different account	No access	
Valid	Invalid	No access	
Invalid	Blank	No access	
Invalid	Valid	No access	
Invalid	Invalid	No access	

❑ **Alternative Flow:** Instead of clicking OK, the user could click Cancel. The system should reset the screen, blanking the user name and password text boxes.

❑ **Notes:** In all cases that do not give the user access, the system should deny access in exactly the same way so the user cannot learn, for example, that he has guessed a valid user name but an invalid password. That would give a ne'er-do-well a valid user name to attack and that would be bad.

Note that this use case specifies the user's actions with enough detail that a relatively inexperienced user could follow it.

Exercise 10 Solution

When a heavy hitter such as a Vice President attacks, you need to call in your Executive Champion. Ideally he can point to your requirements document and show that you did, in fact, consider farbulistic granilation and that everyone agreed the allowance was sufficient. If you didn't consider this issue, you may need to put in some extra study to give your Executive Champion ammunition to fend off the attack.

If your Executive Champion doesn't have enough clout to fight off the Super Villain, you could be in trouble.

One project I worked on really did have Super Villains and Executive Champions at that level in a pretty big company (many tens of thousands of employees). I won't bore you with the details but our Executive Champion and Customer Champion spent a huge amount of time fending off attacks for about two years before the project finished.

Chapter 5

Exercise 1 Solution

Figure A-3 shows one possible solution.

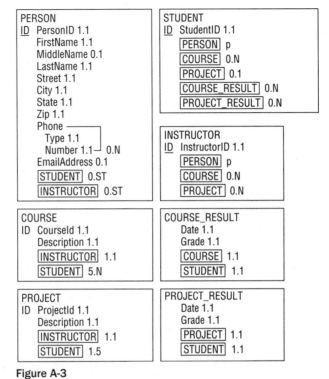

```
PERSON                          STUDENT
ID  PersonID 1.1                ID  StudentID 1.1
    FirstName 1.1                   [PERSON] p
    MiddleName 0.1                  [COURSE] 0.N
    LastName 1.1                    [PROJECT] 0.1
    Street 1.1                      [COURSE_RESULT] 0.N
    City 1.1                        [PROJECT_RESULT] 0.N
    State 1.1
    Zip 1.1
    Phone                       INSTRUCTOR
       Type 1.1                 ID  InstructorID 1.1
       Number 1.1┘ 0.N              [PERSON] p
    EmailAddress 0.1                [COURSE] 0.N
    [STUDENT] 0.ST                  [PROJECT] 0.N
    [INSTRUCTOR] 0.ST

COURSE                          COURSE_RESULT
ID  CourseId 1.1                    Date 1.1
    Description 1.1                 Grade 1.1
    [INSTRUCTOR] 1.1               [COURSE] 1.1
    [STUDENT] 5.N                   [STUDENT] 1.1

PROJECT                         PROJECT_RESULT
ID  ProjectId 1.1                   Date 1.1
    Description 1.1                 Grade 1.1
    [INSTRUCTOR] 1.1               [PROJECT] 1.1
    [STUDENT] 1.5                   [STUDENT] 1.1
```

Figure A-3

❏ In the STUDENT class, COURSE and PROJECT have cardinality 0.N and 0.1, respectively. This doesn't capture the fact that at least one of these two attributes must include at least one value.

❏ Similarly in the INSTRUCTOR class, does not capture the fact that at least one of the COURSE or PROJECT attributes must include at least one value.

Exercise 2 Solution

Figure A-4 shows an inheritance diagram for the Person, Student, and Instructor entities. It also shows the relationship between the Person and Phone entities.

The Phone entity doesn't have a primary key because it doesn't make sense to search for just a Phone entity by itself. Instead, you can find the Phone entities corresponding to a Person entity. That means Phone is a weak entity so it is surrounded by a thick rectangle and its identifying relationship is drawn with a thick arrow.

Appendix A: Exercise Solutions

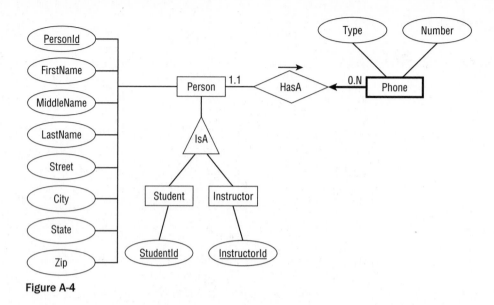

Figure A-4

Figure A-5 shows one possible ER diagram for the college course data.

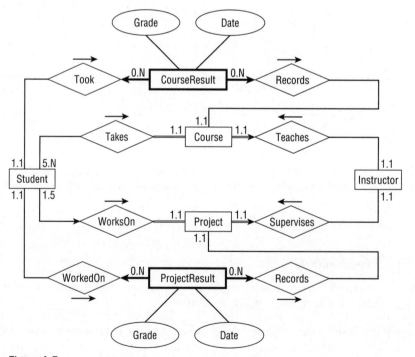

Figure A-5

The diagram's constraints are:

- ❑ It doesn't make sense to look for a particular CourseResult so it doesn't have a primary key. Instead you can look for CourseResults associated with a Student or with a Course. That means CourseResult is a weak entity so it is drawn with a thick rectangle and it is connected to its identifying relationships with thick arrows.

- ❑ Similarly ProjectResult is a weak entity.

- ❑ A Course must be involved in a relationship with a Student (or else the Course is canceled) so its line leading toward Student is double (a participation constraint).

- ❑ Similarly a Project must be involved in a relationship with a Student so its line leading toward Student is double (a participation constraint).

- ❑ A Course must be involved in a relationship with an Instructor (someone has to teach it) so its line leading toward Instructor is double (a participation constraint). A Course can have only one Instructor so the line is also an arrow (a key constraint).

- ❑ Similarly a Project must be involved in a relationship with exactly one Instructor so its line leading toward Instructor is a double arrow (participation and key constraint).

- ❑ A Student can work on at most one Project at a time so its line leading to Project is an arrow (key constraint).

Special notes:

- ❑ The Student entity's relationships with Course and Project do not indicate that a Student must be involved with at least one Course or a Project.

- ❑ Similarly the Instructor entity's relationships with Course and Project do not indicate that an Instructor must be involved with at least one Course or a Project.

Exercise 3 Solution

Figure A-6 shows one possible solution.

Notice the way this model handles the fact that Student and Instructor inherit from Person. The Persons table holds the basic Person information and a PersonId. The Students and Instructors tables include PersonId foreign keys to link to the corresponding basic Person data.

Note also the different approach used for the Student/Course and Instructor/Course relationships. Because a course has exactly one instructor, the Instructors and Courses tables are connected with a simple one-to-many relationship. In contrast, a course has many students so the relationship uses an intermediate StudentCourses table to connect the two to build a many-to-many relationship. (The same reasoning applies to the Student/Project and Instructor/Project relationships.)

Finally, notice the difference between the Student/Course and Student/Project relationships. A student can be enrolled in any number of courses but at most one project so the first is a many-to-many relationship while the second is a one-to-one relationship.

Unfortunately this solution doesn't capture every aspect of the system either. In particular, it doesn't indicate that a Student must be enrolled in at least one Course or a Project. Similarly it doesn't show that

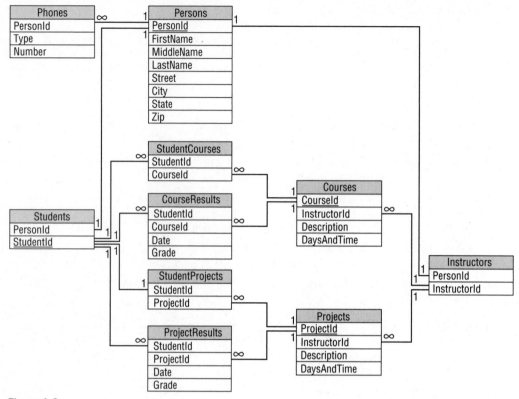

Figure A-6

an Instructor must teach at least one Course or supervise at least one Project. The model also doesn't include data type, required, and other domain data. All of this should be noted in separate documents.

Exercise 4 Solution

Figure A-7 shows one possible solution.

Special notes: The semantic object model actually does a pretty good job of capturing the Mike's Trikes data. About the only item that isn't described explicitly is the manager's role. In this model, you can deduce the manager at any given time by examining the manager's shift data. If Mike needed a more explicit record of who is managing during a salesperson's shift or when a contract was sold, the model would need to be modified.

Exercise 5 Solution

Figure A-8 shows an inheritance diagram for the Person, Customer, Salesperson, and Manager entities. It also shows the relationship between the Person and Phone entities.

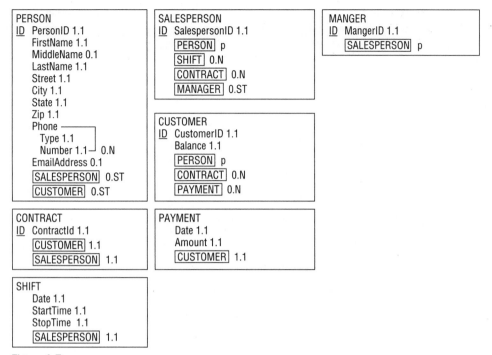

PERSON
ID PersonID 1.1
    FirstName 1.1
    MiddleName 0.1
    LastName 1.1
    Street 1.1
    City 1.1
    State 1.1
    Zip 1.1
    Phone ──────
        Type 1.1   │
        Number 1.1 ──┘ 0.N
    EmailAddress 0.1
    [SALESPERSON] 0.ST
    [CUSTOMER] 0.ST

SALESPERSON
ID SalespersonID 1.1
    [PERSON] p
    [SHIFT] 0.N
    [CONTRACT] 0.N
    [MANAGER] 0.ST

MANGER
ID MangerID 1.1
    [SALESPERSON] p

CUSTOMER
ID CustomerID 1.1
    Balance 1.1
    [PERSON] p
    [CONTRACT] 0.N
    [PAYMENT] 0.N

CONTRACT
ID ContractId 1.1
    [CUSTOMER] 1.1
    [SALESPERSON] 1.1

PAYMENT
    Date 1.1
    Amount 1.1
    [CUSTOMER] 1.1

SHIFT
    Date 1.1
    StartTime 1.1
    StopTime 1.1
    [SALESPERSON] 1.1

Figure A-7

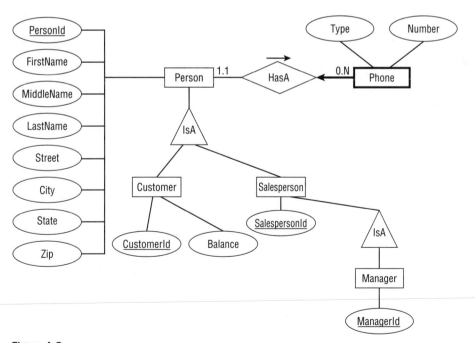

Figure A-8

421

The Phone entity doesn't have a primary key because it doesn't make sense to search for just a Phone entity by itself. Instead, you can find the Phone entities corresponding to a Person entity. That means Phone is a weak entity so it is surrounded by a thick rectangle and its identifying relationship is drawn with a thick arrow.

Figure A-9 shows one possible ER diagram for Mike's Trikes.

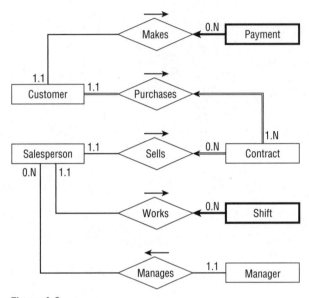

Figure A-9

The diagram's constraints are:

❏   Payment is a weak entity because you look up payments via the Customer who made them. Payment is drawn with a thick rectangle and a thick arrow pointing toward its identifying relationship.

❏   Shift is also is a weak entity because you look up shift data via the Salesperson who works them. Shift is drawn with a thick rectangle and a thick arrow pointing toward its identifying relationship.

❏   A Customer must be involved in at least one Contract (we don't make a Customer record until Customer Purchases Contract) so its line leading toward Contract is double (a participation constraint).

❏   A Contract must have exactly one Customer and exactly one Salesperson so the lines leading out of Contract toward those other entities are double (participation constraint) and arrows (key constraint).

Special notes:

❏   This diagram does not emphasize the fact that a `Manager` is also a `Salesperson` so a manager could play the role of the `Salesperson` in the diagram. You could add the `Manager Works Shift` relationship but that would complicate the diagram.

Exercise 6 Solution

Figure A-10 shows one possible solution.

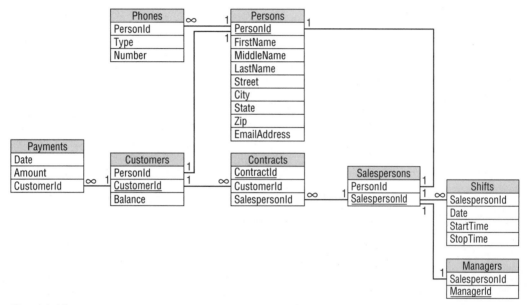

Figure A-10

Notice how this model builds the inheritance hierarchy. The Customers and Salespersons tables use PersonId foreign key fields to link to their corresponding Persons records. The Managers table uses a SalespersonId foreign key field to link to Salespersons records.

As usual, the model doesn't capture all of the information available about the situation. In particular, it doesn't indicate that a Customers record must be associated with at least one Contracts record. You should write down this and other facts such as field data types and domain information in separate documents.

Exercise 7 Solution

Figure A-11 shows one possible solution.

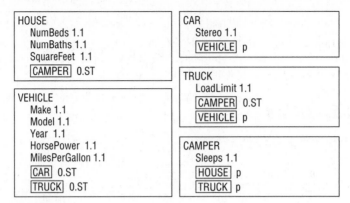

Figure A-11

Exercise 8 Solution

Figure A-12 shows one possible solution.

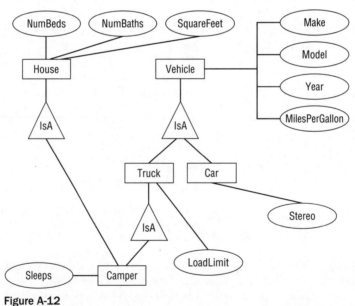

Figure A-12

Chapter 6

Exercise 1 Solution

The following chart describes the Phones table.

Field	Required	Data Type	Domain	Sanity Checks
PersonId	Yes	ID	Persons.PersonId	
Type	Yes	String	List: Cell, Home, Fax	
Number	Yes	String	Phone numbers	

The following chart describes the Persons table.

Field	Required	Data Type	Domain	Sanity Checks
PersonId	Yes	ID	Any ID	
FirstName	Yes	String	Any string	
MiddleName	No	String	Any string	
LastName	Yes	String	Any string	
Street	Yes	String	Any string	
City	Yes	String	Any string	
State	Yes	String	List: (states)	
Zip	Yes	String	ZIP or ZIP+4 format	Verify ZIP or ZIP+4 format
EmailAddress	No	String	Valid email address	Contains one @ symbol
MedicalNotes	?	String	Any string	
IceQualified?	?	Yes/No	Yes or No	
RockQualified?	?	Yes/No	Yes or No	
JumpQualified?	?	Yes/No	Yes or No	

The following chart describes the Guides table.

Field	Required	Data Type	Domain	Sanity Checks
PersonId	Yes	ID	Persons.PersonId	
GuideId	Yes	ID	Any ID	
IceInstructor?	Yes	Yes/No	Yes or No	
RockInstructor?	Yes	Yes/No	Yes or No	
JumpInstructor?	Yes	Yes/No	Yes or No	

The following chart describes the Explorers table.

Field	Required	Data Type	Domain	Sanity Checks
PersonId	Yes	ID	Persons.PersonId	
ExplorerId	Yes	ID	Any ID	

The following chart describes the Organizers table.

Field	Required	Data Type	Domain	Sanity Checks
PersonId	Yes	ID	Persons.PersonId	
OrganizerId	Yes	ID	Any ID	

The following chart describes the Adventures table.

Field	Required	Data Type	Domain	Sanity Checks
AdventureId	Yes	ID	Any ID	
ExplorerId	Yes	ID	Explorers.ExplorerId	
EmergencyContact	Yes	ID	Persons.PersonId	
OrganizerId	Yes	ID	Organizers.OrganizerId	
TrekId	Yes	ID	Treks.TrekId	
DateSold	Yes	Date	Any date	Before the trek's start date. Between January 1, 2000 and December 31, 2050 (or some other very early and late dates).
IncludeAir?	Yes	Yes/No	Yes or No	
IncludeEquipment?	Yes	Yes/No	Yes or No	
TotalPrice	Yes	Currency	Monetary amount > $0	Price > $250 (or some minimum sane value).
Notes	?	Yes/No	Yes or No	

The following chart describes the Treks table.

Field	Required	Data Type	Domain	Sanity Checks
TrekId	Yes	ID	Any ID	
GuideId	Yes	ID	Guides. GuideId	

Field	Required	Data Type	Domain	Sanity Checks
Description	Yes	String	Any string	Length > 100 (anything shorter couldn't say enough).
Locations	Yes	String	List of locations	Length > 5.
StartLocation	Yes	String	A location	Length > 5.
EndLocation	Yes	String	A location	Length > 5.
StartDate	Yes	Date	Any date	StartDate is on or before EndDate. Between January 1, 2000 and December 31, 2050 (or some other very early and late dates).
EndDate	Yes	Date	Any date	EndDate is on or after StartDate. Between January 1, 2000 and December 31, 2050 (or some other very early and late dates).
Price	Yes	Currency	Monetary amount > $0	Price > $250 (or some minimum sane value). Price > some minimum price per day times the number of days (EndDate–StartDate).
MaxExplorers	Yes	Number	Number > 0	Number > 0. Number < 20 (or some maximum sane amount).
IceRequired?	Yes	Yes/No	Yes or No	
RockRequired?	Yes	Yes/No	Yes or No	
JumpRequired?	Yes	Yes/No	Yes or No	

Exercise 2 Solution

The following list describes business rules that can be implemented in field or table checks for the Phones table:

- ❑ **Type:** Verify that the type is one of Home, Work, Cell, or Fax. Alternatively if you think this list might change in the future, you could put these values in a lookup table.

- ❑ **Number:** Verify that the value has a valid phone number format. In the United States, you would probably want to verify that it is a 10-digit number of the format ###-###-#### and you should allow for an extension.

The following list describes business rules that can be implemented in field or table checks for the Persons table:

- ❑ **FirstName/MiddleName/LastName:** Verify that this combination is unique. This will prevent you from adding the same person twice, perhaps as an explorer and as an emergency contact.

427

It would also be natural to try to validate the EmailAddress field in a field check. Unfortunately valid email address formats are quite complicated so this probably doesn't belong in the simpler field and table checks.

Similarly it might be nice to look up the explorer's City, State, and Zip values to make sure they are compatible. If you build a table listing all of the possible combinations, this wouldn't be a hard check but it would be an enormous table so it's probably not worth all of the extra effort. (Although for bonus points you could probably use a Web Service to perform this check over the Internet. If you don't know what a Web Service is, don't worry about it.)

You could also look up the State value in a list built into a field check. Though it's unlikely that the list of allowed states will change often, this list is so long that it's easier to manage in a separate lookup table rather than in a very long field check. (And who knows, Canada may eventually be officially recognized as "The Maple Leaf State.") (Just kidding! But this does bring up a whole series of questions about non-US explorers. This model ignores those issues completely.)

The Explorers, Organizers, and Guides tables should verify that their records are unique. That means checking uniqueness for the Explorers table's PersonId/ExplorerId fields, the Organizers table's PersonId/OrganizerId fields, and the Guides table's PersonId/GuideId fields.

The following list describes business rules that can be implemented in field or table checks for the Adventures table:

- ❏ **(Table):** Verify that the trek has room for this explorer.
- ❏ **(Table):** Verify that the explorer's IceQualified?, RockQualified?, and JumpQualified? values include those required for this trek.
- ❏ **ExplorerId/TrekId:** Verify that this combination is unique. An explorer should not buy the same trek twice. (We're assuming that the same trip on different dates gets a different record in the Treks table. Some people may very well want to go to the same places again.)
- ❏ **EmergencyContact:** Verify that the EmergencyContact is not going on the same trek listed for this Adventures record.
- ❏ **IncludeAir?/Notes:** If IncludeAir? is Yes, the Notes field should include flight information such as the explorer's starting airport and meal preferences. The database can probably not verify that the notes make sense (who knows if the low sodium meal is available on that flight?) but it can verify that the Notes entry has some minimum length if IncludeAir? is Yes.

The Adventures table would be a natural place to try to deal with the discounts for purchasing airline tickets or renting equipment. You would set TotalPrice equal to the trek's cost minus any discounts. (Note that this model doesn't have room to hold information about the equipment rented. The full model would need more order-related information along those lines.)

In any case, the discount schedule seems likely to change so it's better handled later, not in a simple field or table check.

The following list describes business rules that can be implemented in field or table checks for the Treks table:

- ❏ **(Table):** Verify that the guide's IceQualified?, RockQualified?, JumpQualified?, IceInstructor?, RockInstructor?, and JumpInstructor? values include those required for this trek.

Exercise 3 Solution

The following list summarizes business rules that should be extracted from the database's structure:

❑ If you really want to validate email addresses, it would be better to do so outside of the field and table checks. You could put this code in a stored procedure, code library, or middle tier.

❑ If you use a lookup table to validate phone number types (Home, Work, Cell, or Fax), do so here.

❑ If you're going to perform a complex City/State/Zip lookup, this is where to do it. You might use a huge table or you might call a Web Service over the Internet.

❑ If you use a lookup table to validate State values, do so here.

❑ This is where you would calculate an adventure's TotalPrice. You would look up discount information stored in a separate table and perform the calculation. You could put this code in a stored procedure, code library, or middle-tier layer.

❑ The fact that one of the company's owners asked which calculation would give the customer the biggest discount if they both purchase airline tickets and rent equipment (adding the two discounts and take 15% off gives the biggest discount) further implies that they might someday change the way they perform this calculation. That gives you more reason to extract this rule from the database so it's easier to change later.

❑ If the adventure's IncludeAir? value is Yes, you could try to parse the Notes field to see if the flight and meal information is present. I've seen several systems that make these sorts of checks, mostly because their requirements changed after the database was built and they couldn't easily modify the database. If you really need this check, you should move the flight and meal information into separate fields so they are easier to find and examine.

Exercise 4 Solution

The PhoneTypes table would have only one field: Type. The records would initially include Home, Work, Cell, and Fax.

The States table would have only one field: State. The records would list all of the allowed State values: AL, AK, AS,..., WY.

The DiscountParameters table would have two fields: Type and Amount. Type would give the discount type (Air or Equipment) and Amount would be the discount amount (15% or 5%).

An additional Parameters table would have two fields: Name and Value. This table would hold parameters used in other calculations so they would be easier to update than they would be if they were embedded in check constraints. The following table describes the initial values in this table.

Name	Value	Purpose
MinimumDate	January 1, 2000	Sanity check date for DateSold, StartDate, and EndDate.
MaximumDate	December 31, 2000	Sanity check date for DateSold, StartDate, and EndDate.
MinimumTotalPrice	$250	Sanity check price for an Adventure's TotalPrice.
MinimumTrekPrice	$250	Sanity check price for a Trek's Price.

Name	Value	Purpose
MinimumPricePerDay	$100	Sanity check minimum price per day for a Trek's Price.
MaximumExplorers	20	Sanity check maximum number of explorers on a trek.

Chapter 7

Exercise 1 Solution

a. The list isn't in 1NF because it violates these 1NF rules:

1. Each column must have a unique name.
The two Email fields have the same name.

2. The order of the rows and columns doesn't matter.
The order of the Email columns represents the student's preferred email address.

3. Each column must have a single data type.
The MajorOrSchool field holds both majors and schools.

5. Each column must contain a single value.
The Name field contains the student's first and last names together.

Let's take these rules one at a time.

1. Each column must have a unique name.

The two Email fields have the same name. You could fix this problem by giving them different names. For example, you could name them Email1 and Email2. The numbers would indicate the student's preferred email address solving the problem with Rule 2. This is the approach taken by the Phone1 and Phone2 fields so it might work, right?

Not really. There's another equally important issue here. These two Email fields represent the same kind of data with only a minor difference: priority. Aside from the student's preference of which comes first, the two fields hold identical values. How do we know you won't want to add a third email address later? You've already got two, why not three or four? Simply renaming the fields solves the duplicate name issue but locks you in to exactly two email addresses. Not only would that prevent you from adding more email addresses, but in many cases the second field would be empty. It's also flirting with 1NF rule number 6: Columns cannot contain repeating groups.

A better solution to the multiple Email field problem would be to pull those fields into a new StudentEmails table.

While we're thinking about multiple fields holding the same kind of data, let's take a closer look at the Phone1, PhoneType1, Phone2, and PhoneType2 fields. Though they have different names, they also represent the same kind of information and you're probably even more likely to want a third phone number than you are to want a third email

address. Though these fields technically don't violate 1NF (aside from Rule 6), it's probably worthwhile moving them into a new StudentPhones table.

2. The order of the rows and columns doesn't matter.

The order of the Email columns represents the student's preferred email address. The new
StudentEmails table should have a Priority column to capture the student's preference.
Similarly the new StudentPhones table should have a Priority column to indicate the stu-
dent's preference.

3. Each column must have a single data type.

The MajorOrSchool field holds both majors and schools. It should be split into Major and
School fields. Note that a student has a school whether he has a major or not so the School
field should always contain a value while the Major field may contain null.

5. Each column must contain a single value.

The Name field contains the student's first and last names together. Here you need to
decide whether the name value is atomic. In other words, will you *ever* need to do something with just a first name or just a last name? Chances are good that you'll want to at
least be able to search for last names (so you can easily look up students) so you should
split this field into FirstName and LastName fields.

b. Figure A-13 shows a relational diagram for this model.

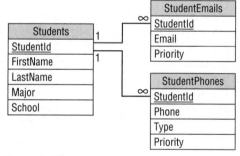

Figure A-13

Exercise 2 Solution

a. The list isn't in 1NF because it violates these 1NF rules:

2. The order of the rows and columns doesn't matter.
   The order of the rows represents the rows' priorities.

5. Each column must contain a single value.
   The Items column contains a comma-separated list of values.

b. The following table shows one way to convert the list into 1NF.

Location	Item	Priority
Grocery store	milk	1
Grocery store	eggs	1
Grocery store	bananas	1
Office supply store	paper	2
Office supply store	pencils	2
Office supply store	divining rod	2
Post Office	stamps	3
Computer store	flash drive	4
Computer store	8″ floppy disks	4

The primary key for this table is the combination Location/Item.

Exercise 3 Solution

a. The list isn't in 2NF because it violates the 2NF rule:

   2. All of the non-key fields depend on all of the key fields.

     The Priority field depends on Location but not Item. That's why its values are repeated so many times in the table.

b. The solution is to pull the non-key field (Priority) out into a new table and use the key field that it depends on (Location) as the link to the original data. Figure A-14 shows the new relational design.

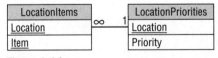

Figure A-14

Figure A-15 shows the new tables holding the original data.

Exercise 4 Solution

a. The list isn't in 3NF because it violates the 3NF rule:

   2. It contains no transitive dependencies.

LocationItems	
Location	Item
Grocery store	milk
Grocery store	eggs
Grocery store	bananas
Office supply store	paper
Office supply store	pencils
Office supply store	divining rod
Post Office	stamps
Computer store	flash drive
Computer store	8" floppy disks

LocationPriorities	
Location	Priority
Grocery store	1
Office supply store	2
Post Office	3
Computer store	4

Figure A-15

In this table, the Department field depends on the Project. Because those fields are not key fields, this is a transitive dependency.

b. The solution is to pull the dependent field (Department) out into a new table and use the field that it depends on (Project) as the link to the original data. Figure A-16 shows the new relational design.

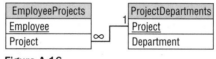

Figure A-16

Figure A-17 shows the new tables holding the original data.

Employee	Project
Bill Michaels	Network Routing
Mandy Ponem	Network Routing
Mike Mix	Net Services Analysis
Deanna Fole	Survey Design
Julie Wish	Survey Design
Alice Most	Work Assignment
Josh Farfar	Work Assignment

Project	Department
Network Routing	Network Lab
Net Services Analysis	Human Factors
Survey Design	Human Factors
Work Assignment	Network Lab

Figure A-17

Exercise 5 Solution

a. The table isn't in 5NF because it violates the 5NF rule:

2. It contains no related multi-values dependencies.

In this table, Person determines Food (the type the person can make), Person determines Tools (those in the person's kitchen), and Tool partially determines Food (you can't make muffins without a muffin tin). This makes a related multi-value dependency.

Figure A-18 shows an ER diagram for this model.

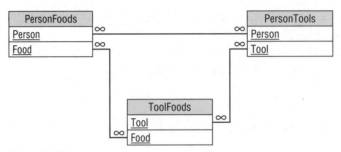

Figure A-18

b. The solution is to break the single table into three new tables that record the three different relationships: Person/Food, Person/Tool, and Tool/Food. Figure A-19 shows the new relational model.

PersonFoods	
Person	Food
Alice	Muffins
Alice	Omelets
Alice	Pancakes
Bob	Muffins
Bob	Omelets
Bob	Pancakes
Cyndi	Omelets

PersonTools	
Person	Tool
Alice	Muffin tin
Alice	Omelet pan
Alice	Pancake griddle
Bob	Omelet pan
Cyndi	Muffin tin
Cyndi	Pancake griddle

ToolFoods	
Tool	Food
Muffin tin	Muffins
Omelet pan	Omelets
Pancake griddle	Pancakes

Figure A-19

Exercise 6 Solution

Figure A-20 shows the matching between normal forms and their rules.

Chapter 8

Exercise 1 Solution

The following ShipClasses table contains the allowed combinations of Ship and Class.

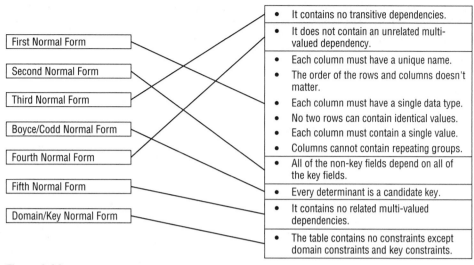

Figure A-20

Ship	Class
Luxury Liner	1st Class
Luxury Liner	2nd Class
Luxury Liner	3rd Class
Luxury Liner	4th Class
Luxury Liner	5th Class
Schooner	1st Class
Schooner	2nd Class
Tuna Boat	1st Class

Because the validation involves two fields, this must be a two-field foreign key constraint. In the Trips table, the combination of fields Ship/Class will be a foreign key referencing the ShipClasses table's Ship/Class fields.

Exercise 2 Solution

The Students table holds information about students so it is an object table. Similarly the Departments table holds information about the school's departments and the Classes table holds information about classes so they are also object tables.

The StudentClasses table links the Students and Classes tables so it is a link table. Similarly the DepartmentClasses table links the Departments and Classes tables so it is also a link table.

Exercise 3 Solution

This table is trying to hold information about three different concepts: the first player, the second player, and the match they will play.

To fix it, create a Players table with fields PlayerId, Name, and Rank. Put all of the player information in this table for all of the Player1 and Player2 entries. This is an object table holding information about players.

Then create a Matches table that has fields PlayerId1, PlayerId2, and MatchTime. This is a link table that links the Players table to itself. It also holds extra information about the link: the times of the matches.

Exercise 4 Solution

a. Average minutes late for an airline at a particular airport.

This will require finding and averaging up to a few hundred values so it should be possible to calculate as needed.

b. Average minutes late for all airlines at a particular airport.

This will require finding and averaging several hundred values. It may still be possible to perform this calculation as needed.

c. Average minutes late for an airline across the country.

This could require a *lot* of calculations. If this is a common query (for example, if lots of people are asking for this information all over the country hundreds of times per day), it might be better to store and update the information as planes take off and land rather than calculating it as needed.

d. Average minutes late for all airlines across the entire country.

This will require a huge number of calculations. This could take quite a while even if the database isn't heavily used so it might be best to store this value rather than calculating it as needed.

Of course, as long as you're going to store some of these values, you might want to just store them all so you can treat them uniformly.

Chapter 9

Exercise 1 Solution

Figure A-21 shows an ER diagram to represent Parcheesi matches.

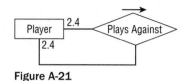

Figure A-21

Exercise 2 Solution

Figure A-22 shows a relational model for recording information about Parcheesi matches. PlayerId1 finished first, PlayerId2 finished second, PlayerId3 finished third, and PlayerId4 finished fourth.

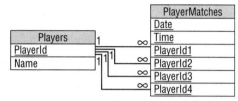

Figure A-22

Exercise 3 Solution

Figure A-23 shows an ER diagram that represents the relationships between Match, Move, and Ply.

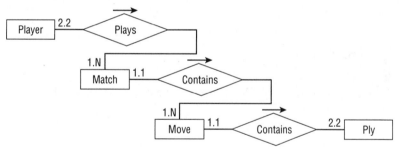

Figure A-23

Exercise 4 Solution

Figure A-24 shows a relational model for recording chess Match, Move, and Ply data.

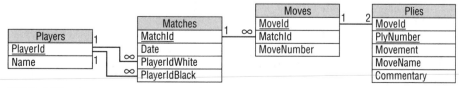

Figure A-24

You can model the one-to-two relationship between Moves and Plies by making the domain of the PlyNumber field include the values 1 and 2. You can implement that as a field-level check constraint on PlyNumber. Note that the fact that MoveId/PlyNumber is the Plies table's primary key ensures that each move cannot contain two plies with the same PlyNumber.

Exercise 5 Solution

Figure A-25 shows the chess model without the Moves table.

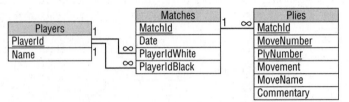

Figure A-25

The new diagram doesn't explicitly show that there should be exactly two plies per move. It has converted the old one-to-two relationship into a new one-to-many relationship.

The database still needs to verify that there are only two plies per move. You can still use a field-level check constraint to verify that the PlyNumber is either 1 or 2. The fact that MatchId/MoveNumber/PlyNumber is the Plies table's primary key ensures that any move in a given match cannot contain two plies with the same PlyNumber.

Exercise 6 Solution

The network solution described earlier in Chapter 9 and shown in Figure A-26 uses two tables. The Nodes table holds node IDs and coordinates. The Links table holds link times and the IDs of the nodes that the link connects.

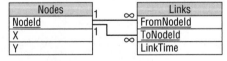

Figure A-26

This exercise is slightly different because it is an undirected network. In other words, each link has the same "value" no matter which direction you cross it. The solution shown in Figure A-26 isn't perfect because the FromNodeId and ToNodeId fields imply a direction for the link. To use this design you would either need to recognize that a Links record connecting node1 to node2 also represents a link connecting node2 with node1. Or you could insert two records for each link with the order of the node IDs switched, but that would double the number of records and all of that duplication screams out, "I'm not normalized!"

In normalization terms, FromNodeId and ToNodeId store the same kind of data. For a directed network, the two fields are not exactly the same thing so there's some benefit to using two fields with different names to store their data and differentiate them.

Normalization purists would say that the link's node data should be moved into a new table with an extra field to tell you which was the "from" node and which was the "to" node. For a directed network, the extra layer of indirection seems like a lot of work for little benefit. In addition to making you follow extra links to find the data, you would also need to perform some new validations to ensure that every link corresponded to exactly two nodes.

However, this more normalized design works somewhat better for an undirected network because moving the link's nodes into a new table removes the implication that one is the "from" node and one is the "to" node.

You still need a way to ensure that each link has two nodes, however. One way to do that is to give the new table a NodeNumber field to indicate which node this is, make the domain of NodeNumber be the numbers 1 and 2, and make LinkId/NodeNumber the primary key. That ensures that any link can have only two nodes. This design is shown in Figure A-27.

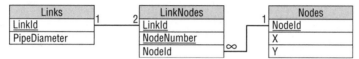

Figure A-27

This is the same as the normalized design for a directed network. The only difference is that in the undirected network you treat the NodeNumber field as a simple index to ensure that a link has two nodes whereas in a directed network you use that field to tell which node is "from" and which is "to."

Exercise 7 Solution

This is fairly straightforward temporal data. Figure A-28 shows a model to hold cheese item data. A CheeseItem record would probably hold other information such as the quantity of cheese purchased, the lot number, and so forth.

Figure A-28

Exercise 8 Solution

Figure A-29 shows the new model to hold cheese item data. Instead of a SellByDate, this version stores the date the cheese was made and a link leading to the shelf life.

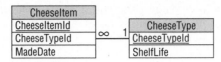

Figure A-29

In the model, the CheeseItem table is the same size as the model for Exercise 7 and there's a new table, so you could ask if this is an improvement. In terms of looking up expiration data for a particular cheese item, however, this model isn't an improvement. It takes more space and requires an extra lookup plus a calculation (MadeDate + ShelfLife) to find the cheese item's sell-by date.

However, this model provides more consistency because it ensures that each item of a particular kind of cheese uses the same shelf life.

Chapter 10

Exercise 1 Solution

This table has a lot of problems. Specific problems include:

❑ The Name field includes two logical fields, FirstName and LastName, so the table isn't even in First Normal Form.

❑ Your client plans to look up the state from the Zip value. Why doesn't he also look up the city? The table should be changed to either also look up the city or have separate City, State, and Zip fields (the second option is a lot easier).

❑ The two phone number fields are not differentiated. In other words, how do you know which number is a home phone, cell phone, or work phone? Which is the daytime number and which is the evening number? These fields should be moved into a Phones table with an additional field indicating the type of the phone number.

❑ Two phone numbers is also an arbitrary limit. Some day a customer will probably want to leave more than two numbers. When you create the Phones table, you should not restrict a customer to two entries.

❑ The Address field has a bad name because Address implies that the field contains an entire address when in fact it only contains the street information. This field's name should be something like Street or StreetAddress.

❑ The Stuff field has a terrible name because "Stuff" could mean just about anything! This field's name should be changed to Interests.

❑ The freshly renamed Interests field lists more than one value. (The fact that the name is plural is a hint.) This field's data should be moved into a new CustomerInterests table. You should also make an Interests lookup table to list the allowed values so CustomerInterests can use it as a foreign key constraint.

❑ Planning for future changes, you might also suggest adding an Email field.

Your client's assumption that you can just build Orders and other tables implies the plan isn't very well thought out. This project definitely needs a lot more planning and a complete database design before you start slapping tables together. This kind of homegrown project also rarely includes documentation of any kind so you'll need to do a lot of documentation work early in the project. (Though this type of project often provides many hours of lucrative consulting later for debugging, it's the frustrating kind of consulting.)

Exercise 2 Solution

Because this client is opening a new store, you should wonder if they will grow even more in the next few years. Blu-ray is also a brand new technology and, if it becomes as popular as current growth indicates, demand for rentals could skyrocket.

This database will need extra testing at very high loads to verify that the database design can meet ever-increasing performance demands.

In contrast, a well-established party rental store probably won't experience explosive growth in the near future because it's been around for a while and it isn't selling new technology. You still need to thoroughly test their application but your load testing doesn't need to run at loads as far beyond the current level.

Exercise 3 Solution

This table is hyper-normalized. Though you can break a street address into name, number, prefix, and so forth, there are very few applications where that is necessary. If you will only ever need to use the address information to send mail to someone, you can combine all of this information in a single Street field. You can even include the apartment or suite number.

Similarly you can probably combine the Zip and PlusFour fields into a single Zip field. If you're only going to use the ZIP Code to write addresses, there's no need to use separate fields.

The Floor and Neighborhood information is also probably not useful. (Although if your business is renting apartments, you might want to be able to search for ground floor apartments or apartments within a certain neighborhood. In that case, these fields might make sense.)

Here's the new list of fields:

- ❑ CustomerId
- ❑ Street
- ❑ City
- ❑ State
- ❑ Zip

Exercise 4 Solution

In this model, the Phones table is fairly unconstrained because it allows a person to have any number of any type of phone number. All of the fields are required. Some other validations that you could build into the database include:

Field	Constraint	Implementation
PersonId	Exists	Foreign key match to Persons.PersonId.
Type	Enumerated value	Foreign key match to new PhoneTypes table.
Number	Format	Let the database verify that the value has format ###-###-####.

In the Persons table, every field except MiddleName should be required. The table can implement the following constraints:

Field	Constraint	Implementation
State	Enumerated value	Foreign key match to new States table.
Zip	Format	Let the database verify that the value has format #### or ####-####.

All of the fields in the Courses and Projects tables should be required, although you may want to allow a blank InstructorId and DaysAndTime so you can create a course before you're ready to schedule it. This table should also have a foreign key constraint requiring that the InstructorId exist in the Instructors table.

The Students and Instructors tables should require all fields. They should also have a foreign key constraint requiring that their PersonId fields have values that exist in the Persons table.

StudentCourses and StudentProjects are linking tables used to implement many-to-many relationships. Their fields should be required and foreign key constraints should verify that their values exist in the corresponding tables.

CourseResults and ProjectResults are also linking tables that implement many-to-many relationships. They should require all fields and foreign key constraints should verify that their ID values exist in the corresponding tables.

CourseResults and ProjectResults should also use constraints to verify that the Grade fields contain acceptable values. If Grade is numeric, a check constraint should verify that it is between 0 and 100 (or whatever scale the school uses). If the Grade value includes A+, A, A-, B+, and so forth, the tables should use foreign key constraints to verify that the Grade exists in a new PossibleGrades table.

Finally, you could check that the Date fields in the CourseResults and ProjectResults tables come after the corresponding student's enrollment date.

Chapter 11

Exercise 1 Solution

The following table summarizes the Course entity's fields.

Field	Req'd?	Data Type	Domain
Title	Yes	String	Any string
Description	Yes	String	Any string.
MaximumParticipants	Yes	Integer	> 0
Price	Yes	Currency	> 0
AnimalType	Yes	String	One of Cat, Dog, Bird, Bat, and so on.
Dates	Yes	String	List of dates.
Time	Yes	Time	Between 8am and 11pm.
Location	Yes	String	One of Room 1, Room 2, yard, arena, and so on.
Trainer	No	Reference	The Employee teaching the course.
Students	No	Reference	Customers table.

Because the Dates and Time fields are required, we cannot create a course until it is scheduled.

A more complex validation for new records should verify that there are no other courses scheduled for the same location with overlapping dates and times.

Exercise 2 Solution

The following table summarizes the Employee entity's fields.

Field	Req'd?	Data Type	Domain
FirstName	Yes	String	Any first name.
LastName	Yes	String	Any last name.
Street	Yes	String	Any street name and number. Not validated.
City	Yes	String	Any city name. Not validated?
State	Yes	String	Foreign key to States table.
Zip	Yes	String	Valid ZIP Code. Not validated?
Email	No	String	Valid email address. If provided, send the customer a monthly email newsletter.
HomePhone	No	String	Valid 10-digit phone number.
CellPhone	No	String	Valid 10-digit phone number.
SocialSecurityNumber	Yes	String	Valid Social Security number.
Specialties	No	String	Zero or more of: Dog, Cat, Horse, Bird, Fish, Snail, and so on.

Exercise 3 Solution

Alicia and The Pampered Pet employees think of work shift assignments as coming in one week batches. Alicia posts schedules one week at a time.

However, the database may not actually need to create records representing weeks of assignments. Instead it can track individual work assignments that represent an employee working certain hours on a given day. The interactive interface and any work assignment reports will gather the assignments for a particular week and display the results in the familiar week-at-a-time format.

That means the Shift entity can be relatively simple:

Field	Req'd?	Data Type	Domain
Employee	Yes	Reference	Refers to the assignment's employee.
Date	Yes	Date	Valid dates. For new records, verify that the date is on or after today.
StartTime	Yes	Time	$> = 6am$.
StopTime	Yes	Time	$> = StartTime + 1$ hour, and $< = 11pm$.

Exercise 4 Solution

The following table summarizes the Customer entity's fields.

Field	Req'd?	Data Type	Domain
FirstName	Yes	String	Any first name.
LastName	Yes	String	Any last name.
Street	See notes	String	Any street name and number. Not validated.
City	See notes	String	Any city name. Not validated?
State	See notes	String	Foreign key to States table.
Zip	See notes	String	Valid ZIP Code. Not validated?
Email	See notes	String	Valid email address. If provided, send the customer a monthly email newsletter.
HomePhone	See notes	String	Valid 10-digit phone number.
CellPhone	No	String	Valid 10-digit phone number.
Pets	No	String	Pet names, ages, and types.

The system only creates customer records in one of the following circumstances:

❑ The customer enrolls in a course. In that case, we require either a home or cell phone number so we can contact the customer in case there's a change in schedule or some other unexpected event occurs (for example, Sveta contracts Capgras syndrome and won't work with Charlie anymore).

❑ The customer wants to receive postal mailings about sales and courses. In that case, the address information is required.

❑ The customer wants to receive email about sales and courses. In that case, the email address is required.

❑ We are shipping items to the customer. In that case, the address information and at least one phone number is required.

Exercise 5 Solution

Like the Shift entity, TimeEntry is simpler than it might appear. Users typically think of timekeeping as a weekly chore so they tend to think of a week's worth of time entries. However, individually each time entry is quite simple. The interactive timekeeping interface and any related reports (including printing payroll checks) will gather the assignments for a particular week and display the results appropriately.

The following table summarizes the TimeEntry entity's fields.

Field	Req'd?	Data Type	Domain
Employee	Yes	Reference	The employee who worked (or at least pretended to work).
Date	Yes	Date	$\leq$ now.
StartTime	Yes	Time	$\leq$ now.
StopTime	Yes	Time	$\leq$ now, and $>$ StartTime.
PaidDate	No	Date	$\leq$ now.

The PaidDate field records the date on which the employee's check was printed covering this time entry.

A more complex check for new records should verify that no existing record for this employee has an overlapping date and times.

Exercise 6 Solution

The Vendor entity gives the name of a company that provides Pampered Pet products. (Peter Piper picked a peck of Pampered Pet products.) It includes information about a contact person at the company.

The following table summarizes the Vendor entity's fields.

Field	Req'd?	Data Type	Domain
CompanyName	Yes	String	Any company name.
ContactFirstName	Yes	String	Any first name.
ContactLastName	Yes	String	Any last name.
Street	Yes	String	Any street name and number. Not validated.
City	Yes	String	Any city name. Not validated?
State	Yes	String	Foreign key to States table.
Zip	Yes	String	Valid ZIP Code. Not validated?
ContactEmail	No	String	Valid email address.
ContactPhone	Yes	String	Valid 10-digit phone number.
Notes	No	String	Miscellaneous instructions and notes.

Chapter 12

Exercise 1 Solution

Food items could be treated like any other inventory item, although their expiration dates would probably be much shorter. Some items might not even be counted in inventory if they expire quickly. For example, the database will need an entry for coffee so you can add one to an order but there's no point trying to update the QuantityInStock every time someone makes a new pot.

Exercise 2 Solution

An easy solution would be to add a new Certifications attribute to the EMPLOYEE class listing the courses that the employee can teach. This would be a foreign key field referring to COURSE classes. In the ER model, the Employee entity would have a new relationship with the Course entity. This would be a moderately hard change but probably doable.

Alternatively you could create a new Instructor subclass that inherits from Employee. This would require creating a new class/entity so it would be harder.

Exercise 3 Solution

Add a new StoreId attribute to the Order entity. That part wouldn't be too hard. At a minimum, you would also need to add a Store entity to look up allowed store IDs. That would be a little harder. If you also want to store real information about each store, such as an Address (which would require a link to the Addresses table), the change would be a lot harder.

Exercise 4 Solution

You could add a link between the Course entity and the Address entity. This wouldn't be too hard but it does require a new relationship so it would be harder than adding a new attribute to the Course entity.

Exercise 5 Solution

It would be easy to store these as Course entities with a Price of $0. The Pampered Pet could advertise them just like any other course. Probably no one would care if people attended without creating Customer entities.

Exercise 6 Solution

Adding more addresses to an order would make the Order/Address relationship many-to-many. You would need to add an intermediate table to represent the Order/Address pairs and replace the existing one-to-many relationship with two new one-to-many relationships. This would be a fairly difficult change.

Exercise 7 Solution

The easy solution would be to add a Phone attribute to the Order entity. However, Figure 12-9 shows that the design already has a Phone entity associated with the Person entity. Rather than creating a new attribute, it would be slightly more complicated but more flexible to reuse the Phone entity.

Before doing any of this, however, it would be worth asking the customers whether they will ever need to allow multiple phone numbers for an order. After all, they're adding one and there's nothing to stop them from adding another, particularly because the Person entity already allows any number of phone numbers.

Unfortunately adding multiple phone numbers to the Order entity would create a many-to-many relationship (one order can have many phone numbers and one phone number might be used to place any number of orders, probably by the same customer). To implement this, you would need to make an OrderPhone entity and two new one-to-many relationships. That would be a much harder change than simply adding a new Phone attribute to the Order entity.

Exercise 8 Solution

The obvious solution is to add a new Department attribute to the InventoryItem entity. However, that would create a functional dependency in that entity's attributes. InventoryItem already has a ShelfLocation field that tells where the item is when it is on display in the store. That location is in some department so adding a new Department attribute would partially duplicate that data and that could lead to inconsistent data. For example, an item could be listed as shelved in the Fish department but its Department field could be set to Reptile.

A better solution would be to make a new Departments entity that maps ShelfLocation values to departments. This requires adding a new table and a new relationship between InventoryItem and Departments so it would be fairly difficult.

Exercise 9 Solution

This would require a couple of changes. First, you would need to add effective date attributes to the Address entity. You would also need to change the user interface significantly to let the user decide which of a customer's addresses to use for any given operation. If the program simply uses the address that was in effect when an order was placed, that might be manageable.

Overall, however this change seems like a lot of trouble and the need is so unclear that I would ask the customers why they wanted to do this and try to talk them out of it if they don't have a good reason.

Exercise 10 Solution

The discount applied to an order would need to be recorded so the simplest solution would be to add a new Discount attribute to the Order entity.

More complicated solutions could track types of discounts to ensure consistency. Then, for example, the employee entering an order would enter a coupon or discount code rather than the actual discount percentage so entering in an incorrect discount would be less common. This solution would require creating a new Discounts entity and a relationship between it and the Order entity so it would be a more complicated solution.

Exercise 11 Solution

Figure A-30 shows one possible solution. It uses the CompetitorRobot entity to implement the Competitor/Robot relationship and it uses the RobotMatch entity to implement the Robot/Match relationship.

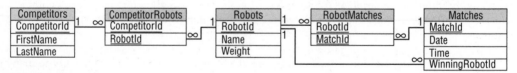

Figure A-30

Exercise 12 Solution

Figure A-31 shows one possible relational design.

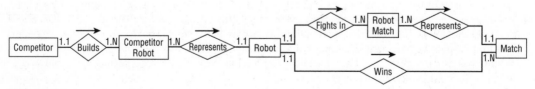

Figure A-31

Chapter 13

Exercise 1 Solution

The following list describes the primary keys and required fields for each table:

❑ **Competitors** — The CompetitorId field is the primary key. Other required fields are FirstName, LastName, Street, City, State, Zip.

❑ **CompetitorRobots** — This is an intermediate table. Its primary key includes both of its fields. Both of its fields are also foreign key constraints to other tables so they are completely constrained.

❑ **Robots** — The RobotId field is the primary key. Name and Class must be required in order to compete. The Weight, MaxSpeed, and Chassis fields could also be required.

❑ **RobotMatches** — This is an intermediate table. Its primary key includes both of its fields. Both of its fields are also foreign key constraints to other tables so they are completely constrained.

❑ **Matches** — The MatchId field is the primary key. Date, Time, and Location are also required. WinningRobotId cannot be required because the Matches record will probably be created before the match occurs and at that time the winner isn't known (unless it's a fixed fight).

❑ **RobotWeapons** — This table lists the weapons that are built into each robot (chainsaw, axe, grapple, laser cannon). Both of its fields are part of the primary key so both are required. The RobotId field is a foreign key constraint referring to the Robots table so it is completely constrained.

Exercise 2 Solution

The following list describes sanity checks for each table:

❑ **Competitors** — Zip should have a valid ZIP Code format similar to either 12345 or 12345-6789.

❑ **CompetitorRobots** — None.

❑ **Robots** — If present, Weight > 0 and Weight < 10,000 lbs. If present, Speed > = 0 and Speed < 30 mph.

❑ **RobotMatches** — None.

❑ **Matches** — When created, Date > = today. Time > 8am and Time < 11pm.

❑ **RobotWeapons** — None.

Exercise 3 Solution

The following list describes lookup tables for each table's fields:

❑ **Competitors** — You could build a full City/State/Zip lookup table but it would be big and hard to maintain. You could use the trick described in this chapter of using a table to validate common

City/State/Zip values but allow values not in the table, but competitors in Robot Wars come from all over the country so there's no good list of the most likely City/State/Zip combinations.

❑ **CompetitorRobots** — Both of this table's fields are used in foreign key constraints already.

❑ **Robots** — Chassis should be one of 4 Wheel, 6 Wheel, Tank Tread, Hovercraft, and so forth. Class should be one of Light, Medium, Heavy, Under $1000, and so forth. The allowed values should be moved into new Chasses and Classes lookup tables.

❑ **RobotMatches** — Both of this table's fields are used in foreign key constraints already.

❑ **Matches** — Location should be one of Arena 1, Arena 2, Pond, and so forth. These values should be added to a Locations lookup table.

❑ **RobotWeapons** — WeaponType should be one of Chainsaw, Axe, Rail Gun, Plasma Cannon, and so forth. Those values should be added to a WeaponTypes table.

Exercise 4 Solution

The three somewhat more complicated business rules that I thought of that really should be implemented in some manner are:

❑ Two matches should not be scheduled for the same place at the same time. This can be implemented as a uniqueness constraint on the Matches table's combined Date/Time/Location values. (This assumes the matches fit in nice time slots so we don't need to worry about them overlapping.)

❑ A robot should not be scheduled for two matches at the same time.

❑ Because competitors must control their robots during a match, none of a competitor's robots should not be scheduled for two matches at the same time. (If two robots share multiple co-owners, the team could split up and be in two matches at once but that would make the database just plain ugly. If that sort of change is required, you'll be glad you provided this check in a stored procedure, a middle tier, or some other place that's reasonably easy to change.)

Some other possible rules that I thought of include:

❑ A competitor can have no more than one robot in each match.

❑ A competitor can have no more than one robot in each class.

❑ A robot can have no more than two weapons.

❑ Weight, speed, chassis, and weapons could be part of what determines class. For example, classes could include Heavy, Light & Fast, Wheeled, or Single Weapon. Those definitions would be complicated and would probably change regularly.

❑ How the matches are assigned could be part of a set of business rules. For example, it could be single elimination, double elimination (if a robot can be repaired), winners and losers brackets, or a giant brawl.

Exercise 5 Solution

Figure A-32 shows the new relational model with the lookup tables added.

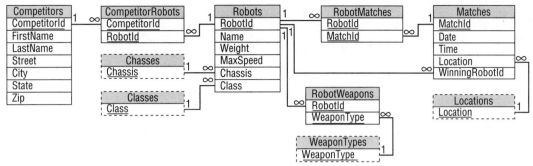

Figure A-32

Chapter 14

Exercise 1 Solution

This table isn't in 1NF because it contains two columns that hold multiple values. The Show column holds the names of all shows at a particular venue and the Times column holds all of the times for shows at a location.

Figure A-33 shows a relational design that stores this data in 1NF.

Shows
ShowName
Time
Venue
Seating

Figure A-33

The following table shows the data in this new format.

ShowName	Time	Venue	Seating
Sherm's Shark Show	11:15	Sherman's Lagoon	375
Sherm's Shark Show	3:00	Sherman's Lagoon	375
Meet the Rays	1:15	Sherman's Lagoon	375
Meet the Rays	6:00	Sherman's Lagoon	375
Deb's Daring Dolphins	11:00	Peet Amphitheater	300
Deb's Daring Dolphins	12:00	Peet Amphitheater	300

ShowName	Time	Venue	Seating
Deb's Daring Dolphins	6:30	Peet Amphitheater	300
The Walter Walrus Comedy Hour	2:00	Peet Amphitheater	300
The Walter Walrus Comedy Hour	5:27	Peet Amphitheater	300
Flamingo Follies	2:00	Ngorongoro Wash	413
Wonderful Waterfowl	3:00	Ngorongoro Wash	413

This table contains so much redundant information that there must be something wrong with it.

Exercise 2 Solution

The solution to Exercise 1 isn't in 2NF because some non-key fields depend on only some of the primary key fields. A particular show only occurs in one location (it would be hard to move the dolphins to different amphitheaters for different shows) so the Venue and Seating fields depend only on Show and not on Time.

The solution is to move the Venue and Seating data into a new table connected to the original table by the ShowName. Because the original table now only holds show time information, I'm going to rename it ShowTimes and call the new table Shows. Figure A-34 shows the result.

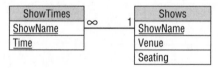

Figure A-34

Figure A-35 shows the new tables holding their data.

ShowTimes			Shows		
Sherm's Shark Show	11:15		Sherm's Shark Show	Sherman's Lagoon	375
Sherm's Shark Show	3:00		Meet the Rays	Sherman's Lagoon	375
Meet the Rays	1:15		Deb's Daring Dolphins	Peet Amphitheater	300
Meet the Rays	6:00		The Walter Walrus Comedy Hour	Peet Amphitheater	300
Deb's Daring Dolphins	11:00		Flamingo Follies	Ngorongoro Wash	413
Deb's Daring Dolphins	12:00		Wonderful Waterfowl	Ngorongoro Wash	413
Deb's Daring Dolphins	6:30				
The Walter Walrus Comedy Hour	2:00				
The Walter Walrus Comedy Hour	5:27				
Flamingo Follies	2:00				
Wonderful Waterfowl	3:00				

Figure A-35

Exercise 3 Solution

The solution to Exercise 2 isn't in 3NF because the Shows table contains a transitive dependency: the Seating field is determined by the Venue field. In the original table, the dependency isn't obvious because the same Venue and Seating values are not repeated. In Figure A-35 the problem is shown by the repeated Venue/Seating pairs in the Shows table.

The solution is to move the seating information into a new table to match venues with their capacities. The new table should use the Venue field to link back to the Shows table. Because this table describes the venues, I'll call it Venues. (Clever, huh?) Figure A-36 shows the new design.

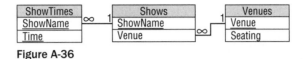

Figure A-36

Figure A-37 shows the data in the new tables.

Figure A-37

Exercise 4 Solution

Changing show names, time, or venue names is difficult for the design shown in Figure A-36 because those fields are used as primary keys. To increase the database's flexibility, all you need to do is make artificial keys (ID numbers) for the tables. Because the ShowName was only in the ShowTimes table to provide a link to the Shows table, it is no longer needed in ShowTimes. Similarly the Venue field in the Shows table was only there to link to the Venus table so Venue is no longer needed in the Shows table.

Figure A-38 shows the more flexible design.

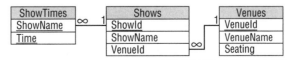

Figure A-38

Figure A-39 shows the data in the new tables. The ShowId values are between 1 and 6 and the VenueId values are between 101 and 103 so it's easy to see which are which.

ShowTimes

11:15	1
3:00	1
1:15	2
6:00	2
11:00	3
12:00	3
6:30	3
2:00	4
5:27	4
2:00	5
3:00	6

Shows

1	Sherm's Shark Show	101
2	Meet the Rays	101
3	Dep's Daring Dolphins	102
4	The Walter Walrus Comedy Hour	102
5	Flamingo Follies	103
6	Wonderful Waterfowl	103

Venues

101	Sherman's Lagoon	375
102	Peet Amphitheatre	300
103	Ngorongoro Wash	413

Figure A-39

Notice that the tables contain no repeated data other than their ID values so you can easily change a show's name or time, or a venue's name.

Chapter 15

These exercises ask you to do something and there's no reasonable way to put answers for them here. If you visit the book's Web site at wrox.com, you can download the Access database I created for these exercises and then you can compare them to your own.

Chapter 16

These exercises ask you to do something and there's no reasonable way to put answers for them here. If you visit the book's Web site, you can download the MySQL Workbench solutions and the database creation scripts I built for these exercises, and then you can compare them to your own.

Chapter 17

Exercise 1 Solution

The following code creates the Venues, Shows, and ShowTimes tables. Note that you must create the tables in this order because you cannot create a foreign key constraint that refers to a table that doesn't yet exist.

```
CREATE TABLE Venues(
  VenueId     INT             NOT NULL,
  VenueName   VARCHAR(45)     NOT NULL,
  Seating     INT             NOT NULL,
```

```
       PRIMARY KEY (VenueId)
);

CREATE TABLE Shows(
   ShowId      INT          NOT NULL,
   ShowName    VARCHAR(45)  NOT NULL,
   VenueId     INT          NOT NULL,

   PRIMARY KEY (ShowId),

   INDEX fk_Shows_Venues (VenueId),

   CONSTRAINT fk_Shows_Venues
     FOREIGN KEY (VenueId)
     REFERENCES Venues (VenueId)
     ON DELETE NO ACTION
     ON UPDATE NO ACTION
);

CREATE TABLE ShowTimes(
   ShowId      INT          NOT NULL,
   Time        TIME         NOT NULL,

   PRIMARY KEY (ShowId, Time),

   INDEX fk_ShowTimes_Shows (ShowId),

   CONSTRAINT fk_ShowTimes_Shows
     FOREIGN KEY (ShowId)
     REFERENCES Shows (ShowId)
     ON DELETE NO ACTION
     ON UPDATE NO ACTION
);
```

Exercise 2 Solution

The following code inserts the values for the aquarium show schedule. Note that the statements must insert data in tables used as foreign key constraints before inserting the values that refer to them. For example, the statement that creates the Sherman's Lagoon Venues record must come before the Sherm's Shark Show record that refers to it.

Also note that some of the text contains an apostrophe so that text is delimited by double quotes instead of apostrophes. For example, the text `"Sherman's Lagoon"` contains an apostrophe. Alternatively you could double-up the apostrophes to indicate characters that are part of the text value as in `'Sherman''s Lagoon'` (here `''` are two apostrophes, not a double quote).

```
INSERT INTO Venues VALUES (101, "Sherman's Lagoon", 375);
INSERT INTO Venues VALUES (102, "Peet Amphitheater", 300);
INSERT INTO Venues VALUES (103, "Ngorongoro Wash", 413);

INSERT INTO Shows VALUES (1, "Sherm's Shark Show", 101);
```

455

```
INSERT INTO Shows VALUES (2, "Meet the Rays", 101);
INSERT INTO Shows VALUES (3, "Deb's Daring Dolphins", 102);
INSERT INTO Shows VALUES (4, "The Walter Walrus Comedy Hour", 102);
INSERT INTO Shows VALUES (5, "Flamingo Follies", 103);
INSERT INTO Shows VALUES (6, "Wonderful Waterfowl", 103);

INSERT INTO ShowTimes VALUES (1, "11:15");
INSERT INTO ShowTimes VALUES (1, "15:00");
INSERT INTO ShowTimes VALUES (2, "13:15");
INSERT INTO ShowTimes VALUES (2, "18:00");
INSERT INTO ShowTimes VALUES (3, "11:00");
INSERT INTO ShowTimes VALUES (3, "12:00");
INSERT INTO ShowTimes VALUES (3, "18:30");
INSERT INTO ShowTimes VALUES (4, "14:00");
INSERT INTO ShowTimes VALUES (4, "17:27");
INSERT INTO ShowTimes VALUES (5, "14:00");
INSERT INTO ShowTimes VALUES (6, "15:00");
```

Exercise 3 Solution

The following statement updates the Flamingo Follies time:

```
UPDATE Shows, ShowTimes SET Time = "14:15"
WHERE Shows.ShowId = ShowTimes.ShowId
  AND Time= "14:00"
  AND ShowName = "Flamingo Follies";
```

The following statement updates the Sherm's Shark Show time:

```
UPDATE Shows, ShowTimes SET Time = "15:15"
WHERE Shows.ShowId = ShowTimes.ShowId
  AND Time= "15:00"
  AND ShowName = "Sherm's Shark Show";
```

Exercise 4 Solution

The following code produces the desired result in MySQL:

```
SELECT
    ShowName AS "Show",
    LPAD(DATE_FORMAT(Time, "%l:%i %p"), 8, " ") AS Time,
    VenueName AS Location
FROM Shows, ShowTimes, Venues
WHERE Shows.ShowId = ShowTimes.ShowId
  AND Shows.VenueId = Venues.VenueId
ORDER BY "Show", TIME(Time);
```

Exercise 5 Solution

The following code produces the desired result in MySQL:

```
SELECT
    LPAD(DATE_FORMAT(Time, "%l:%i %p"), 8, " ") AS Time,
    ShowName AS "Show",
    VenueName AS Location
FROM Shows, ShowTimes, Venues
WHERE Shows.ShowId = ShowTimes.ShowId
  AND Shows.VenueId = Venues.VenueId
ORDER BY TIME(Time), "Show";
```

Chapter 18

Exercise 1 Solution

One order in which you could build these tables is: MpaaRatings, Genres, Movies, Persons, MovieProducers, MovieDirectors, RoleTypes, MovieActors.

Exercise 2 Solution

The following code shows one possible SQL script for creating the movie database:

```
CREATE DATABASE MovieDb;
USE MovieDb;

CREATE TABLE MpaaRatings (
    MpaaRaiting        VARCHAR(5)     NOT NULL,
    Description        VARCHAR(40)    NOT NULL,
    PRIMARY KEY (MpaaRaiting)
);

CREATE TABLE Genres (
    Genre              VARCHAR(10)    NOT NULL,
    Description        VARCHAR(40)    NOT NULL,
    PRIMARY KEY (Genre)
);

CREATE TABLE Movies (
    MovieId            INT            NOT NULL     AUTO_INCREMENT,
    Title              VARCHAR(40)    NOT NULL,
    Year               INT            NOT NULL,
    MpaaRating         VARCHAR(5)     NOT NULL,
    Review             TEXT           NULL,
    NumStars           INT            NULL,
    Minutes            INT            NOT NULL,
```

```
    Description         TEXT            NULL,
    Genre               VARCHAR(10)     NULL,
    TrailerUrl          VARCHAR(255)    NULL,
    PRIMARY KEY (MovieId),
    INDEX FK_Movies_Ratings (MpaaRating ASC),
    INDEX FK_Movies_Genres (Genre ASC),
    CONSTRAINT FK_Movies_Ratings
      FOREIGN KEY (MpaaRating)
      REFERENCES MovieDb.MpaaRatings (MpaaRaiting)
      ON DELETE NO ACTION
      ON UPDATE NO ACTION,
    CONSTRAINT FK_Movies_Genres
      FOREIGN KEY (Genre)
      REFERENCES MovieDb.Genres (Genre)
      ON DELETE NO ACTION
      ON UPDATE NO ACTION
);

CREATE TABLE Persons (
    PersonId            INT             NOT NULL AUTO_INCREMENT,
    FirstName           VARCHAR(40)     NOT NULL,
    LastName            VARCHAR(40)     NOT NULL,
    PRIMARY KEY (PersonId)
);

CREATE TABLE MovieProducers (
    MovieId             INT             NOT NULL,
    PersonId            INT             NOT NULL,
    PRIMARY KEY (MovieId, PersonId),
    INDEX FK_Producers_Persons (PersonId ASC),
    INDEX FK_Producers_Movies (MovieId ASC),
    CONSTRAINT FK_Producers_Persons
      FOREIGN KEY (PersonId)
      REFERENCES MovieDb.Persons (PersonId)
      ON DELETE NO ACTION
      ON UPDATE NO ACTION,
    CONSTRAINT FK_Producers_Movies
      FOREIGN KEY (MovieId)
      REFERENCES MovieDb.Movies (MovieId)
      ON DELETE NO ACTION
      ON UPDATE NO ACTION
);

CREATE TABLE MovieDirectors (
    MovieId             INT             NOT NULL,
    PersonId            INT             NOT NULL,
    PRIMARY KEY (MovieId, PersonId),
    INDEX FK_Directors_Persons (PersonId ASC),
    INDEX FK_Directors_Movies (MovieId ASC),
    CONSTRAINT FK_Directors_Persons
      FOREIGN KEY (PersonId)
      REFERENCES MovieDb.Persons (PersonId)
      ON DELETE NO ACTION
```

```
      ON UPDATE NO ACTION,
    CONSTRAINT FK_Directors_Movies
      FOREIGN KEY (MovieId)
      REFERENCES MovieDb.Movies (MovieId)
      ON DELETE NO ACTION
      ON UPDATE NO ACTION
);

CREATE TABLE RoleTypes (
    RoleType              VARCHAR(40)    NOT NULL,
    PRIMARY KEY (RoleType)
);

CREATE TABLE MovieActors (
    MovieId            INT           NOT NULL,
    PersonId           INT           NOT NULL,
    CharacterName      VARCHAR(40)   NOT NULL,
    RoleType           VARCHAR(40)   NULL,
    Review             TEXT          NULL,
    NumStars           INT           NULL,
    PRIMARY KEY (MovieId, PersonId, CharacterName),
    INDEX FK_Actors_Persons (PersonId ASC),
    INDEX FK_Actors_RoleTypes (RoleType ASC),
    INDEX FK_Actors_Movies (MovieId ASC),
    CONSTRAINT FK_Actors_Persons
      FOREIGN KEY (PersonId)
      REFERENCES MovieDb.Persons (PersonId)
      ON DELETE NO ACTION
      ON UPDATE NO ACTION,
    CONSTRAINT FK_Actors_RoleTypes
      FOREIGN KEY (RoleType)
      REFERENCES MovieDb.RoleTypes (RoleType)
      ON DELETE NO ACTION
      ON UPDATE NO ACTION,
    CONSTRAINT FK_Actors_Movies
      FOREIGN KEY (MovieId)
      REFERENCES MovieDb.Movies (MovieId)
      ON DELETE NO ACTION
      ON UPDATE NO ACTION
);

DROP DATABASE MovieDb;
```

Chapter 19

Exercise 1 Solution

The following table shows a backup schedule. In this case, you have time for a full backup every night so you may as well use it.

Night	Off-Peak Start	Off-Peak End	Off-Peak Hours	Backup Type
Monday	11:00pm	4:00am	5	Full
Tuesday	11:00pm	4:00am	5	Full
Wednesday	11:00pm	4:00am	5	Full
Thursday	11:00pm	4:00am	5	Full
Friday	11:00pm	6:00am	7	Full
Saturday	9:00pm	6:00am	9	Full
Sunday	9:00pm	4:00am	7	Full

Exercise 2 Solution

The following table shows a new backup schedule. Now you can make a full backup only on Saturday night and on other nights you only have time for an incremental backup of changes since the previous night's backup.

Night	Off-Peak Start	Off-Peak End	Off-Peak Hours	Backup Type
Monday	12:00am	3:00am	3	Incremental from Sunday
Tuesday	12:00am	3:00am	3	Incremental from Monday
Wednesday	12:00am	3:00am	3	Incremental from Tuesday
Thursday	12:00am	3:00am	3	Incremental from Wednesday
Friday	12:00am	5:00am	5	Incremental from Thursday
Saturday	10:00pm	5:00am	7	Full
Sunday	10:00pm	3:00am	5	Incremental from Saturday

This backup schedule is pretty full so you should probably start thinking about other strategies to use if your database continues to grow. For example, you might need to perform some backups during peak hours (naturally during the "off-peak" peak hours) or you could partition the database so areas handling different time zones are stored separately so you can back them up separately.

Chapter 20

Exercise 1 Solution

An order entry clerk doesn't need to read or update any existing order records so you don't need to set privileges for individual fields in the Orders or OrderItems tables. (Although you may want the user interface program to read previous orders so it can copy their values.)

The clerk will need to read existing Customers records for existing customers and create Customers records for new customers. Many applications also allow the clerk to update customer data when creating a new order so the clerk needs Update access to the Customers table. The clerk should not change the CustomerId field, however, because that would disconnect the customer from previous orders. (In general, you should not update primary key values because that causes this kind of problem.)

The clerk needs Read access to the InventoryItems table to select the items that the customer wants to buy. (If there isn't enough inventory, assume the clerk creates the order anyway and sets the order's status to Back Order.)

The clerk also needs Read access to the OrderStatuses table to pick an initial status.

The following table lists the privileges that an order entry clerk needs for each table.

Table or Field	Privileges
Customers	C
CustomerId	R
FirstName	RU
LastName	RU
Street	RU
City	RU
State	RU
Zip	RU
Phone	RU
CreditCardType	RU
CreditCardNumber	RU
Orders	C
OrderId	–
CustomerId	–
OrderDate	–
ShippedDate	–
OrderStatus	–
OrderItems	C
OrderId	–
SequenceNumber	–
ItemId	–

Table or Field	Privileges
Quantity	–
InventoryItems	–
ItemId	R
Description	R
Price	R
QuantityInStock	R
OrderStatuses	–
OrderStatus	R

The following SQL statements create an order entry clerk with appropriate privileges:

```
CREATE USER EntryClerk IDENTIFIED BY 'secret';

-- Revoke all privileges for the user.
REVOKE ALL PRIVILEGES, GRANT OPTION FROM EntryClerk;

-- Grant needed privileges.
GRANT INSERT, SELECT ON ShippingDb.Customers TO EntryClerk;
GRANT UPDATE (FirstName, LastName, Street, City, State, Zip, Phone,
    CreditCardType, CreditCardNumber)
  ON ShippingDb.Customers TO EntryClerk;
GRANT INSERT ON ShippingDb.Orders TO EntryClerk;
GRANT INSERT ON ShippingDb.OrderItems TO EntryClerk;
GRANT SELECT ON ShippingDb.InventoryItems TO EntryClerk;
GRANT SELECT ON ShippingDb.OrderStatuses TO EntryClerk;
```

Exercise 2 Solution

A customer service clerk must be able to read everything to give information about an existing order. This clerk doesn't need to create records but needs to be able to update and delete Orders and OrderItems records for orders that have not yet shipped.

Though the clerk can update Customers data, the CustomerId should never change because that would disconnect it from previous orders.

Note that it doesn't make sense for the clerk to update Orders data. Changing OrderId would disconnect the items from the order, changing CustomerId would disconnect the order from the customer, changing OrderDate would be revising history (popular with politicians but not a good business practice), and changing ShippedDate and OrderStatus is the shipping clerk's job.

This clerk should also not be able to change an OrderItems record's OrderId value because it would disconnect the item from the order.

Whether the clerk can delete Customers records is a business rule. In this case, assume the clerk cannot delete customers so you don't need to worry about old orders without corresponding Customers records.

Finally, whether the clerk can update OrderItems records or should just delete old records and create new ones is another business rule. In this case, it will probably be easier for the user interface application to delete the old records and create new ones so the clerk needs Create, Read, and Delete privileges for the OrderItems table.

The following table lists the privileges that a customer service clerk needs for each table.

Table or Field	Privileges
Customers	–
CustomerId	R
FirstName	RU
LastName	RU
Street	RU
City	RU
State	RU
Zip	RU
Phone	RU
CreditCardType	RU
CreditCardNumber	RU
Orders	D
OrderId	R
CustomerId	R
OrderDate	R
ShippedDate	R
OrderStatus	R
OrderItems	CD
OrderId	R
SequenceNumber	R
ItemId	R
Quantity	R
InventoryItems	–
ItemId	R

Table or Field	Privileges
Description	R
Price	R
QuantityInStock	R
OrderStatuses	–
OrderStatus	R

The following SQL statements create a customer service clerk with appropriate privileges:

```
CREATE USER ServiceClerk IDENTIFIED BY 'secret';

-- Revoke all privileges for the user.
REVOKE ALL PRIVILEGES, GRANT OPTION FROM ServiceClerk;

-- Grant needed privileges.
GRANT SELECT ON ShippingDb.Customers TO ServiceClerk;
GRANT UPDATE (FirstName, LastName, Street, City, State, Zip, Phone,
    CreditCardType, CreditCardNumber)
  ON ShippingDb.Customers TO ServiceClerk;
GRANT SELECT, DELETE ON ShippingDb.Orders TO ServiceClerk;
GRANT INSERT, SELECT, DELETE ON ShippingDb.OrderItems TO ServiceClerk;
GRANT SELECT ON ShippingDb.InventoryItems TO ServiceClerk;
GRANT SELECT ON ShippingDb.OrderStatuses TO ServiceClerk;
```

Exercise 3 Solution

The inventory manager's main task is to order new inventory and maintain the InventoryItems table. That requires Create, Read, Update, and Delete privileges on that table.

To change an order's status from Back Ordered to Ordered, the inventory manager must look in the Orders table to find orders in the Back Ordered status, look up the items for that order, and see if there is now enough inventory to fulfill the order. That means the manager must be able to look at the Orders table's OrderId and OrderStatus fields, and update the OrderStatus field. The manager must also be able to look at the OrderItems table's OrderId, ItemId, and Quantity fields.

The following table lists the privileges that an inventory manager needs for each table.

Table or Field	Privileges
Customers	–
CustomerId	–
FirstName	–
LastName	–

Table or Field	Privileges
Street	–
City	–
State	–
Zip	–
Phone	–
CreditCardType	–
CreditCardNumber	–
Orders	–
OrderId	R
CustomerId	–
OrderDate	–
ShippedDate	–
OrderStatus	RU
OrderItems	–
OrderId	R
SequenceNumber	–
ItemId	R
Quantity	R
InventoryItems	CD
ItemId	R
Description	RU
Price	RU
QuantityInStock	RU
OrderStatuses	–
OrderStatus	R

The following SQL statements create a customer service clerk with appropriate privileges:

```
CREATE USER ServiceClerk IDENTIFIED BY 'secret';

-- Revoke all privileges for the user.
REVOKE ALL PRIVILEGES, GRANT OPTION FROM ServiceClerk;

-- Grant needed privileges.
```

```
GRANT SELECT ON ShippingDb.Customers TO ServiceClerk;
GRANT UPDATE (FirstName, LastName, Street, City, State, Zip, Phone,
    CreditCardType, CreditCardNumber)
  ON ShippingDb.Customers TO ServiceClerk;
GRANT SELECT, DELETE ON ShippingDb.Orders TO ServiceClerk;
GRANT INSERT, SELECT, DELETE ON ShippingDb.OrderItems TO ServiceClerk;
GRANT SELECT ON ShippingDb.InventoryItems TO ServiceClerk;
GRANT SELECT ON ShippingDb.OrderStatuses TO ServiceClerk;
```

Sample Database Designs

When you break a data model down into small pieces, there are really only three types of data relationships: one-to-one, one-to-many, and many-to-many (modeled with one-to-many relationships). If you think in those terms, then you really don't need examples. Just break the problem into small enough pieces and start assembling these three kinds of relationships. (Inheritance and subtyping forms another kind of logical relationship that you can also model.)

However, it may be useful to see more complete examples that include several different entities associated in typical ways. This appendix is intended to show you those kinds of examples.

Note that many different problems can be modeled in very similar ways. For example, consider a typical library. It has one or more copies of a whole bunch of books and lends them to patrons for a specific amount of time. Patrons can renew a book once and pay late fees if a book isn't returned on time.

Now consider a business that rents party supplies such as tables, chairs, big tents, dunk tanks, doves, and so forth. Like a library, this business has multiple copies of many of these items (it probably has dozens of tables and hundreds of chairs). Also like a library, this business "loans" (for a fee) its items to customers and charges a late fee if an item isn't returned on time.

Though a library and a party rental store are very different organizations, the structure of their databases is quite similar.

As you look at the examples in this appendix, think about variations that might use a similar structure. Though your application may not fit these examples exactly, you may find an example that uses a similar structure.

Also note that different applications might use very different database designs for the same data. The exact fields and sometimes even the tables included in the design depend on the application's focus.

For example, consider a large company's employee data. If you're building an application to assign employees to tasks for which they are qualified, your database will probably have an EmployeeSkills table that matches employee records to their skills. You'll also need a Tasks table that describes tasks and lists the skills that they require.

In contrast, suppose you need to build a human resources application that tracks employee payroll deductions for retirement contributions, medical coverage, and so forth. Although this application deals with the same employees, it doesn't need skill or task data so it doesn't need the EmployeeSkills or Tasks tables. It also needs new employee data not required by the work assignment project such as employee Social Security number, bank account number, next of kin, and anniversary date.

These two applications deal with the same physical entities (employees) but have very different data needs.

Because the types of data that you might need to store in a particular table depends on your application, these examples don't try to be exhaustive. For employee data, a table might include a few fields such as FirstName, LastName, and HireDate to give you an idea of what the table might include but you'll have to fill in the details for your application.

The following sections each describe a single example database design and give some ideas for variations that you may find useful. In particular, many of these models can include all sorts of address information such as Street, Suite, Building, Office, MailStop, City, State, Zip, PostalCode, Phone, and Extension. To keep the models simple, some tables include a single Address entry to represent address information. You should use whatever address information is appropriate for your application.

Books

The entities in a books database include the books themselves, authors, and publishers. Depending on your application, you may also want to include information about the book's various editors (acquisitions editors, managing editors, production editors, technical editors, and copy editors), artists, photographers, and all of the other people associated with the book. If the book is a compilation (for example, a collection of articles or short stories), the "Editor" who put it all together is similar to the author of the work as a whole.

Some of these people may be associated with the publisher. For example, many editors work for a particular publisher, although others are hired by a publisher as contractors and editors often move from one publisher to another over time so, if you want to record these types of associations, you will probably need to allow a separate publisher affiliation for each book.

Books may have many printings and editions. Different printings contain few or no differences. Different editions may contain completely different content or may come in different media such as paperback, hardcover, audio CD, video, DVD, PDF file, large print edition, and so forth.

Figure B-1 shows a simple book database design that models books, authors, and publishers. Book categories include Cooking, Home & Garden, Science Fiction, Professional, Bodice Ripper, and so forth. Recall that dashed lines represent lookup tables.

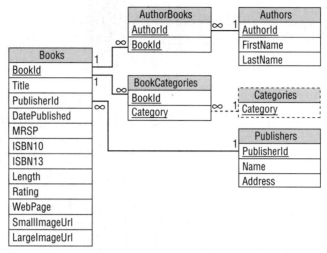

Figure B-1

Figure B-2 shows a more complex design that includes media and edition information. The LengthUnit depends on an item's medium. For example, the DVD and Video media have length measured in minutes whereas printed books have length measured in pages.

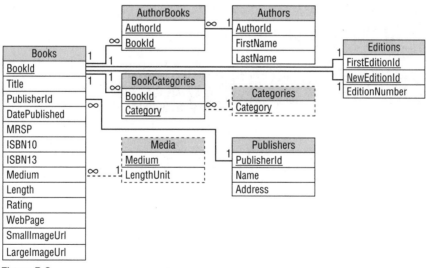

Figure B-2

Figure B-3 generalizes the author data to include other types of people such as editors, artists, and photographers.

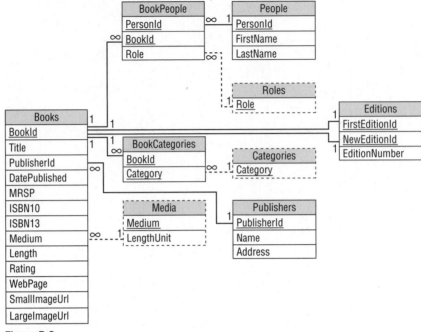

Figure B-3

DVD and Movies

In many ways, DVDs and movies are similar to books. All of them are created by a team of people who may work on other projects as well, all of them are owned by some sort of entity (publisher or studio), and all have similar basic information such as lengths and URLs. Many of the details are different (movies have actors instead of authors and directors instead of editors) but some of the basic structure of the data is similar.

Figure B-4 shows a version of Figure B-3 that has been modified to hold movie data. To avoid confusion, this model uses the word "job" to represent a person's responsibility in the project (Actor, Director, Producer, Grip, Best Boy, and so forth) and "actor role" to represent a part played by an actor.

Notice that a single person may appear in more than one MoviePeople records for a movie. For example, an actor may play more than one role and may be the director. (I suppose an actor could also be a crew member but it's hard to imagine Orlando Bloom catering or Julia Roberts stringing cables.)

Notice also the one-to-one relationship between the MoviePeople and ActorRoles records. Each Actor-Roles record represents a single role in a particular movie. If someone later shoots a remake of a movie, this model assumes that each of the characters gets a new ActorRoles record because the characters will represent new interpretations of the originals. If the ActorRoles records are abbreviated enough that they will be the same for different versions, you could make this a one-to-many relationship. You might also want to add version information similar to the Editions table in Figure B-3.

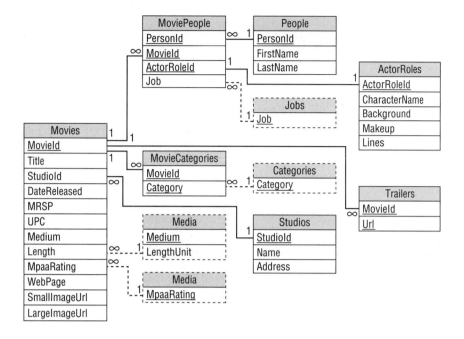

Figure B-4

(I'll know a lot more about the movie industry so I can build better models after Steven Spielberg makes a movie out of this book.)

Music and CDs

Though music collections, books, and movies all have similarities (for example, they are all produced by a team of people), there are some important differences. Songs are grouped by album and albums are grouped by band. Some or all of a band may participate in any given song on an album. Over time, the members of a band may change (except for ZZ Top) and one artist may be in many bands or even the same band more than once (in case they have a falling out and then later decide to make a reunion tour when the money runs out).

Although you could make similar distinctions for books (you could group books by series and you might define working combinations of authors), it doesn't make as much sense unless your application really needs to focus on that kind of information.

Figure B-5 shows a design to hold music album data.

In this model, roles might include such values as Lead Singer, Writer, and Costume Designer. The Instruments table holds values such as Electric Guitar, Drums, Zither, and Didgeridoo.

Notice that one person may play multiple roles in the same song. Typically this will be singer and song writer but really nimble artists may play multiple instruments.

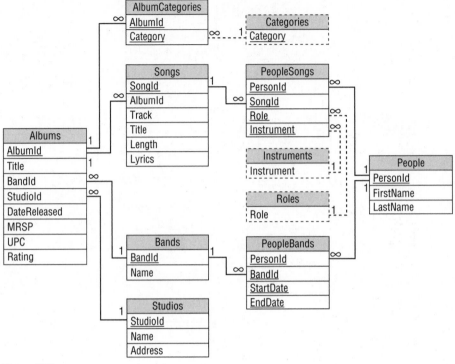

Figure B-5

Documents

Before you rush out and build a document management system, you might consider using one that is already available. Systems such as Visual Source Safe (msdn.microsoft.com/en-us/vstudio /aa718670.aspx), Concurrent Versions System (CVS — www.nongnu.org/cvs), and Subversion (subversion.tigris.org) manage multiple document versions quite effectively. They may not provide all of the features that you might add (such as advanced keyword queries) but they provide enough features to be quite useful without all of the work of building your own system.

However, Figure B-6 shows a data model that you could use to manage multiple document versions. This model assumes that a single author makes each version of a document and that multiple versions have major and minor version numbers as in 1.0, 1.1, 2.0, and so forth. The model allows you to store keywords and comments for the document as a whole and for each version.

The DocumentVersions table's Content field can hold either the complete document version or a list of differences between this version and the previous one.

Customer Orders

Several of the examples described throughout this book include data to record customer orders. Figure B-7 shows one of the simpler variations. It assumes a customer has a single address and all orders for that customer are shipped to that address.

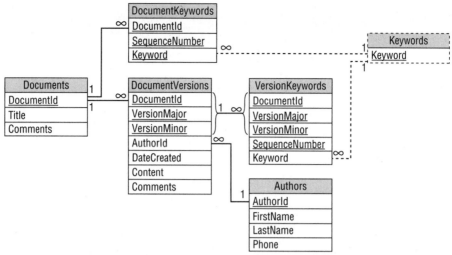

Figure B-6

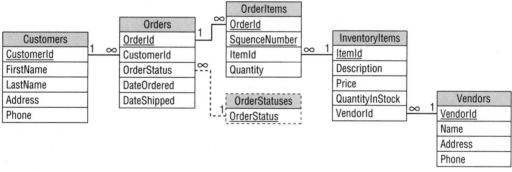

Figure B-7

Employee Shifts and Timesheets

Employee shifts and timesheet records are very similar. Both record a date and either hours scheduled or worked for an employee. Figure B-8 shows a simple model for storing shift and timesheet data.

Employees, Projects, and Departments

Figure B-9 shows a model for storing employee, project, and department data. This model assumes that an employee can be in any number of projects but only one department. The DepartmentRoles table contains values such as Manager, Secretary, Member of Technical Staff, and Sycophant. The ProjectRoles table contains values such as Project Manager, Lead Developer, Toolsmith, and Tester. The primary key for EmployeeProjects includes the ProjectRole field so a single employee can play multiple roles in a single project (for example, Project Manager and Doomsayer).

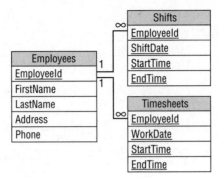

Figure B-8

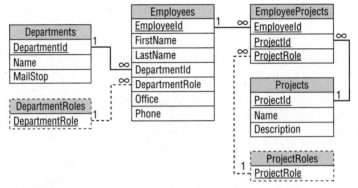

Figure B-9

You can use this design for matrix management with only a few changes. In matrix management, an employee has a *functional manager* who coordinates employees who have similar functions (mechanical engineering, optical design, software development, and so forth). The functional manager guides the employee's career development and handles project reviews.

Project managers determine what the employee does on a particular project.

For example, an electronics technician might be in the Electronics department, report to a functional manager in that department, work on several projects in various other departments, and report to project managers in those departments.

If each functional department has a single manager, you can use Figure B-9 by simply adding the functional managers as members of their departments with DepartmentRole set to Functional Manager. If there is not a simple one-to-one relationship between departments and functional managers, you can add a FunctionalId field to the Employees table as shown in Figure B-10.

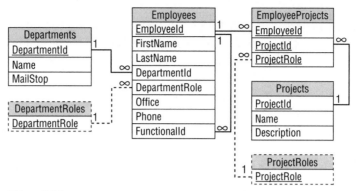

Figure B-10

Employee Skills and Qualifications

Employee skills and qualifications are important when certain jobs require them. For example, machining a particular glass part might require a technician who is certified to use a computerized ultrasonic cutter.

Depending on your application, some qualifications may expire. For example, a Red Cross CPR certification expires one year after it is issued. The design shown in Figure B-11 assumes that all skills expire. If a skill does not expire, you can set its ValidDuration to a really large value such as 300 years. If none of the skills you track expire, you can remove the ValidDuration field.

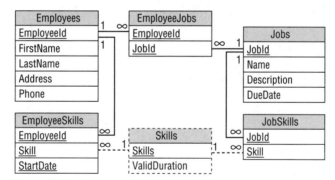

Figure B-11

In a more formal setting, you might need to add more fields to the EmployeeSkills table. For example, you might need to track a certification number, issuing agency, and so forth to prove an employee has a certain skill.

Note that this design tracks employee skills but doesn't do anything with them. It would be up to the user interface application to ensure that only employees with the proper skills are assigned to a given job.

Identical Object Rental

Just about any situation where something is given to a customer for a limited period of time can be modeled as a rental. For example, equipment rentals, DVD rentals, hourly contractors, and hotel rooms can all be treated as different kinds of rentals.

Figure B-12 shows a design that holds data for simple rental of identical objects. For example, a DVD rental store has many copies of each DVD and you don't really care which copy of a DVD the customer gets.

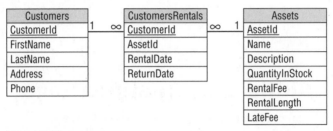

Figure B-12

If you want to track specific instances of rented assets (for example, to keep track of the number of times each copy of a DVD is rented), you can add an AssetInstances table as shown in Figure B-13.

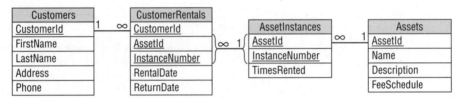

Figure B-13

There are many variations on rental and late fees. A DVD rental store might charge a nightly fee and no late fees. A store that rents heavy equipment such as backhoes and excavators might charge an hourly fee and large late fees. A public library might charge no rental fee and a small daily late fee. (My library charges no fees for children's books.)

Distinct Object Rental

Figure B-14 shows a rental variation that is more appropriate for a company that hires its employees as contractors.

Unlike DVD rental and libraries, contractor "rental" models distinct entities because different contractors are not alike. (Unless you're the army or a mega-corporation that treats people as interchangeable "assets.")

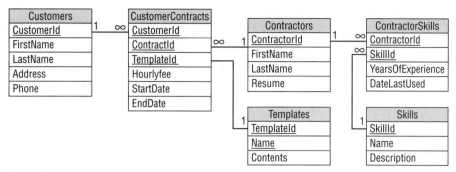

Figure B-14

Other businesses can model distinct entities in a similar manner, although the exact details will usually differ. For example, Figure B-15 shows a model designed for hotel reservations.

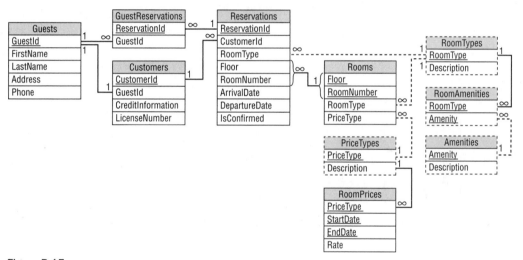

Figure B-15

A customer calls and makes a reservation. Initially the reservation is for a type of room, not a particular room. When the guests check in, the clerk fills in the floor and room number.

A Guest is a person staying in the room (there can be several people in the same room). A Customer is a person who pays for a reservation (only one person pays). If the IsConfirmed field has the value True, the reservation is confirmed for late arrival so the hotel will hold the room and charge the Customer's credit card if they show up at midnight. (Although I've had my room sold to another customer despite being confirmed for late arrival.)

A Room Type defines the amenities in the room. Amenities include such things as hot tubs, balconies, bathrooms, non-smoking, pets allowed, and king-sized heart-shaped rotating beds.

A Price Type defines the prices for a room. Price Types include values such as Business, Preferred, Frequent Visitor, Walk In, and Chump Whose Flight Was Canceled At The Last Minute And Is Desperate. (Hotels typically code price types as A, B, C, and so forth so the Chump doesn't notice he's paying four times as much as the family from Des Moines who booked three months in advance.)

Students, Courses, and Grades

Figure B-16 shows a model for storing student, course, and grade data.

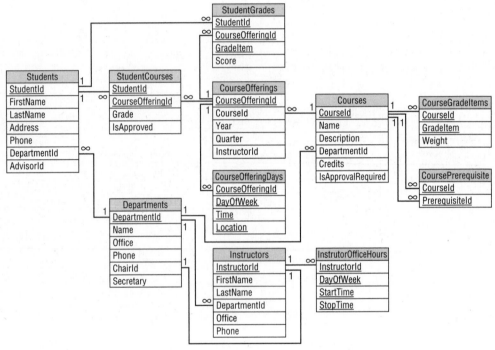

Figure B-16

A Course represents a type of class (Introduction to Database Design). A Course Offering is a particular instance of a Course (the 2010 winter term Introduction to Database Design class on Tuesdays and Thursdays from 9:00 to 10:30 in Building 12, room B-16).

A Grade Item is something in the course that receives a grade, such as Quiz 1, Midterm, and Term Paper 2. The CourseGradeItem table's Weight field lets you assign different weights to different Grade Items (for example, the Final is worth 50% of the total grade).

Grade Items are somewhat tricky because a StudentGrades record should have an appropriate GradeItem value. You might like to make the record's combined CourseOfferingId/GradeItem be a foreign key into the CourseGradeItems table but that table uses CourseId as a key, not CourseOfferingId. Ensuring that the CourseGradeItems record has a valid GradeItem must be handled as a business rule.

This database will probably be stored in two pieces: an online piece holding the current school year's data and a data warehouse piece holding older data. The data would undergo final consistency checks before it is moved form the current database to the warehouse. For example, you would verify that students have grades for every CourseGradeItem defined for their classes.

Other Students fields in the online database would probably record summary information. For example, a GPA field could record the student's grade point average for courses in the data warehouse. That field would be redundant because you could recalculate it from the data in the data warehouse, but placing it in the online database would let you avoid opening the data warehouse for day-to-day queries.

Teams

Figure B-17 shows a relatively simple data model for team sports. This design is based on a typical volleyball league. Players belong to a team and teams play in tournaments.

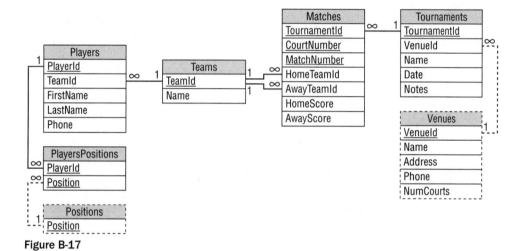

Figure B-17

This model allows each player to be associated with several positions. You can include special "positions" such as captain, coach, and water boy, or you can add them as new fields in the Players or Teams table depending on your needs.

Tournaments occur at venues that have a given number of courts. A match is a game between two teams. (In practice, a match will include several games so the scores may be games won rather than points won. In a really serious competition, you would need to expand the model to save scores for individual games in a match so you can compare points head-to-head in case there's a tie based on games alone. In fact, official volleyball record sheets include so much detail that you can figure out exactly when each point was made by each team and every player's location at the time.)

In a normal tournament, teams play against each other in pools. For example, six teams might play a round-robin against each other on each of two courts. Then the top two teams from each pool would enter single-elimination playoffs.

You can modify the simple design shown in Figure B-17 to handle non-tournament situations. For example, in many soccer leagues teams play one game a week so there isn't really a notion of a tournament. In that case, you can pull the relevant tournament fields (VenueId, Date, Notes) into the Matches table. You might also want to make some cosmetic changes such as changing "court" to "field" or "pitch."

Individual Sports

An individual sport such as running doesn't need all of the team information recorded in the previous model. Instead its database can focus on individual statistics and accomplishments.

Figure B-18 shows a model to hold running information. If you only store basic race information, you can treat races like any other run. If you're more competitive and want to record race data such as finishing position, position in age group, mile times, number of bathroom breaks, and so forth, you can add new Races and RunnerRaces tables similar to the Runs and RunnerRuns.

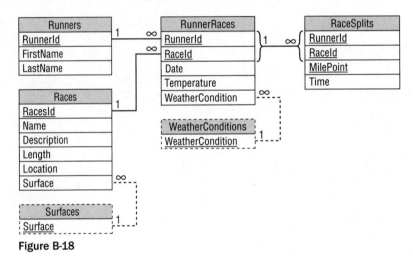

Figure B-18

Vehicle Fleets

Fleet tracking can be quite complex. Different parts of a business might want to track the vehicles' cargo and weights, current location, special equipment and tools, leases, repairs and maintenance, mileage, equipment, drivers, taxes, fuel use and taxes, and so forth.

For this example, you should know a little about the International Fuel Tax Agreement (IFTA). IFTA is an agreement among most U.S. States and Canadian Provinces to distribute fuel taxes fairly.

Each state and province charges a different tax rate on various kinds of fuel such as gasoline, diesel, propane, E-85, A55, and several others. (Perhaps the list will soon include hydrogen.) The taxes are included in the price at the pump and you've been paying them for years, probably without thinking about it.

The system is simple and makes sense until you consider a big fleet of vehicles that buys fuel in one state and then drives mostly in another state. For example, suppose your business is in St. Louis, Missouri but you do most of your driving across the river in Illinois. Fuel is cheaper in Missouri so you buy yours there. Illinois screams, "No fair! You're paying fuel taxes to Missouri but using our roads!" Enter ITFA.

Each quarter, you need to file IFTA tax forms listing every mile you drove and every drop of fuel you purchased in every state or province. You then need to pay any extra taxes that you owe based on how much tax you paid in each state and where you drove. In this example, you probably owe Illinois some money. (The net result is there's much less incentive for you to cross borders to buy fuel. The IFTA agency gathers all of these records from fleets all over North America, performs lengthy calculations, and then makes the states pay each other the differences between their taxes collected and what they should have collected based on miles driven. The numbers tend to cancel out so the grand totals aren't necessarily big.)

Figure B-19 shows a model designed to hold license, permit, fuel, and mileage data. Each field marked with an asterisk should be validated against a States lookup table but, to keep the model simple (relatively simple, anyway), the States table and its links aren't shown.

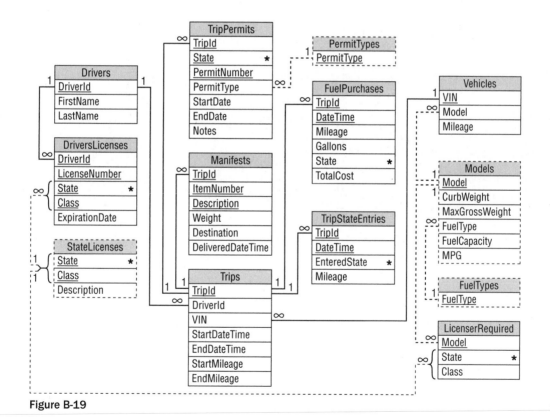

Figure B-19

The model's FuelPurchases table records the states in which fuel is purchased. The TripStateEntries records the mileages at which a vehicle entered a new state. By subtracting Mileage values in subsequent TripStateEntries, you can calculate the number of miles driven in each state.

Another interesting case is modeling jobs, employees, and vehicles with special requirements, tools, and skills. Employees have tools (such as wrenches, ohm meters, and chainsaws) and skills (such as the ability to fix dishwashers, install phones, and juggle). Vehicles have equipment such as pipe benders and threaders, cherry pickers, and pole setters.

Finally, jobs require certain skills and tools. For example, if you need to haul a lot of logs, you need a vehicle with a tree grapple and an employee who has tree grappling as a skill. ("Tree grappling" sounds like a wrestling move but it's not.)

Figure B-20 shows a data model to store this information. The model is simplified and leaves out a lot of information. For example, you may need to add job addresses, appointments, length, and so forth.

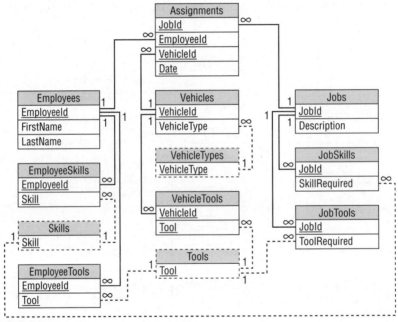

Figure B-20

(Note that assigning a tool to an employee implies that the employee can use the tool. You wouldn't give a defibrillator to an employee who didn't know how to use it. However, if you also want to model employees signing equipment in and out, you might need to make this assumption explicit by giving the employee a Defibrillator skill.)

This model assumes that multiple employees may be assigned to a single job. You could allow an Assignments record to have a null VehicleId value to allow two employees to ride in the same vehicle.

Of course, once you have this data stored, someone will need to figure out a way to match employees, vehicles, and jobs to get the most work done as efficiently as possible.

Contacts

The most obvious application that needs to store contact information is an address book, but many other applications can store contact information, too. Most complex applications that involve interaction among customers, employees, vendors, and other people can benefit from a contact database. For example, an order placement and processing application can use contact data to keep track of customer calls that place orders, change orders, request returns, and register complaints.

Figure B-21 shows a general contact data model. An application can use these tables to remember contacts at different times covering different topics.

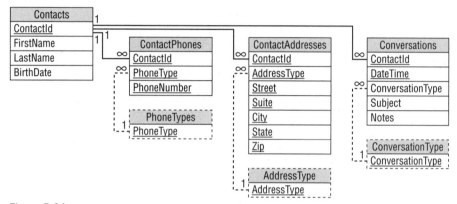

Figure B-21

If you want to integrate contact data in an application involving multiple employees, you may want to add an EmployeeId field to the Conversations table so you know who talked to the customer. You might also want to add fields to refer to a customer order to help further define the conversation. That would allow you to search for all of the conversations related to a particular order.

Passengers

There are several ways you might like to model vehicles with passengers. For example, typically city buses don't take reservations and don't care where passengers sit as long as the number of passengers doesn't exceed the vehicle's capacity (which in larger cities equals approximately two passengers per cubic foot of space).

Figure B-22 shows a simple design to track the number of passengers on a bus.

A route defines the stops that a bus will take. The information for each stop includes the time it should take to get to that stop and the duration of time that the bus should ideally wait at that stop.

A trip represents a bus traveling over a route. The TripStops records correspond to RouteStops records and record actual times and passenger counts (although in practice I don't know how often drivers record passenger numbers).

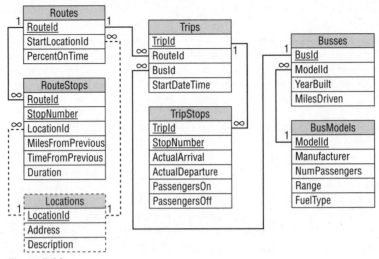

Figure B-22

Figure B-23 shows a slightly more complex model that allows passengers to reserve room on a bus but not to reserve individual seats. This model is intended for long distance common carriers such as long-distance buses (Greyhound, Trailways) and railroads. In this model, the customer makes reservations to assure that a seat is available on each leg of the trip but specific seats are not assigned.

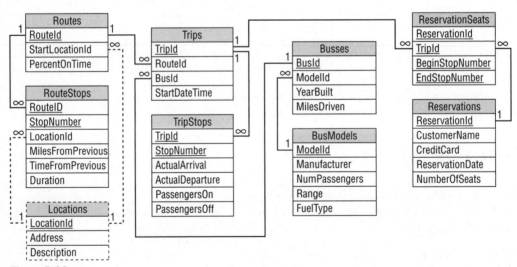

Figure B-23

This model is very similar to the previous one except it includes Reservations and ReservationSeats tables. Each Reservations record records information about a customer's trip. A ReservationSeats record holds information about a set of seats on a particular bus trip. The collection of ReservationSeats records corresponding to a particular Reservations record contains all of the information about the buses that a passenger's trip will use.

You can model airline and other travel where passengers have previously assigned seats using a very similar model. The only change you need (at least to model this part of the system) is to add assigned seat information to the ReservationSeats data. You could also add meal selection and other special information to each seat.

Note that these databases are typically enormous. For example, a typical large airline runs several thousand flights per day holding up to a few hundred passengers each. That means the Trips and TripStops tables grow by a few thousand records per day and the ReservationSeats table might grow by a few hundred thousand records per day. If you allow passengers to reserve seats up to a year in the future, the database must be able to hold several hundred million records.

Keeping such a large and quickly changing database running efficiently 24 hours a day is a Herculean effort. It may require huge disk farms, segmented data, special route-finding algorithms, and massive backup and warehousing processes. In other words, don't try this at home.

Recipes

This may seem like a silly example but it demonstrates how to store a set of instructions that require special equipment (ingredients).

A recipe database needs to store basic information about recipes such as their names, difficulty, and tastiness rating. It also needs an ingredient list and instructions. Figure B-24 shows a simple recipe database design. This model assumes the Difficulty and Rating fields are simple numeric values (for example, on a 1 to 10 scale). If you wanted to, you could change them to values such as Easy, Medium, and Hard, and make them foreign keys to lookup tables.

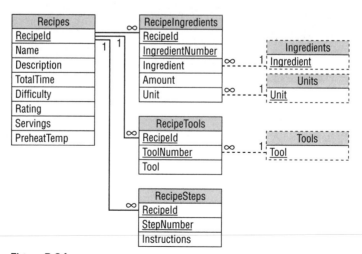

Figure B-24

You can use this design to store information about other assembly tasks (putting together skateboards, tuning a car, and so forth) or more generally for giving instructions (troubleshooting a wireless network).

Unfortunately generalizing this model to pull information out of the steps is trickier than it might initially seem. For example, you might like to make an instruction record refer to an ingredient and then tell you what to do with it as in, "Oatmeal, 2 cups, mix." That instruction would work but others are more complex.

For example, a recipe might ask you to mix different ingredients in separate bowls and then combine them. To break that information out, you would probably need to record the bowls as equipment and then somehow associate ingredients with each bowl. Some recipes call for even more complex steps such as separating eggs, scalding milk, caramelizing sugar, changing temperatures during cooking, and even lighting food on fire.

With enough time and effort, you might be able to write a cooking language to let you represent all of these operations (you could call it CML — Cooking Markup Language) but what would you have gained? Breaking instructions down to that level would let you do things such as finding all recipes that require you to perform certain tasks such as "powderizing" oatmeal in a food processor but how often will you need to perform those kinds of searches?

The simpler model already lets you search for specific tools, ingredients, and temperatures so it's probably best to stick with that model unless you have a very specialized need with well-defined steps. If necessary, you can add keywords to the recipes to let you search for particular unusual tools and techniques such as flambé and fossil-shaped gelatin molds.

Glossary

This appendix contains a glossary of useful database terms. You may find them handy when you read other books and articles about databases. You may also want to look for database and related glossaries online and in print. For example, "The DAMA Dictionary of Data Management" (Mark Mosley editor, Technics Publications, LLC, 2008) contains an excellent data management glossary.

For a list of relational database management systems in addition to those mentioned here, see en.wikipedia.org/wiki/List_of_relational_database_management_systems. For a comparison of relational database management system features, see en.wikipedia.org/wiki/Comparison_of_relational_database_management_systems.

1NF   See "First Normal Form."

2NF   See "Second Normal Form."

3NF   See "Third Normal Form."

4NF   See "Fourth Normal Form."

5NF   See "Fifth Normal Form."

6NF   See "Domain Key Normal Form."

ACID   Acronym for a set of database properties needed for reliable transactions. ACID stands for Atomicity, Consistency, Isolation, Durability (see the entries for those terms).

ADO   ActiveX Data Objects. A Microsoft collection of classes that allows programs to interact with databases. ADO is built on top of OLE DB (see "OLE DB").

alternate key   A candidate key that is not used as the table's primary key.

API   Application Programming Interface. A library of routines that a program can use to perform specialized tasks such as manipulating a database or drawing graphics.

association object   In a semantic object model, an object used to represent a relationship between two other objects.

atom   A piece of data that cannot be meaningfully divided. For example, a Social Security number of the form 123-45-6789 contains three pieces but they don't have any separate meaning so the number as a whole is an atom. (Unless your application groups records by, say, the middle two digits of a Social Security number. That would be weird.)

atomic transaction   A possibly complex series of actions that is considered as a single operation by those not involved directly in performing the transaction.

atomicity   The requirement that tasks within a transaction occur as a group as if they were a single complex task. The tasks are either all performed or none of them are performed. It's all or nothing.

attribute   The formal database term for column (see "column").

b+tree   (Pronounced "bee plus tree.") A self-balancing tree data structure that allows efficient searching of indexes. A b+tree stores data records only in leaf nodes.

BCNF   See "Boyce-Codd Normal Form."

BLOB   Binary Large Object. A data type that can hold large objects of arbitrary content such as video files, audio files, images, and so forth. Because the data can be any arbitrary chunk of binary data, the database does not understand its contents so you cannot search in these fields.

Boyce-Codd Normal Form (BCNF)   A table is in BCNF if every determinant is also a candidate key (minimal superkey). See "determinant" and "candidate key."

b-tree   (Pronounced "bee tree.") A self-balancing tree data structure that allows efficient searching of indexes. A b-tree stores data records in internal and leaf nodes.

business rule   Business-specific rule that constrains the data. For example, "all orders require a valid existing Customers record" and "orders for $50 or more get free shipping" are business rules.

candidate key   A minimal superkey (see "superkey"). In other words, the fields in a candidate key uniquely define the records in a table and no subset of those fields also uniquely defines the records.

cardinality   A representation of the minimum and maximum allowed number of values for an attribute. In semantic object models, written as L.U where L and U are the lower and upper bounds. For example, 1.10 means an attribute must occur between 1 and 10 times.

catalog   A directory storing metadata.

check constraint   A record-level validation that is performed when a record is created or updated.

column   A piece of data that may be recorded for each row in a table. The corresponding formal database term is attribute.

commit   Makes changes made within a transaction permanent.

composite index   An index that includes two or more fields. Also called a compound index or concatenated index.

composite key   A key that includes two or more fields. Also called a compound key or concatenated key.

composite object   In a semantic object model, an object that contains at least one multi-valued non-object attribute.

compound index   An index that includes two or more fields. Also called a composite index or concatenated index.

compound key   A key that includes two or more fields. Also called a composite key or concatenated key.

compound object   In a semantic object model, an object that contains at least one object attribute.

concatenated index   An index that includes two or more fields. Also called a compound index or composite index.

concatenated key   A key that includes two or more fields. Also called a compound key or composite key.

consistency   The requirement that a transaction should leave the database in a consistent state. If a transaction would put the database in an inconsistent state, the transaction is canceled.

CRUD   Acronym for the four main database operations: Create, Read, Update, Delete. These operations correspond to the SQL statements INSERT, SELECT, UPDATE, and DELETE.

CSV file   Comma Separated Value file. A text file where each row contains the data for one record and field values are separated by commas.

cursor   An object that allows a program to work through the records returned by a query one at a time. Some databases allow cursors to move forward and backward through the set of returned records whereas others allow only forward movement.

cyclic dependency   Occurs in a table when field A depends on field B, field B depends on field C, and field C depends on field A.

DAO   Data Access Objects. A Microsoft collection of classes that allows programs to interact with databases. DAO is in many ways similar to ADO, although ADO is newer.

Data Definition Language   The SQL commands that deal with creating the database's structure such as CREATE TABLE, CREATE INDEX, and DROP TABLE.

data dictionary   A list of descriptions of data items to help developers stay on the same track.

Data Manipulation Language   The SQL commands that manipulate data in a database. These include INSERT, SELECT, UPDATE, and DELETE.

data mart   A smaller data warehouse that holds data of interest to a particular group. Also see "data warehouse."

data mining   Digging through data (usually in a data warehouse or data mart) to identify interesting patterns.

data scrubbing   Processing data to remove or repair inconsistencies.

data type   The type of data that a column can hold. Types include numbers, fixed-length strings, variable-length strings, and so forth.

data warehouse   A repository of data for offline use in building reports and analyzing historical data. Also see "data mart."

database   An entity that holds data in some useful way and provides CRUD methods (see "CRUD"). Modern databases also provide sophisticated methods for joining, sorting, grouping, and otherwise manipulating the data.

database administrator   Someone who manages the database, optimizes performance, performs backups, and so forth.

DBA   Database Administrator.

DBMS   Database Management System. A product or tool that manages any kind of database, not just relational databases.

DDBMS   Distributed Database Management System. See "DBMS."

DDL   See "Data Definition Language."

DELETE   SQL command that removes a row from a table. The Delete in CRUD.

deletion anomaly   Occurs when deleting a record can destroy information.

determinant   A field that at least partly determines the value in another field.

dimensional database   A database that treats the data as if it is stored in cells within a multi-dimensional array (see "multi-dimensional array").

distributed database   A database with pieces stored on multiple computers on a network.

DKNF   See "Domain Key Normal Form."

DML   See "Data Manipulation Language."

document-oriented database   A database oriented around documents. For example, a file system or a Web site.

domain   The values that are allowed for a particular column. For example, the domain of the Average-Speed field in a database of downhill speed skiers might allow values between 0 and 200 miles per hour (although if your average speed is 0, you might consider another sport).

490

Domain Key Normal Form (DKNF)   A table is in DKNF if it contains no constraints except domain constraints and key constraints.

durability   The requirement that a completed transaction is safely recorded in the database and will not be lost even if the database crashes.

Edgar Codd   IBM researcher who laid the groundwork for modern relational databases and SQL starting in 1970.

entity   In entity-relationship modeling, an object or item of interest such as a customer, invoice, vehicle, or product.

entity integrity   Requires that all tables have a primary key. The values in the primary key fields must be non-null and no two records can have the same primary key values.

entity-relationship diagram (ER diagram)   A diagram that shows entities (rectangles), their attributes (ellipses), and the relationships among them (diamonds).

ER diagram   See "entity-relationship diagram."

field   Another informal term for column (see "column").

Fifth Normal Form (5NF)   A table is in 5NF if it is in 4NF and contains no related multi-valued dependencies.

First Normal Form (1NF)   A table is in 1NF if it satisfies basic conditions to be a relational table.

flat file   A plain old text file used to store data. A flat file isn't very fancy and provides few tools for querying, sorting, grouping, and performing other database operations but flat files are very easy to use.

foreign key   One or more columns that are related to values in corresponding columns in another table. For example, the Orders table's CustomerId column might be a foreign key referring to the Customers table's CustomerId column. To maintain consistency, no Orders record could have a CustomerId value that is not in some record in the Customers table.

Fourth Normal Form (4NF)   A table is in 4NF if it is in BCNF and contains no unrelated multi-valued dependencies.

HOLAP   Hybrid Online Analytical Processing. A combination of MOLAP and ROLAP. Typically this combines relational storage for some data and specialized storage for other data. The exact definition of HOLAP isn't clear so you can use it as a conversation starter at cocktail parties. Also see "OLAP."

hybrid object   In a semantic object model, an object that contains a combination of multi-valued and object attributes. For example, it might contain a multi-valued group attribute that includes an object attribute.

hypercube   A multi-dimensional array (see "multi-dimensional array"). To be a true hyper*cube*, each dimension should have the same length or number of entries.

identifier   In a semantic object model, one or more attributes that are used to identify individual objects. Indicated by writing ID to the left of the attribute(s), underlined if the identifier is unique.

index   A data structure that uses one or more columns to make looking up values on those columns faster.

INSERT   SQL command that creates a new record in a table. The Create in CRUD.

insertion anomaly   Occurs when you cannot store certain kinds of information because it would violate the table's primary key constraints.

instance   A particular occurrence of an entity. For example, if VicePresident is an entity (class) then Dan Quayle is an instance of that class.

isolation   The requirement that no one should be able to peek into the database and see changes while a transaction is underway. Anyone looking at the data will either see it as it is before the transaction or after the transaction but cannot see the transaction partly completed.

JDBC   Java Database Connectivity. An API for manipulating databases from Java programs.

join   A query that selects data from more than one table, usually using a JOIN or WHERE clause to indicate which records in the two tables go together.

JOLAP   Java Online Analytical Processing. A Java API for online analytical processing. Also see "OLAP."

key   One or more fields used to locate or arrange the records in a table. Also see "index."

key constraint   In an ER diagram, a key constraint means an entity can participate in at most one instance of a relationship. For example, during flight a pilot can fly at most one hang glider.

lock   Used to control access to part of the database. For example, while one user updates a row, the database places a lock on the row so other users cannot interfere with the update. Different databases may lock data by rows, table, or disk page.

many-to-many relationship   A relationship where one object of one type may correspond to many objects of another type and vice versa. For example, one COURSE may include many STUDENTs and one STUDENT may be enrolled in many COURSEs. Normally you implement this kind of relationship by using an intermediate table that has one-to-many relationships with the original tables.

MDAC   Microsoft Data Access Components. A group of Microsoft tools and APIs that provides tools for interacting with many kinds of databases.

memo   A text data type that can hold very large chunks of text.

metabase   A database that stores metadata.

metadata   Data about the database such as table names, column names, column data types, column lengths, keys, and indexes. Some relational databases allow you to query tables that contain the database's metadata.

MOLAP   Multidimensional Analytical Processing. The "classic" version of OLAP and is sometimes referred to as simply OLAP. See "OLAP."

multi-dimensional array   A multi-dimensional rectangular block of cells containing values. Picture a row of bricks where each brick is a cell. A wall made of bricks arranged in rows and columns (which would not be very architecturally sound) would be a two-dimensional array. A series of walls closely packed together (which would be architecturally useless) would be a three-dimensional array. Use your imagination for higher dimensions.

multi-valued dependency   When one field implies the values in two other fields that are unrelated. For example, a table has a multi-valued dependency if field A implies values in field B, and field A implies values in field C, but the values in fields B and C are not related.

MySQL   An open source relational database management system. See `www.mysql.com`.

normalization   The process of transforming the database's structure to minimize the changes of certain kinds of data anomalies.

null   A special column value that means "this column has no value."

object   An instance of an item of interest to the data model. See "instance."

object database   See "object-oriented database."

object database management systems (ODBMS)   A product or tool for managing object-oriented databases. See "object-oriented database."

object store   See "object-oriented database."

object-oriented database   A database that provides tools to allow a program to create, read, update, and delete objects. The database automatically handles object persistence (changes to the object are automatically saved) and concurrency (two users accessing the same object will not interfere with each other).

object-relational database (ORD)   A database that provides relational operations plus additional features for creating, reading, updating, and deleting objects.

object-relational database management system (ORDBMS)   See "object-relational database."

object-relational mapping   A translation layer that converts objects to and from entries in a relational database.

ODBC   Open Database Connectivity. A standard database interface that allows many database products to use data stored in different kinds of databases.

ODBMS   Object Database Management System. See "object database management system."

OLAP   Online Analytical Processing. A data mining approach for performing multi-dimensional queries.

OLE DB   Object Linking and Embedding, Database. A Microsoft API that allows programs to manipulate databases. OLE DB is part of MDAC.

one-to-many relationship   A relationship where one object of one type may correspond to many objects of another type. For example, one INSTRUCTOR may teach many COURSEs but each COURSE has only one INSTRUCTOR.

one-to-one relationship   Occurs when one record in a table corresponds to exactly one record in another table.

OODBMS   Object-Oriented Database Management System. See "object database management system."

Oracle   An enterprise-level relational database management system. See `www.oracle.com/database/index.html`.

ORD   Object-Relational Database. See "object-relational database."

ORDBMS   Object-Relational Database Management System. See "object-relational database."

participation constraint   In an ER diagram, a participation constraint means every entity in an entity set must participate in a relationship set. The constraint is drawn with a thick or double line. For example, during flight a hang glider must participate in the "Pilot Flies HangGlider" relationship.

PL/SQL   Procedural Language/Structured Query Language. Oracle's extension to SQL used to write stored procedures in Oracle.

primary key   A candidate key that is singled out as the table's "main" method for uniquely identifying records. Most databases automatically build an index for a table's primary key and enforce uniqueness.

primary key constraint   Requires that each table's primary key behavior be valid. In particular, this requires that no two records in a table can have exactly the same primary key values and that all records' primary key values not be null.

query   A SQL SELECT statement that extracts data from a database.

RDBMS   Relational Database Management System. A product or tool that manages a relational database such as SQL Server, MySQL, and Informix.

record   Another informal term for row (see "row").

referential integrity   Requires that relationships among tables be consistent. For example, foreign key constraints must be satisfied. You cannot accept a transaction until referential integrity is satisfied.

relation   The database theoretical term for a table. For example, the Customer table is a relation holding attributes FirstName, LastName, Street, City, State, and ZipCode.

relational database   A database that stores data in tables containing rows and columns, and that allows queries representing relationships among records in different tables.

relationship   An association between two tables. For example, if an order contains several order items, there is a one-to-many relationship between Orders and OrderItems tables. Don't confuse this term with "relation."

replication   The process of storing data in multiple databases while ensuring that it remains consistent. For example, one database might contain a master copy of the data and other satellite databases might hold read-only copies to let clerks view data quickly without impacting the main database.

report   The results of a query displayed in a nice format. Sometimes this term is used to mean the format that will produce the report when data is added to it.

ROLAP   Relational Online Analytical Processing. OLAP performed with a relational database. See "OLAP."

rollback   Undoes changes performed within a transaction before the transaction is committed.

row   A group of related column values in a table. The corresponding formal database term is tuple. Also see "record."

Second Normal Form (2NF)   A table is in 2NF if it is in 1NF and every field that is not part of the primary key depends on every part of the primary key.

SELECT   SQL command that selects data from a database. The Read in CRUD.

semantic attribute   A characteristic of a semantic object.

semantic class   A named collection of attribute sufficient to specify an entity of interest.

semantic object (SO)   An instance of a semantic class with specific attribute values.

semantic object model (SOM)   A model that uses classes, objects, and relationships to provide understanding of a system. Classes have attributes that describe instances. Object attributes provide the relationships among objects.

simple object   In a semantic object model, an object that has only single-valued simple attributes.

SOM   See "semantic object model."

splay tree   A self-balancing tree data structure that allows efficient searching of indexes.

SQL   See "Structured Query Language."

SQL Server   Microsoft's enterprise-level relational database management system. See www.microsoft.com/sql/default.mspx.

SQLJ   A standard Java language extension for embedding SQL statements in Java programs. The code must be run through a preprocessor before they can be compiled. Also see "JDBC."

stored procedure   A piece of code stored in the database that can be executed by various pieces of code such as check constraints or application code. Stored procedures are a good place to store business logic that should not be built into the database's structure.

Structured Query Language   An industry standard English-like language for building and manipulating relational databases.

subclass object   An object that represents a subset of the objects in a larger class. For example, the Vehicle class could have the Truck subclass, which could have its own PickupTruck subclass, which could in turn have its own BrokenPickupTruck class.

superkey   A set of fields that uniquely define the records in a table. (Not a key that wears a cape and fights crime.)

table   A collection of rows holding similar columns of data. The corresponding formal database term is *relation*.

temporal database   A database that associates times with data. See "valid time."

Third Normal Form (3NF)   A table is in 3NF if it is in 2NF and it contains no transitive dependencies.

transaction   A series of database operations that should be treated as a single atomic operation so either they all occur or none of them occur. Also see "commit" and "rollback."

Transact-SQL   Microsoft's version of SQL used in SQL Server. See "SQL."

transitive dependency   When one non-key field's value depends on another non-key field's value. Typically this shows up as duplicated data. For example, suppose a table holds people's favorite book information and includes fields Person, Title, and Author. The primary key is Person but Title determines Author so there is a transitive dependency between Title and Author.

trigger   A stored procedure that executes when certain conditions occurs such as when a record is created, modified, or deleted. Triggers can perform special actions such as creating other records or validating changes.

TSQL   See "Transact-SQL."

tuple   The formal database term for a record or row (see "row").

unique constraint   Requires that the values in one or more columns be unique within a table. **UPDATE** SQL command that changes the values in a record's fields. The Update in CRUD.

update anomaly   Occurs when a change to a row leads to inconsistent data.

valid time   The time during which a piece of data is valid in a temporal database.

view   The result of a query that can be treated as if it were a virtual table. For example, you could define views that return only selected records from a table or that return only certain columns.

weak entity   In an ER diagram, an entity that cannot be identified by its own attributes. Instead you need to use the attributes of some other associated entity to find the weak entity. Drawn with a bold or double rectangle and attached to its *identifying relationship* by a bold or double arrow.

XML   Extensible Markup Language. A language that uses nested tokens to represent hierarchical data.

Index

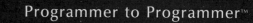